# Mastering Proxmox

## Third Edition

Build virtualized environments using the Proxmox VE
hypervisor

**Wasim Ahmed**

BIRMINGHAM - MUMBAI

# Mastering Proxmox

## *Third Edition*

First published: July 2014

Second edition: May 2016

Third edition: November 2017

Production reference: 1141117

Published by Packt Publishing Ltd.
Livery Place
35 Livery Street
Birmingham
B3 2PB, UK.

ISBN 978-1-78839-760-5

www.packtpub.com

# Credits

**Author**
Wasim Ahmed

**Copy Editors**
Safis Editing
Madhusudan Uchil

**Reviewers**
Nicolas Ledez
Jorge Moratilla Porras

**Project Coordinator**
Virginia Dias

**Commissioning Editor**
Vijin Boricha

**Proofreader**
Safis Editing

**Acquisition Editor**
Rahul Nair

**Indexer**
Francy Puthiry

**Content Development Editor**
Sharon Raj

**Graphics**
Kirk D'Penha

**Technical Editors**
Vishal Kamal Mewada
Khushbu Sutar

**Production Coordinator**
Nilesh Mohite

# About the Author

**Wasim Ahmed**, born in Bangladesh and now a citizen of Canada, is a veteran of the IT world. He first came into close contact with computers in 1992 and never looked back. Wasim has a deep understanding of networks, virtualization, big data storage, and network security.

By profession, Wasim is the CEO of a global IT support and cloud service provider based in Calgary, Alberta. He serves many companies and organizations through his company on a daily basis. Wasim's strength comes from his experience, which comes from learning and serving continually. Wasim strives to find the most effective solution at the most competitive price. He has built over 20 enterprise production virtual infrastructures using Proxmox and the Ceph storage system.

Wasim and his team are notorious for not simply accepting a technology based on its description alone, but putting it through rigorous testing to check its validity. Any new technology that his company provides goes through months of continuous testing before it is accepted. Proxmox made the cut superbly.

*This book, Mastering Proxmox – Third Edition, would not have been possible without the support and wholehearted cooperation of the team at Packt Publishing. I wish to acknowledge my indebtedness to each of the team members who walked me through the process of the major undertaking that was writing this book.*

*I also would like to acknowledge the support and dedication of the Proxmox VE developer team, who made this great hypervisor available to all of us. Their vision and attention to detail has enabled Proxmox VE to mature in a very short period of time since its first release.*

*I am thankful to the global community of Proxmox users, whose combined experiences have allowed me to learn many different scenarios in which Proxmox is used today.*

*Finally, I would like to acknowledge Charles McCrea, whose friendship and support played an important role in bringing this book to completion.*

# About the Reviewers

**Nicolas Ledez** has been working as a system administrator since 2000. He has been in big businesses such as Orange (a French telecom company) and in small organizations too. His skills are in DevOps, Linux, Ruby, Python, Ansible, Chef, Saltstack, and others. Currently, he is a DevOps architect at Cozy Cloud. You can find him on the internet with the pseudonym `nledez`.

**Jorge Moratilla Porras** has a bachelor's degree in computer science and has been working for internet companies since 1998. He has been working as a contractor for companies such as Sun Microsystems and Oracle. His passions are teaching and improving workloads using automation techniques. He has been working as a Sun Microsystems certified instructor and field engineer for several years. He has a large background working with products such as Sun Solaris, Linux, LDAP services, and CheckPoint. Recently, he has been working with configuration management products such as Puppet and Chef on his assignments and has been taking part in Madrid DevOps (a group of technicians devoted to continuous deployment and DevOps culture) as coordinator. He promotes the adoption of a culture of continuous improvement in enterprise and startups as the baseline to do great things. You can meet him at talks and hangouts that he organizes in the community.

He has collaborated as a reviewer on other Packt titles as well:

- *Configuration Management with Chef-Solo* by *Naveed ur Rahman*
- *Proxmox Cookbook* by *Wasim Ahmed*

*I would like to thank my wife, Nuria, and sons, Eduardo and Ruben, for being so understanding and supportive while I was reviewing this book. Also, I would like to thank my dear mom, Milagros, and dad, Toñi, who put in all their effort to give me an education. Finally, I would also like to thank all those who have contributed to my personal and professional development through the years.*

# www.PacktPub.com

For support files and downloads related to your book, please visit www.PacktPub.com. Did you know that Packt offers eBook versions of every book published, with PDF and ePub files available? You can upgrade to the eBook version at www.PacktPub.com and as a print book customer, you are entitled to a discount on the eBook copy. Get in touch with us at service@packtpub.com for more details.

At www.PacktPub.com, you can also read a collection of free technical articles, sign up for a range of free newsletters and receive exclusive discounts and offers on Packt books and eBooks.

https://www.packtpub.com/mapt

Get the most in-demand software skills with Mapt. Mapt gives you full access to all Packt books and video courses, as well as industry-leading tools to help you plan your personal development and advance your career.

## Why subscribe?

- Fully searchable across every book published by Packt
- Copy and paste, print, and bookmark content
- On demand and accessible via a web browser

# Customer Feedback

Thanks for purchasing this Packt book. At Packt, quality is at the heart of our editorial process. To help us improve, please leave us an honest review on this book's Amazon page at https://www.amazon.com/dp/1788397606.

If you'd like to join our team of regular reviewers, you can email us at customerreviews@packtpub.com. We award our regular reviewers with free eBooks and videos in exchange for their valuable feedback. Help us be relentless in improving our products!

# Table of Contents

# Preface

Based on the foundation laid out by the first edition and second edition, this book, *Mastering Proxmox, Third Edition*, brings updated information and details of the new features of Proxmox VE 5.0. Since the first edition of this book was published, Proxmox has been through many changes. With this third edition, I am confident that readers will be able to upgrade their skills while building and managing even better Proxmox clusters. This book shows the inner workings of Proxmox, including virtual network components, shared storage systems, the Proxmox firewall, high availability, and other features.

## What this book covers

Chapter 1, *Understanding Proxmox VE and Advanced Installation*, introduces Proxmox VE in general and shows the advanced options available during installation.

Chapter 2, *Creating a Cluster and Exploring the Proxmox GUI*, explains how to create a cluster and shows the layout of the graphical user interface.

Chapter 3, *Proxmox under the Hood*, explains the Proxmox directory structure and configuration files.

Chapter 4, *Storage Systems*, explains how Proxmox interacts with storage and various supported storage systems.

Chapter 5, *Installing and Configuring Ceph*, shows how to deploy and configure a fully functional Ceph cluster along with Proxmox.

Chapter 6, *KVM Virtual Machines*, covers creating and managing KVM-based virtual machines.

Chapter 7, *LXC Virtual Machines*, covers creating and managing LXC containers.

Chapter 8, *Network of Virtual Networks*, explains the different networking components used in Proxmox to build virtual networks.

Chapter 9, *The Proxmox VE Firewall*, explains the built-in firewall feature of Proxmox.

Chapter 10, *Proxmox High Availability*, explains the high availability or redundancy feature of Proxmox and how to configure it.

Chapter 11, *Monitoring the Proxmox Cluster*, shows how to configure the Zabbix-based network monitoring option.

Chapter 12, *Proxmox Production-Level Setup*, explains different components in a production-level setup.

Chapter 13, *Back Up and Restore Virtual Machines*, explains the backup and restore features of Proxmox for disaster planning.

Chapter 14, *Updating/Upgrading Proxmox*, explains how to keep a Proxmox cluster up to date.

Chapter 15, *Proxmox Troubleshooting*, lists real incidents that may arise in a Proxmox cluster, with solutions.

Chapter 16, *Rescuing Proxmox*, shows ways to rescue a Proxmox cluster should a disaster occur.

# What you need for this book

Since we will be working with a Proxmox cluster throughout the book, it will be extremely helpful to have a working Proxmox cluster of your own. A very basic cluster of two to three nodes, along with a storage node, will do just fine. If learning to implement Ceph in a Proxmox cluster, then a small cluster of two or three nodes for Ceph will also be extremely helpful.

# Who this book is for

This book is for readers who want to build and manage a virtual infrastructure based on Proxmox as the hypervisor. Whether the reader is a veteran in the virtualized industry but has never worked with Proxmox, or somebody is just starting out on a promising career in this industry, this book will serve them well. Due to the advanced nature of this book, prior conceptual knowledge of server virtualization, networking, and hypervisors is required.

# Conventions

In this book, you will find a number of text styles that distinguish between different kinds of information. Here are some examples of these styles and an explanation of their meaning. Code words in text, database table names, folder names, filenames, file extensions, pathnames, dummy URLs, user input, and Twitter handles are shown as follows: "The keyring that we need to copy is located in `/priv/ceph.client.admin.keyring`."

A block of code is set as follows:

```
allow-vmbr1 ens21
iface ens21 inet manual
    ovs_type OVSPort
    ovs_bridge vmbr1
```

Any command-line input or output is written as follows:

```
# apt-get install openvswitch-switch
```

**New terms** and **important words** are shown in bold. Words that you see on the screen, for example, in menus or dialog boxes, appear in the text like this: "Open vSwitch bridge and interface under the **Create** tab of the **Network** menu of the node."

Warnings or important notes appear like this.

Tips and tricks appear like this.

# Reader feedback

Feedback from our readers is always welcome. Let us know what you think about this book-what you liked or disliked. Reader feedback is important for us as it helps us develop titles that you will really get the most out of. To send us general feedback, simply email feedback@packtpub.com, and mention the book's title in the subject of your message. If there is a topic that you have expertise in and you are interested in either writing or contributing to a book, see our author guide at www.packtpub.com/authors.

# Customer support

Now that you are the proud owner of a Packt book, we have a number of things to help you to get the most from your purchase.

# Downloading the color images of this book

We also provide you with a PDF file that has color images of the screenshots/diagrams used in this book. The color images will help you better understand the changes in the output. You can download this file from `https://www.packtpub.com/sites/default/files/downloads/MasteringProxmoxThirdEdition_ColorImages.pdf`.

# Errata

Although we have taken every care to ensure the accuracy of our content, mistakes do happen. If you find a mistake in one of our books-maybe a mistake in the text or the code-we would be grateful if you could report this to us. By doing so, you can save other readers from frustration and help us improve subsequent versions of this book. If you find any errata, please report them by visiting `http://www.packtpub.com/submit-errata`, selecting your book, clicking on the **Errata Submission Form** link, and entering the details of your errata. Once your errata are verified, your submission will be accepted and the errata will be uploaded to our website or added to any list of existing errata under the Errata section of that title. To view the previously submitted errata, go to `https://www.packtpub.com/books/content/support` and enter the name of the book in the search field. The required information will appear under the **Errata** section.

# Piracy

Piracy of copyrighted material on the internet is an ongoing problem across all media. At Packt, we take the protection of our copyright and licenses very seriously. If you come across any illegal copies of our works in any form on the internet, please provide us with the location address or website name immediately so that we can pursue a remedy. Please contact us at `copyright@packtpub.com` with a link to the suspected pirated material. We appreciate your help in protecting our authors and our ability to bring you valuable content.

# Questions

If you have a problem with any aspect of this book, you can contact us at `questions@packtpub.com`, and we will do our best to address the problem.

# 1
# Understanding Proxmox VE and Advanced Installation

**Virtualization**, as we all know today, is a decades-old technology that was first implemented in the mainframes of the 1960s. Virtualization was a way to logically divide the mainframe's resources for different application processing. With the rise in energy costs, running under-utilized server hardware is no longer a luxury. Virtualization enables us to do more with less, thus saving energy and money while creating a virtual green data center without geographical boundaries.

A **hypervisor** is a piece of software, hardware, or firmware that creates and manages virtual machines. It is the underlying platform or foundation that allows a virtual infrastructure to be built. In a way, it is the very building block of all virtualization. A bare metal hypervisor acts as a bridge between physical hardware and the virtual machines by creating an abstraction layer. Because of this unique feature, an entire virtual machine can be moved over a vast distance over the internet and be made available to function exactly the same. A virtual machine does not see the hardware directly; instead, it sees the layer of the hypervisor, which is the same no matter what hardware the hypervisor has been installed on.

The **Proxmox Virtual Environment** (**VE**) is a cluster-based hypervisor and one of the best-kept secrets in the virtualization industry. The reason is simple. It allows you to build an enterprise business-class virtual infrastructure at a small business-class price tag without sacrificing stability, performance, and ease of use. Whether it is a massive data center to serve millions of people, or a small educational institution, or a home serving important family members, Proxmox can handle configuration to suit any situation.

If you have picked up this book, you are no doubt familiar with virtualization, and perhaps well versed with other hypervisors, such as VMware, Xen, Hyper-V, and so on. In this chapter and upcoming chapters, we will see the mighty power of Proxmox from the inside out. We will examine scenarios and create a complex virtual environment. We will tackle some heavy day-to-day issues and show resolutions that might just save the day in a production environment. We will also learn how to deploy a highly redundant storage system using Ceph to store virtual machines. So strap yourself in and let's dive into the virtual world with the mighty hypervisor, Proxmox VE.

# Understanding Proxmox features

Before we dive in, it is necessary to understand why one should choose Proxmox over the other mainstream hypervisors. Proxmox is not perfect, but stands out among other contenders with its hard-to-beat features. The following are some of the features that make Proxmox a real game changer.

## It is free!

Yes, Proxmox is free! To be more accurate, Proxmox has several subscription levels, among which the community edition is completely free. One can simply download the Proxmox ISO at no cost and raise a fully functional cluster without missing a single hypervisor feature and without paying anything. The main difference between the paid and community subscription level is that the paid subscription receives updates, which go through additional testing and refinement. In a production cluster with a real workload, it is highly recommended to purchase a subscription from Proxmox or Proxmox resellers.

## Built-in firewall

Proxmox VE comes with a robust firewall ready to be configured out of the box. This firewall can be configured to protect the entire Proxmox cluster down to a virtual machine. The per-VM firewall option gives you the ability to configure each VM individually by creating individualized firewall rules, a prominent feature in a multi-tenant virtual environment. We will learn about this feature in detail in Chapter 9, *The Proxmox VE Firewall*.

# Open vSwitch

Licensed under Apache 2.0, Open vSwitch is a virtual switch designed to work in a multi-server virtual environment. All hypervisors need a bridge between VMs and the outside network. Open vSwitch enhances the features of the standard Linux bridge in an ever-changing virtual environment. Proxmox fully supports Open vSwitch which allows you to create an intricate virtual environment, all the while reducing virtual network management overhead. For details on Open vSwitch, refer to `http://openvswitch.org/`.

We will learn about Open vSwitch management in Proxmox in `Chapter 8`, *Network of Virtual Networks*.

# The graphical user interface

Proxmox comes with a fully functional **graphical user interface** (**GUI**) out of the box. The GUI allows an administrator to manage and configure almost all the aspects of a Proxmox cluster. The GUI has been designed keeping simplicity in mind, with functions and features separated into menus for easier navigation. The following screenshot shows an example of the Proxmox GUI dashboard:

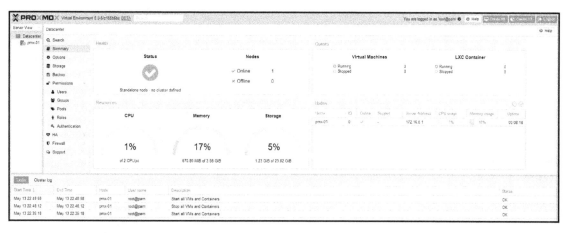

We will dissect the Proxmox GUI dashboard in `Chapter 2`, *Creating a Cluster and Exploring the Proxmox GUI*.

# KVM virtual machines

A **Kernel-based Virtual Machine (KVM)** is a kernel module that is added to Linux for full virtualization to create isolated, fully independent virtual machines. KVMs are not dependent on the host operating system in any way, but they do require the virtualization feature in BIOS to be enabled. A KVM allows a wide variety of operating systems for virtual machines, such as Linux and Windows. Proxmox provides a very stable environment for KVM-based VMs. We will learn how to create KVM VMs and also how to manage them in Chapter 6, *KVM Virtual Machines*.

# Linux containers, or LXC

Introduced in Proxmox VE 4.0, **Linux containers**, or **LXCs**, allow multiple Linux instances on the same Linux host. All the containers are dependent on the host Linux operating system and only Linux flavors can be virtualized as containers. There are no containers for the Windows operating system. LXC replaces prior OpenVZ containers, which were the primary containers in the virtualization method in the previous Proxmox versions. If you are not familiar with LXC or want details on it, refer to https://linuxcontainers.org.

We will learn how to create LXC containers and manage them in Chapter 7, *LXC Virtual Machines*.

# Storage plugins

Out of the box, Proxmox VE supports a variety of storage systems to store virtual disk images, ISO templates, backups, and so on. All plugins are quite stable and work great with Proxmox. Being able to choose different storage systems gives an administrator the flexibility to leverage the existing storage in the network. As of Proxmox VE 5.0, the following storage plugins are supported:

- The local directory mount points
- LVM
- LVM thin
- NFS
- iSCSI
- GlusterFS

- Ceph **RADOS Block Devices (RBD)**
- ZFS over iSCSI
- ZFS

We will learn the usage of different storage systems and the types of files they can store in detail in Chapter 4, *Storage Systems*.

# Vibrant culture

Proxmox has a growing community of users who are always helping others learn Proxmox and troubleshoot various issues. With so many active users around the world, and through active participation of Proxmox developers, the community has now become a culture of its own. Feature requests are continuously being worked on, and the existing features are being strengthened on a regular basis. With so many users supporting Proxmox, it sure is here to stay.

 Visit the following link for the official Proxmox forum: https://forum. proxmox.com.

# The basic installation of Proxmox

The installation of a Proxmox node is very straightforward. Simply accept the default options, select localization, and enter the network information to install Proxmox VE. We can summarize the installation process in the following steps:

1. Download the ISO from the official Proxmox site and prepare a disc with the image (http://proxmox.com/en/downloads).

2. Boot the node with the disc and hit *Enter* to start the installation from the installation GUI, as shown in the following screenshot:

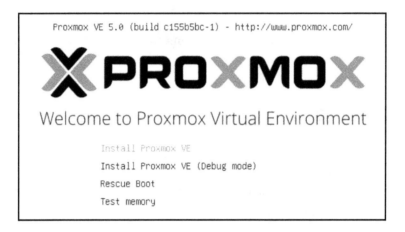

If an optical drive to use the installation disc is unavailable, we can also install Proxmox from a USB drive.

3. Progress through the prompts to select options or type in information.
4. After the installation is complete, access the Proxmox GUI dashboard using the IP address, as `https://<proxmox_node_ip>:8006`.

In some cases, it may be necessary to open the firewall port to allow access to the GUI over port `8006`.

# The advanced installation option

Although the basic installation works in all scenarios, there may be times when the advanced installation option is necessary. Only the advanced installation option provides you the ability to customize the main OS drive.

A common practice for the operating system drive is to use a mirror RAID array using a controller interface. This provides drive redundancy if one of the drives fails. This same level of redundancy can also be achieved using a software-based RAID array, such as ZFS. Proxmox now offers options to select ZFS-based arrays for the operating system drive right at the beginning of the installation. For details on ZFS, if you are not familiar, refer to `https://en.wikipedia.org/wiki/ZFS`.

It is common to ask why one should choose ZFS software RAID over tried-and-tested hardware-based RAID. The simple answer is flexibility. Hardware RAID is locked, or fully dependent, on the hardware RAID controller interface that created the array, whereas ZFS creates software-based RAID which is not dependent on any hardware, and the array can easily be ported to different hardware nodes. Should a RAID controller failure occur, the entire array created from that controller is lost unless there is an identical controller interface available for replacement. The ZFS array is only lost when all the drives or a maximum tolerable number of drives are lost in the array.

Besides ZFS, we can also select other filesystem types, such as **ext3**, **ext4**, or **xfs**, from the same advanced option. We can also set the custom disk or partition sizes through the advanced option. The following screenshot shows the installation interface with the target hard disk selection page:

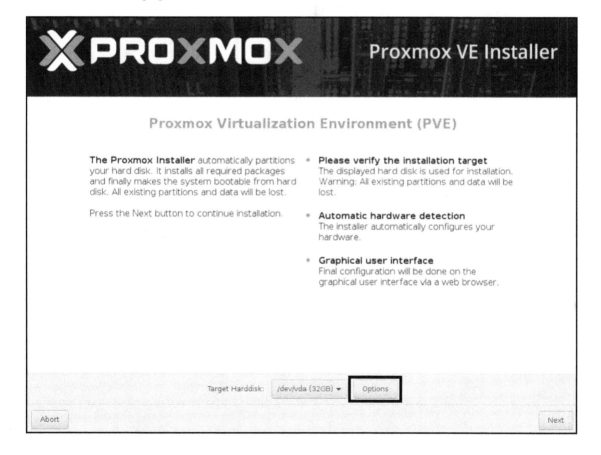

Click on **Options,** as shown in the preceding screenshot, to open the advanced options for the hard disk. The following screenshot shows the option window with supported filesystem drop-down menu:

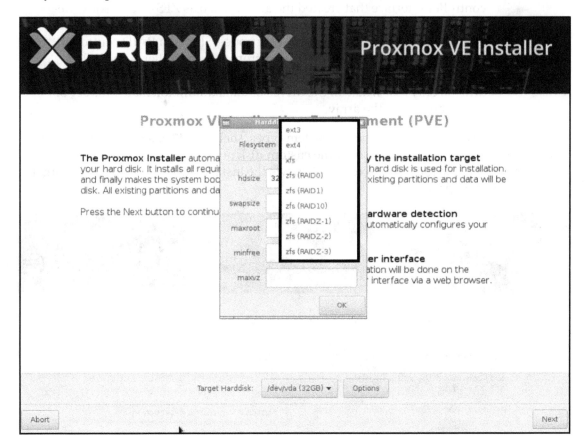

We are going to select the ZFS mirror or RAID1, for the purpose of this book, in order to create a demo cluster from scratch. In the preceding screenshot, we selected **zfs (RAID1)** for mirroring, and the two drives, **Harddisk 0** and **Harddisk 1**, to install Proxmox. The installer will auto-select the installed disk drive, as shown in the following screenshot:

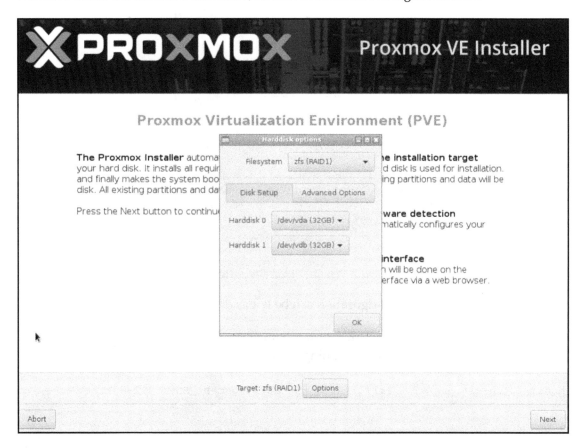

The **Advanced Options** include some ZFS performance-related configurations such as **compress**, **checksum**, and **ashift** or alignment shift, as shown in the following screenshot:

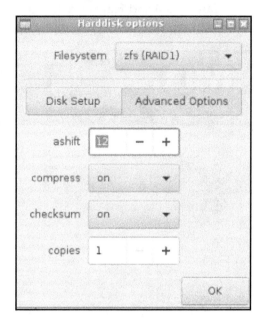

For most environments, this configuration can be left as default.

If you are unfamiliar with ZFS advanced tuning, then the following link may be helpful to get some insight on ZFS performance tuning options:

http://open-zfs.org/wiki/Performance_tuning#Alignment_Shift_.28ashift.29

If we pick a filesystem such as EXT3, EXT4, or XFS instead of ZFS, the **Harddisk options** dialog box will look like the following screenshot, with a different set of options:

Selecting a filesystem gives us the following advanced options:

- **hdsize**: This is the total drive size to be used by the Proxmox installation.
- **swapsize**: This defines the swap partition size.
- **maxroot**: This defines the maximum size to be used by the root partition.
- **minfree**: This defines the minimum free space that should remain after the Proxmox installation.
- **maxvz**: This defines the maximum size for the data partition. This is usually `/var/lib/vz`.

From Proxmox VE version 5, we can select the interface that will be used for management. This is very useful when a node has multiple network interfaces and we want to intentionally use a particular interface for cluster management. The following screenshot shows the management network interface selection screen during Proxmox installation:

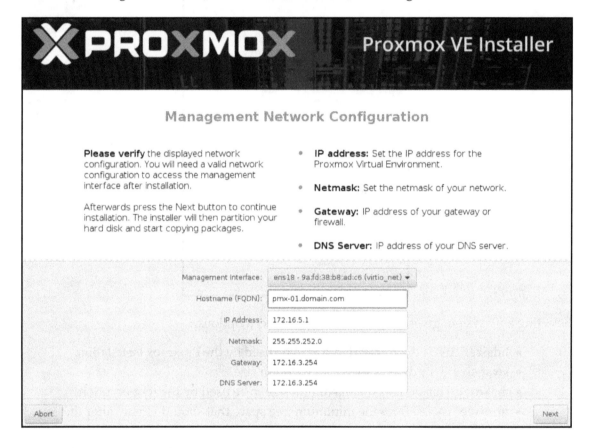

# Debugging the Proxmox installation

Debugging features are part of any good operating system. Proxmox has debugging features that will help you during a failed installation. Some common reasons are unsupported hardware, conflicts between devices, ISO image errors, and so on. Debugging mode logs and displays installation activities in real time. When the standard installation fails, we can start the Proxmox installation in debug mode from the main installation interface, as shown in the following screenshot:

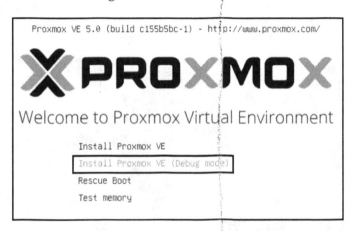

The debug installation mode will drop us in the prompt, as shown in the following screenshot:

```
Proxmox startup
mounting proc filesystem
mounting sys filesystem
comandline: BOOT_IMAGE=/boot/linux26 ro ramdisk_size=16777216 rw quiet splash=verbose proxdebug
loading drivers:  shpchp i2c_piix4 pata_acpi mac_hid qemu_fw_cfg floppy virtio_blk pcspkr serio_raw psmouse input_leds
searching for cdrom
testing cdrom /dev/sr0
found proxmox cdrom
Debugging mode (type exit or CTRL-D to continue startup)
/ #
```

To start the installation, we need to press *Ctrl + D*. If there is an error during the installation, we can simply press *Ctrl + C* to get back to this console to continue with our investigation. From the console, we can check the installation log using the following command:

```
# cat /tmp/install.log
```

At times, it may be necessary to edit the loader information when normal booting does not function. This is a common case when Proxmox is unable to show the video output due to UEFI or a nonsupported resolution. In such cases, the booting process may hang. From the main installation menu, we can press *E* to enter edit mode to change the loader information, as shown in the following screenshot:

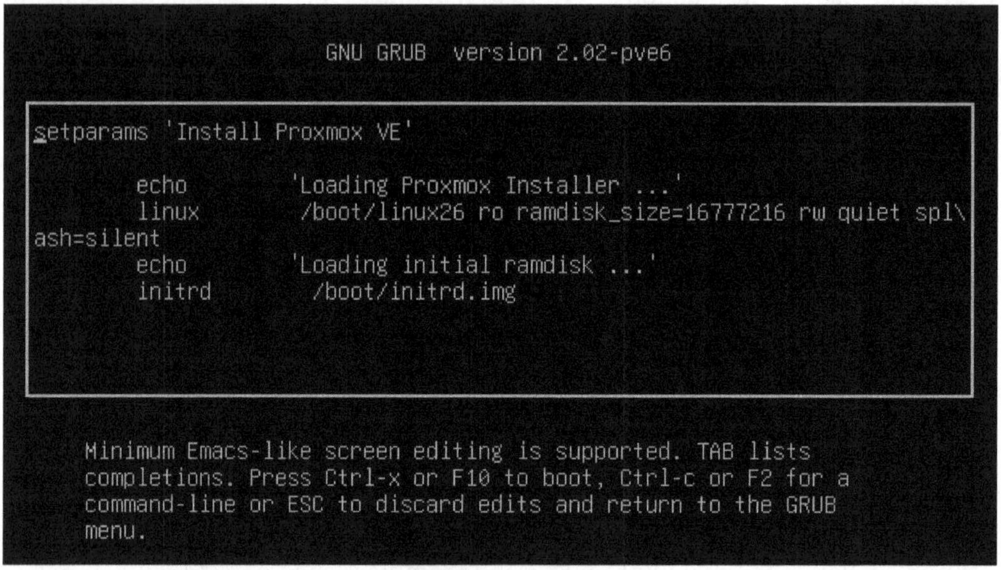

```
                    GNU GRUB   version 2.02-pve6

setparams 'Install Proxmox VE'

        echo         'Loading Proxmox Installer ...'
        linux        /boot/linux26 ro ramdisk_size=16777216 rw quiet spl\
ash=silent
        echo         'Loading initial ramdisk ...'
        initrd       /boot/initrd.img




    Minimum Emacs-like screen editing is supported. TAB lists
    completions. Press Ctrl-x or F10 to boot, Ctrl-c or F2 for a
    command-line or ESC to discard edits and return to the GRUB
    menu.
```

One way to continue with booting is to add the `nomodeset` argument by editing the loader. The loader should look as follows after the edit:

```
linux/boot/linux26 ro ramdisk_size=16777216 rw quiet nomodeset
```

# Proxmox subscription and repositories

Proxmox itself is completely free to download and deploy without any cost. But a subscription offers an added level of stability to any node used in a production environment. Both free and subscribed versions have separate repositories and receive updates differently.

Updates or packages released through the subscribed or Enterprise repository go through additional testing and debugging before they are released. This is not to say the updates or packages in the free repository are full of bugs and are released without testing. All Proxmox patches, updates, and packages are taken through the complete development cycle, including testing, before they are released. But Enterprise packages go through much more comprehensive debugging and testing. This level of tests is mandatory for an enterprise-class network environment where a small issue can cost a company a lot of money. A highly stable environment is usually not needed in a home-based platform or small business environment. The subscription menu allows you to activate a purchased subscription on a node. So from a stability point of view, the enterprise version is without a doubt the best choice for any production environment cluster. The price of an enterprise subscription varies depending on the level of Proxmox support provided through tickets, portal, and phone.

Free repository users can only reach out for support through the official Proxmox forum. Proxmox developers quite often lend their expertise to address issues posted on the forum by users. There is no portal or ticket system available for free users. Since this is a free community forum, some issues may not get answered in time.

 Even with the free version, Proxmox is still very stable. Do not let the subscription level fool you into thinking that the free version is not even worth considering.

Both free and enterprise versions can be mixed in the same environment. For example, some critical nodes actively serving users can be on the enterprise version, while any non-critical nodes, such as nodes used for testing, backup, and so on, can be on the free version. Upon logging in through the free non-subscription Proxmox node through the GUI, we will be presented with the following notification:

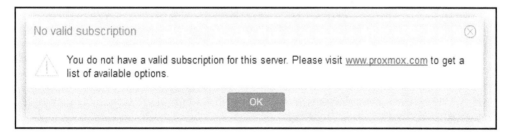

There are three package repositories for Proxmox:

- Proxmox VE Enterprise repository

- Proxmox VE No-Subscription or Free repository
- Proxmox VE Test repository

# Proxmox VE Enterprise repository

As the name suggests, this repository is for nodes with paid subscriptions. By default, the Enterprise Repository is enabled in Proxmox. The repository information is in the file `/etc/apt/sources.list.d/pve-enterprise.list`. We can disable the Enterprise Repository by simply commenting it out with the # symbol in the following line:

```
deb https://enterprise.proxmox.com/debian jessie pve-enterprise
```

When disabling the Enterprise Repository, the No-Subscription Repository must be enabled in order to receive updates, patches, and packages. If you're using the Enterprise Repository on a mission-critical node and a subscription has been purchased, the subscription key can be uploaded through the Proxmox GUI by clicking on the **Upload Subscription Key** button under the **Node | Subscription** menu, as shown in the following figure:

Copy and paste the subscription key and then click on **OK**. Proxmox will automatically check the validity of the key and activate the subscription for the node. A fully subscribed node appears similarly to the following screenshot, under subscriptions in the GUI:

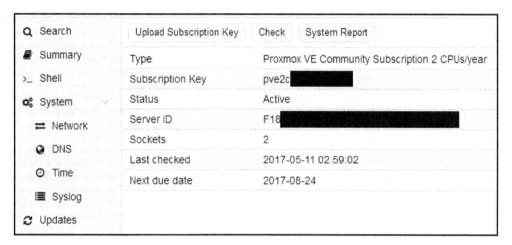

Let's look at the details provided through the **Subscription** page.

# Type

This shows the name of the Proxmox subscription level. There are four levels of subscription available: **Community**, **Basic**, **Standard**, and **Premium**. The higher the level, the more support add-ons are included.

# Subscription key

This is the alphanumeric subscription key the customer receives after purchasing any subscription. The key is formatted in two parts: pveXx-XXXXXXXXXX. The first portion of the key indicates which level of subscription this key belongs to and for how many server sockets. For example, in the previous screenshot, the subscription key is for a Community-level subscription for a server with two sockets. If this were the Premium-level subscription for a server with four sockets, the key would appear as pve4p-XXXXXXXX.

All letters and numbers after the – are unique to each key and should not be shared with unauthorized personnel or made public.

# Status

This shows the current status of the subscription key.

# Server ID

This uniquely generated ID belongs to one node only. When a subscription key is activated on a particular server, the key gets associated with this unique ID. When a node needs to be reinstalled without any hardware changes in it, the key can be reapplied to the server without being reissued or reactivated. But if the key is to be applied to other server hardware or if any major component (such as the CPU, motherboard, or memory) in the server has been changed, then a new unique ID will be generated. In that case, the key will need to be reissued or reactivated. This reissuing can be done by the user on the Proxmox customer site or by the authorized reseller from whom the subscription key has been purchased.

# Sockets

This shows the physical CPU socket count of the server node.

# Last checked

This shows the date and time of the last key validation check performed automatically by the node or manually by the user.

# Next due date

This shows the expiration date of the subscription key, by which the key needs to be renewed. If the key is not renewed and expires, the Proxmox node will still continue to function properly. But it will not receive any updates from the Enterprise Repository.

# Proxmox VE No-Subscription repository

This repository includes updates and packages free of cost. If using this repository, changes must be made to activate it. After disabling the Enterprise Repository, by following the instructions in the previous section, add the following line to the file `/etc/apt/sources.list`:

```
deb http://download.proxmox.com/debian jessie pve-no-subscription
```

## Proxmox VE Test repository

This repository largely contains packages for testing purposes only. It is mainly used by Proxmox developers to test new packages and allow interested users to test them as well. Under no circumstances should this repository be used in a production environment. To enable this repository, add the following line to `/etc/apt/sources.list`:

```
deb http://download.proxmox.com/debian jessie pvetest
```

 Proxmox has the very best prices per subscription in the virtualization product industry. The operating cost of a Proxmox cluster is minimal as compared to a giant virtual product, such as VMWare. Proxmox provides big-business virtualization at a small-business cost. For details of different subscription levels, refer to `http://proxmox.com/proxmox-ve/pricing`.

# Summary

In this chapter, we looked at why Proxmox is a better option as a hypervisor, what advanced installation options are available during an installation, and why we choose software RAID for the operating system drive. We also looked at different subscription levels and their benefits. We learned about the presence of the debugging features to investigate when an installation does not proceed as usual.

In next chapter, we will take a closer look at the Proxmox GUI and see how easy it is to centrally manage a Proxmox cluster from a web browser.

# 2

# Creating a Cluster and Exploring the Proxmox GUI

Proxmox VE can be used independently without being part of a cluster. But in order to truly use Proxmox at its full potential, a cluster enables many more advanced features such as centralized management, high availability, and live migration. We will look into the features in later chapters. When multiple Proxmox nodes are in the same cluster, they can all be managed and monitored by logging in to the Proxmox GUI through any member node. There is no master-slave scheme in Proxmox. All nodes works together by sharing the same configuration.

## Creating a Proxmox cluster

A cluster is nothing but a group of Proxmox servers or nodes, sharing resources. A Proxmox cluster can contain up to 32 physical nodes. If network latency permits, the number of nodes can be higher. But any number of nodes higher than 32 may cause an unstable situation within the cluster.

As of Proxmox VE 5, we cannot create clusters through the graphical interface. The entire process of cluster creation must be done through the CLI. Proxmox provides a tool to create and add nodes to a cluster called **Proxmox VE Cluster Manager** or **pvecm**.

 When naming a cluster, keep in mind that it can be a maximum of 15 characters and only—can be used as a special character.

To create a new cluster, log in to any available Proxmox node through SSH and run the following command:

```
# pvecm create <clustername>
```

For our first demo cluster, we are going to run the following command to create a cluster named pmx-cluster:

```
# pvecm create pmx-cluster
```

After successfully creating the cluster, we can quickly check it through the following command:

```
# pvecm status
```

The following screenshot shows the result after running the pvecm command:

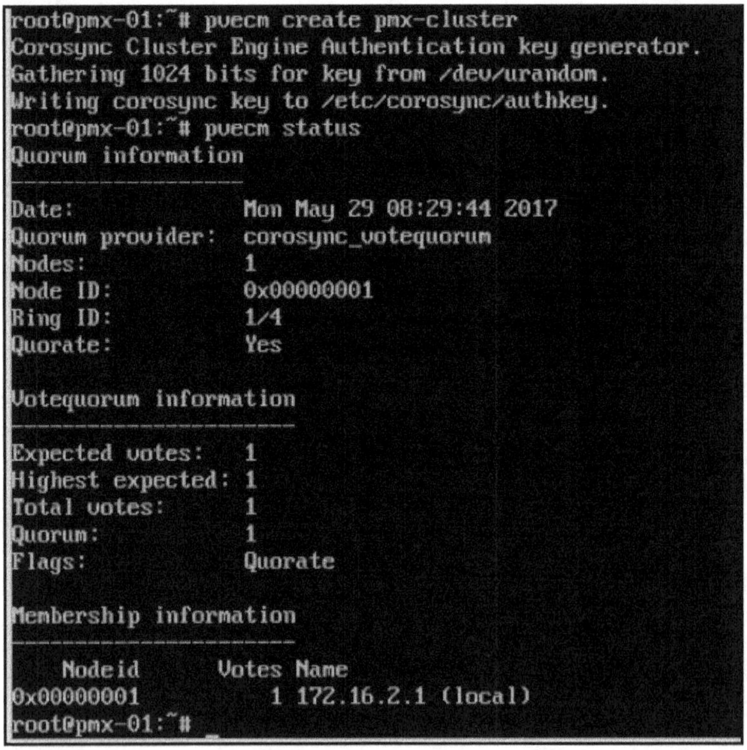

```
root@pmx-01:~# pvecm create pmx-cluster
Corosync Cluster Engine Authentication key generator.
Gathering 1024 bits for key from /dev/urandom.
Writing corosync key to /etc/corosync/authkey.
root@pmx-01:~# pvecm status
Quorum information
------------------
Date:             Mon May 29 08:29:44 2017
Quorum provider:  corosync_votequorum
Nodes:            1
Node ID:          0x00000001
Ring ID:          1/4
Quorate:          Yes

Votequorum information
----------------------
Expected votes:   1
Highest expected: 1
Total votes:      1
Quorum:           1
Flags:            Quorate

Membership information
----------------------
    Nodeid      Votes Name
0x00000001          1 172.16.2.1 (local)
root@pmx-01:~#
```

As shown in the previous screenshot, we have created a new cluster from *node 1*. We are now going to add a second node into the cluster. To add a member node, log in to the node through SSH, and then run the following command:

```
# pvecm add <existing_member_ip>
```

If there is more than one member node in the cluster already, then the IP address in the command can be any of those nodes. As mentioned earlier, there is no master-slave scheme in a Proxmox cluster. All nodes share the same cluster configuration and information. For our demo cluster, we are going to add our second node into the cluster using the following command, where 172.16.2.1 is the assigned IP address of the first node in the cluster:

```
# pvecm add 172.16.2.1
```

The command will initiate the process of adding the node into the cluster and will display results as it progresses. The command also starts or restarts necessary services. The only user prompt that is necessary in the beginning of the process is to enter the destination node's root credentials. The following screenshot shows the command to add a node and the process it progresses through:

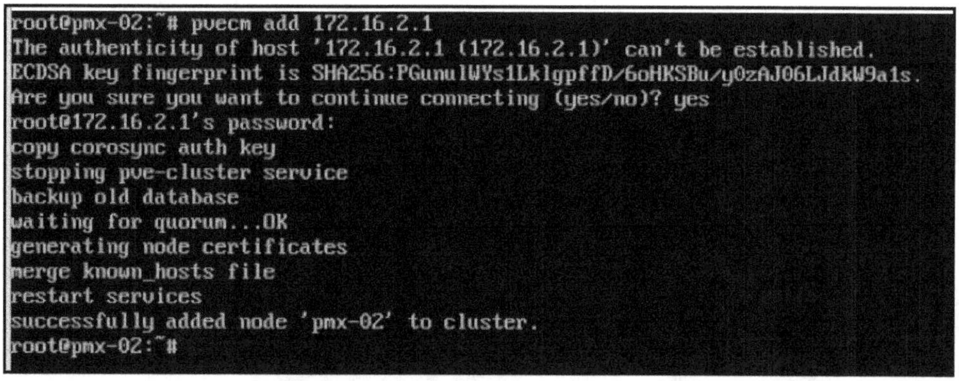

```
root@pmx-02:~# pvecm add 172.16.2.1
The authenticity of host '172.16.2.1 (172.16.2.1)' can't be established.
ECDSA key fingerprint is SHA256:PGunulWYs1LklgpffD/6oHKSBu/y0zAJO6LJdkW9a1s.
Are you sure you want to continue connecting (yes/no)? yes
root@172.16.2.1's password:
copy corosync auth key
stopping pve-cluster service
backup old database
waiting for quorum...OK
generating node certificates
merge known_hosts file
restart services
successfully added node 'pmx-02' to cluster.
root@pmx-02:~#
```

Sometimes it may be necessary to rejoin a member node with the same hostname and IP address into the cluster for any number of reasons, such as a hostname change or reinstall. The node-joining command will produce an error, as shown in the following screenshot, if the node has the same network information as it had previously:

```
root@pmx-02:~# pvecm add 172.16.2.1
detected the following error(s):
* authentication key '/etc/corosync/authkey' already exists
* cluster config '/etc/pve/corosync.conf' already exists
* corosync is already running, is this node already in a cluster?!
root@pmx-02:~#
```

The reason this error occurs is the cluster configuration already has a node listed in it with the same hostname and IP address. In such cases, we can add an option at the end of the node-joining command as follows:

```
# pvecm add <existing_mode_ip> -f
```

The command will forcefully rewrite the cluster configuration, recreate the SSH authentication key, and join the member node. We can see the list of member nodes in the cluster using the following command:

```
# pvecm nodes
```

We can also use the pvecm command to remove or detach a member node from the cluster. This command should be run from any node in the cluster except from the node being detached.

> Before removing a node from the cluster, ensure that all virtual machines have been moved to other nodes of the cluster, because after the node is detached, all VMs residing in the node will become inaccessible from the rest of the nodes in the cluster.

The following command will remove a node from the Proxmox cluster:

```
# pvecm delnode <hostname/IP>
```

# Exploring the Proxmox GUI

The Proxmox GUI allows users to interact with the Proxmox cluster graphically using menus and a visual representation of the cluster status. Even though all of the management can be done from the CLI, it can be overwhelming at times, and managing a cluster can become a daunting task. To properly utilize a Proxmox cluster, it is very important to have a clear understanding of the Proxmox GUI. The GUI can be accessed through any member nodes in the cluster. From Proxmox VE 4.2, the GUI has been updated to Sencha Ext JS 6, adding a new level of cluster visibility along with aesthetic appeal. We can now gather a lot more, at-a-glance data while managing more details through the GUI.

In this chapter, we are going to explore the different parts of the Proxmox web GUI, such as how the menu system is organized and the menus' functions. The GUI can be easily accessed from just about any browser though a URL similar to `https://<node_ip>:8006`. For our demo cluster, we are going to access the GUI through the link: `https://172.16.2.1:8006`.

The following screenshot shows an example of the Proxmox GUI for our demo cluster:

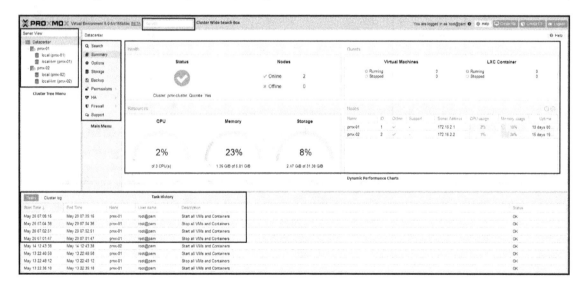

# The GUI menu system

The Proxmox GUI is a single-page administration control panel. This means that no matter which feature one is managing, the browser does not open a new page or leave the existing page. Menus on the admin page change depending on which feature is being administered. For example, in the preceding screenshot, the cluster known as Datacenter is selected, so the main menu only shows cluster-specific menus. If a node is selected, the main menu looks like the following screenshot, displaying node-specific menus:

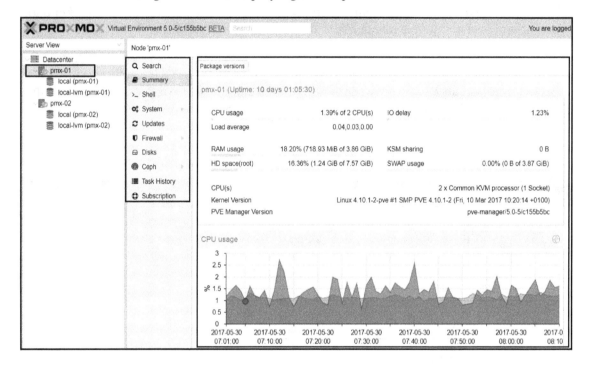

The following chart is a visual representation of the Proxmox GUI menu system. Some menu options are system settings that need to be set up once during installation and do not need any regular attention, such as DNS, time and services. Other menu items require regular visits to ensure a healthy cluster environment, such as **Summary**, **Syslog**, **Backup**, and **Permissions**:

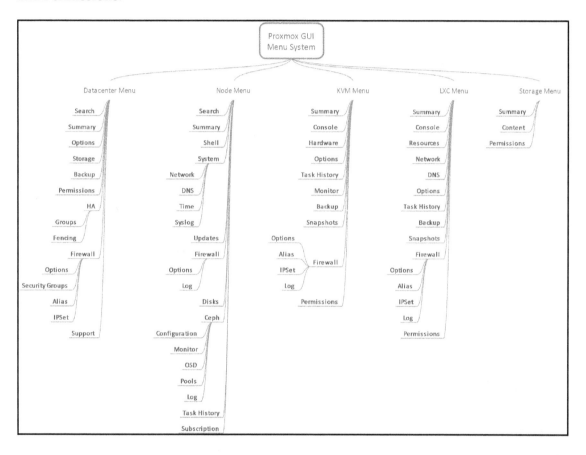

# Cluster tree view

By default, the Proxmox GUI displays the cluster tree menu in the **Server View** mode. No matter which view mode is selected, it does not change the main menu system. There are a total of four modes that we can change the tree views to, as shown in the following screenshot:

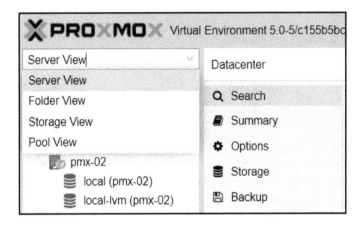

## Server View

This is the default tree view, which shows the complete list of all nodes and the resources they contain. Nodes can be uncollapsed to view the resources they contain, such as virtual machines, containers, and the storage connected to them.

## Folder View

This view separates different resources in a folder-like manner, such as **Nodes**, **Pools**, virtual machine, and **Storage**. The following screenshot shows our demo cluster in **Folder View**:

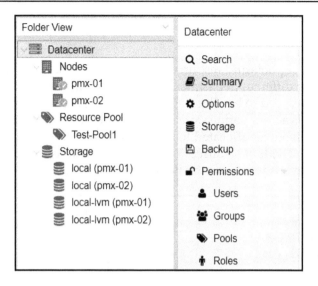

# Storage View

This view shows the list of nodes with only storage devices attached to them. It does not show any virtual machines or other resources. This is a great view for storage administrators to manage storage throughout the cluster. The following screenshot shows the **Storage View** of our demo cluster:

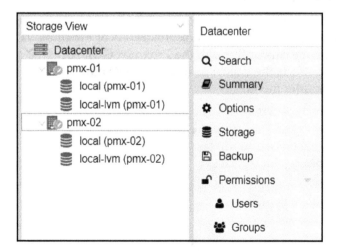

# Pool View

This view shows a list of pools and resources allocated on those pools. In the Proxmox GUI, we can create pools for different departments, customers, or just about any requirement where certain resources need to be allocated for specific parties and managed separately. The advantage of this is access permissions can be set at the pool level where an authorized person can access all resources allocated to that pool. This eliminates the need to set permissions for each individual resource. To cancel permissions, simply delete it from the pool. The following screenshot shows the **Pool View** for our demo cluster:

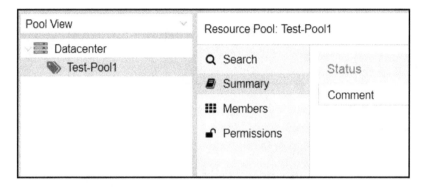

# The Datacenter menu

In the Proxmox GUI, **Datacenter** is the main-level folder of the Proxmox nodes/VMs tree. Each data center can only hold one Proxmox cluster. As of Proxmox VE 5, it is not possible to manage more than one cluster through the Proxmox GUI. Any task performed through the **Datacenter** menu affects the cluster as a whole. Let's now look at the various options available in the **Datacenter** menu.

# Datacenter | Search

It is very easy to manage a cluster with a small number of virtual machines with an even smaller number of Proxmox and storage nodes. When maintaining a large number of virtual machines and Proxmox nodes, the search feature can save a lot of time for an administrator spent in scrolling and manually looking for a particular resource. This is where the **Search** menu option can come in handy. The following screenshot shows a search result after typing a node name in the **Search** box in our example cluster:

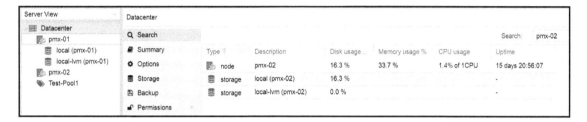

The **Search** box under **Datacenter** | **Search** shows the results in real time as you type in the box. It can search with any string in the **Type** or **Description** columns. It can be the partial name of a VM, VMID, or VM Type (qemu, lxc).

Wildcards are not supported in search strings. The **Datacenter** search page also shows a complete list of all resources of the cluster. Prior to version 4.3 this information was available under **Datacenter** | **Summary**.

It is worth mentioning here that there is another cluster-wide search option available that is accessible from anywhere in the GUI menu system. It is located at the top of the GUI page next to Proxmox version information, as shown in the following screenshot:

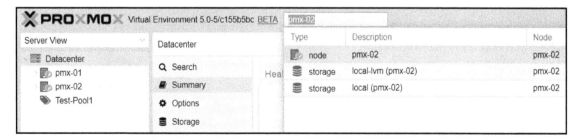

This search box functions exactly like the **Search** option under the **Datacenter** menu.

# Datacenter | Summary

Starting from Proxmox VE version 4.3, the **Summary** menu in **Datacenter** now displays much more information, including real-time cluster performance data showing real-time clusters, rather than showing a list of all the member nodes in the Proxmox cluster. The following screenshot shows the node list in the **Summary** menu for our demo cluster:

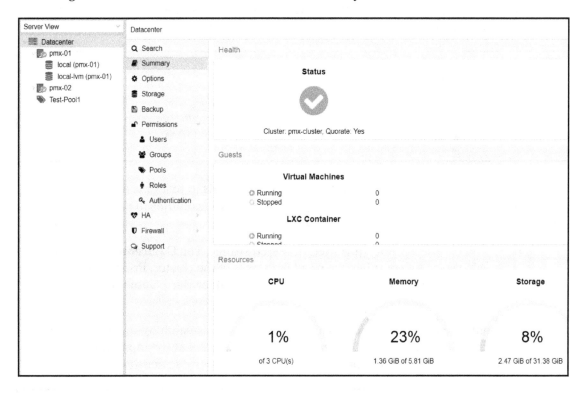

# Datacenter | Options

**Options** in the **Datacenter** menu allows you to set the **Keyboard Layout** language, **HTTP proxy**, default **Console Viewer**, and **Email from address** format that the Proxmox node sends root emails from. We can also change the default **MAC address prefix** for all auto-created MAC addresses within the cluster from this menu. The following screenshot shows the **Options** menu for our demo cluster:

# Datacenter | Storage

The **Storage** menu is probably one of the most important menu options in the GUI. This is where the Proxmox cluster and storage system come together. This is the menu to attach or detach various storage systems with Proxmox. In `Chapter 4`, *Storage Systems*, we are going to dive deeper into the Proxmox storage system. The following screenshot shows attached **Storage** in a Proxmox cluster:

# Datacenter | Backup

Cluster-wide backup schedules are created through this menu. No backup tasks can be directly performed here. A good backup plan is the first line of defense against any disaster that can cause major or minor data loss. In our ultra-modern digital world, data is much more valuable than ever before. Every virtual environment administrator struggles with a backup strategy of their virtual environment.

The fine line between granular files and an entire virtual machine backup is somewhat diminished in a virtual environment. To take the daily struggle of a backup plan out of the equation, Proxmox added an excellent backup system right in the hypervisor itself.

 As of Proxmox VE 5.0, we can only schedule backup tasks up to 1 week. Although the backup feature cannot back up individual files inside a virtual machine, it works well while backing up an entire virtual machine.

Proxmox backups can be scheduled over multiple storage systems, multiple days, and time. In Chapter 13, *Back Up and Restore Virtual Machines*, we will learn what backup and restore options are available in Proxmox as part of disaster planning.

# Datacenter | Permissions

This **Permissions** menu allows you to set cluster-wide access permission levels to a user. The menu also shows you a complete list of all the permissions already assigned to users. The same permissions can be set from the virtual machine and storage specific permission menus. When setting permissions from the **Datacenter** | **Permissions** menu, we have to type in the path for the entity we want to set the permission for. For example, the following screenshot shows virtual machines assigned to some users:

| Datacenter | | | | |
|---|---|---|---|---|
| Q  Search | Add ∨   Remove | | | |
| ▣  Summary | Path ↑ | User/Group | Role | Propag... |
| ⚙  Options | /vms/101 | vps_ygsidetm@pve | PVEVMUser | true |
| ▤  Storage | /vms/102 | meggioue@pve | PVEVMUser | true |
| ▣  Backup | /vms/103 | sgvhsghl@pve | PVEVMUser | true |
| ⚲  Permissions | /vms/104 | vps_qyliwndj@pve | PVEVMUser | true |
|  | /vms/105 | rwtqzkcn@pve | PVEVMUser | true |
| ▲  Users | /vms/106 | duvitrcr@pve | PVEVMUser | true |
| 👥  Groups | /vms/108 | dbugdbwv@pve | PVEVMUser | true |

Following are the paths formats for user permission level for VMs, storages and pool:

- To assign the user permission level for both the KVM and LXC virtual machines, the path format is /vms/<vm/lxc_id>.
- To assign the user permission level for storage, the path format is /storage/<storage_name>.
- To assign the user permission level for pools, the path format is /pool/<pool_name>.

The group permission level can also be set from this **Permissions** menu. Before we can create permissions for users or groups, we have ensured the user or group exists through the **Users** and **Groups** menu under **Permissions**. The following screenshot shows the permission-creating dialog box:

## Datacenter | Permissions | Users

This menu allows the user creator to assign different permission levels for a Proxmox cluster or virtual machine access. Changes to user details, removal of users and changing passwords, and assigning groups are also performed from this menu. The following screenshot shows the user-creation window with some example data:

The Proxmox user management allows you to set a user's access expiration date. This is very useful when giving a user temporary access, which must be deactivated after a certain number of days. This option is good for temporary access, such as contracted employees or vendor access.

## Datacenter | Permissions | Groups

This menu helps you create, edit, and remove groups only. When the same permission is to be granted to multiple users, it is easier to assign those users to a group and then assign the permission level to that group only instead of all the users individually. This saves a lot of time and makes user management much simpler. The following screenshot shows a list of three groups in the example cluster:

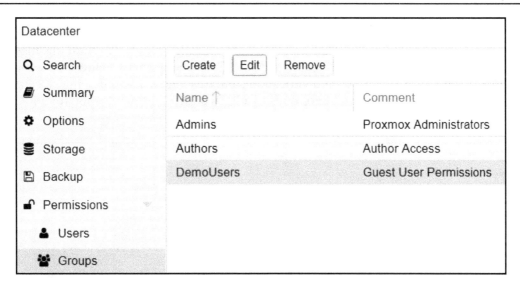

## Datacenter | Permissions | Pools

Pools in a Proxmox cluster are a way of grouping different entities, such as storage and virtual machines. For example, in a multi-tenant virtual environment, we can assign storage to virtual machines that belong to a client in a separate pool so that it is easy to view resources assigned to that client. We can create, edit, or remove pools from this menu.

## Datacenter | Permissions | Roles

This menu only shows predefined roles or permission levels that come with Proxmox 4.1. There are no options to edit or add new levels. The menu also shows defined privileges for each role. These roles can be assigned to users or user groups to set different user permission levels.

### Datacenter | Permissions | Authentication

By default, Proxmox creates the PAM and PVE authentication realm. Through this menu, we can create a new authentication realm, such as LDAP and an Active Directory server. We can also configure two-factor authentication from this menu. The following screenshot shows the authentication menu with options to add two-factor authentication for a PAM realm:

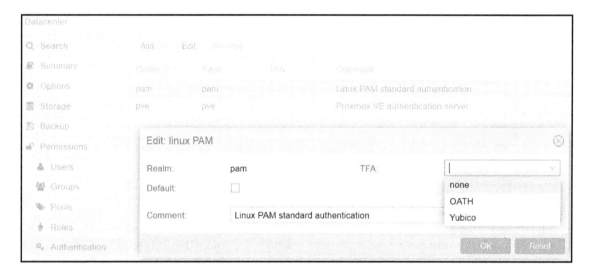

## Datacenter | HA

**High Availability** (**HA**) has never been easier than it is in Proxmox VE 5. It is now much simpler to configure all through the GUI. In simple words, an HA-enabled virtual machine is automatically moved to a different node during node failure. We will learn how to configure and leverage HA in Chapter 10, *Proxmox High Availability*.

# Datacenter | Firewall

The Proxmox built-in firewall is one of the most prominent features in recent versions. It allows firewall rules down to the virtual machine level while protecting with cluster-wide rules. A firewall works at both the cluster and virtual machine level, which can be configured to allow or deny connections to and from specific IP addresses. Any firewall rules under the Datacenter menu apply to the entire cluster. Chapter 9, *The Proxmox VE Firewall*, has been dedicated to learning about the firewall feature in greater length.

# Datacenter | Support

This menu tab shows support options that are available when there is a paid subscription applied to a node. Without any paid subscription-level node in the cluster, the menu displays no support information, as shown in the following screenshot:

Refer to the *Proxmox subscription and repositories* section in Chapter 1, *Understanding Proxmox VE and Advanced Installation,* for information on the benefits of having a paid subscription.

# Node-specific menus

Node-specific menu options are specific to each node in the cluster. New menu tabs become available as each node is selected from the left-hand side navigation pane.

# Node | Search

This is similar to the **Search** option in the datacenter-specific menu; this search option limits the scope of your search to the selected node.

# Node | Summary

The **Summary** menu option for a node is a visual representation of real-time data of the node's health. It shows vital information, such as uptime and resource consumption. The **Summary** menu also shows CPU usage, server load, memory usage, and network traffic in a very easy-to-understand graph. An administrator can get the necessary information of a node just by glancing at the summary. The graphs can be viewed on an hourly, daily, weekly, monthly, and yearly basis. The following screenshot shows the summary of node pmx-01 in our demo cluster:

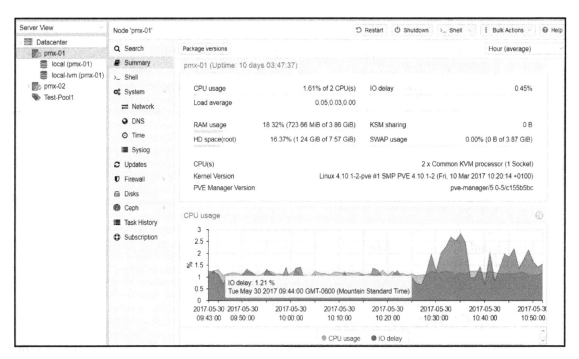

# Node | Shell

This menu opens the shell console of the node right in the same browser instead of a pop-up window. One of the benefits of opening the shell inside the browser is that sometimes a console opened in a pop-up window does not resize well. That makes the console partially visible, which can be a great annoyance at times when trying to manage the node through the CLI. A console opened through this **Shell** option will always resize to the full view of the console. The following screenshot shows the **Shell** window of our node pmx-01:

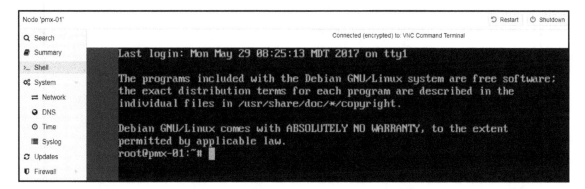

We can still open the console separately in a browser window using the existing **Shell** button in the upper-right corner of the GUI, as shown in the following screenshot:

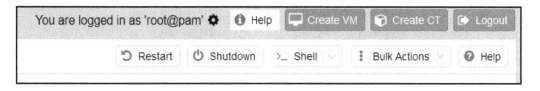

# Node | System

This menu displays the status of all the vital services in the node. We can also start or stop a specific service from this menu without going through the CLI. During troubleshooting or node maintenance, services may need to start or stop, or the status of a service may be unknown. This menu lists all running or stopped services for the node. The following screenshot shows services running in one of the nodes in our example cluster:

Node 'pmx-01'

| Name ↑ | Status | Description |
|---|---|---|
| corosync | running | Corosync Cluster Engine |
| cron | running | Regular background program processing daemon |
| ksmtuned | running | Kernel Samepage Merging (KSM) Tuning Daemon |
| postfix | exited | Postfix Mail Transport Agent |
| pve-cluster | running | The Proxmox VE cluster filesystem |
| pve-firewall | running | Proxmox VE firewall |
| pve-ha-crm | running | PVE Cluster Ressource Manager Daemon |
| pve-ha-lrm | running | PVE Local HA Ressource Manager Daemon |
| pvedaemon | running | PVE API Daemon |
| pvefw-logger | running | Proxmox VE firewall logger |
| pveproxy | running | PVE API Proxy Server |
| pvestatd | running | PVE Status Daemon |
| spiceproxy | running | PVE SPICE Proxy Server |
| sshd | running | OpenBSD Secure Shell server |
| syslog | running | System Logging Service |
| systemd-ti... | running | Network Time Synchronization |

Sidebar menu: Search, Summary, Shell, System, Network, DNS, Time, Syslog, Updates, Firewall, Disks, Ceph, Task History, Subscription

Toolbar: Start, Stop, Restart

## Node | Network

The **Network** menu acts as the glue between all virtual machines, nodes, and shared storage systems. Without a proper **network interface card** (**NIC**) or **virtual NIC** (**vNIC**) and a virtual bridge setup, no communication can take place. A deeper understanding of this menu will allow you to create a very complex web of clusters, nodes, and virtual machines. We will take a closer look at the network components later in this book in Chapter 8, *Network of Virtual Networks*. The following screenshot shows the node **Network** menu with some interfaces already configured:

| Node 'pmx-01' | | | | | | | | | ↻ Restart |
|---|---|---|---|---|---|---|---|---|---|

| | Create | Revert  Edit  Remove | | | | | | | |
|---|---|---|---|---|---|---|---|---|---|
| Q Search | Name ↑ | Type | Active | Autostart | Ports/Slaves | IP address | Subnet mask | Gateway | Comment |
| ▲ Summary | ens18 | Network Device | Yes | No | | | | | |
| >_ Shell | vmbr0 | Linux Bridge | Yes | Yes | ens18 | 172.16.2.1 | 255.255.25... | 172.16.3.254 | |
| ⚙ System | | | | | | | | | |
| ⇄ Network | | | | | | | | | |
| ❂ DNS | | | | | | | | | |

The concept of a virtual network depends on the building blocks of the virtual bridge, virtual NIC, and virtual LAN. Network virtualization is the future of physical networks as server virtualization had been for physical servers. The Proxmox virtual network provides a hardware abstraction layer, making the virtual network much more flexible and compatible.

## Node | DNS

The **DNS** menu for the node allows you to set the default DNS server address to be used by all virtual machines in the node. The **DNS** settings are very important for containers as they will use the nodes for their access to the internet.

## Node | Time

Through this menu, we can define the time zone and current time where the node is physically located. This is a useful feature when cluster nodes are spread across regions. For a healthy cluster, it is very important for all nodes' times to be in sync with each other.

## Node | Syslog

The **Syslog** option allows an administrator to view the system log in real time. Syslog gives feedback as it happens in the node. It also allows you to scroll up to view logs from the past. More importantly, if an error occurs in the node, **Syslog** gives that information in real time with the time and date stamp. This helps pinpoint an issue exactly when it occurs. An example of a scenario when **Syslog** information can come in handy is that if a node cannot connect to a storage system, the **Syslog** screen will show you the error that is preventing the connection. The following screenshot shows the **Syslog** record of our node pmx-01:

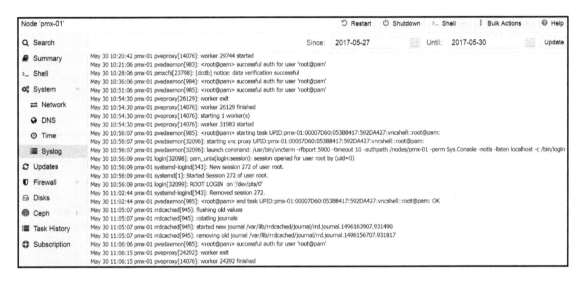

# Node | Updates

The Proxmox node can be updated right from the GUI through the **Updates** tab. Each node checks daily for any available updates and alerts the administrator through an email if there are any new updates. It is important to keep all the nodes up to date by updating regularly. The **Updates** menu enables upgrading by just using a few mouse clicks. The following screenshot shows the node's **Updates** menu with some pending upgrades available for one of the nodes in our example cluster:

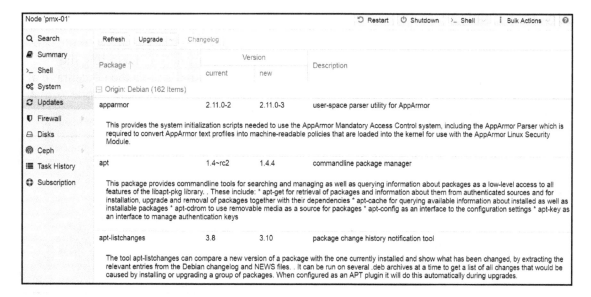

> Always update one node at a time. Some updates require the node to be restarted. If uptime is important, then migrate all the running virtual machines to a different node before restarting the upgraded node.

# Node | Firewall

The **Firewall** menu for a node allows you to manage rules specific to virtual machines in that node only. When a VM is migrated or moved to a different node, the rules from the previous node will no longer apply to that VM. We will take a look at the firewall menu in detail in `Chapter 9`, *The Proxmox VE Firewall*.

# Node | Disks

The **Disks** menu shows information about physically installed disk drives in the node. As of Proxmox version 5, the disk menu can show **S.M.A.R.T.** information, including the model and a serial number of the drive. For SSDs, the menu also displays the percentage of remaining life. The following screenshot shows the disk menu of a production node with a Proxmox operating system SSD and Ceph HDD installed:

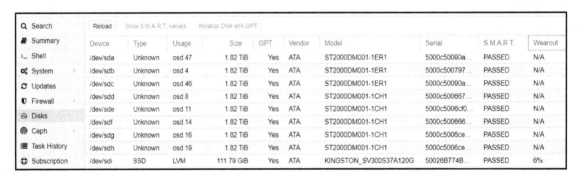

| | | Device | Type | Usage | Size | GPT | Vendor | Model | Serial | S.M.A.R.T. | Wearout |
|---|---|---|---|---|---|---|---|---|---|---|---|
| Q Search | Reload | Show S.M.A.R.T. values | Initialize Disk with GPT | | | | | | | | |
| ▤ Summary | | | | | | | | | | | |
| >_ Shell | | /dev/sda | Unknown | osd.47 | 1.82 TiB | Yes | ATA | ST2000DM001-1ER1 | 5000c50090a... | PASSED | N/A |
| ✿ System | | /dev/sdb | Unknown | osd.4 | 1.82 TiB | Yes | ATA | ST2000DM001-1ER1 | 5000c500797... | PASSED | N/A |
| ⟳ Updates | | /dev/sdc | Unknown | osd.46 | 1.82 TiB | Yes | ATA | ST2000DM001-1ER1 | 5000c50090a... | PASSED | N/A |
| ▯ Firewall | | /dev/sdd | Unknown | osd.8 | 1.82 TiB | Yes | ATA | ST2000DM001-1CH1 | 5000c500667... | PASSED | N/A |
| ⊟ Disks | | /dev/sde | Unknown | osd.11 | 1.82 TiB | Yes | ATA | ST2000DM001-1CH1 | 5000c5006cf0... | PASSED | N/A |
| | | /dev/sdf | Unknown | osd.14 | 1.82 TiB | Yes | ATA | ST2000DM001-1CH1 | 5000c500666... | PASSED | N/A |
| ☻ Ceph | | /dev/sdg | Unknown | osd.16 | 1.82 TiB | Yes | ATA | ST2000DM001-1CH1 | 5000c5006ce... | PASSED | N/A |
| ☰ Task History | | /dev/sdh | Unknown | osd.19 | 1.82 TiB | Yes | ATA | ST2000DM001-1CH1 | 5000c5006ce... | PASSED | N/A |
| ✛ Subscription | | /dev/sdi | SSD | LVM | 111.79 GiB | Yes | ATA | KINGSTON_SV300S37A120G | 50026B774B... | PASSED | 6% |

# Node | Ceph

Proxmox seamlessly integrates the **Ceph** RBD storage to store virtual disk images. The superb resilience of Ceph and its extremely low price makes it a truly enterprise-class storage system to rely on. We will learn how to install and configure a Ceph cluster and manage it through Proxmox GUI properly to realize its full potential in `Chapter 5`, *Installing and Configuring Ceph*. We will also look at the **Ceph** menu in that chapter. The **Ceph** menu in the Proxmox GUI displays real-time Ceph cluster data, as shown in the following screenshot:

# Node | Task History

The **Task History** menu displays all the user tasks performed in the node. The following screenshot shows the task history of the node pmx-01 in our example cluster:

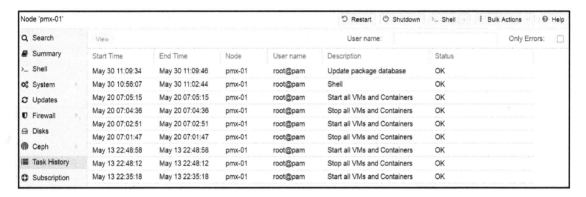

By typing in the username in the **User name:** textbox, we can filter the history for a specific user. This is very useful in a multi-user cluster where many users manage their own set of virtual machines. We can also only view tasks with errors by clicking on the **Only Errors:** checkbox.

# Node | Subscription

This menu shows information on the subscription or no-subscription level of the node. This menu is also used to apply new subscriptions or check an existing subscription key expiry. The following screenshot shows subscription information of a production Proxmox node:

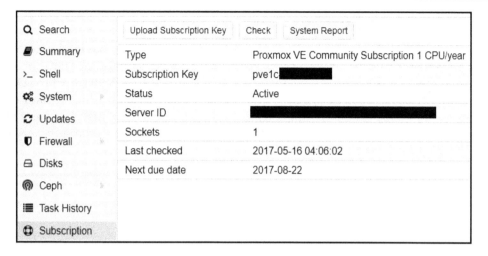

To apply or reapply a subscription key, click on the **Upload Subscription Key** button and enter the key you got directly from Proxmox or an authorized reseller, and then click on **OK,** as shown in the following screenshot:

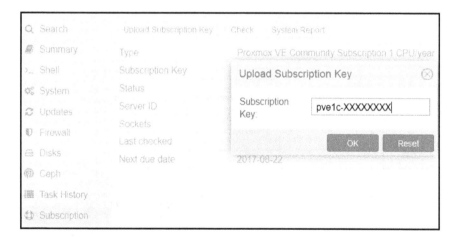

# KVM menu

This menu is exclusive to KVM-based virtual machines. The menu tab is visible when a KVM virtual machine is selected from the left-hand navigation pane.

# KVM VM | Summary

This menu tab represents similar information as the one accessed by navigating to **Node** | **Summary**. Valuable information can be gathered that shows the real-time status of a KVM-based virtual machine. One additional feature this menu has is the **Notes** textbox. Double-clicking on the **Notes** textbox brings up a multiline textbox where an administrator can enter data, such as the department, the intended usage of the VM, or just about any other information that needs to be on hand. The following screenshot shows the summary of one of the KVM VMs in our example cluster:

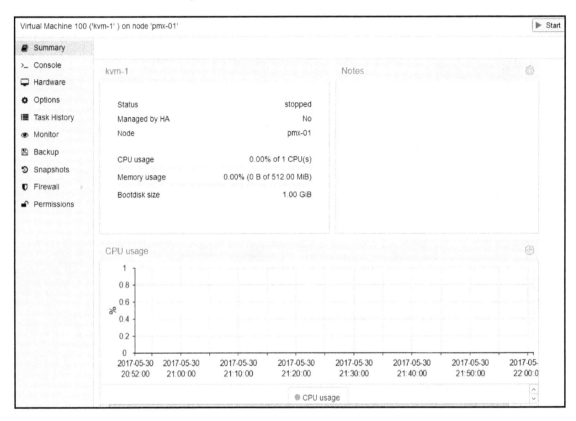

# KVM | Console

Similar to the shell console option of the node-specific menu, the KVM console menu also shows the VM within the browser using `noVNC`. Virtual Network Computing or VNC is a cross-platform system to share graphical user interface across network which also transmits keyboard and mouse signals. This allows an user to access an interface remotely. VNC requires java in order to function. To eliminate the shortfall of java, noVNC was born. noVNC relies on HTML5 operate so it works through any HTML5 supported browser. To open the VM console in a separate browser, we need to click on a viewer from the **Console** drop-down menu, as shown in the following screenshot:

When the VM video adapter is not set to **SPICE**, the option to select the **SPICE** console is disabled. **SPICE** (known as **Simple Protocol for Independent Computing Environment**) is a protocol that allows you to access a virtual machine or any physical machine remotely. **SPICE** can be used to access both Windows and Linux-based machines. Unlike noVNC, where a browser can be used to access a VM remotely, SPICE requires client software locally. Learn more about SPICE from here: `http://www.spice-space.org/index.html`.

# KVM | Hardware

The initially created virtual machine is always never the final configuration. As the functions of a VM rise, it becomes necessary to add virtual drives or network interfaces. The **Hardware** menu tab under the virtual machine is where the adding and removing of devices happens. Through the **Add** menu, additional CD drives, hard drives, and network interfaces (bridge, vNIC, and so on) can be added to a virtual machine. The following screenshot shows the configured hardware for our example KVM VM #100:

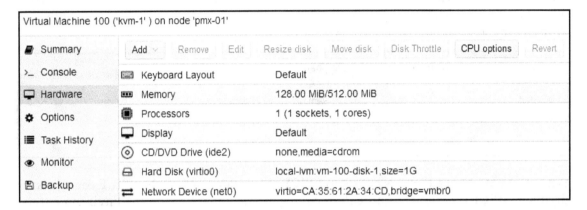

Besides the **Add** menu, other menus, such as **Remove**, **Edit**, **Resize disk**, and **Move disk**, are also available through the **Hardware** menu. All these additional menus, except the **Add** menu, require a hardware item to be selected. **Resize disk** and **Move disk** will be enabled for clicking when a virtual drive is selected. We will cover these in detail in Chapter 6, *KVM Virtual Machines*.

> **Move disk** is the safest way to move a virtual hard drive from one storage to another. If the virtual disk is on shared storage, then live migration of the virtual disk is possible, helping save a lot of time.

We will explore KVM virtual machine configuration in detail in Chapter 6, *KVM Virtual Machines*.

# KVM | Options

The **Options** menu under the virtual machine allows further tweaking, such as changing the name and boot order. Most of the options here can be left to default.

If you want the virtual machine to autostart as soon as the Proxmox node reboots, set the **Start at boot** option to **Yes**.

The following screenshot shows the **Options** menu for a KVM VM:

| Virtual Machine 100 ('kvm-1' ) on node 'pmx-01' | |
|---|---|
| **Summary** | Edit   Revert |
| **Console** | Name | kvm-1 |
| **Hardware** | Start at boot | Yes |
| **Options** | Start/Shutdown order | order=any |
| **Task History** | OS Type | Linux 4.X/3.X/2.6 Kernel |
| | Boot Order | Disk 'virtio0', CD-ROM, Network |
| **Monitor** | Use tablet for pointer | Yes |
| **Backup** | Hotplug | Disk, Network, USB, Memory, CPU |
| **Replication** | ACPI support | Yes |
| **Snapshots** | SCSI Controller Type | VirtIO SCSI |
| **Firewall** | BIOS | Default (SeaBIOS) |
| | KVM hardware virtualization | No |
| **Permissions** | Freeze CPU at startup | No |
| | Use local time for RTC | No |
| | RTC start date | now |
| | SMBIOS settings (type1) | uuid=ff166b1f-2603-4b88-b4a5-1dc211b7b12a |
| | Qemu Agent | No |
| | Protection | No |

# KVM VM | Task History

The **Task History** menu shows all the tasks performed for a specific VM. This functionality is identical to the node-specific task history, where it shows all the tasks for all the KVM virtual machines in the node.

# KVM | Monitor

The **Monitor** menu in a KVM is an interface used to interact with a running KVM virtual machine directly through the **QEMU Monitor Protocol** (**QMP**). We can initiate monitor commands through the Proxmox monitor interface and see the result on the same page. There are a large number of commands used to perform various tasks through the **Monitor** menu. For example, in the following screenshot, we've entered the `info pci` command to view the PCI devices that the VM sees at this moment:

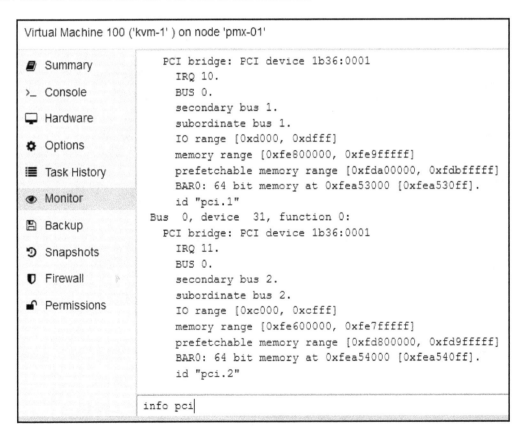

The monitor is a great way to debug a KVM VM-related issue due to the ability to gather a vast amount of debugging data, including the memory core dump, CPU info, and so on. We can also inject configurations, such as balloon memory configuration, additional CPUs, and USB devices through this **Monitor** menu into a running KVM VM. Type `help` to view a list of all the commands usable with **Monitor**.

# KVM | Backup

A backup system is only as good as the ability to restore the backup. Both the backing up and restoring can be done from a single menu under the virtual machine named **Backup**. It also allows backups, browsing, and manual deletion of any backups. All these are done from a single interface with a few mouse clicks. Due to the importance of a backup strategy in a virtual environment, we will take a look at the Proxmox backup system in detail in `Chapter 13`, *Back Up and Restore Virtual Machines*. This menu is usually used to manually perform a backup task for a particular VM.

# KVM VM | Snapshot

Proxmox **Snapshots** is a way to roll back a virtual machine to a previous state. Although it provides similar protection to Proxmox **Backup**, it comes with speed. Proxmox **Snapshots** is extremely fast when compared to Proxmox **Backup**, thus allowing a user to take several snapshots a day. The following screenshot shows the **Snapshots** menu with a snapshot taken after a clean installation of the operating system in the virtual machine:

A common scenario where **Snapshots** can be used is when a software developer wants to test the software or available patches that need to be applied. They can take a snapshot, execute the program, and, if anything goes wrong, simply roll back to the previous state. It creates a snapshot in the RAM itself, so the virtual machine is preserved.

 Never fully depend on snapshots only. A snapshot is not a full backup. It is merely a state where the virtual machine is frozen in time. Always do a full backup of virtual machines for maximum protection. Snapshots are never included in the full VM backup. Snapshots are also never automatically deleted. As more and more snapshots are created, they will accumulate over time, consuming storage space.

We will look into the **Snapshots** option as a backup strategy in Chapter 13, *Back Up and Restore Virtual Machines*.

# KVM | Firewall

Unlike the **Datacenter** | **Firewall** feature, which applies to the whole cluster, the KVM firewall applies to the selected VM only. The KVM VM firewall allows you to configure each virtual machine with its own set of firewall rules, thus isolating each VM from the other even further. In a multi-tenant environment where there are many levels of users, this firewall option helps you prevent a VM from accessing another VM. In Chapter 9, *The Proxmox VE Firewall*, we will take a look at the VM firewall in detail.

# KVM | Permissions

The **Permissions** menu allows the management of user permissions for a particular virtual machine. It is possible to give multiple users access to the same virtual machine. Just click on **Add** to add users or groups already created by navigating to the **Datacenter** | **Users and Datacenter** | **Groups** menus. The following screenshot shows that our example VM has one user permission:

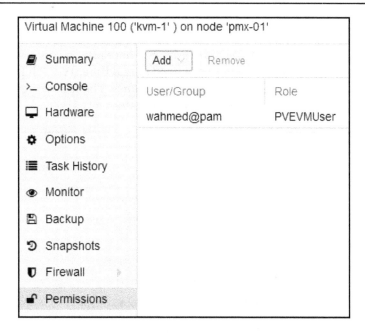

# LXC container menu

This menu is specific to only LXC-based containers. The menu tab is visible when an LXC container is selected from the left-hand navigation pane.

## LXC container | Summary

Like the **Summary** menu under the KVM-specific menus, this shows the stats, notes, and usage graph of an LXC container. Data can be viewed on an hourly, daily, weekly, monthly or yearly basis.

# LXC container | Resources

Additional resources for LXC Containers are adjusted here after a container is created. Changes in the resources get applied to a container in real time. We will look into container resource management in `Chapter 7`, *LXC Virtual Machines*. The following screenshot shows the resources currently allocated for our example container `#101`:

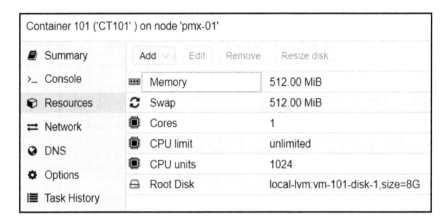

# LXC container | Network

The **Network** menu for a container shows the currently assigned network interface. We can add a new interface or make changes to any existing interface from this menu. The following screenshot shows the **Network** menu for our example container:

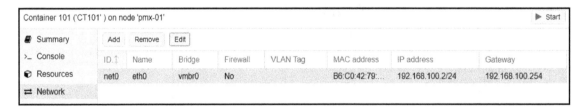

# LXC container | DNS

Similar to the **DNS** menu under the node-specific menus, the **DNS** menu for a container is used to configure the **DNS search domain** and **DNS server address**. Additionally, we can change the **Hostname** of the container. The following screenshot shows the **DNS** menu for our container `#101`:

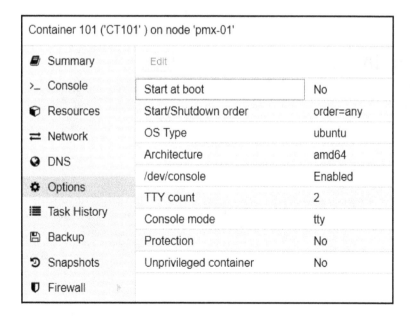

Container 101 ('CT101' ) on node 'pmx-01'

| Summary | Edit | |
| --- | --- | --- |
| Console | Hostname | CT101 |
| Resources | DNS domain | domain.com |
| Network | DNS server | 8.8.8.8 |
| DNS | | |

# LXC container | Options

Similar to the **Options** menu under KVM VMs, this menu provides additional configuration options for containers. Options such as autostart during node boot, **Start/Shutdown order**, and selection of the **OS Type** in the container are available through this **Options** menu. The following screenshot shows the **Options** menu for our  container #101:

Container 101 ('CT101' ) on node 'pmx-01'

| Summary | Edit | |
| --- | --- | --- |
| Console | Start at boot | No |
| Resources | Start/Shutdown order | order=any |
| Network | OS Type | ubuntu |
| DNS | Architecture | amd64 |
| | /dev/console | Enabled |
| Options | TTY count | 2 |
| Task History | Console mode | tty |
| Backup | Protection | No |
| Snapshots | Unprivileged container | No |
| Firewall | | |

Details about these options will be discussed later in the book in Chapter 7, *LXC Virtual Machines*.

## LXC container | Task History

The **Task History** menu shows a list of all the tasks performed on the selected container. Similar to the **Task History** menu under KVM VMs, the container's task history provides a means to search for tasks performed by specific users or only shows tasks with errors.

## LXC container | Backup

This menu is identical to the **Backup** menu under KVM VMs, where we can perform a manual backup of a selected container, remove a backup file, or restore a container from a list of backup files. The details of the backup and restore strategy will be covered in detail in Chapter 13, *Back Up and Restore Virtual Machines*.

## LXC container | Snapshots

This menu offers identical functionality as KVM **Snapshots**, where we can create snapshots of the container or roll back to a previous state. More about snapshots will be covered in Chapter 13, *Back Up and Restore Virtual Machines*.

## LXC container | Firewall

Similar to the KVM-specific **Firewall** menu, this menu enables and manages firewall rules for a particular LXC container. More will be discussed in Chapter 9, *The Proxmox VE Firewall*.

## LXC container | Permissions

Similar to the KVM-specific **Permissions** menu, we can set different permission levels for a container through this menu. Refer to the **Permissions** menu under the KVM-specific menu as they are identical for both the KVM and LXC virtual machines.

# Pool menu

This menu is visible when a **Pool** is selected from the left-hand navigation pane. Let's now look at each of the options in detail.

# Pool | Summary

The **Summary** menu for the pool only shows the **Comment** description for the pool, as shown in the following screenshot:

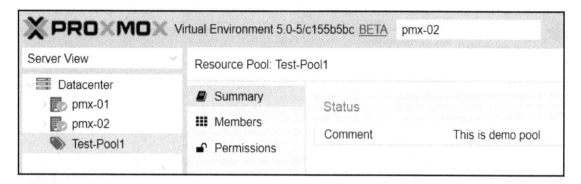

We cannot, however, change the description or add a note from the **Pools** menu. This task can be done through the **Datacenter** | **Permissions** | **Pools** menu. From there, select the desired pool and change the description. This is also the same menu to add new pools to the cluster. The following screenshot shows the pool edit dialog box for our demo pool, Test-Pool1:

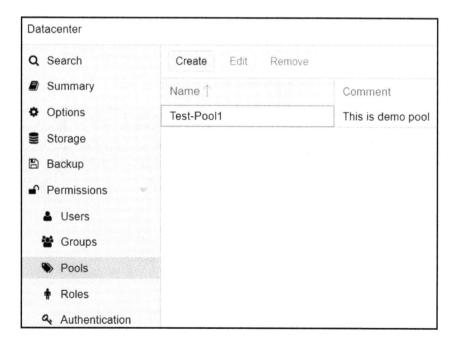

# Pool | Members

This menu shows all the resources currently allocated to the selected pool. We can allocate virtual machines or storage to a pool. For example, in our demo pool named `Test-Pool1`, we have a container #101 and local storage allocated, as shown in the following screenshot:

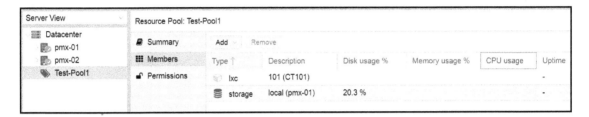

New resources can be added through the **Add** drop-down menu. We can only add virtual machines and storage to a pool. To add a KVM or LXC container, simply click on the **Add** button and select a virtual machine from the dialog box, as shown in the following screenshot:

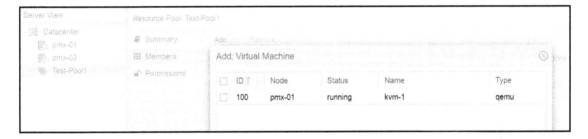

Conveniently, the dialog box will only show virtual machines that have not been added to the pool yet. For our example in the previous screenshot, container #101 has been already added to the pool so the dialog box only shows 100 available virtual machines. The procedure to add storage to a pool is the same as adding a virtual machine.

## Pool | Permissions

The **Permissions** menu under **Pools** is the same as the KVM and LXC virtual machine permissions. With these permissions, we can assign a user to a pool and all the resources under that pool become accessible to that user. This eliminates any need of assigning permissions individually by resources. For example, if a user requires access permissions to multiple virtual machines, we can put those virtual machines in a pool and give the user permissions to that pool only. The following screenshot shows that in our example pool named `Test-Pool1`, the user `wahmed` has been given administrative permissions to manage the pool:

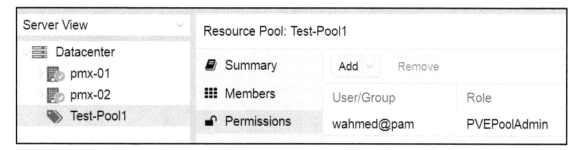

# Summary

In this chapter, we learned how to create a Proxmox cluster and explored the graphical user interface of Proxmox VE. We learned about how the menu system is divided into different entities and what features are used to manage resources in a Proxmox cluster. We also saw different modes of the viewing option to browse all the resources in a Proxmox cluster.

Being equipped with the knowledge of the Proxmox GUI and its features paves the way for much more advanced topics in the coming chapters. Although Proxmox provides many management options through the CLI, a great deal of time is still spent on the Proxmox GUI for day-to-day cluster management.

In the next chapter, we will see what is under the hood of Proxmox. We will see how the Proxmox directory structure is laid out to store vital configuration files and what the Proxmox cluster filesystem is and why it is important.

# 3
# Proxmox under the Hood

In the previous chapter, we saw how the Proxmox GUI looks and also looked at its features. In this chapter, we will take a look how configuration files hold a Proxmox virtualization platform together, and the files to be used for advanced configuration and how they are used to troubleshoot a Proxmox platform. Proxmox is built on Debian Linux, which is very stable with a large active community. So, it inherited the heavy dependency on configuration or `.conf` files as a primary means to store various configurations. The Proxmox GUI provides you with the ability to manage a cluster, but does not provide direct access to any configuration files. Any direct changes by advanced users have to be done through a **command-line interface** (**CLI**). Commonly used scenarios, such as adding special arguments to configuration files, is done through the CLI. In this chapter, we will cover the following topics:

- The Proxmox cluster file system, or pmxcfs
- The Proxmox directory structure
- Configuration files' location and their functions
- Arguments and syntaxes used in configuration files

# The Proxmox cluster file system

Proxmox is a cluster-based hypervisor. It is meant to be used with several server nodes. By using multiple nodes in a cluster, we provide redundancy or high availability to the platform while increasing uptime. A production virtual environment may have several dozens to several hundreds of nodes in a cluster. As an administrator, it may not be a realistic scenario to change configuration files in the cluster one node at a time. Depending on the number of nodes in a cluster, it may take several hours just to change one small argument in a configuration file of all the nodes. To save precious time, Proxmox implemented the clustered filesystem to keep all the configuration files or any other common files shared by all the nodes in the cluster, in a synchronous state. Its official name is **Proxmox Cluster file system** (**pmxcfs**). The pmxcfs is a database-driven filesystem used to store configuration files. Any changes made to any files or copied/deleted in this filesystem get replicated in real time to all the nodes using corosync. The Corosync Cluster Engine is a group communication system used to implement high availability within an application. You can learn more about corosync by visiting the link: `http://corosync.github.io/corosync/`.

Any file added to this filesystem almost instantly gets replicated to all the nodes in the cluster, thus saving an enormous amount of time for a system administrator.

 The pmxcfs filesystem is a database-driven filesystem used to store the Proxmox cluster configuration files or any other files commonly shared by all the nodes in the Proxmox cluster. To know more about pmxcfs, visit the following Proxmox Wiki:
`http://pve.proxmox.com/wiki/Proxmox_Cluster_file_system_(pmxcfs)`

The pmxcfs filesystem is mounted at the following path:

```
# /etc/pve
```

All cluster-related files are stored in this folder path.

# Proxmox directory structure

Proxmox comes with a distinct directory structure where all the configuration files and other necessary files are stored. This makes finding those configuration files in time of need very easy. The following table shows the location of the files stored and their functions:

| Filename/location | File function |
| --- | --- |
| `/etc/pve/datacenter.cfg` | Proxmox VE data center configuration file. Used to change options such as the default language, keyboard layout, default console, and so on. |
| `/etc/pve/corosync.conf` | Main cluster configuration file. Prior to Proxmox VE 4.0, this was known as `cluster.conf` and can also be used to change the vote of a particular node. |
| `/etc/pve/storage.cfg` | PVE storage configuration file. This holds all the information of a local or shared storage system. |
| `/etc/pve/user.cfg` | User list and access control configuration for all users and groups in the cluster. |
| `/etc/pve/authkey.pub` | Public key used by the ticket system. |
| `/etc/pve/ceph.conf` | When a Ceph cluster is integrated with Proxmox, this configuration file is generated for the Ceph cluster. |
| `/etc/pve/vzdump.cron` | Cluster-wide backup tasks that are not specific to a single node. This file should not be edited manually. All the entries are auto created from the **Backup** menu on the GUI. |

| | |
|---|---|
| `/etc/pve/priv/shadow.cfg` | Shadow password file that holds all usernames and their encrypted passwords. |
| `/etc/pve/priv/authkey.key` | Private key used by the ticket system. |
| `/etc/pve/priv/ceph.client.admin.keyring` | Authentication keyring for a Ceph cluster. This is only created when Ceph is integrated with Proxmox. |
| `/etc/pve/priv/ceph/<storage_id>.keyring` | Keyring used to attach the Ceph RBD storage. We will take a look at Ceph in `Chapter 4`, *Storage Systems*. |
| `/etc/pve/firewall/<vmid>.fw` | Firewall rules for all VMs. |
| `/etc/pve/nodes/<name>/pve-ssl.pem` | Public SSL key for the web server. Used to access the Proxmox web GUI. |
| `/etc/pve/nodes/<name>/priv/pve-ssl.key` | Private SSL key. |
| `/etc/pve/nodes/<name>/host.fw` | Firewall rules for the Proxmox host. |
| `/etc/pve/nodes/<name>/qemu-server/<vmid>.conf` | Virtual machine configuration data for KVM VMs. |
| `/etc/pve/nodes/<name>/lxc/ <vmid>.conf` | Virtual machine configuration data for LXC containers. |
| `/etc/pve/.version` | File versions' data to detect file modifications. |
| `/etc/pve/.members` | Information nodes that are members of the cluster. |
| `/etc/pve/.vmlist` | List of all VMs in the cluster. |
| `/etc/pve/.clusterlog` | Last 50 entries of the cluster log. |
| `/etc/pve/.rrd` | Most recent entries of RRD data. |

Any changes made to these files or any other files inside pmxcfs mounted under the /etc/pve folder get replicated automatically the moment the changes are made. For this reason, we will have to take extra care of what we do to these files. For example, if we delete a .conf file from one node by mistake, it will also be deleted from all the other nodes in the Proxmox cluster.

 A regular manual backup of the /etc/pve folder should be a common practice in case the cluster needs rebuilding after any disaster or accidental file deletion/change.

On a regular day-to-day basis, a system administrator will not need to access these files from the command line since almost all of these are editable from the Proxmox GUI. But knowing the location of these files and what they hold might save the day when the GUI becomes inaccessible for whatever reason.

# Dissecting the configuration files

We now know where all the important files that hold a Proxmox cluster together are placed. We will go inside some of these files for a better understanding of what they do and what command arguments they use. You can use any Linux editor to view/edit these configuration files. In this book, we will use #nano to view and edit configuration files.

During the learning process, it will be a good idea to make a backup of the configuration files before editing them. In case something goes wrong, you will be able to replace it with the original working configuration file. Simply copy the configuration file using the following command:

```
# cp /etc/pve/<config_file> /home/<any_folder>
```

We can also use the SCP command to back up files to another node:

```
# scp /etc/pve/<config_file> <user>@<ip_or_hostname>:/<folder>
```

# The cluster configuration file

The `corosync.conf` configuration file stores parameters needed for a cluster operation. Any empty lines or lines starting with # in this configuration file are completely ignored. The following code is what our `corosync.conf` file currently looks like in our example cluster with two Proxmox nodes. The Proxmox cluster configuration file is located under `/etc/pve/corosync.conf`:

```
logging {
  debug: off
  to_syslog: yes
}

nodelist {
  node {
    name: pmx-02
    nodeid: 2
    quorum_votes: 1
    ring0_addr: pmx-02
  }

  node {
    name: pmx-01
    nodeid: 1
    quorum_votes: 1
    ring0_addr: pmx-01
  }

}

quorum {
  provider: corosync_votequorum
}

totem {
  cluster_name: pmx-cluster
  config_version: 2
  ip_version: ipv4
  secauth: on
  version: 2
  interface {
    bindnetaddr: 172.16.2.1
    ringnumber: 0
  }

}
```

We are now going to dig into `corosync.conf` to describe the functions of the parameters. This configuration file is automatically created when a new Proxmox cluster is created. There are four segments in this file, which are as follows:

- `logging {  }`
- `nodelist {  }`
- `quorum {  }`
- `totem {  }`

# logging { }

This segment contains configuration parameters used for logging. According to the parameters in our example cluster, debugging is off and logs are transferred to `syslog`. If we want to turn debugging on and transfer logs to a `logfile` instead of `syslog`, our parameters will appear as follows:

```
logging {
   debug: on
   to_logfile : yes
   to_syslog : no
   timestamp : on
}
/var/log/<filename>.log {
   daily
   rotate 5
   copytruncate
}
```

We can also attach a `timestamp` to all the log entries. Note that if we want to pass logs to a `logfile`, we need an additional `logfile {  }` segment along with the `logrotate` and `copytruncate` parameters.

# nodelist { }

As the name implies, this segment is where all the member nodes of a Proxmox cluster are listed. Each node is separated by the `node {  }` subsegment. The following are the three main parameters as they appear in our cluster configuration file:

```
nodeid
```

This parameter shows the numeric order of the member nodes as they get added to the cluster. This is optional for IPv4 but mandatory when using IPv6. Each `nodeid` must be unique in the cluster configuration file. If no `nodeid` parameter is used when using IPv4, then the cluster automatically calculates this ID from the 32-bit IPv4 address. With IPv6, this calculation cannot happen since IPv6 is more than 32 bit.

 Warning! Never use `nodeid` instead of `0` as it is reserved by `corosync.conf`.

`quorum_votes`

This option shows the number of votes that the node must cast to form a quorum. In a Proxmox cluster, this is no more than one vote per node. Whatever this number is, it should be equal for all nodes. There are simply no reasons to use anything other than 1.

`ring0_addr`

This line basically specifies the IP address or the hostname of the node. The actual format of this option is `ringX_addr`, where `X` is the ring number. When multiple network interfaces are used for redundancy purposes, the redundant ring protocol is implemented in corosync. Each of the interfaces is assigned a unique `ringnumber`. This unique `ringnumber` tells the interface to connect to the corresponding ring protocol. For example, in our example cluster, if we use the second interface for redundancy, the `node { }` segment will appear as follows:

```
node {
  nodeid: 2
  quorum_votes: 1
  ring0_addr: 172.16.0.71
  ring1_addr: 192.168.0.71
}
```

# quorum { }

This segment tells the cluster which quorum algorithm to use to form a quorum. As of corosync version 2.3.5, there is only one provider available, which is `votequorum`. This algorithm ensures that there are no split-brain situations and a quorum is formed only when majority votes are cast. There are no additional options available for this segment.

# totem { }

This segment specifies parameters for totem protocols. Corosync consists of the totem **Single Ring Protocol (SRP)** and totem **Redundant Ring Protocol (RRP)**. This segment also includes a { } subsegment interface to specify the bind address and ring number.

 When only one interface is used for cluster communication, totem SRP is implemented. In this protocol, only the ring number 0 is used. When multiple interfaces are used for redundancy, totem RRP is implemented, where more than one ring number and interfaces are used.

The following parameters show the name of the Proxmox cluster that is created by Proxmox during our example cluster creation:

```
cluster_name: pmx-cluster
```

We can also see the cluster name from the **Datacenter** I **Summary** menu.

```
config_version: 2
```

This parameter specifies the version number of the configuration file after each cluster-wide change, such as adding or removing member nodes. When any changes are made manually directly to the file, then it is mandatory to increase the version number manually. Failure to do so will cause the cluster configuration to fail. In that case, the cluster filesystem in /etc/pve/ may be inaccessible since the node will not be able to start the pve-cluster service. The config number should only increase incrementally.

```
ip_version: IPv4
```

This parameter specifies the version of IP to be used. By default, IPv4 is used. To use version 6 of IP, simply use the option IPv6.

```
secauth: on
```

This parameter tells the cluster to use the SHA1 authentication for encrypting all transmitted messages. Although this option adds extra overhead for all transmitted messages, thus reducing the total throughput, it is important to use encryption to protect the cluster from invaders. By default, this parameter is enabled in Proxmox.

Note that the `secauth` parameter for corosync is deprecated. It is recommended by the corosync maintainers to use `crypto_hash` and `crypto_cipher`. But as of Proxmox 5, `secauth` is still used by default. The following is an example of how the recommended setting will appear in the totem segment:

```
totem {
  crypto_hash: sha1
  crypto_cipher: aes256
}
```

At the time of writing this book, Proxmox developers have not confirmed whether `crypto_hash` and `crypto_cipher` can be safely used instead of `secauth`.

```
version: 2
```

This parameter specifies the version of the configuration. Currently, the only version for this parameter is 2. This is not the version increment of the configuration file whenever any changes are made. This number must not be changed manually.

Besides the parameters mentioned earlier, there are a few other parameters available in the totem segment for various purposes. The following table shows some of these parameters and their functions:

| Parameter | Description |
|-----------|-------------|
| rrp_mode | Available options: `none`, `active`, and `passive`.<br>This parameter specifies redundant protocol modes. When there is only one interface, corosync automatically chooses none. With multiple interfaces, we can set it to `active`, which offers a lower latency at the cost of less performance. We can also set the mode to `passive`, which offers a significant performance boost at the cost of CPU usage. |
| netmtu | Available options: `1500` to `8982`.<br>This specifies the MTU of an interface. It is useful when jumbo frames are used. Linux adds an 18-byte header to the network data packets. So, even though hardware can support 9,000 MTUs, it is wise to set MTUs to 8,982. This way, after Linux adds additional headers, the total MTU does not go beyond 9,000 and hardware will not misbehave. These MTU tips apply to all situations where jumbo frames are intended. |
| transport | Available options: `udp`, `udpu`, and `iba`.<br>This specifies the transport protocol. By default, corosync uses UDP. If InfiniBand and network are used with RDMA, then we can specify `iba` instead of `udp`. |

# interface { }

This is the subsegment of the totem segment where the information regarding the network interface is specified. By default, Proxmox only enters the `bindnetaddr` and `ringnumber` parameters in this subsegment:

```
bindnetaddr : <ip/network_address>
```

These parameters specify the IP address or network address that corosync should bind to. This can be any IP address of a node in the cluster. Usually, this is the IP address of the node where the initial Proxmox cluster creation command was executed:

```
ringnumber: 0
```

This parameter specifies a separate ring number for each network interface. A unique `ringnumber` for each interface allows unique identification of which ring should use which interface. For example, with a single interface where totem SRP is applied, there is only one ring with `ringnumber: 0`. With dual interfaces and totem RRP applied, there are two rings with `ringnumber: 0` and `ringnumber: 1`. Note that the ring number must start from 0.

Although the primary use of multiple rings is redundancy, it can be used for other purposes too, such as connecting nodes in different locations to a single Proxmox cluster. We can achieve this by implementing VPN, such as OpenVPN, IPSEC, or tinc. We can create a dedicated network on a separate VLAN and create a new ring to bind to that network. This way, corosync will send multicast data on both networks.

There are a few other advanced parameters available that are not used by default. The following table shows some of these parameters and their functions:

| Parameter | Description |
| --- | --- |
| mcastaddr | This specifies a multicast address, which is used by corosync. The address can be IPv4 or IPv6 when IPV6 is used. This parameter is usually not needed if the `cluster_name` parameter has already been used in the `corosync.conf` configuration file. But when both are used, `mcastaddr` will have a higher priority over `cluster_name`. By default, the Proxmox cluster configuration, `mcastaddr`, is not used. |

| | |
|---|---|
| `mcastport` | This specifies the UDP port number for a multicast address. Corosync uses two ports for multicasts: one for receiving and the other for sending. We only need to specify the receiving port since the sending port is automatically calculated using the formula `mcastport - 1`. For example, if we specify the receiving port number `5405`, then corosync will use `5404` for sending. This is very important to note in a multi-cluster environment on the same network. |

If we put all the totem parameters we have seen so far together, the `corosync.conf` for our example cluster will appear as follows if redundant interfaces have been used:

```
totem {
   cluster_name: pmx-cluster
   config_version: 4
   ip_version: ipv4
   crypto_hash: sha1
   crypto_cipher: aes256
   version: 2
   rrp_mode: passive
    interface {
   bindnetaddr: 172.16.2.71
   ringnumber: 0
   mcastaddr: 224.1.1.1
   mcastport: 5405
   }
   Interface {
   bindnetaddr: 172.16.20.71
   ringnumber: 1
   mcastaddr: 224.1.1.2
   mcastport: 5408
   }
}
```

# Storage configuration file

This is the configuration file where storage to be used with Proxmox are specified. The configuration file is located under `/etc/pve/storage.cfg`. We will take a look at the different storage systems in Chapter 4, *Storage Systems*. The following is the possible content of the storage configuration file with various storage systems supported by Proxmox:

```
dir: local
   path /var/lib/vz
   content images,iso,vztmpl,rootdir
   maxfiles 0
```

```
nfs: nfs_share_name
  path /mnt/pve/nfs-server
  server 192.168.145.11
  export /mnt/pmxnas01
  options vers=3
  content iso,vztmpl
  maxfiles 1

iscsi: nas-iscsi-01
  target iqn.2015-12.org.example.istgt:pmxtgt01
  portal 192.168.145.11
  content none

lvm: nas-lvm-01
  vgname nas-lvm-01
  base nas-iscsi-01:0.0.0.scsi-330000000391132dd
  shared
  content images

nfs: vm-nfs-01
  path /mnt/pve/vm-nfs-01
  server 192.165.145.11
  export /mnt/pmxnas01
  options vers=3
  content images,vztmpl,backup,rootdir
  maxfiles 1

zfspool: zfs-01
  enable
  pool zfs_pool
  content images, rootdir
```

Almost all the settings in `storage.cfg` can be changed from the Proxmox GUI without using any CLI. Attached storage abides by the following common format in `storage.cfg`:

```
storage_type : storage_name
  path </path to folder>
  target <target file name> (for iSCSI)
  portal <server IP address> (for iSCSI)
  vgname <volume group name> (for LVM)
  base <base volume group> (for LVM)
  server <storage server IP address>
  export </shared location on NFS server>
  content <type of files the storage can hold>
  maxfile <maximum number of old backup to keep>
```

# User configuration files

The `user.cfg` file holds all user, group, and access control information in the cluster and is located under `/etc/pve/user.cfg`. It follows the following format to store all information:

- For user information, the format is as follows:

    ```
    <type>:<user>@realm:enable:expiry:f_name:l_name:email:comment
    ```

- For group information, the format is as follows:

    ```
    <type>:<group_name>:user@realm:comment
    ```

- For pool information, the format is as follows:

    ```
    <type>:<pool_name>:<assigned_resource>:user@realm:comment
    ```

- For access control information, the format is as follows:

    ```
    <type>:<assigned_resource>:user@realm:comment:<assigned_role>
    ```

Based on this format, the following is what our `user.cfg` file looks like in our example cluster:

```
user:wahmed@pam:1:0:Wasim:Ahmed:wahmed@symmcom.com:::
user:root@pam:1:0:::admin@domain.com:::

group:Authors:wahmed@pam:Author Access:
group:DemoUsers::Guest User Permissions:
group:Admins::Proxmox Administrators:

pool:Test-Pool1:This is demo pool:101:local:


acl:1:/pool/Test-Pool1:wahmed@pam:PVEPoolAdmin:
acl:1:/vms/100:wahmed@pam:PVEVMUser:
```

Note that the `user.cfg` file does not hold any user passwords. This information is stored in `/etc/pve/priv/shadow.cfg` in an encrypted form. All the content in this configuration file can be managed through the Proxmox GUI. Whenever we create a new user/group or assign roles, the configuration file gets updated. If the GUI becomes inaccessible, this file can be manually edited.

# The password configuration file

The password configuration file is located under `/etc/pve/priv/shadow.cfg` and stores all the passwords for users in the cluster. The format is rather simple but the function of this file is very crucial. The format to store password information is as follows:

```
<user_name>:<encrypted_password>
```

Notice that the password file is in a `/priv` folder inside `/etc/pve`. Sensitive information, such as passwords, private authorization keys, and known hosts, are kept in the `/etc/pve/priv` folder. When a new user is created through the Proxmox GUI, a new entry is added here.

# KVM virtual machine configuration file

The `vmid.conf` file stores configuration information for each virtual machine and is located at `/etc/pve/nodes/<name>/qemu-server/<vmid.conf>`. The directory structure divides all VM configuration files into categories based on nodes. For example, the configuration file for our VM `#100` is stored in the following location:

```
# /etc/pve/nodes/pmx-01/qemu-server/100.conf
```

When we migrate a VM from one node to another, Proxmox just moves the configuration file to the destination node. If the VM is powered on during the migration, then the entire memory content of the VM is also migrated to the destination node. For our VM 100, if we migrate it to `pmx-02`, the second node in the cluster, then the location of the `100.conf` file will be as follows:

```
# /etc/pve/nodes/pmx-02/qemu-server/100.conf
```

 If a node with virtual machines in it becomes inaccessible, simply moving the `<vm_id>.conf` files to a different node will allow access to all the VMs from a different node. Any files of the folder inside `/etc/pve` can be seen from any node in the cluster.

We will now take a look at a `<vm_id>.conf` file itself to see what makes up a virtual machine behind the scenes. This configuration file follows a simple `option:value` format. The following is the configuration file of our VM `#100`:

```
balloon: 128
bootdisk: virtio0
cores: 1
ide2: none,media=cdrom
kvm: 0
memory: 512
name: kvm-1
net0: virtio=CA:35:61:2A:34:CD,bridge=vmbr0
numa: 0
ostype: l26
parent: Clean_Install
scsihw: virtio-scsi-pci
smbios1: uuid=ff166b1f-2603-4b88-b4a5-1dc211b7b12a
sockets: 1
virtio0: local-lvm:vm-100-disk-1,size=1G

[Clean_Install]
balloon: 128
bootdisk: virtio0
cores: 1
ide2: none,media=cdrom
kvm: 0
memory: 512
name: kvm-1
net0: virtio=CA:35:61:2A:34:CD,bridge=vmbr0
numa: 0
ostype: l26
scsihw: virtio-scsi-pci
smbios1: uuid=ff166b1f-2603-4b88-b4a5-1dc211b7b12a
snaptime: 1496204459
sockets: 1
virtio0: local-lvm:vm-100-disk-1,size=1G
```

Since our virtual machine also has a snapshot, the configuration also embeds the specification of the virtual machine as it was during the snapshot. Almost all the options in this file can be set through the Proxmox GUI under the KVM virtual machine **Options** menu tab. Some option values, such as arguments, have to be added through the CLI. The following table shows some of the possible options. The values can be used as virtual machine configurations:

| Options | Description | Possible values |
| --- | --- | --- |
| args | Allows you to pass arguments to a VM. Features such as sound can be activated using KVM arguments. Refer to section 2.2.6.2 for more details on arguments used in the KVM. | See section 2.2.6.2 |
| autostart | Auto-restarts a virtual machine after crash. The default value is 0. | 1; 0 |
| balloon | Targeted RAM for a VM in MB. | Integer number |
| boot | Default boot device | c=hdd; d=cd-rom; n=network |
| bootdisk | Enables booting from a specific disk. | ide; sata; scsi; virtio |
| core | Number of cores per socket. The default value is 1. | Integer number |
| cpu | Emulated CPU types. The default value is kvm64. | 486; kvm32; kvm64; qemu32; qemu64; conroe; haswell; nehalem; opteron_G1/2/3/4/5; penryn; sandybridge; westmere; athlon; core2duo; coreduo; host; pentium; pentium2; pentium3; phenom |
| cpuunits | This is the CPU weight of the VM. This value is used by the kernel fair scheduler. The larger the value is, the more CPU time a VM will get. Note that this value is relative to the weights of all other running VMs in the cluster. The default value is 1000. | Integer 0 to 500000 |
| description | Notes for VM | Plain text |
| freeze | Freezes the CPU at startup | 1; 0 |
| hostpci(n) | This option allows a VM direct access to the host hardware. When this option is used, it is not possible to migrate the VM. Caution should be used for this option as it is still in the experimental stage. It is not recommended for a production environment. | HOSTPCIDEVICE Syntax for HOSTPCIDEVICE is bus: <pci_device_number> Get pci_device_number using #lspci |
| hotplug | Enables hotplug for disk and network devices. The default value is 0. | 1; 0 |

| | | |
|---|---|---|
| ide(n) | Allows the volume to be used as an IDE disk or CD-ROM. The n in ide(n) is limited to 0 to 3. | `[volume=]image_name;` `[media=cdrom,disk]; [cyls=c,heads=h,` `secs=s,[trans=t]];` `[snapshot=on,off];` `[cache=none,writethrough,writeback,` `unsafe,directsync];` `[format=f];[backup=yes|no],` `[rerror=ignore, report,stop];` `[werror=enospc,ignore,` `report,stop]; [aio=native,threads]` |
| kvm | Enables/disables the KVM hardware virtualization. This option disables any hardware acceleration within a VM. A possible usage scenario is when you are setting up a nested virtualized cluster. The default value is 1. | `1; 0` |
| lock | Enables locking/unlocking of a VM. | `backup; migrate; rollback; snapshot` |
| memory | Allocated amount of RAM for the VM. | Integer number from `16` to `N` |
| migration_downtime | Value in seconds for the maximum tolerated downtime for migration. The default value is **0.1**. | Number `0` to `N` |
| migration_speed | Value for the maximum speed in MB/s for VM migrations. Set the value to `0` for no limit. The default value is `0`. | Integer number from `0` to `N` |
| name | Name for the VM. | Text |
| net(n) | Specified network devices. `MODEL=XX:XX:XX:XX:XX:XX,` `[bridge=<dev>], [rate=<mbps>], [tag=<vlanid>]` | `MODEL= e1000, i82551, i82557b,` `i82559er, ne2k_isa, ne2k_pci,` `pcnet, rtl8139, virtio` |
| onboot | Enables/disables VM auto-start during the host node reboot. | `1; 0` |
| sata(n) | Allows the volume to be used as a SATA disk or CD-ROM. N in sata(n) is limited to 0 to 5. | `[volume=]volume], [media=cdrom,` `disk];` `[cyls=c,heads=h,secs=s,trans=t]` `[snapshot=on, off]; [cache=none,` `writethrough, writeback, unsafe,` `directsync]; [format=f]; [backup=yes,` `no]; [rerror=ignore, report, top];` `[werror=enospc, ignore, report,` `stop]; [aio=native, threads]` |
| scsi(n) | Allows the volume to be used as an SCSI disk or CD-ROM. N in scsi(n) is limited to 0 to 13. | `[volume=volume], [media=cdrom,` `disk];[cyls=c,heads=h,` `secs=s,trans=t] [snapshot=on, off];` `[cache=none, writethrough,` `writeback, unsafe, directsync];` `[format=f]; [backup=yes, no];` `[rerror=ignore, report, stop];` `[werror=enospc, ignore, report,` `stop]; [aio=native, threads]` |
| scsihw | SCSI controller type. The default value is `lsi`. | `lsi;megasas;virtio-scsi-pci` |

| shares | This is the value-allocated amount of RAM for autoballooning. The larger this value is, the more RAM the VM will get. The value 0 disables this option. The default value is 1000. | Integer from 0 to 50000 |
|---|---|---|
| sockets | Number of CPU sockets. The default value is 1. | Integer from 1 to N |
| startdate | This option sets the initial date of the real-time clock. | now \| YYYY-MM-DD \| YYYY-MM-DDTHH:MM:SS |
| startup | This option sets the behavior for VM startup and shutdown. Order is a positive integer number, which sets the order in which the VMs will start. Shutdown follows the order value in reverse. The delay of startup and shutdown can be set through up and down in seconds. | [order=+ Int], [up=+ Int], [down=+ Int] |
| tablet | Enables/disables the USB tablet device in a VM. Without this option, if running a lot of console-only VMs on one host, disabling this feature can save context switches. The default value is 1. | 1; 0 |
| unused(n) | Unused volumes in a VM. When a virtual drive is deleted from a VM, the volume does not get deleted instantly. Instead, the status changes to unused:<volume_name>. At a later time, if the volume is needed, it can be reattached to the VM by changing the option to ide(n): \| scsi(n): \| sata(n):. | string |
| usb(n) | Enables pass-through direct access to a USB device. N can be set to 0 to 4. When this option is used, it is no longer possible to migrate the VM. | HOSTUSBDEVICE Syntax for HOSTUSBDEVICE is <vendor_id:product_id> Get pci_device_number from command #lsusb -t |
| vga | VM display type | cirrus \| std \| vmware \| qxl |
| virtio(n) | Allows the volume to be used as a VirtIO disk. The n in virtio(n) is limited to 0 to 15. | [volume=volume]; [media=cdrom, disk], [cyls=c,heads=h, secs=s,trans=t]; [snapshot=on, off]; [cache=none, writethrough, writeback, unsafe, directsync]; [format=f]; [backup=yes, no]; [rerror=ignore, report, stop]; [werror=enospc, ignore, report, stop]; [aio=native, threads] |

# Arguments in the KVM configuration file

Arguments in a virtual machine configuration file are a way to extend the capability of the VM beyond just the default. For example, sound is not enabled for a VM by default. In order to give a VM the ability to play audio/video, an argument has to be passed through the VM configuration file. The following are some examples of arguments that can be used in a Proxmox VM configuration file. Arguments can be added in the following format:

```
args: -<device_arguments_1> -<device_arguments_2> . . . .
ballon: 512
bootdisk: virtio0
cores: 1
ide2: none,media=cdrom
. . . .
. . . .
```

Enable a serial device in a VM using the following code:

```
args: -serial /dev/ttyS0
```

Enable sound in a Windows XP VM using the following code:

```
args: -device AC97,addr=0x18
```

Enable sound in Windows 7 and later VMs using the following code:

```
args -device intel-hda,id=sound5,bus=pci.0,addr=0x18 -device had-
micro,id=sound5-codec0,bus=sound5.0,cad=0 -device had-duplex,id=sound5-
codec1,bus=sound5.0,cad=1
```

Enable UUID in a VM using this line of code:

```
args -uuid f1234a93-20d32-2398-129032ds-2322
```

Enable support for `aio=native` in a VM:

```
args: -drive file=/dev/VGGRP/VOL,if=virtio,index=1,cache=none,aio=native
```

# LXC container configuration file

From Proxmox VE 4.0, OpenVZ has been dropped in favor of LXC containers. LXC is derived from OpenVZ for the mainline kernel. One of the main advantages of LXC is that it can be used on top of the standard Linux kernel without needing a special kernel, as is the case for OpenVZ.

When using LXC, keep in mind that live migration of a container is not possible as of Proxmox VE 5.0. The container will need to be powered off to commit offline migration.

The following is the LXC configuration file of the container #101 in our example cluster, which is located in /etc/pve/lxc/101.conf:

```
arch: amd64
cores: 1
hostname: CT101
memory: 512
nameserver: 8.8.8.8
net0: name=eth0,bridge=vmbr0,gw=192.168.100.254,hwaddr=B6:C0:42:79:3E:D5,ip=192.168.100.2/24,type=veth
ostype: ubuntu
rootfs: local-lvm:vm-101-disk-1,size=8G
searchdomain: domain.com
swap: 512
```

LXC container configuration is much simpler than OpenVZ. As with OpenVZ, there are no User Bean Counters in LXCs. It is worth noting here that if your existing cluster is pre-Proxmox VE 5 and has OpenVZ containers running, they cannot be seamlessly upgraded to LXCs during the Proxmox upgrade. All OpenVZ containers must be powered off, commit a full backup, and then restored in the upgraded Proxmox VE 5. We will take a look at the upgrade process in detail later in this book in Chapter 14, *Updating/Upgrading Proxmox*.

Like a KVM configuration file, LXC also uses an option and value format of the configuration in its file. Parameters added by default during the LXC creation in Proxmox are mostly self explanatory. Most of these parameters for LXC can be changed through the Proxmox GUI. LXC itself has got quite a few configuration parameters, which cannot be controlled through the GUI, but they can be added manually through the CLI, depending on the requirement. A comprehensive list of all the possible configuration parameters for LXC can be found at the link: http://man7.org/linux/man-pages/man5/lxc.container.conf.5.html.

# Version configuration file

The version configuration file shows the version numbers of configuration files in the cluster and is located under /etc/pve/.version. Every time a configuration file is edited, the version number increments in the .version file. The following is the .version file in our cluster at this moment:

```
{
"starttime": 1496068086,
"clinfo": 6,
"vmlist": 11,
"corosync.conf": 2,
"corosync.conf.new": 3,
"storage.cfg": 1,
"user.cfg": 18,
"domains.cfg": 1,
"priv/shadow.cfg": 1,
"datacenter.cfg": 1,
"vzdump.cron": 1,
"ha/crm_commands": 1,
"ha/manager_status": 1,
"ha/resources.cfg": 1,
"ha/groups.cfg": 1,
"ha/fence.cfg": 1,
"status.cfg": 1,
"kvstore": {
"pmx-01": {
"tasklist": 18924}
,
"pmx-02": {
"tasklist": 18689}
}
}
```

There are no manual configurations or editing required in this file.

# Member nodes

Located under /etc/pve/.members, the member node file shows all the member nodes that are part of the Proxmox cluster. It is a great way to see the cluster status when the Proxmox GUI becomes inaccessible for any reason. The following is the .members file in our basic cluster:

```
{
"nodename": "pmx-01",
"version": 6,
"cluster": { "name": "pmx-cluster", "version": 2, "nodes": 2, "quorate": 1 },
"nodelist": {
  "pmx-02": { "id": 2, "online": 1, "ip": "172.16.2.2"},
  "pmx-01": { "id": 1, "online": 1, "ip": "172.16.2.1"}
  }
}
```

```
"nodename": "pm4-2"
```

The nodename section shows the current node where the .members file is being accessed:

```
"version": 4
```

The .members file has its own version numbering system. Like the .version file, every time .members is changed, the version increases incrementally. For example, when a node is added or removed from the cluster, the version number moves upward:

```
"cluster": { "name": "pmx-cluster", "version": 2, "nodes": 2, "quorate": 1
},
```

The previous code shows the cluster information, such as the cluster name, cluster version, number of member nodes, and number of votes (quorate) needed to form a quorum.

```
"nodelist": {  }
```

Nodes mentioned in the node list section provide information about each node, such as the ID, online/offline status, and IP address.

# Virtual machine list file

Located under `/etc/pve/.vmlist`, the virtual machine list file stores a list of all the virtual machines within the Proxmox cluster. The `.vmlist` file uses the following format to store the list:

```
"<vmid>": { "node": "<nodename>", "type": "<vm_type>", "version": <int> }
```

We have two virtual machines and one template in our basic cluster. The following screenshot shows the information stored in the `.vmlist` file:

```
{
"version": 11,
"ids": {
"100": { "node": "pmx-01", "type": "qemu", "version": 5 },
"101": { "node": "pmx-01", "type": "lxc", "version": 10 }}

}
```

This list allows you another way to view the virtual machines list in the cluster in all the nodes. We can have a hard copy of this file if disaster strikes, making the cluster inaccessible through GUI, or we need to rebuild a virtual environment.

# The cluster log file

This is a log file for the cluster itself and is located under `/etc/pve/.clusterlog`. It mostly maintains a log of login authentication of users.

# Ceph configuration files

Ceph is a kind of a distributed object and file storage system, which fully integrates with Proxmox. Out of the box, Proxmox comes with the Ceph cluster management option through the GUI and a whole array of features to make the integration as seamless as possible. We will dive deep into Ceph in Chapter 4, *Storage Systems*. Ceph can be installed on its own hardware using operating systems such as Ubuntu, or it can coexist with Proxmox on the same node. Whether it's coexisting or on its own cluster, Proxmox nodes need access to the Ceph configuration file to connect. The configuration file is located in /etc/pve/ceph.conf for the Proxmox+Ceph coexisting node. For non-coexisting Proxmox nodes, the file needs to be stored in /etc/ceph/ceph.conf. In the coexisting node, Proxmox creates a symbolic link of the Ceph configuration file in /etc/ceph/ceph.conf.

Besides the configuration file, Ceph also uses authentication keys, which are stored in the following directories:

```
/etc/pve/priv/ceph.client.admin.keyring
/etc/pve/priv/ceph.mon.keyring
/etc/pve/priv/ceph/<rbd_storage_id>.keyring
```

In order to connect a **Ceph RBD** storage, Proxmox requires a separate keyring. The <rbd_storage_id>.keyring is simply a copied and renamed version of ceph.client.admin.keyring. Without this keyring, Proxmox will not be able to connect to Ceph. We will look at details of Ceph in Chapter 5, *Installing and Configuring Ceph*.

# Firewall configuration file

As of Proxmox 5, a fully functional firewall is integrated with a Proxmox cluster. It is very powerful and comes with a granular customization down to a single virtual machine. Firewall rules can be created separately for a cluster, node, and virtual machine. The following table shows the firewall rules' file location:

| Cluster-wide firewall rules | /etc/pve/firewall/cluster.fw |
|---|---|
| Node firewall rules | /etc/pve/nodes/<node_id>/host.fw |
| VM/CT firewall rules | /etc/pve/firewall/cluster.fw |

All the firewall rules can be managed through the Proxmox GUI firewall menu without editing using the command line. We will take a look at the firewall in detail later in this book in Chapter 9, *The Proxmox VE Firewall*.

It is worth mentioning that the Proxmox firewall should be not a substitute for the main gateway firewall where the internet enters the facility. There should be a dedicated firewall between the WAN and the local network. The Proxmox firewall enhances security by allowing you to prevent inter-VM communication and by fine-tuning the incoming and outgoing network traffic.

# Summary

In this chapter, we looked at the location of the important configuration files needed to run a Proxmox cluster. We also looked at the configuration files from inside to have a better understanding of the parameters used and other possible values for different parameters. As mentioned earlier, most of these configuration files can be changed via the Proxmox GUI. But when the GUI becomes inaccessible for any reason, knowing where these files are located can save a tremendous amount of time by accessing them through the CLI.

In the next chapter, we will take a look at the various storage systems that can be used with Proxmox and the different types of disk images and their use cases.

# 4
# Storage Systems

A storage system is a medium to store data for simultaneous access by multiple devices or nodes in a network. As server and desktop virtualization becomes the norm, a proper, stable storage system today is much more critical for a virtual environment. In terms of Proxmox, a storage system is where virtual disk images are stored for both KVM and container-based virtual machines.

Although a Proxmox cluster can function fully with **Direct Attached Storage (DAS)** or a local storage system in the same Proxmox node, a shared storage system has many benefits in a production environment, such as increased manageability, seamless storage expansion, and redundancy, just to name a few. In this chapter, we will cover the following topics:

- Local versus shared storage
- Virtual disk image types
- Storage types supported by Proxmox
- Commercial and free shared storage options
- FreeNAS as a low-cost shared storage option

Local or shared, a storage system is a vital component of a Proxmox cluster. A storage system is where all the virtual machines reside. Therefore, a deeper understanding of different storage systems will allow an administrator to properly plan storage requirements for any cluster environment.

# Local storage versus shared storage

Shared storage is not absolutely necessary in a Proxmox cluster environment, but without a doubt, it makes storage management a simpler task. In a small business environment, it may be adequate not to have 24/7 uptime and 100% reliability, so a local storage system will suffice. In most enterprise virtual environments with critical data, shared storage is the only logical choice due to the benefits it brings to the whole cluster operation. The following are considered benefits of using shared storage:

- Live migration of a virtual machine
- Seamless expansion of multi-node storage space
- Centralized backup
- Multilevel data tiering
- Central storage management

# Live migration of a virtual machine

This is probably one of the important sought-after reasons to go for a shared storage system. **Live migration** is when a virtual machine can be moved to a different node without shutting it down first. **Offline migration** is when the virtual machine is powered off prior to migration. The hardware and operating systems of Proxmox nodes need updates, patches, and replacements occasionally. Some updates require an immediate reboot while some require none at all. The primary function of Proxmox nodes in a cluster is to run virtual machines. When a node needs to be rebooted, all the running VMs must be stopped or migrated to other nodes. Then, migrate them back to the original node after the reboot cycle is complete. In Proxmox, a powered-on VM cannot be migrated using live migration without powering it down first if the VM is on the local disk of the node in question. If a total Proxmox node failure occurs for any reason, all the VMs stored in that node will be completely unavailable until the node is fixed or replaced. This is because VMs cannot be accessed to be moved to a different node until the issue node is powered up.

In most cases, shutting down all the VMs just to reboot the host node is not an option. This causes too much downtime depending on the number of VMs the node handles. In order to migrate locally stored VMs, they must be stopped and then migration should be initiated from the Proxmox GUI. Migration from one local storage to another local storage takes a long time, depending on the size of the VM, since Proxmox moves an entire image file using rsync to relocate the VM to another node. Let's take a look at the following diagram of a cluster with 40 locally stored virtual machines with 10 on each of the four Proxmox nodes:

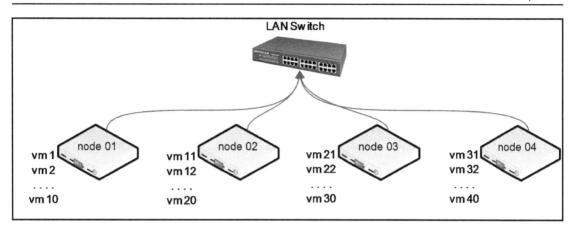

In the preceding overly simplified diagram, there are four Proxmox nodes with 10 virtual machines on each. If **node 01** needs to reboot to apply an update or hardware upgrade, all the 10 virtual machines have to be stopped, the node needs to be rebooted, and then all the virtual machines must be powered up. If **node 01** fails completely, then all these 10 virtual machines will be inaccessible until **node 01** is back on again.

So clearly, a cluster setup with local storage for virtual machines can cause unwanted downtime when migration is needed. Now, let's take a look at the following diagram where four Proxmox nodes with 40 virtual machines are stored on a shared storage system:

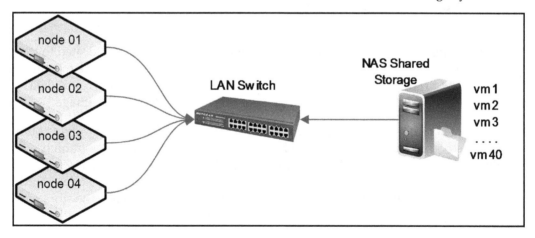

In the preceding diagram, all the 40 virtual machines are stored on a shared storage system. The Proxmox node only holds the configuration files for each virtual machine. In this scenario, if **node 01** needs to be rebooted due to a security patch or update, all the virtual machines can be simply migrated to another node without powering down a single virtual machine. A virtual machine user will never notice that their machine has actually moved to a different node. If a total Proxmox node failure occurs, the virtual machine configuration file can simply be manually moved from `/etc/pve/nodes/node01/qemu-server/<vmid>.conf` to `/etc/pve/nodes/node02/qemu-server/<vmid>.conf`.

We can also leverage another feature in Proxmox known as high availability to automate the VM configuration file to move during node failure. Refer to `Chapter 10`, *Proxmox High Availability*, to learn about this feature.

Since all the virtual machine configuration files are in a **Proxmox clustered file system (pmxcfs)**, they can be accessed from any node. Refer to `Chapter 3`, *Proxmox under the Hood*, for details on the pmxcfs. With virtual machine image files on shared storage, Proxmox migration does not have to move all the image files using rsync from one node to another, which allows much faster virtual machine migration.

The rsync is an open source program and network protocol for Unix-based systems. It provides nonencrypted or encrypted incremental file transfers from one location to another.

When live-migrating a VM, keep in mind that the more memory (RAM) allocated to the VM, the longer it will take to live-migrate a powered-on virtual machine since the migration process will need to copy the entire memory contents. Failure to do so may cause data corruption since the data in memory may not have been written to the disk image.

It should be noted that shared storage can cause a single point of failure if a single node-based shared storage solution is set up, such as FreeNAS or NAS4Free without high availability configured. Using multinode or distributed shared storage such as Ceph, Gluster, or DRBD, the single point of failure can be eliminated. On a single-node shared storage, all virtual machines are stored on one node. If node failure occurs, the storage will become inaccessible by a Proxmox cluster, thus rendering all the running virtual machines unusable.

As of Proxmox VE 5.0, LXC containers cannot be live-migrated. They will need to be powered off to commit offline migration. KVM VMs can be live-migrated without shutting down.

# Seamless expansion of multinode storage space

Digital data is growing faster than ever before in our modern 24/7 digitally connected world. The growth has been exponential since the introduction of virtualization. Since it is much easier to set up a virtual server at a moment's notice, an administrator can simply clone a virtual server template, and within minutes, a new virtual server is up and running while consuming storage space. If left unchecked, this regular creating and retiring of virtual machines can force a company to grow out of available storage space. A distributed shared storage system is designed keeping this very specific requirement in mind.

In an enterprise environment, storage space should increase on demand without shutting down or interrupting critical nodes or virtual machines. Using a multinode or distributed shared storage system, virtual machines can now go beyond few-node local clusters to scattered multiple nodes spanned across geographical regions. For example, Ceph or Gluster can span across several racks and comprise well over several petabytes of usable storage space. Simply add a new node with a full bay of drives and then tell the storage cluster to recognize the new node to increase storage space for the entire cluster. Since shared storage is separated from the virtual machine host nodes, storage can be increased or decreased without disturbing any running virtual machines. In Chapter 5, *Installing and Configuring Ceph*, we will see how we can integrate Ceph into a Proxmox cluster.

# Centralized backup

Shared storage makes centralized backup possible by allowing each virtual machine host node to create a backup in one central location. This helps a backup manager or an administrator to implement a solid backup plan and manage the existing backups. Since a Proxmox node failure will not take the shared storage system down, virtual machines can be easily restored to a new node to reduce downtime.

Always use a separate node for backup purposes. It is not a wise practice to store both virtual machines and their backups on the same node.

# Multilevel data tiering

Data tiering is a concept where different files can be stored on different storage pools based on their performance requirements. For example, a virtual file server can provide very fast service if its VM is stored in an SSD storage pool, whereas a virtual backup server can be stored on slower HDD storage since backup files are not frequently accessed and thus do not require very fast I/O. Tiering can be set up using different shared storage nodes with different performance levels. It can also be set up on the same node by assigning volumes or pools to specific sets of drives.

# Central storage management

By separating shared storage clusters from primary Proxmox clusters, we can manage two clusters without them interfering with each other. Since shared storage systems can be set up with separate nodes and physical switches, managing them based on different authorizations and permissions becomes an easier task. NAS, SAN, and other types of shared storage solutions come with their own management programs from where an administrator or operator can check storage cluster health, disk status, free space, and so on. The Ceph storage is configured via CLI, but Proxmox has integrated a great deal of Ceph management options within the Proxmox GUI, which makes Ceph cluster management much easier. Using the API, Proxmox can now collect the Ceph cluster data and display it through the Proxmox GUI, as shown in the following screenshot:

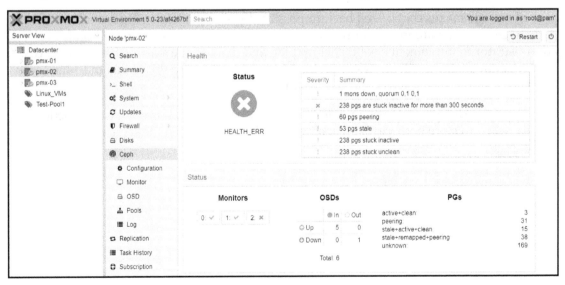

Other NAS solutions such as FreeNAS, OpenMediaVault, and NAS4Free also have a GUI that simplifies management. The following screenshot is an example of the hard drive status from a FreeNAS GUI window:

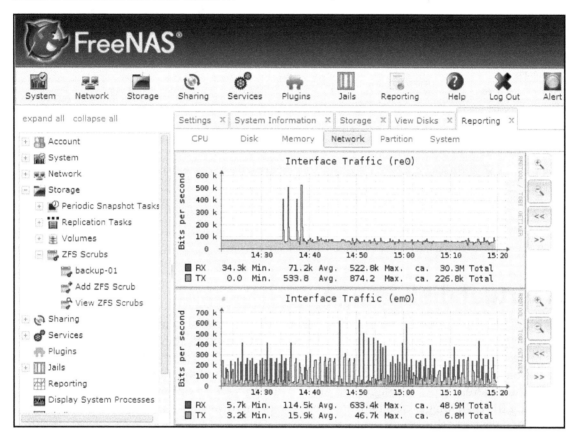

# Local and shared storage comparison

The following table is a comparison of both the local and shared storage for a quick reference:

| Features | Local storage | Shared storage |
|---|---|---|
| VM live migration | No | Yes |
| High availability | No | Yes, when used in distributed shared storage |
| Cost | Lower | Significantly higher |
| I/O performance | Native disk drive speed | Slower than the native disk drive speed |
| Skill requirements | No special storage skills required | Must be skilled in the shared storage option used |
| Expandability | Limited to available drive bays of a node | Expandable over multiple nodes or racks when multinode or distributed shared storage is used |
| Maintenance complexity | Virtually maintenance free | Storage nodes or clusters require regular monitoring |

# A virtual disk image

A virtual disk image is a file or group of files in which a virtual machine stores its data. In Proxmox, a VM configuration file can be recreated and used to attach a disk image. But if the image itself is lost, it can only be restored from a backup. There are different types of virtual disk image formats available to be used with a virtual machine. It is essential to know the different types of image formats in order to have an optimally performing VM. Knowing the disk images also helps prevent the premature shortage of space, which may occur by over-provisioning virtual disks.

# Supported image formats

Proxmox supports the .raw, .qcow2, and .vmdk virtual disk formats. Each format has its own set of strengths and weaknesses. The image format is usually chosen based on the function of the virtual machine, storage system in use, performance requirement, and available budget. The following screenshot shows the menu where we can choose an image type during virtual disk creation through the GUI:

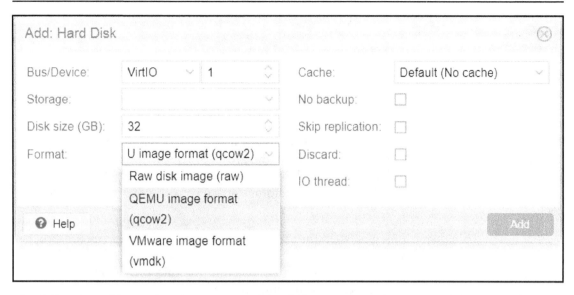

The following table is a brief summary of the different image formats and their possible usage:

| Image type | Storage supported | Strength | Weakness |
| --- | --- | --- | --- |
| .qcow2 | NFS and directory | Allows dynamic virtual storage of image files. Stable and secure. Most feature rich among image types. | Complex file formats with additional software layers. High I/O overhead. |
| .raw | LVM, RBD, iSCSI, and directory | No additional software layer. Direct access to image files. Stable, secure, and fastest. | Fixed virtual image only. Cannot be used to store dynamic images. VM takes longer to back up due to the size of image files. |
| .vmdk | NFS and directory | Works exceptionally well with the VMware infrastructure. Allows dynamic virtual storage of image files. | Additional software layer, thus slower performance. Not fully tested with Proxmox. |

Proxmox is very forgiving with setting up virtual machines with the wrong image format. You can always convert these image types from one format to another. Conversion can be done from both the CLI and GUI. Virtual disk image conversion is explained later in this chapter.

# The .qcow2 images

The .qcow2 type is a very stable VM image format. Proxmox fully supports this file format. A VM disk created using .qcow2 is much smaller since by default it creates thin-provisioned disk images. For example, an Ubuntu VM created with 50 GB storage space may have an image file with a size around 1 GB. As a user stores data in the VM, this image file will grow gradually. The .qcow2 image format allows an administrator to over-provision VMs with the .qcow2 disk image file. If not monitored regularly, the shared storage will run out of space to accommodate all the growing virtual image files. Available storage space should be regularly monitored in such an environment. It is a good practice to add additional storage space when the overall storage space consumption reaches around 80%.

Thin provisioning is when the virtual disk image file does not preallocate all the blocks, thus keeping the size of the image file to only what we want. As more data is stored in the virtual machine, the thin-provisioned image file grows until it reaches the maximum size allocated. Thick provisioning, on the other hand, is when the virtual disk image file preallocates all the blocks, thus creating an image file that is exactly the size set when creating it.

The .qcow2 format also has a very high I/O overhead due to its additional software layer. Thus, it is a bad choice of image format for a VM such as a database server. Any data being read or written into the image format goes through the .qcow2 software layer, which increases the I/O, making it slower. A VM backup created with a .qcow2 image can only be restored to an NFS or local directory.

When budget is the main concern and storage space is very limited, .qcow2 is an excellent choice. This image type supports KVM live snapshots to preserve states of virtual machines.

# The .raw image type

The .raw image type is also a very stable and mature VM image format. Its primary strength lies in performance. There is no additional software layer for data to go through. A VM has direct pass-through access to the .raw file, which makes it much faster. Also, there is no software component attached to it, so it is much less problem prone. The .raw format can only create a fixed-size or thick-provisioned VM image file. For example, an Ubuntu VM created with 50 GB storage space will have a 50 GB image file. This helps an administrator to know exactly how much storage is in use, so there is no chance of an uncontrolled out-of-storage situation.

The .raw type is the preferred file format for all Proxmox VMs. A .raw image format VM can be restored to just about any storage type. In a virtual environment, additional virtual disk image files can be added to a virtual machine at any time. So it is not necessary to initially allocate a larger-size .raw virtual disk image file with possible future growth in mind. The VM can start with a smaller .raw image file and add more disk images as needed. For example, a VM with 50 GB data starts with an 80 GB .raw image file. Then, increase the size of the disk image or add more virtual disk images as the need arises. The concept is much like adding new hard drives to a server to increase overall space.

Since all the .raw disk image files are preallocated, there are no risks of over-provisioning beyond the total available storage space. KVM live snapshots are also supported by the .raw image format. There are some shared storage solutions that only support the .raw disk image. Ceph RBD is one example. As of Proxmox VE 4.1, we can only store the .raw virtual disk image on Ceph block devices. But the **Ceph FileSystem (CephFS)** supports all the virtual disk images. CephFS is one of the three storage types supported on the Ceph platform. Currently, there are no direct storage plugins for CephFS in Proxmox, only for RBD. But we can connect CephFS to Proxmox as an NFS share.

# The .vmdk image type

The .vmdk image format is very common in the VMware infrastructure. The main advantage of Proxmox supporting .vmdk is the ease of VM migration from VMware to a Proxmox cluster. A VM created in VMware with the .vmdk image format can easily be configured to be used in a Proxmox cluster and converted. There are no benefits to keeping a virtual disk image file in the .vmdk format, except during a transitional period, such as converting virtual machines from a VMware infrastructure.

# Virtual device types

Virtual device types emulate the bus or device nature of physical drives. Proxmox allows quite a few additional virtual drives to be added to a VM. The following table shows the bus types supported in Proxmox and the maximum number of allowed disk devices per VM by Proxmox:

| Bus/device type | Maximum allowed |
|---|---|
| IDE | 3 |
| SATA | 5 |
| VirtIO | 15 |
| SCSI | 13 |

Out of four supported bus types, the VirtIO bus type gives the maximum performance in almost all situations. VirtIO disk images are recognized by Linux without any additional work during OS installation. However, when installing Windows in a VM, VirtIO drives are not recognized. Additional VirtIO drives need to be added at the time of Windows installation. We will look into best practices for using the VirtIO bus type with Windows OSes later in this chapter.

# Managing disk images

A Proxmox virtual image file can be managed from both the WebGUI and CLI. The WebGUI allows the administrator to use the add, resize (increase only), move, throttling, and delete options, as shown in the following screenshot:

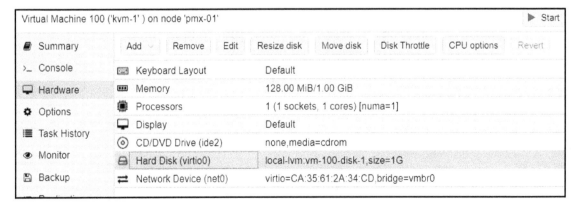

To make any changes to a virtual disk image file, the image must be selected first from the **Hardware** tab, as shown in the preceding screenshot. Virtual machine image files can also be manipulated using CLI commands. The following table shows a few examples of the most common commands used to delete, convert, and resize an image file:

| Command | Function |
|---|---|
| `#qemu-img create -f <type> -o <filename> <size>`<br>`#qemu-img create -f raw -o test.raw size=1024M` | Creates an image file |
| `#qemu-img convert <source> -O <type> <destination>`<br>`#qemu-img convert test.vmdk -O qcow2 test.qcow2` | Converts an image file |
| `#qemu-img resize <filename> <+|-><size>`<br>`#qemu-img resize test.qcow2 +1024M` | Resizes an image file |

# Resizing a virtual disk image

The **Resize disk** option only supports increasing the size of the virtual disk image file. It has no shrink function. The Proxmox **Resize disk** option only adjusts the size of the virtual disk image file. After any resizing, the partition must be adjusted from inside the VM. The safest way to resize partitions is to boot a Linux-based virtual machine with a partitioning ISO image, such as *GParted* (http://gparted.org/download.php), and then resize the partitions using the GParted graphical interface. It is also possible to perform an online partition resizing while the virtual machine is powered on. Resizing a virtual disk image file involves the following three steps:

1. Resize virtual disk image file in Proxmox:
   - **From GUI**: Select the virtual disk, and then click on **Resize disk**.
   - **From CLI**: Run the following command:

     ```
     # qm resize <vm_id> <virtual_disk> +<size>G
     ```

2. Resize the partition of the virtual disk image file from inside the VM:
   - **For Windows VMs**: Resize the disk by going to **Computer Management** under **Administrative Tools**.
   - **For Linux VMs with RAW partitions**: Run the following command:

     ```
     # cfdisk <disk_image>
     ```

- **For Linux VMs with LVM partitions**: Run the following command:

```
# cfdisk </dev/XXX/disk_image>
```

- **For Linux VMs with QCOW2 partitions**: Run the following commands:

```
# apt-get install nbd-client
# qemu-nbd --connect /dev/nbd0 <disk_image>
# cfdisk /dev/nbd0
# qemu-nbd -d /dev/nbd0
```

3. Resize the filesystem in the partition of the virtual disk image file:
   - **For a Linux client with LVM**: Run the following commands:

```
# pvscan   (find PV name)
# pvresize /dev/xxx   (/dev/xxx found from pvscan)
# lvscan (find LVname)
# lvresize -L+<size>G /dev/xxx/lv_<disk>
```

   - **To use 100% free space**: Run the following commands:

```
# lvresize -l +100%FREE /dev/xxx/lv_<disk>
# resize2fs /dev/xxx/lv_<disk> (resize filesystem)
```

 Steps 2 and 3 are necessary only if online resizing is done without shutting down a VM. If GParted or another bootable partitioning medium is used, then only step 1 is needed before booting the VM with an ISO.

# Moving a virtual disk image

**Move disk** allows the image file to be moved to a different storage or converted to a different image type:

In the **Move disk** option menu, just select the **Target Storage** and **Format** type, and then click on **Move disk** to move the image file. Moving can be done live without shutting down the VM.

The **Format** type in the **Move disk** option will be greyed out if the destination storage only supports one image format type. In the preceding screenshot, `ssd-ceph-01` is an RBD storage in a Ceph pool. Since RBD only supports the RAW format, the format type has been greyed out automatically.

Clicking on **Delete source** will delete the source image file after the moving is complete.

Note that if the virtual machine has any snapshots, Proxmox will not be able to delete the source file automatically. In such cases, the disk image has to be manually deleted after the snapshots are removed. The source image will be listed as **Unused disk 0**, as shown in the following screenshot, after the moving is done for a disk image with snapshots:

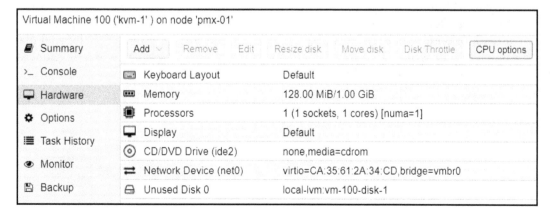

# Throttling a virtual disk image

Proxmox allows throttling or setting a limit on the read/write speed and **input/output operations per second (IOPS)** for each virtual disk image. By default, there are no set limits. Each disk image will try to read and write at the maximum speed achievable in the storage where the disk image is being stored. For example, if a disk image is stored on a local storage, it will try to perform read and write operations at about 110 MB/s since that is the theoretical limit of a SATA drive. This performance will vary in different storage options. In a multi-tenant or large environment, if all the disk images are not throttled without any limit, this may put pressure on the network and/or storage bandwidth. By throttling, we can control the bandwidth that each disk image can utilize. The **Disk Throttle** option is available on the **Hardware** tab of a VM. The following screenshot shows the **Disk Throttle** dialog box with the option to set limits:

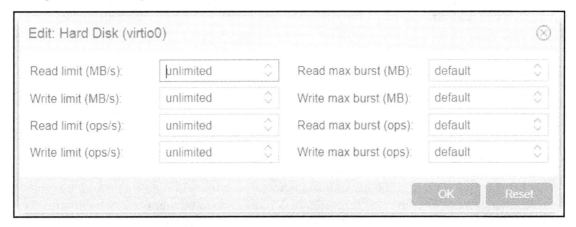

When it comes to disk throttling, there's no one-size-fits-all limit. The set limit is going to vastly vary for different storage used in the cluster environment and the amount of load each VM carries. Depending on the type of storage used, it may be necessary to just set write or read, or both, limits. For example, a Ceph storage cluster with an SSD journal may have a much higher write speed than the read speed. So throttling a VM with a higher read limit while setting a lower write limit may be a viable option.

As mentioned earlier, we can set a limit based on MB/s or OP/s. Setting the MB/s limit is much simpler since we can quantify the read/write speed of a disk drive or network in megabytes much more easily. For example, a standard SATA drive can achieve a theoretical speed of 115 MB/s while a gigabit network can achieve about 100 MB/s. Knowing the performance in IOPS or OP/s requires some extra steps. In some storage systems, we can integrate some forms of monitoring, which can present us the IOPS data in real time. For others, we need to calculate the IOPS data to know the performance matrix of the storage system used. The complete details of the IOPS calculation are beyond the scope of this book. But the following guidelines should serve as a starting point to calculate the OP/s of different storage devices:

OP/s for a single 7200-RPM SATA disk:

$$IOPS = 1/(avg.\ latency\ in\ seconds + avg.\ seek\ time\ in\ seconds)$$

Based on the previous formula, we can calculate IOPS of a standard SSD device. To get the average latency and seek time of a device, we can use the Linux tool `ioping`. It is not installed in Proxmox by default. We can install it using the following command:

```
# apt-get install ioping
```

The `ioping` tool is similar to the `iperf` command but for disk drives. The following command will show the IO latency of our example SSD device:

```
# ioping /dev/sda
```

The following screenshot shows that the result of `ioping` for average latency is `1.79` milliseconds or 0.00179 seconds:

```
--- /dev/sdh (block device 111.8 GiB) ioping statistics
5 requests completed in 4.01 s, 558 iops, 2.18 MiB/s
min/avg/max/mdev = 1.52 ms / 1.79 ms / 2.40 ms / 312 us
```

To get the average seek time of a device, we need to run the following `ioping` command:

```
# ioping -R /dev/sda
```

The following screenshot shows that the result of `ioping` for average seek time is `133` microseconds or 0.000133 seconds:

```
--- /dev/sdh (block device 111.8 GiB) ioping statistics ---
21.9 k requests completed in 3.00 s, 7.50 k iops, 29.3 MiB/s
min/avg/max/mdev = 27 us / 133 us / 3.02 ms / 128 us
```

Using the gathered results, we can calculate the IOPS or OP/s of the SSD device, as follows:

$$IOPS = 1 / (0.00179 + 0.000133) = 520$$

If we know the maximum IOPS a storage medium can provide, we can tweak each VM with OP/s throttling to prevent IO issues in the cluster. As of Proxmox VE 4.1, we cannot set a cluster-wide throttling limit. Each disk image needs manual throttling separately.

## Caching a virtual disk image

Caching a virtual disk image provides performance and in some instances protection against an ungraceful VM shutdown. Not all caching is safe to use. For optimum VM performance, it is important to be aware of the various caching offered in Proxmox. This option is available under the VM **Hardware** tab in the disk image creation or edit dialog box. The following screenshot shows the disk image's edit dialog box with the caching drop-down menu for the .raw disk image of our example VM:

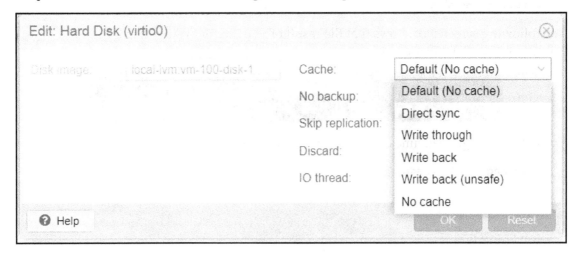

As of Proxmox VE 5.0, the following caching options are available:

| Cache option | Description |
| --- | --- |
| **Direct sync** | In this cache option, the Proxmox host does not do any caching, but a VM disk image uses the write-through cache. In this cache, writes are only acknowledged when data has been committed to the storage device. **Direct sync** is recommended for VMs that do not send flushes when required. This is a safer cache as data is not lost during a power failure but it is also slower. |
| **Write through** | In this cache option, the Proxmox host page cache is enabled while the VM disk write cache is disabled. This cache provides good read performance but slow write performance due to the write cache being disabled. This is a safer cache as it ensures data integrity. This cache is recommended for local or direct attached storage. |
| **Write back** | In this cache option, both read and write caching is done by the host. Writes are acknowledged by the VM disk as completed as soon as they are committed to the host cache regardless of whether they have been committed to storage or not. Data loss will occur for VMs in this cache. |
| **Write back (unsafe)** | This cache is the same as **Write back** except that all flushes are completely ignored by the guest VM. This is the fastest cache although the most unsafe. This cache should never be used in a production cluster. Usually, this cache is used to speed up OS installation in a VM. After the VM installation, this cache should be disabled and reverted to a different safer cache option. |
| **No cache** | This is the default caching option in Proxmox. In this option, no caching occurs at the host level, but the guest VM does write-back caching. The VM disk directly receives a write acknowledgment from the storage device in this cache option. Data can be lost in this cache during an abrupt host shutdown due to a power failure. |

Not all cache types will provide the same performance in all virtual environments. Every VM's workload is different. So choosing various cache types and observing the performance of the VM is necessary to find out which caching works best for a particular VM.

# VirtIO bus type for Windows VMs

VirtIO disk images are automatically recognized by Linux VMs since all Linux flavors come equipped with VirtIO drivers. Windows operating systems, however, do not. We can follow two methods to use the VirtIO disk type with Windows.

First, download the VirtIO drivers for Windows in ISO format from the following link:

```
https://fedoraproject.org/wiki/Windows_Virtio_Drivers
```

After downloading the ISO image file, simply upload it to a storage attached to Proxmox so we can make it available to any VM. Note that the ISO image holds drivers for not just the VirtIO disk device but also the VirtIO network interface.

## Installing VirtIO drivers during Windows installation

In the first method, we can load the VirtIO drivers during Windows installation through the following steps:

1. Add two CD/DVD drives when creating the Windows VM. The first drive is to load the Windows installer and the other one to load the VirtIO ISO image.

2. Start Windows installation and click on **Load driver** as shown in the following screenshot:

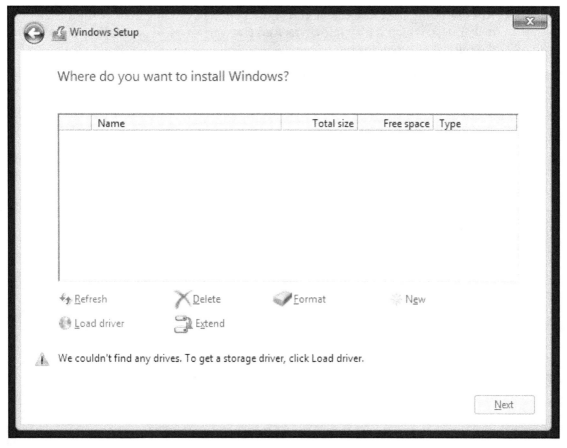

3. Go to **Browse** to select the drive with the VirtIO ISO image, and then navigate to the driver folder. The driver for the VirtIO disk image is usually stored in `\\<DriveLetter>\viostor\<windows_version>\amd6`.

4. After selecting the folder, it should show you the available drivers for the VirtIO disk image, which is also known as **Red Hat VirtIO SCSI controller**, as shown in the following screenshot:

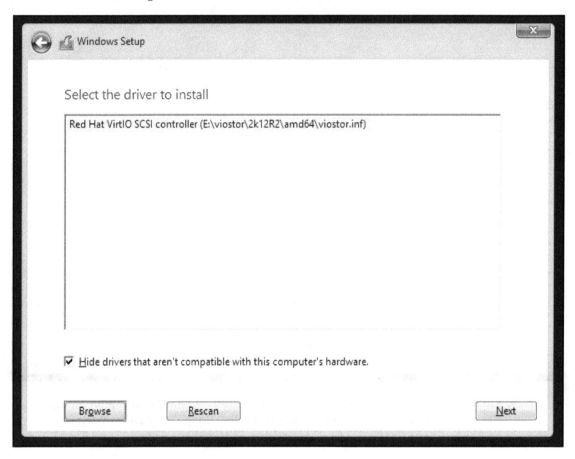

5. Select the driver and continue with the Windows installation as usual.

## Installing VirtIO drivers after Windows installation

This method is useful when Windows is already installed on a VM and you need to convert existing IDE/SATA disk images to VirtIO type. In this method, the VirtIO driver must be loaded before the main OS disk image is changed to the VirtIO bus type. The following steps are how we can change the bus type of the main Windows OS disk image after Windows has already been installed on a non-VirtIO disk:

1. Create a small additional disk image.
2. Log in to Windows and load the VirtIO drive ISO image.
3. Install drivers so the additional VirtIO disk image is recognized and configured by Windows.
4. Shut down Windows, change the main OS disk image to VirtIO type, and delete the additional disk image.
5. Restart Windows.

# Storage types in Proxmox

Proxmox has excellent plugins for the mainstream storage options. In this section, we are going to see which storage plugins are integrated into Proxmox and also see how to use them to connect to different storage types in Proxmox. The following are the storage types that are natively supported as of Proxmox VE 5.0:

* Directory
* LVM
* NFS
* ZFS
* Ceph RBD
* GlusterFS

# Directory

The `Directory` storage is a mounted folder on the Proxmox local node. It is mainly used as local storage. But we can also mount a remote folder in a different node and use that mount point to create a new `Directory` storage. By default, this location is mounted under `/var/lib/vz`.

Any VM stored in this `Directory` storage does not allow live migration. The VM must be stopped before migrating to another node. All virtual disk image file types can be stored in the `Directory` storage. To create a new storage with a mount point, go to `Datacenter` | **Storage**, and click on **Add** to select the `Directory` plugin. The following screenshot shows the **Add: Directory** storage dialog box, where we can add storage named `local-iso`, which is mounted at `/mnt/iso`, to store the ISO and container templates:

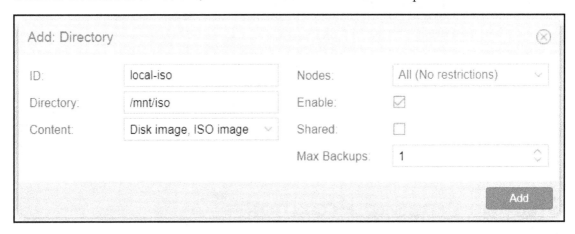

For locally mounted storage, selecting the **Shared** checkbox is not necessary. This option only pertains to a shared storage system, such as NFS and RBD.

# iSCSI

**Internet Small Computer Systems Interface**, which stands for **iSCSI**, is based on Internet Protocol, which allows the transmission of SCSI commands over a standard IP-based network. iSCSI devices can be set up locally or over a vast distance to provide storage options. We cannot store virtual disk images directly on an iSCSI device, but we can configure LVM storage on top of the iSCSI devices and then store disk images. An attached iSCSI device appears as if it were physically connected even if the device is stored in another remote node.

For more details on iSCSI, refer to the following link:

```
http://en.wikipedia.org/wiki/ISCSI
```

We will assume that you already have an iSCSI device created in a remote node using FreeNAS or any other Linux distribution. To add the device to Proxmox, we are going to use the iSCSI storage plugin, which we can find by navigating to the Datacenter | **Storage** | **Add** menu. As shown in the following screenshot, we are adding an iSCSI target named test1-iSCSI, which is configured in a remote node, 172.16.2.10:

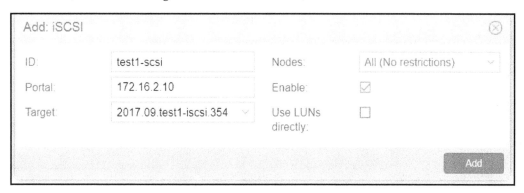

Note that using LUNs directly is not recommended, although the option to enable them is available. It is known to cause an iSCSI device error when accessed directly.

# Logical Volume Management

**Logical Volume Management** (**LVM**) provides a method of storage space allocation by using one or more disk partitions or drives as the underlying base storage. LVM storage requires a base storage to be set up and function properly. We can create LVM storage with local devices as backing or network backing with iSCSI devices. LVM allows scalable storage space since the base storage can be on the same node or on a different one. LVM storage only supports the RAW virtual disk image format. We can only store virtual disk images or containers on LVM storage.

For more details on LVM, refer to the following link:

```
http://en.wikipedia.org/wiki/Logical_Volume_Manager_(Linux)
```

If the LVM disk array is configured using local direct-attach disks in the node, VMs stored on this storage cannot be migrated live without powering down. But by connecting iSCSI devices from a remote node, and then creating the LVM storage on top of the iSCSI volume, we can make live migration possible since the storage is now considered shared storage. FreeNAS is an excellent option to create LVM plus iSCSI shared storage at no license cost. It comes with a great graphical user interface and many features, which go far beyond just LVM or iSCSI.

To add LVM storage, go to `Datacenter` I **Storage** I **Add**, and select the **LVM** storage plugin. The following screenshot shows the LVM dialog box, where we are using the iSCSI device `test1-iscsi`, that we added in the previous section, to create LVM storage:

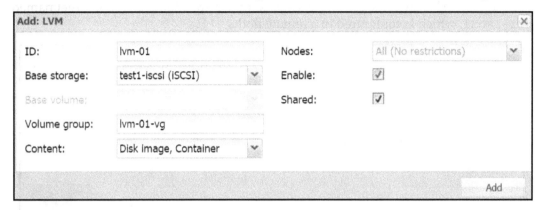

# NFS

**Network File System** (**NFS**), in short, is a well-matured filesystem protocol originally developed by Sun Microsystems in 1984. Currently, version 4 of the NFS protocol is in effect. But it was not as widely accepted as version 3 due to a few compatibility issues. But the gap is closing fast between version 3 and 4. Proxmox, by default, uses version 3 of the NFS protocol, while administrators can change to version 4 through the use of options in `storage.cfg`. NFS storage can store the `.qcow2`, `.raw`, and `.vmdk` image formats, providing versatility and flexibility in a clustered environment. NFS is also the easiest to set up and requires the least amount of upfront hardware cost, thus allowing a budget-conscious small business or a home user to get their hands on a stable shared storage system for the Proxmox cluster.

Care should be taken when using NFS version 4 instead of version 3 in Proxmox. There are still a few bugs that exist in NFSv4, such as kernel panic during system startup while mounting the NFSv4 share.

The NFS server can be configured on just about any Linux distribution and then connected to a Proxmox cluster. An NFS share is nothing but a mount point on the NFS server, which is read by the Proxmox NFS plugin. We can also use FreeNAS to serve as the NFS server, and thus take advantage of the FreeNAS features and GUI to easily monitor the shared storage. Due to the simplicity of the NFS configuration, this is probably the most widely used storage option in the virtualization world. Almost all network admins have used an NFS server at least once in their career.

In the following screenshot, we are connecting an NFS storage named `nfs-01` from the remote server `172.16.2.10`:

After entering the IP address of the remote server, the **Export** drop-down menu will scan the remote server for all the NFS shares and display them in the list. In our example, the mount point found from the dialog box is in `/nfs-vol/nfs-01`.

# ZFS

ZFS was originally developed by Sun Microsystems. ZFS storage is a combination of filesystem and LVM, providing high-capacity storage with important features, such as data protection, data compression, self-healing, and snapshots. ZFS has built-in software-defined RAID, which makes the use of hardware-based RAID unnecessary. A disk array with ZFS RAID can be migrated to a completely different node, and then entirely imported without rebuilding the entire array. We can only store `.raw` format virtual disk images on the ZFS storage. For more details on ZFS, refer to `http://en.wikipedia.org/wiki/ZFS`.

As of Proxmox VE 4.1, a ZFS storage plugin is included, which leverages the use of ZFS natively in Proxmox cluster nodes. A ZFS pool supports the following RAID types:

- **RAID-0 pool**: Requires at least one disk
- **RAID-1 pool**: Requires at least two disks
- **RAID-10 pool**: Requires at least four disks
- **RAIDZ-1 pool**: Requires at least three disks
- **RAIDZ-2 pool**: Requires at least four disks

ZFS uses pools to define storage. Pools can only be created through a CLI. As of Proxmox VE 5.0, there are no ZFS management options in the GUI. All ZFS creation and management must be done through the CLI. Once the pools are created, they can be attached to Proxmox through the Proxmox GUI. In our example, we are going to create a RAID1 mirrored pool named `zfspool1` and connect it to Proxmox. The command used to create the ZFS pool is as follows:

```
# zpool create <pool_name> <raid_type> <dev1_name> <dev2_name> ...
```

So, for our example pool, the command will appear as follows:

```
# zpool create zfspool1 mirror /dev/vdd /dev/vde
```

The following options are available for RAID types:

| RAID type | Option string to use |
| --- | --- |
| RAID0 | no string |
| RAID 1 | mirror |
| RAIDZ-1 | raidz1 |
| RAIDZ-2 | raidz2 |

To verify that the pool is created, run the following command:

```
# zpool list
```

The following screenshot shows the ZFS pool list as it appears for our example ZFS node:

We can use the pool directly, or we can create a dataset inside the pool and connect the dataset separately to Proxmox as an individual storage. The advantage of this is to isolate the different types of stored data in each dataset. For example, if we create a dataset to store VM images and another dataset to store backup files, we can turn on compression for the VM image dataset to compress the disk image files while keeping compression off for the backup-storing dataset since the backup files are already compressed, thus saving valuable resources. Each ZFS dataset can be configured individually with its own set of configuration options. If we compare a `zpool` with a directory, datasets are like subdirectories inside the main directory. The following command is used to create a dataset inside a ZFS pool:

```
# zfs create <zpool_name>/<zfs_dataset_name>
```

Datasets must be mounted in a directory before they can be used. By default, a new `zfs` pool or dataset gets mounted under the root directory. The following command will set a new mount point for a dataset:

```
# zfs set mountpoint=/mnt/zfs-vm zfspool1/zfs-vm
```

To enable compression for the dataset, we can run the following command:

```
# zfs set compression=on zfspool1/zfs-vm
```

The ZFS pool will only function locally from the node where the pool is created. Other nodes in the Proxmox cluster will not be able to share the storage. By mounting a ZFS pool locally and creating the NFS share, it is possible to share the ZFS pool between all the Proxmox nodes. We can mount a `zfs` dataset in a directory and use that directory to configure the Proxmox node as the NFS server.

The process of mounting and sharing needs to be done through a CLI only. From the Proxmox GUI, we can only attach the NFS share with the underlying ZFS pool. In order to serve the NFS share, we need to install the NFS server in the Proxmox node using the following command:

```
# apt-get install nfs-kernel-server
```

Enter the following line of code in /etc/exports:

```
/mnt/zfs/   172.16.0.71/24(rw,nohide,async,no_root_squash)
```

Start the NFS service using the following command:

```
# service nfs-kernel-server start
```

To share the NFS-enabled ZFS pool through the Proxmox GUI, we can simply follow the steps laid out for the NFS storage in the previous section. To add a ZFS pool or dataset to the Proxmox cluster through the GUI, we need to log in to the GUI of the node where the ZFS pool is created. In our two-node example cluster, we have the ZFS pools in node #1, so we will have to access the GUI for that node. Otherwise, the ZFS pools or datasets cannot be added from different node GUIs. We can find the ZFS storage plugin option by navigating to the Datacenter | **Storage** | **Add** menu. Click on the **ZFS** plugin to open the dialog box. The following screenshot shows the ZFS storage dialog box with the zfs pool example and dataset in the drop-down menu:

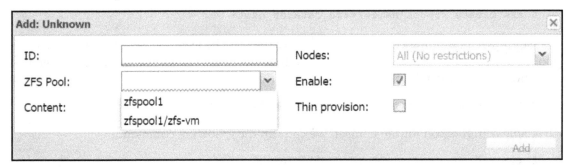

By combining the ZFS pool with an NFS share, we can create a shared storage with complete ZFS features, thus creating a flexible shared storage to be used with all the Proxmox nodes in the cluster. Using this technique, we can create a backup storage node, which is also manageable through the Proxmox GUI. This way, during a node crisis, we can also migrate VMs to the backup nodes temporarily. The previous steps are applicable to any Linux distribution and not just a Proxmox node. For example, we can set up a *ZFS+NFS* server using Ubuntu or CentOS Linux to store virtual disk images or templates. If you are using FreeNAS or a similar storage system, then the steps for ZFS laid out in this section are not required. The entire process of ZFS creation is completed using the FreeNAS GUI.

# Ceph RBD

**RADOS Block Device** (**RBD**) storage is provided by the Ceph distributed storage system. It is the most complex storage system, which requires multiple nodes to be set up. By design, Ceph is a distributed storage system and can be spanned over several dozen nodes. RBD storage can only store .raw image formats. To expand a Ceph cluster, simply add a hard drive or a node and let Ceph know about the new addition. Ceph will automatically rebalance data to accommodate the new hard drive or node. Ceph can be scaled to several petabytes or more. Ceph also allows multiple pool creations for different disk drives. For example, we can store database servers' VM images on an SSD-driven pool and back up server images on a slower-spinning drive pool. Ceph is the recommended storage system for medium-to-large cluster environments due to its resilience against data loss and the simplicity of storage expandability.

As of Proxmox VE Version 4.1, the Ceph server has been integrated into Proxmox to coexist on the same node. The ability to manage Ceph clusters through the Proxmox GUI has also been added. Later in this chapter, we will learn how to create a Ceph cluster and integrate it with Proxmox. Ceph is a truly enterprise storage solution with a learning curve. Once the mechanics of Ceph are understood, it is also one of the easiest to maintain. To know more about Ceph storage, refer to http://ceph.com/docs/master/start/intro/. There's more to come in Chapter 5, *Installing and Configuring Ceph*.

# GlusterFS

GlusterFS is a powerful, distributed filesystem, which can be scaled to several petabytes under a single mount point. Gluster is a fairly new addition to Proxmox that allows GlusterFS users to take full advantage of the Proxmox cluster. GlusterFS uses stripe, replicate, or distribute mode to store files. Although distribute mode offers the option of scalability, note that in stripe mode, when a GlusterFS node goes down, all the files in that server become inaccessible. This means that if a particular file is saved by the GlusterFS translator in that server, only that node holds the entire data of that file. Even though all the other nodes are operational, that particular file will no longer be available. GlusterFS can be scaled up to petabytes inside a single mount. The GlusterFS storage can be set up with just two nodes and supports NFS, thus allowing you to store any image file format.

To know more about GlusterFS, visit the following link:

http://docs.gluster.org/en/latest/

We can install Gluster on the same Proxmox node or on a remote node using any Linux distribution to create a shared storage. Gluster is a great option for a two-node, stable storage system, such as DRBD. The biggest difference is that it can be scaled out to increase the total storage space. For a lower-budget virtual environment with redundancy requirements, Gluster can be an excellent option. In a two-node Gluster setup, both the nodes sync with each other and when one node becomes unavailable, the other node simply takes over. The installation of Gluster is rather complex.

To learn more about how to set up a GlusterFS cluster, refer to the following link:

`http://gluster.readthedocs.org/en/latest/Quick-Start-Guide/Quickstart/`

In this section, we will see how to connect a GlusterFS cluster to Proxmox using the Gluster plugin. We can find the plugin option by navigating to `Datacenter` | **Storage** | **Add**. Click on the **GlusterFS** plugin to open the storage creation-dialog box, as shown in the following screenshot:

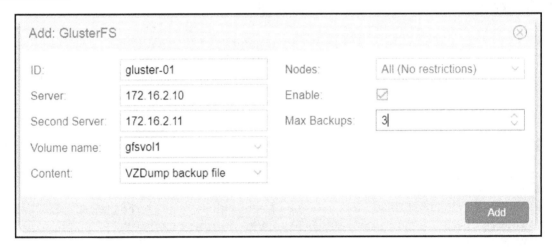

The following table shows the type of information needed and the values used for our example to attach GlusterFS:

| Items | Type of value | Example value |
|---|---|---|
| **ID** | New name of storage. | `gluster` |
| **Server** | IP address of the first Gluster node. | `172.16.0.171` |
| **Second Server** | IP address of the second Gluster node. | `172.16.0.172` |
| **Volume name** | Drop-down menu to select available volumes on the Gluster node. | `gfsvol11` |
| **Content** | Selects the type of files to be stored. | `VZDump backup file` |
| **Nodes** | Selects nodes that can access the storage. | **All (No restrictions)** |
| **Enable** | Enables or disables the storage. | Enabled |
| **Max Backups** | Maximum number of recent backup files can be stored. Older backups will be deleted automatically during the backup process. | 2 |

Since Gluster does not have the built-in software-defined RAID option, each Gluster node will require some form of RAID for drive redundancy per node. Like NFS on top of ZFS, which we learned earlier in this chapter, we can also put Gluster on top of ZFS and provide drive redundancy that way. Note that this will create some overhead since resources will be consumed by ZFS.

# Noncommercial/commercial storage options

We have discussed which virtual machine image formats and storage types are supported by Proxmox. To better acquaint ourselves for test or practice labs, we are now going to take a look at what noncommercial and commercial options we have out there in order to set up a storage system for the Proxmox-clustered environment. By noncommercial, I mean they are free without any primary features missing and without any trial limits.

These noncommercial options will allow you to set up a fully functional shared storage system with some hard work. Commercial versions usually come with full support from the provider company and, in some cases, an ongoing **service-level agreement** (**SLA**) contract. The following list is by no means a complete one, but a guideline to guide you in the direction where you need to plan and implement a Proxmox cluster environment. Each of these products can provide everything you need to set up shared storage:

| Noncommercial | | Commercial | |
|---|---|---|---|
| Solaris+napp-IT | www.napp-it.org/ | Nexenta | www.nexenta.com |
| FreeNAS | www.freenas.org | Falconstor | www.falconstor.com |
| GlusterFS | www.gluster.org | EMC2 | www.emc.com |
| Ceph | www.ceph.com | Open-E DSS | www.open-e.com |
| | | NetApp | www.netapp.com |

A question often asked is "Can I set up a Proxmox production cluster environment using only noncommercial solutions?". The short answer is *yes*!

It is indeed possible to create an entire complex Proxmox cluster using only noncommercial storage solutions. However, you have to be prepared for the unexpected and spend a significant amount of time learning the system. Commercial solutions aside, just studying a system will give an administrator an advantage when unforeseen issues arise. The main difference between these noncommercial and commercial solutions is the company support behind it. Typically, noncommercial solutions only have community-driven support through forums and message boards. Commercial offerings come with technical support, with the response time varying from anything between immediate to 24 hours.

 The trade-off of using noncommercial open source solutions is the money that is saved, which usually gets substituted by the time spent on research and mistakes.

# Summary

In this chapter, we took a look at the storage options that are supported by Proxmox and their advantages and disadvantages. We also saw the types of virtual image files that can be used with Proxmox and when to use them. We learned how to configure different storage options using NFS, ZFS, RBD, and Gluster as storage backends. Storage is an important component for Proxmox clustering because this is where virtual machines are created and operate from. A properly implemented storage system is crucial to making any cluster a successful one. With proper planning of different storage requirements and by choosing the right format and option, a lot of hassle and frustration can be minimized later on.

In the next chapter, we will see how to install and configure a Ceph storage system and integrate it with a Proxmox cluster.

# 5
# Installing and Configuring Ceph

Ceph is a distributed, highly scalable storage system which provides block, object, and file-based storage in the same storage cluster. Ceph is open source and designed to run on off the shelf commodity hardware. Currently, Ceph **RADOS Block Device** (**RBD**) block storage is fully supported by Proxmox. The Ceph **Reliable Autonomic Distributed Object Store** (**RADOS**) provides features such as replication, snapshot, and other block storage abilities. There are numerous reasons to consider Ceph as a storage backend. The following are some of the highlights of why one should consider Ceph over other storage systems:

- Ceph is *free*
- Ceph is a highly scalable, reliable, distributed storage system
- Ceph RBD is seamlessly integrated with Proxmox clusters
- Ceph can be managed and monitored through a dedicated Ceph menu in the Proxmox GUI
- Ceph can tolerate multiple simultaneous drive failures
- As the Ceph cluster grows in size, so does the performance

Visit the official link to learn about Ceph in detail if you are new to Ceph or want to know more about it: `http://ceph.com/`.

When compared to other storage systems, such as ZFS, GlusterFS, and so on, Ceph is a complex system. It requires extensive knowledge to properly maintain a Ceph cluster. Despite its complexity, Ceph also offers the highest level of redundancy spanned over multiple nodes and not just drive redundancy. In this chapter, we are going to learn how to install and configure Ceph to work with a Proxmox cluster.

 Proxmox VE 5.0 comes with Ceph Luminous, which is not yet fully production ready. If your existing environment is built on Proxmox VE 4.x, then do not upgrade just yet. Try Proxmox VE 5.0 on a test environment first instead.

# Ceph components

Before we dive in, let's take a look at some key components that make up a Ceph cluster. These components are what makes Ceph, and it is important to have a proper understanding of what they are.

# A physical node as cluster member

A physical node is the actual server hardware that holds one or more Ceph components.

# Maps

In Ceph, maps hold information, such as a list of participating nodes in a cluster and their locations, and data paths, and a list of OSDs with certain data chunks. There are several maps in a Ceph cluster, such as a cluster map, an **object storage daemon** (**OSD**) map for a list of OSDs, a monitor map for known monitor nodes, a **placement group** (**PG**) map for the location of objects or data chunks, and a CRUSH map to determine how to store and retrieve data by computing the data storage location.

# A cluster map

A cluster map is a map of devices and buckets that compose a Ceph cluster. Ceph uses a bucket hierarchy to define nodes or node locations, such as a room, rack, shelf, host, and so on. For example, let's say there are four disk drives used as four OSDs in the following bucket hierarchy:

```
Bucket datacenter = dc01
|
Bucket room = 101
|
Bucket rack = 22
|
Bucket host = ceph-node-1
|
Bucket osd = osd.1, osd.2, osd.3, osd.4
```

In the preceding example, we can see that `osd.1` to `osd.4` are in the node `ceph-node-1`, which is in rack number `22`, which is in room number `101`, which is in data center `dc01`. If `osd.3` fails, and there is an on-site technician, then an administrator can quickly give the technician the previous bucket hierarchy to identify the exact disk drive location to replace it. There can be several hundreds of OSDs in a cluster. A cluster map helps you pinpoint a single host or disk drive using the bucket hierarchy.

# A CRUSH map

**Controlled Replication Under Scalable Hashing** (**CRUSH**) is an algorithm used in Ceph to store and retrieve data by computing data storage locations within the cluster. It does so by providing a per-device weight value to distribute data objects among storage devices. The value is auto assigned, based on the actual size of the disk drive being used. For example, a 2 TB disk drive may have an approximate weight of 1.81. The drive will keep writing data until it reaches this weight. By design, CRUSH distributes data evenly among weighted devices to maintain a balanced utilization of storage and device bandwidth resources. A CRUSH map can be customized by a user to fit any cluster environment of any size.

For more details on CRUSH maps, refer to the following link:

```
http://ceph.com/docs/master/rados/operations/crush-map/
```

# Monitor

A Ceph **monitor** (**mon**) is a cluster monitor daemon node that holds the OSD map, PG map, CRUSH map, and monitor map. Monitors can be set up on the same server node with OSDs or on a fully separate machine. For a stable Ceph cluster, setting up separate nodes with monitors is highly recommended. Since monitors only keep track of everything that happens within the cluster and not the actual read/write of cluster data, a monitor node can be very underpowered and thus less expensive. To achieve a healthy status of the Ceph cluster, a minimum of three monitors need to be set up. A healthy status is when every status in the cluster is OK, without any warnings or errors. Note that with the recent integration of Ceph with Proxmox, the same Proxmox node can be used as a monitor. Starting from Proxmox 3.2, it is possible to set up Ceph monitors on the same Proxmox node, thus eliminating the need to use a separate node for monitors. Monitors can also be managed from the Proxmox GUI.

For details on Ceph monitors, visit the following link:

```
http://ceph.com/docs/master/man/8/ceph-mon/
```

# OSD

The OSD is the actual storage media or partition within media, such as HDD/SSD, that stores the actual cluster data. OSDs are responsible for all the data replication, recovery, and rebalancing. Each OSD provides the monitoring information for Ceph monitors to check for heartbeats. A Ceph cluster requires a minimum of two OSDs to be in the `active+clean` state. The Ceph cluster provides feedback on the cluster status at all times. An `active+clean` state expresses an error- or warning-free cluster. Refer to the PG section for other states a Ceph cluster can achieve. As of Proxmox version 5.0, OSDs can be managed through the Proxmox GUI.

## OSD journal

In Ceph, any I/O writes are first written to a journal before they are transferred to the actual OSD. Journals are simply smaller partitions that accept smaller bits of data at a time while the backend OSDs catch up with the writes. By putting journals on faster-access disk drives, such as SSDs, we can increase a Ceph operation significantly, since user data is written to a journal at a higher speed while the journal sends short bursts of data to OSDs, giving them time to catch up. Journals for multiple OSDs can be stored in one SSD per node. Alternatively, OSDs can be divided into multiple SSDs. For a small cluster of up to eight OSDs per node, using an SSD improves performance. However, while working with a larger cluster with a higher number of OSDs per node, collocating the journal with the same OSDs increases performance instead of using SSDs. The combined write speed of all the OSDs together outperforms the speed of one or two SSDs as a journal.

The important thing to remember about a journal is that the loss of a journal partition causes OSD data loss. For this reason, it is highly recommended that you use an enterprise-grade SSD device. At the time of writing, the Intel DC S3700 SSD is known to work fine as a Ceph journal SSD device.

# Metadata server

A **metadata server** (**MDS**) stores meta information for the **Ceph FileSystem** or **CephFS**. The Ceph block and object storage do not use MDS. So in a cluster, if block and object are the only types that are going to be used, it will not be necessary to set up an MDS server. Like a monitor, MDS needs to be set up on a different machine of its own to achieve high performance. As of Proxmox version 5.0, MDS cannot be managed or created from the Proxmox GUI.

The CephFS is not fully standardized yet and is still in the development phase. It should not be used to store mission-critical data. It is mostly stable, but unforeseen bugs may still cause major issues, such as data loss. Note that there have not been many reports of mass data loss due to an unstable CephFS installation. Two of the virtual machines used to write this book have been running for more than 11 months without any issues.

There should be two MDS nodes in a cluster to provide redundancy, because the loss of an MDS node will cause the loss of data on CephFS and will render it inaccessible. Two MDS nodes will act as *active+passive* when one node failure is taken over by another node, and vice versa. To learn about MDS and CephFS, visit `http://docs.ceph.com/docs/master/cephfs/`.

# PG

The main function of a PG is to combine several objects into a group and then map the group to several OSDs. A per-group mechanism is much more efficient than a per-object mechanism, since the former uses fewer resources. When data is retrieved, it is far more efficient to call a group than to call an individual object in a group. The following diagram shows how PGs are related to OSDs:

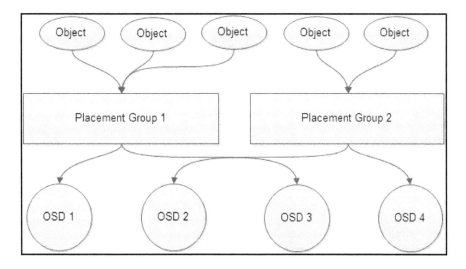

For better efficiency, we recommend a total of 50 to 100 PGs per OSD for all pools. Each PG will consume some resources of the node, such as CPU and memory. A balanced distribution of PGs ensures that all the nodes, and OSDs in the nodes, are not out of memory, or that the CPU does not face overload issues. A simple formula to follow while allocating PGs for a pool is as follows:

*Total PGs = (OSD x 100) / Number of Replicas*

The result of the total PG should be rounded up to the nearest power of two. In a Ceph cluster with *3* nodes (replicas) and *24* OSDs, the total PG count should be as follows:

*Total PGs = (24 x 100) / 3 = 800*

If we divide *800* by *24*, which is the total number of OSDs, then we get *33.33*. This is the number of PGs per replica per OSD. Since we have three replicas, we multiply *33.33* by *4* and get *99.99*. This is the total number of PGs per OSD in the previous example. The formula will always calculate the PGs per replica. For a three-replica setup, each PG is written thrice, and thus, we multiplied the PG of *33.33* by *3* to get the total number of PGs per OSD. Let's take a look at another example to calculate PG. The following setup has *150* OSDs, *3* Ceph nodes, and *2* replicas:

*Total PGs = (150 x 100) / 2 = 7500*

If we divide *7500* by *150*, the total number of OSDs that we get is *50*. Since we have *2* replicas, we multiply *50* by *2* and get *100*. So, each OSD in this cluster can store *100* PGs. In both examples, our total PG per OSD was within the *50-100* recommended range. Always round up the PG value to remove any decimal point.

To balance the available hardware resources, it is necessary to assign the right number of PGs. The PG number will vary depending on the number of OSDs in a cluster. The following table shows a PG suggestion made by Ceph developers:

| Number of OSDs | Number of PGs |
| --- | --- |
| Fewer than 5 OSDs | 128 |
| Between 5-10 OSDs | 512 |
| Between 10-50 OSDs | 1024 |

Selecting the proper number of PGs is crucial since each PG will consume node resources. Too many PGs for the wrong number of OSDs will actually penalize the resource usage of an OSD node, while very few assigned PGs in a large cluster will put data at risk. A rule of thumb is to start with the lowest number of PGs possible, and then increase them as the number of OSDs increases. For details on Placement Groups, visit `http://docs.ceph.com/docs/master/rados/operations/placement-groups/`.

There's a great PG calculator created by Ceph developers to calculate the recommended number of PGs for various sizes of Ceph clusters at `http://ceph.com/pgcalc/`.

# Pools

Pools are like logical partitions where Ceph stores data. When we set a PG or the number of replicas, we actually set them for each pool. When creating a Ceph cluster, three pools are created by default: data, metadata, and RBD. The data and metadata pools are used by the Ceph cluster, while the pool RBD is available to store the actual user data. PGs are set on a per-pool basis. The formula that we discussed earlier in the PG section calculates the PGs required for one pool. So, when creating multiple pools, it is important to modify the formula a bit so that the total PG stays within *50-100* per OSD.

For instance, in the example of *150* OSDs, *3* Ceph nodes, and *2* replicas, our PG was *7500* for a pool. This gave us *50* PGs per OSD. If we had *3* pools in that setup and each pool had *7500* PGs, then the total number of PGs would have been *150* per OSD. In order to balance the PGs across the cluster, we can divide *7500* by *3* for *3* pools and set a PG of *2500* for each pool. This gives us *2500/150 OSDs = 16 PGs per pool per OSD* or *16 x 3 pools = 48 total PGs per OSD*. Since we have two replicas in this setup, the final total PGs per OSD will be *48 x 2 replicas = 96 PGs*. This is within the recommended *50-100* range of PGs per OSD.

# Ceph components summary

If we want to understand the relationship between all the Ceph components we have seen so far, we can think of it this way: each pool comprises multiple PGs. Each PG comprises multiple OSDs. An OSD map keeps track of the number of OSDs in the cluster and in the nodes they are in. The mon map keeps track of the number of monitors in a cluster to form a quorum and maintains a master copy of the cluster map. A CRUSH map dictates how much data needs to be written to an OSD and how to write or read it. These are the building blocks of a Ceph cluster. The following diagram is an example of how the Ceph components come together to form the storage system:

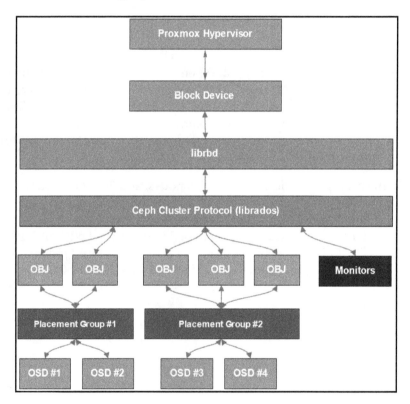

# Virtual Ceph for training

It is possible to set up an entire Ceph cluster in a virtual environment. But this cluster should only be used for training and learning purposes. If you are learning Ceph for the first time and do not want to invest in the physical hardware, then a virtualized Ceph platform is certainly possible. This will eliminate the need to set up the physical hardware to set up Ceph nodes. The procedure to set up a virtual Ceph cluster is exactly the same as for a physical one.

# Installing a Ceph cluster

The following diagram is a basic representation of Proxmox and a Ceph cluster. Note that both the clusters are on separate subnets on separate switches:

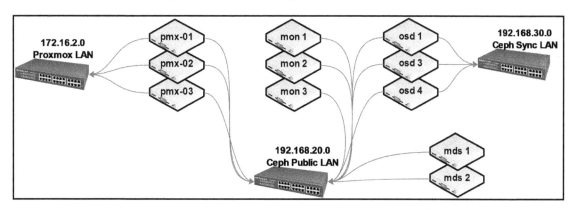

A Ceph cluster should be set up with a separate subnet on a separate switch to keep it isolated from the Proxmox public subnet and for optimal Ceph cluster functioning. The **Ceph Sync LAN** is used by Ceph primarily to sync data between OSDs. The **Ceph Public LAN** is used primarily to serve user requests for data from Ceph into Proxmox VMs. The advantage of this practice is to keep Ceph's internal traffic isolated so that it does not interfere with the traffic of the running virtual machines. On a healthy Ceph cluster with the *active+clean* state, this is not an issue. However, when Ceph goes into self-healing mode due to an OSD or node failure, it rebalances itself by redistributing PGs among remaining OSDs, which causes very high bandwidth consumption. Separating two clusters ensures that the cluster does not slow down significantly due to the shortage of the network bandwidth and the VM remains accessible.

This also provides added security, since the Ceph cluster network is completely hidden from any public access using a separate switch. In our previous example, we have three mons, two MDSs, and three OSD nodes connected to a dedicated switch used only for the Ceph cluster. The Proxmox cluster connects to the Ceph cluster by creating a storage connection through the Proxmox GUI.

# Installing Ceph on Proxmox

As of Proxmox version 5.0, it is possible to install Ceph on the same Proxmox node, thus reducing the number of separate Ceph nodes needed, such as the admin node, monitor node, or OSD node. Proxmox also provides the GUI features that we can use to view the Ceph cluster and manage OSDs, mons, pools, and so on. In this section, we will see how to install Ceph on the Proxmox node. As of Proxmox version 5.0, MDS server and CRUSH map management are not possible from the Proxmox GUI.

## Preparing a Proxmox node for Ceph

Since we are installing Ceph on the same Proxmox node, we will set up the network interfaces for a separate network for Ceph traffic only. We will set up three of our example Proxmox nodes—pmx-01, pmx-02, and pmx-03—with Ceph. On all of the three nodes, we will add the following interfaces section to /etc/network/interfaces. You can use any IP address that suits your network environment. We are going to run the following command from the Proxmox node pmx-01:

```
# nano /etc/network/interfaces
```

Configure all network interfaces according to IP addresses based on your environment. The following is the content of the network configuration for our example cluster after Proxmox and the Ceph network have been configured:

```
# Node pmx-01
# Proxmox Network
auto vmbr0
iface vmbr0 inet static
    address 172.16.2.1
    netmask 255.255.252.0
    gateway 172.16.3.254
    bridge_ports ens18
    bridge_stp off
    bridge_fd 0

# Ceph Public Network
```

```
auto ens19
  iface ens19 inet static
    address 192.168.20.1
    netmask 255.255.255.0

# Ceph Sync Network
auto ens20
  iface ens20 inet static
  address 192.168.30.1
  netmask 255.255.255.0
```

The network interfaces can also be configured through Proxmox GUI. Reboot the node or run the following command to make the new interface active:

**# ifup eth2**

Follow the previous steps and add additional network interfaces with the IP addresses 192.168.10.2 and 192.168.10.3, respectively.

# Installing Ceph

Proxmox added a small command-line utility called pveceph to perform various Ceph-related tasks. Currently, pveceph can perform the following tasks through the command line:

| Command | Task performed |
| --- | --- |
| pveceph install | Installs Ceph on the Proxmox node. |
| pveceph createmon | Creates Ceph monitors and must be run from the node to become a monitor. |
| pveceph createpool <name> | Creates a new pool. It can be used from any node. |
| pveceph destroymon <mon_id> | Removes a monitor. |
| pveceph destroypool <name> | Removes a Ceph pool. |
| pveceph init --network <x.x.x.0/x> | Creates the initial Ceph configuration file based on the network CIDR used. |
| pveceph start <service> | Starts Ceph daemon services, such as mon, OSD, and MDS. |
| pveceph stop <service> | Stops Ceph daemon services, such as mon, OSD, and MDS. |

| | |
|---|---|
| `pveceph status` | Shows the cluster, monitor, MDS server, OSD status, and cluster ID. |
| `pveceph createosd </dev/X>` | Creates OSD daemons. |
| `pvecph destroyosd <osdid>` | Removes OSD daemons. |
| `pveceph purge` | Removes Ceph and all Ceph-related data from the node the command is running from. |

Ceph must be installed and at least one monitor must be created using a command line initially before managing it through the Proxmox GUI. We can perform the following steps to install Ceph on the Proxmox nodes and create the first monitor. Run the following command to install Ceph on all the Proxmox nodes that will be part of the Ceph cluster:

**# pveceph install -version jewel**

Note that at the time of writing this book, the latest version of Ceph was codenamed *Kraken*. However, the Ceph version *Jewel LTS* has been used for the writing of this book, as it is fully supported by Proxmox, as of Proxmox 5.0. Simply change the codename in the command to install the latest Ceph releases when they become available in Proxmox.

Visit the following link for information on Ceph releases and their life cycle:

`http://docs.ceph.com/docs/master/releases/`

Run the following command to create an initial Ceph configuration file on the first Proxmox node. We only need to run this command once, and from one node only:

**# pveceph init --network 192.168.20.0/24**

After running the command, Proxmox will create a Ceph configuration file in `/etc/pve/ceph.conf`. It also creates a symlink of the configuration file in `/etc/ceph/ceph.conf`. This way, any custom changes made to the Ceph configuration file get replicated across all Proxmox nodes.

 Although the Ceph cluster can be managed from the Proxmox GUI, in order to perform advanced tasks, we need to use the CLI. Ceph comes loaded with quite a few commands for various tasks. It is beyond the scope of this book to list all Ceph commands. But a short list of commands used to perform the most common tasks is included later in this chapter.

Run the following command to create the first Ceph monitor on the same node that we just created in the initial configuration file:

```
# pveceph createmon
```

After performing these steps, we can proceed with the Proxmox GUI to further create mons, OSDs, or pools. All the Ceph options can be obtained by navigating to the `Datacenter` | node | **Ceph** menu. The following screenshot shows the content of the `/etc/ceph/ceph.conf` file for our example cluster after creating a Ceph cluster with two mons and no OSDs:

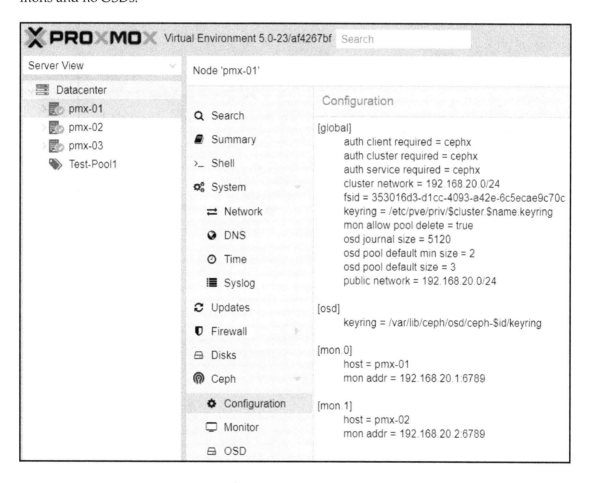

Recall from the previous configuration screenshot that both the cluster and public network are on the same subnet. That is because we have not configured the Ceph sync or cluster network yet. Simply change the IP subnet of the cluster network by changing the Ceph configuration file in `/etc/ceph/ceph.conf` to ask Ceph to sync OSDs on the separate network. For our example cluster, we want the Ceph sync network to be on `192.168.30.0/24`, as shown here:

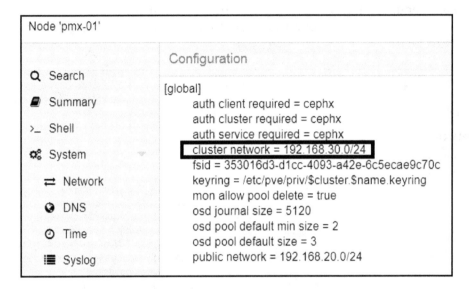

When trying to access the **Ceph** menu through the GUI from a node which is not a Ceph mon, you may see the following error message:

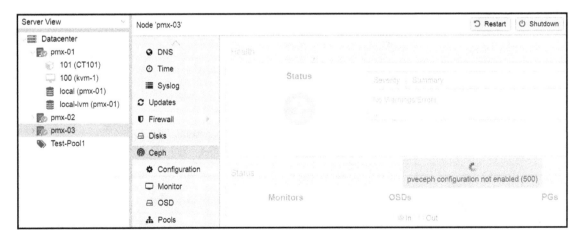

If you do not intend to create any OSD on the node but want to manage the Ceph cluster from a node, then simply install Ceph using the #pveceph command on that node and create a mon. This will enable the node to read the Ceph configuration file and allow managing of the Ceph cluster through the Proxmox GUI.

# Creating mons from the Proxmox GUI

To view and create monitors from the Proxmox GUI, navigate to Datacenter | node | **Ceph** | **Monitor**. Click on **Create** to open the monitor creation dialog box. Select a Proxmox node from the drop-down list and then click on the **Create** button to initiate the monitor creation. We can also quickly check the overall Ceph cluster status from the GUI. The following screenshot shows our example Ceph cluster as seen through the Proxmox GUI after the initial configuration:

From the **Status** interface, we can gather vital pieces of information at a glance. The Ceph cluster contains an error at this moment since there are no OSDs added. It is perfectly normal for the Ceph cluster to show PGs stuck at inactive and unclean, as we have not added any OSDs.

# Creating OSDs from Proxmox GUI

OSDs are actual disk drives where data is stored in a Ceph cluster. All OSD-related tasks can be performed through the `Datacenter` I node I **Ceph** I **OSD** menu. To view the installed disk drives in the node, go to the `Datacenter` I node I **Disks** menu. The following screenshot shows that we have two available drives, `/dev/vdc` and `/dev/vdd`, which can be used to create OSDs in node `pmx-01`:

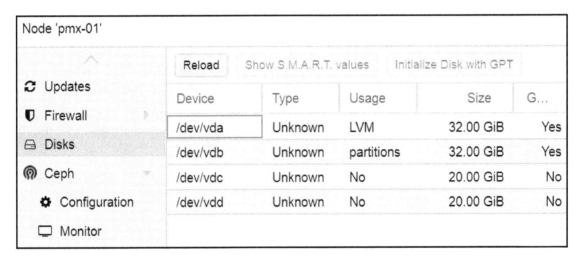

To create an OSD, go to the `Datacenter` I node I **Ceph** I **OSD** menu and click on the **Create OSD** button to open a dialog box, as shown in the following screenshot. Select an available disk drive from the drop-down list, and then click on the **Create** button:

There is no need to select **Journal Disk** if the journal is going to be collocated on the same OSD drive. Click on the **Journal Disk** drop-down button to select a different disk drive to store the OSD journal. A faster drive, such as an SSD, can be used to store the Ceph journal, which makes writing to the Ceph cluster extremely fast in a smaller cluster of fewer than six Ceph nodes. If using a separate drive for journaling, the drive must be partitioned through the CLI before creating the OSD using this dialog box. Follow the same procedure to finish creating OSDs in the node. The following screenshot shows the Ceph **Status** page after creating two OSDs in node pmx-01:

Note that even after adding two OSDs in the node, our Ceph cluster is still degraded and unclean. This is because we only created OSDs in one node. By default, Ceph will try to create three replicas on different nodes. So, we are going to add four more OSDs in the second and third node by following the previous steps. The following screenshot shows our example Ceph cluster with six OSDs on three nodes, with a **Health_OK** status for **Health**:

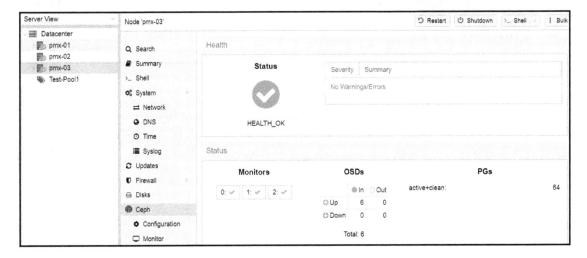

By default, Proxmox creates OSDs with the XFS filesystem. However, sometimes, it is necessary to create OSDs with different filesystem types, such as ext3, btrfs, and so on, due to requirements or performance improvements. As of Proxmox 5.0, we cannot adjust the partition type during the OSD creation through the GUI. It can only be done when creating the OSD through CLI. Enter the following command format using the CLI to create OSDs with different partition types:

```
# pveceph createosd -fstype ext4 /dev/sdX
```

# Managing a Ceph pool using Proxmox GUI

All Ceph pool-related tasks can be performed through the `Datacenter` | node | **Ceph** | **Pools** menu. The pool interface shows information about existing pools, such as the name, replica number, PG number, and per-pool percentage used. Once a pool is created, it cannot be modified or changed in any way from the Proxmox GUI. But a pool can be edited through the CLI. If you are going to strictly use the Proxmox GUI to perform all Ceph-related tasks, then a new pool needs to be created if existing pool configuration needs to be changed, such as changing the replica size or increasing the PG number. When the Ceph cluster is created, a default pool named `rbd` is created with replica size 3 and a total of 64 PGs. This PG number of the `rbd` pool is too low to store any data. So we can create a new pool or we can modify this pool through CLI. When an existing pool holds a lot of data, changing the pool configuration through CLI is the way to go, or else all data will need to be moved to the new pool, which can take a very long time depending on the amount of data being stored.

Replica size is the second most important configuration for a Ceph pool. Basically, replica size defines how many times data will be replicated before it is distributed among OSDs on different nodes. Keep in mind that a higher replica size will consume higher network bandwidth and higher disk storage due to increased replication. For a smaller cluster, a replica size of 2 is best suited from a performance standpoint. However, in a large Ceph cluster with lots of drives and nodes, using a replica size of 3 is recommended.

For the pool `rbd` in our example Ceph cluster, we are going to change the default replica size of 3 to 2 using the following command:

```
# ceph osd pool set rbd size 2
```

We are also going to change the minimum size, or `min_size`, value of the pool. The minimum replica size defines the minimum replicated data that must exist in order for the pool to operate. For example, in the default pool `rbd`, the minimum size is 2. So if multiple HDD failures occur where a set of OSDs that hold two data replicas goes down, the cluster will not come online. But if the minimum size is 1, then as long as the Ceph cluster can see one data replica anywhere in the cluster, even in the case of multiple OSD failures, the cluster will still operate. A minimum size of 1 will ensure that there is always at least one copy of data at all times. We can change the minimum size of a pool using the following command format:

```
# ceph osd pool set rbd min_size 1
```

We are going to increase the PG number of the default pool rbd in order to make it usable to store virtual machine data.

Refer to the Ceph PG calculator at the following link to calculate the number of PGs you need for your Ceph cluster:

```
http://ceph.com/pgcalc/
```

There are two values that need to be set for the PG number of a pool: the actual PG number and the effective PG number. This value is defined with the option pgp_num. The pgp_num must be equal or less than pg_num. We are going to increase the PG number to 256 for our default pool rbd using the following command:

```
# ceph osd pool set rbd pg_num 256
# ceph osd pool set rbd pgp_num 256
```

When changing PG values, it is very important to keep in mind that it is a very intensive process. The Ceph cluster will be under load during this process. When changing the PG value from low to high, it is a wise idea to do it in steps, using smaller PG values incrementally. This is not a problem for a brand new Ceph cluster which is not serving any users yet. But on an established Ceph cluster with many active users, the performance will be noticeable and may cause service interruption.

The replica size, minimum replica size, and PG value are the most important values for a Ceph pool. Changes in these values have the most impact on overall cluster performance and reliability. So to recap, let's run these commands for a hypothetical pool named vm_store. We are going to change the replica size to 3, minimum replica size to 1, PG number to 1024, and effective PG number to 1024 using the following commands:

```
# ceph osd pool set vm_store size 3
# ceph osd pool set vm_store min_size size 1
# ceph osd pool set vm_store pg_num 1024
# ceph osd pool set vm_store pgp_num 1024
```

The following screenshot shows the pool status for our default pool rbd in our example cluster after making necessary changes through CLI:

# Creating a Ceph pool using Proxmox GUI

To create a new pool using the Proxmox GUI, go to Datacenter I node I **Ceph** I **Pools**. Then click on the **Create** button to open the pool-creation dialog box, as shown in the following screenshot. Enter a name for the pool in the **Name** field, the number of replicas in **Size**, and the number of minimum replicas; leave **Crush RuleSet** at 0; and enter the proper PG number. Click on **Create** to start the pool's creation:

# Connecting Ceph to Proxmox

As of Proxmox VE 5.0, we can only connect Ceph block storage (RBD) to Proxmox. We cannot connect Ceph Object Storage or Ceph FileSystem. We can connect Ceph RBD storage to the cluster using the Proxmox GUI. However, there is one step that needs to be completed before Proxmox can successfully read the Ceph storage. Ceph uses authentication for its functioning. Authentication occurs based on keyrings, which are created along with the Ceph cluster. For each Ceph storage, we need to connect to Proxmox, and we need to copy the main Ceph admin keyring to the Proxmox directory. The keyring that we need to copy is located in `/priv/ceph.client.admin.keyring`.

This keyring needs to be copied to the following location and in the following format. The directory `/etc/pve/priv/ceph` does not exist, so it needs to be created first: `/etc/pve/priv/ceph/<storage_id>.keyring`.

For example, we are going to create an RBD storage named `rbd-01`. So, we need to copy the keyring, as shown in the following command:

```
# cp /etc/pve/priv/ceph.client.admin.keyring
/etc/pve/priv/ceph/rbd-01.keyring
```

We can find the Ceph RBD storage plugin option by navigating to `Datacenter` | **Storage** | **Add**. Click on the **RBD (external)** storage plugin to open the dialog box and add the required information, as shown in the following screenshot:

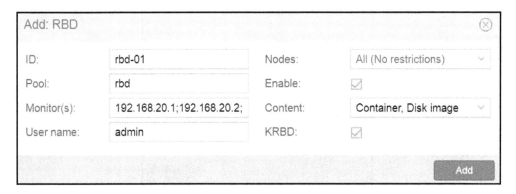

In the preceding screenshot, we are adding an RBD storage named `rbd-01` that will store virtual disk images in the Ceph pool named `rbd`. IP addresses of the Ceph mon nodes are separated by a semicolon in the **Monitor(s)** textbox. There is no need to change the **User name**, as the `admin` is the default user of the Ceph operation. As of Proxmox VE 5.0, we can also use the Ceph RBD storage to store LXC containers. However, it will only work if we select the **KRBD** option in the dialog box. It is possible to store both the LVM and LXC images on a single KRBD-enabled RBD storage, but for maximum performance and isolation, it is highly recommended that you use two separate Ceph pools for KVM and LXC virtual machine disk images, with the **KRBD** option enabled for the LXC container pool. The following screenshot shows the RBD storage status from the Proxmox GUI:

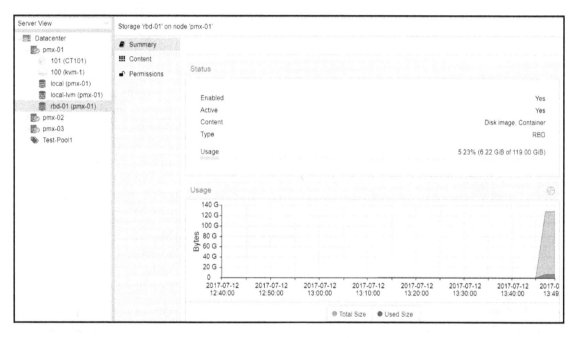

# Ceph command list

The following table shows some of the common Ceph commands used in a cluster:

| Command | Function |
|---|---|
| `#ceph -s` | Displays the Ceph cluster status. |
| `#ceph -w` | Displays the Ceph cluster running log. |
| `#ceph health detail` | Displays a detailed error if there is one. |
| `#ceph osd tree` | Displays a list of all OSDs categorized by nodes. |
| `#ceph set osd noout`<br>`#ceph set osd nodown` | Prevents any OSDs from getting marked out and down, so Ceph does not start rebalancing. It is necessary during maintenance when the node requires a reboot due to updates. |
| `#ceph unset osd noout`<br>`#ceph unset osd nodown` | Must be run after the maintenance is over in order to resume normal operation. |
| `#ceph daemon osd.X config show | grep <item_name>`<br>`Ex: #ceph daemon osd.2 config show | grep threads` | Displays runtime values of Ceph. For example, we can run this command to display all thread-related items in a Ceph cluster. |

| | |
|---|---|
| `#ceph tell osd.* injectargs '<item_name> <value>'` <br> `Ex: #ceph tell osd.* injectargs '-osd-op-threads 8'` | Injects values into items during runtime without restarting any daemons. It is helpful to play around with different values to find optimum numbers. When satisfied, the changes must be entered in `/etc/pve/ceph.conf` or else they will get reset during the node reboot or OSD daemon restart. |
| `#ceph osd lspools` | Lists pools. |
| `#ceph osd pool create <name> <pg> <pgs>` | Creates a pool. |
| `#ceph osd pool delete <name> [<name> --yes-i-really-really-mean-it]` | Deletes a pool. |
| `#ceph osd pool get <name> pg_num` | Gets the number of PGs in a pool. |
| `#ceph osd set pool <pool_name> size <value>` | Changes the replica values of a pool. |

# Summary

In this chapter, we learned what Ceph storage is and how to install and configure it to work with Proxmox cluster to store virtual disk images. We also learned various Ceph commands to manage a Ceph cluster.

In the next chapter, we will learn details about KVM-based virtual machines. We will see how to create and manage KVM virtual machines and their advanced configurations.

# 6
# KVM Virtual Machines

So far, we have familiarized ourselves with the Proxmox graphical user interface, configuration files, and directory structure. We have also learned about the different type of storage supported by Proxmox and how to integrate a Ceph storage cluster in a Proxmox environment. In this chapter, we are going to take it one step further by looking at **Kernel-based Virtual Machine** (**KVM**) and all that it has to offer. We are going to cover some of the following topics:

- Exploring KVM virtual machines
- Creating KVM virtual machines
- Configuring KVM virtual machines
- Migrating KVM virtual machines
- Nested virtual environments
- Proxmox backup/restore system
- Virtual machine snapshots

# Exploring KVM

As the name implies, KVM is merely a virtualization process that adds the hypervisor ability to a Linux kernel. KVM allows you to create fully isolated virtual machines while not being dependent on the host operating system or kernel. The isolation is created by emulating several types of hardware, such as CPU, RAM, sound/video/network cards, PCI bridges, and input devices. In order to create KVM virtual machines, the CPU in the host node must have **hardware virtualization extensions** (**HWE**). KVM/Qemu creates a layer that virtualizes physical hardware, allowing full system virtualization and not kernel-level virtualization, as is the case with OpenVZ and LXC containers. This allows a wide range of operating systems to be virtualized, such as Linux, BSD, Windows, and macOS. One of the main differences between KVM and container-based virtual machines is that a KVM virtual system shares on the hardware level, whereas container-based virtualization shares on the kernel level. Thus, the density of the number of KVM VMs in a node is much lower than containers. KVM is the only choice for non-Linux operating systems and for purpose-built operating systems based on Linux, such as ClearOS, FreeNAS, and Zentyal.

For more information on KVM, refer to the following link:

```
https://en.wikipedia.org/wiki/Kernel-based_Virtual_Machine
```

# Creating a KVM

In Proxmox, we can a create KVM VM in the following ways:

- From scratch using an ISO image
- From a template
- Using network PXE boot

In this chapter, we are only going to take a look at VM creation though ISO images and templates.

# Creating a KVM using an ISO image

The VM creation process is based on simple tab-based dialog boxes. During the process, we have to assign resources and type in necessary information pertaining to the VM. The dialog box can be accessed by clicking on the **Create VM** button located in the top right-hand corner of the screen, as shown in the following screenshot. It can also be accessed by right-clicking on a node and then selecting **Create VM** from the context menu:

In our example cluster, we are going to create a KVM named centos1 in node pmx-01. To progress through the VM creation, simply click on the **Next** button or click on the **Back** button to go back to the previous tab. The following screenshot shows the dialog box after we click on **Create VM** from the Proxmox GUI:

# General tab

The **General** tab of the dialog box is used to mainly assign identification information. Let's have a look at them.

## Node

This is a drop-down list to select in which Proxmox node the VM should be created.

## VM ID

This is the textbox used to enter the numeric ID of the VM. We can also increase or decrease the value of the **VM ID** using the arrows. If we assign an ID that exists in the cluster, the box will show a red border around the box indicating that there is already a VM with the same ID.

## Name

This is the textbox used to enter the name of the VM. We can enter any alphanumeric string with only a dash or – allowed as the special character.

## Resource Pool

This is the drop-down menu used to select a previously created pool. It is only necessary if we want to assign the VM to a specific pool. For our example VM, we are assigning it to pool named `Linux_VMs`.

## Help

The **Help** button will open a new tab with installed documentation created by Proxmox developers. This documentation contains specific information pertaining to the tab. Each **Help** button on different tabs is anchored to a particular section of the documentation. The URL for this KVM documentation is `https://ip_addr:8006/pve-docs/chapter-qm.html`.

# The OS tab

The **OS** tab is used to select the type of guest operating system that will be installed on the VM. This type of selection allows the VM to be aware of the intended operating system and adjust the architecture based on the OS selected. In our example VM, we have selected **Linux 4.X/3.X/2.6 Kernel**, as shown in the following screenshot:

To achieve maximum performance and stability, it is highly recommended you select the proper OS type.

# The CD/DVD tab

Since KVM VMs are fully enclosed and emulate a physical machine, we can only boot the VM or load the operating system using ISO images loaded in a virtual CD/DVD drive or through a physical drive attached to the Proxmox host node. In this tab, we can select whether to use a virtual or physical CD/DVD drive or select an ISO image. The following screenshot shows the dialog box for the **CD/DVD** tab, where we have selected CentOS ISO:

If we only want to create the VM without specifying any disk image, we will need to select the **Do not use any media** option.

# The Hard Disk tab

In this tab, we specify the configuration for the first disk image of the VM. The following screenshot shows the dialog box with the configuration for our example VM:

## Bus/Device

There are two drop-down menus available for this option. One to select the *disk image bus type* and the other to select the *device ID*.

For maximum performance, the VirtIO bus is recommended.

For a Windows VM, it is necessary to select an IDE since Windows does not have a built-in driver for VirtIO. In such cases, we can use the following steps to add VirtIO capability to a Windows VM:

1. Create the VM with IDE and install Windows as usual.
2. Add a second disk image with the VirtIO bus and reboot into Windows.
3. Download the latest VirtIO driver ISO for Windows from the following links and then load it through a virtual CD drive:
   - `https://fedorapeople.org/groups/virt/virtio-win/direct-downloads/stable-virtio/virtio-win.iso`
   - `http://www.linux-kvm.org/page/WindowsGuestDrivers/Download_Drivers`
4. Update the driver for the new hardware found for the VirtIO disk image.
5. Shut down the Windows VM and log in to the Proxmox dashboard.
6. From the **Hardware** tab of the VM, select the IDE image and click on **Remove**. Note that this does not remove the disk image permanently. The disk image will now show as **Unused Disk 0**:

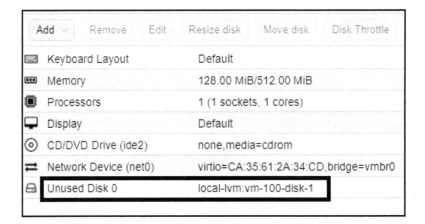

7. Select the **Unused disk 0** and click on **Edit**. This will open up a dialog box with options to select the **Bus/Device** type and other configuration options:

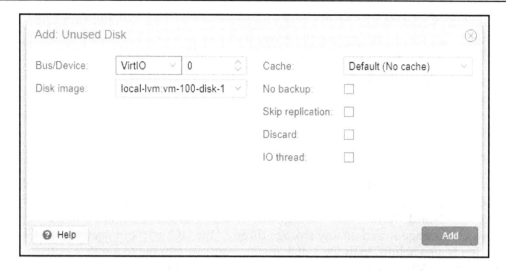

8. From this dialog box, we can select the desired bus type and other configuration options if necessary.

9. Click on the **Add** button to add the disk image back to the VM.

The previous steps are necessary to enable the Windows VM to use a VirtIO disk image. Once the driver is loaded, it is not necessary to reload it for additional VirtIO disk images.

## Storage

This is a drop-down menu to select the storage in which the disk image should be stored. Along with the name of the storage, the drop-down menu shows the total capacity and available storage space of attached storage devices.

## Disk size (GB)

This is a textbox to define the size of the disk storage in GB. The value can only be numeric. We can also use the up and down arrows of the textbox to define the disk image size.

## Format

This is a drop-down menu to select the type of disk image. If we select storage that only supports a certain disk type, then this menu option will be greyed out. For example, in our example cluster, we have selected Ceph RBD storage, which can only store .raw images as of Proxmox 5.0. So the format option is greyed out.

If we select the wrong format of disk image or later our requirement changes to using a different format, we can simply use the **Move disk** option in the **Hardware** tab to change the format. This can also be done through the CLI using the following command format:

```
#qemu-img convert -O <type> <source_image> <destination_image>
```

If we want to convert a .qcow2 disk image to a .raw image, the command would be as follows:

```
#qemu-img convert -O raw vm-101-disk-1.qcow2 vm-101-disk-1.raw
```

This command works great for local, NFS, ZFS, and Gluster storage but is not suitable for RBD. To change the disk image format stored in RBD, use the **Move disk** option in the Proxmox dashboard. Besides RBD storage disk image, this **Move disk** option can be used to move any disk image stored on any storage through the GUI without needing the CLI at all. This option is also helpful to move a disk image from one storage to another without powering off the VM. The move could be from local to shared or vice versa. To move or change the format of a disk image, select the disk image from the **Hardware** tab and click on **Move disk** to open a dialog box:

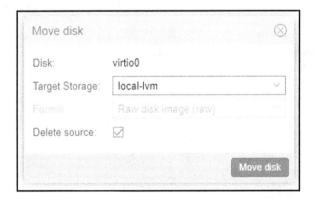

As shown in the previous screenshot, for our example VM we are moving a .raw disk image from RBD to local storage. If we select the **Delete source** option, it will delete the source file automatically after converting or moving is finished. If the option is not selected, then we will have to manually delete the source file. The source file will show up as an unused disk image under the **Hardware** tab of the VM.

# Cache

This drop-down menu allows us to select the cache method to use for the disk image. We have learned about the different cache options in the *Caching a virtual disk image* section in `Chapter 4`, *Storage Systems*. We can change the cache option any time even after the VM is fully created and functioning. After each cache option change, we will need to power-cycle the VM to enable the new cache option.

# No backup

If this option is enabled, the virtual disk image will never be included in the backup. By default, the option is disabled.

# Discard

Disk images in Proxmox are sparse regardless of the image type, meaning the disk image grows slowly as more data gets stored in it. Over time, data gets created and deleted within the filesystem of the disk image. But in a sparse disk image, even after data is deleted, it never reclaims the free space. The VM may report the correct available storage space but Proxmox storage will show higher storage usage. The **Discard** option allows the node to reclaim the free space that does not have any data. This is equivalent to the TRIM option that was introduced in SSD drives. Before this option can be used, we have to ensure that the VM uses the **VirtIO SCSI** controller. We can set the **SCSI Controller Type** under virtual machine's **Options** tab:

| Virtual Machine 102 ('centos1') on node 'pmx-01' | | |
|---|---|---|
| ■ Summary | Edit Revert | |
| >_ Console | Name | centos1 |
| ⬛ Hardware | Start at boot | No |
| ✿ Options | Start/Shutdown order | order=any |
| ☰ Task History | OS Type | Linux 4.X/3.X/2.6 Kernel |
| | Boot Order | Disk 'virtio0', CD-ROM, Network |
| ☞ Monitor | Use tablet for pointer | Yes |
| ▣ Backup | Hotplug | Disk, Network, USB |
| ⇄ Replication | ACPI support | Yes |
| ↺ Snapshots | SCSI Controller Type | VirtIO SCSI |
| ◻ Firewall | BIOS | Default (SeaBIOS) |

The **Discard** option may not be suitable for all environments, storage solutions, and operating systems. Perform enough testing before implementing it in your environment. In some cases, the **Discard** option may cause a VM to lock up, needing to be power-cycled. The VM will need to be power-cycled if the option is enabled after powering it back up.

## IO thread

There are two options for disk images with KVM:

- **IO thread**
- `io=native`

By default, Proxmox uses `io=native` for all disk images unless the **IO thread** option is specifically checked for the disk image.

The **IO thread** option allows each disk image to have its own thread instead of waiting in a queue with everything else. Since disk I/O is no longer waiting due to having its own threads, it does not hold up other tasks or queues related to the VM, which in turn speeds up the VM performance besides providing increased disk performance. The **IO thread** option is fairly new in Proxmox. There were a few reported instances where the VM was locked up due to this option. So perform plenty of testing before implementing this feature in a production environment.

# The CPU tab

This tab allows configuration of a virtual CPU for virtual machines. The following screenshot shows the dialog box with available CPU options:

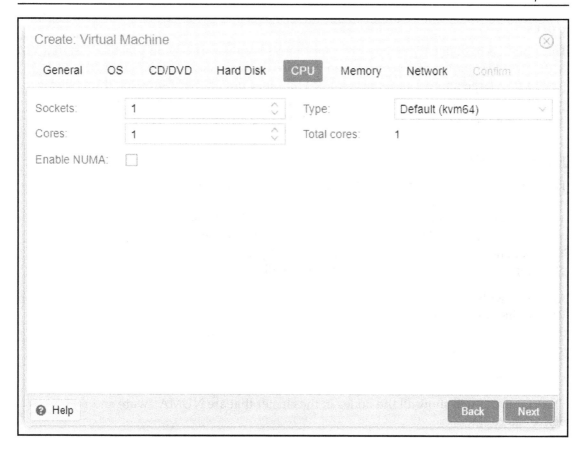

## Sockets

This option is to define the number of sockets the VM can use. We can use more than one socket for the VM even if the physical node does not have enough sockets. This may only be useful if an application in the VM requires us to have more than one socket. But it is not useful at all to increase VM performance in a single-socket Proxmox node.

## Cores

This option is to define the number of cores the VM can use. It is good practice to start a VM with a smaller number of cores and then increase them as needed, depending on load. Assigning a large number of cores to a VM will cause unnecessary stress on the available resources in the node. Usually, VMs can provide good performance with two or four cores unless it is a high-demand VM, such as a remote desktop server or SQL/Exchange server.

## Enabling NUMA

The **non-uniform memory access** (**NUMA**) is not a new approach to handling memory in a multi-CPU environment, although it is a new addition to Proxmox VE. With NUMA, memory can be distributed evenly among CPUs, which increases performance since there is no bottleneck due to all CPUs trying to access the same memory bank. In Proxmox, the NUMA option also enables memory and CPU hot-plugging. Without this option, hot-plugging for CPU and memory will not work at all.

Any node with more than one CPU socket is usually NUMA aware. So enabling NUMA for VMs in this node will benefit VM performance. NUMA will always try to keep the VM in the same CPU package. We can check the NUMA status in the Proxmox cluster using the following command:

```
# numastat
```

This command will show all the nodes in the cluster that are NUMA aware and their performance stats.

## Type

This is a drop-down menu to select the CPU package type. By default, the **Default (kvm64)** CPU type is selected for all VMs. A common use case is when a specific application requires SSE or AVX instructions. By selecting the host CPU type, we can give a VM direct access to the physical CPU.

For the best performance, host type should be used. This way, the VM will be able to access the CPU directly without an emulation layer. This is optimal type in an environment where all nodes are identical. For maximum portability of a VM, it is best to choose the KVM or Qemu CPU types.

# The Memory tab

This tab allows configuration of the memory allocation of the VM. The following screenshot shows the dialog box for our example VM:

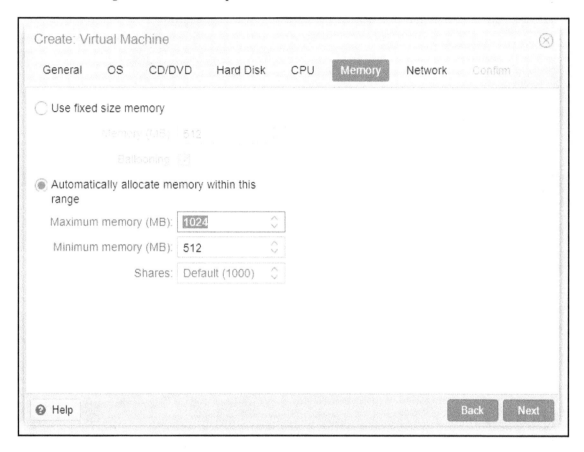

In Proxmox, we can set fixed or dynamic memory for a VM. Automatic range is also known as memory ballooning. For the fixed option, all memory is allocated at once. In the dynamic option, memory is allocated based on the VM, within a preset range. Automatic memory allocation works great for Linux-based guest VMs. But for Windows VMs, memory ballooning consumes a higher amount of CPU resources, causing the VM to slow down. So for windows VMs, it is best to use fixed memory whenever possible.

# The Network tab

This tab allows configuration of the virtual network interface of the VM. The following screenshot shows the dialog box for the network configuration of our example VM:

## Bridged mode

This mode allows a VM to connect to the network using a bridge. The VM does not get direct access to the outside network. We can set the VLAN ID at the node level, which makes it unnecessary to configure it inside the VM. The **Bridged mode** also provides firewall options for the VM. For our example VM, we have selected the default bridge vmbr0 and enabled the **Firewall** option.

# Firewall

To enable the Proxmox firewall for network interfaces, this option needs to be checked. Without this option, no firewall rules will be applied to the VM interface. We will look at the Proxmox firewall in greater detail in `Chapter 9`, *The Proxmox VE Firewall*.

# NAT mode

This mode provides a VM direct access to outside networks. Network traffic does not go through any bridge. If VLAN is used in the physical network, it must be configured inside the VM in order to have the data packets tagged or untagged. The Proxmox firewall option is not available when using NAT mode.

# No network device

This option will create the VM without any network interface configured.

# Model

This is a drop-down menu to select the virtual network interface type. For maximum network performance, the use of VirtIO is highly recommended. Windows does not come with a VirtIO driver. So if this is used for a Windows VM, we have to manually load the driver from the ISO we have downloaded in *The Hard Disk tab* section of this chapter. We can also use Intel E1000 for Windows VMs. From Windows 7 onward, the driver for Intel is included.

# MAC address

By default, all MAC addresses for virtual network interfaces are automatically assigned. By typing a MAC address in this textbox, we can specify a particular MAC address for the interface. This may be necessary when a specific MAC address is required by an application in the guest VM.

# Rate limit (MB/s)

This is a textbox to define the maximum allowable speed of the network interface in megabytes per second. This is a very useful option to limit network resources per VM. Without any value defined, the VM will try to use as much bandwidth as possible.

### Multiqueues

Ordinarily, KVM VMs are single-queued, where sending and receiving packets occurs one at a time and not in parallel. **Multiqueues** remove this bottleneck by allowing sending and receiving in parallel by leveraging virtual CPU cores for parallel queues. **Multiqueues** are especially useful for a VM which is active on numerous clients, for example, a web server. In the Proxmox **Network** tab in the VM creation dialog box, we can enter a numeric value to define how many parallel queues the VM should use. This value should not be more than the allocated vCPU of the VM. For example, if the VM has a virtual core count of four, we can set a **Multiqueues** value of 4. **Multiqueues** increase network performance of a VM greatly since both sending and receiving can happen in parallel.

 Keep in mind that enabling **Multiqueues** will also increase CPU usage of the VM since each queue is dependent on each vCPU.

### Disconnect

If this option is enabled, the virtual network interface will be created along with the VM but will not be activated.

# Creating VM by cloning

When deploying multiple VMs with identical configuration, creating them individually can become a time-consuming process. In such cases, we can clone an existing VM or a template. Cloning creates a fully independent VM with identical configuration. The cloned VM is in no way connected to the VM it was cloned from. The cloning option can be accessed from the context menu by right-clicking on the VM to be cloned:

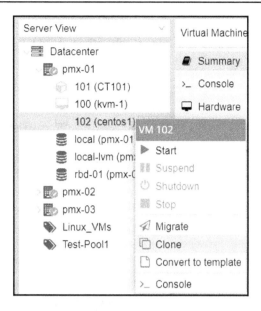

One of the uses of cloning a VM is backup strategy. A VM can be cloned regularly to separate nodes, even on separate storage. In the event that the main node becomes inaccessible, the cloned VM can be up and running in minutes without going through the VM restore process. The following screenshot shows the clone dialog box after clicking on **Clone** from the context menu:

The cloning feature is also useful to keep the master VM up to date or add new applications and so on, because the source VM is still a fully functional VM.

# Creating VMs from a template

Similar to cloning, a template is also a quick way to deploy fully configured VMs without going through the complete VM creation process and manually installing OS and applications. We can create a new VM and install the OS and all other necessary programs before converting it to a template. This way, all new VMs created from the template will be fully configured with OS and programs. What sets template apart from just cloning is that once a VM is converted to a template, it cannot be powered up again. If the template VM needs any changes, a new VM must be created, configured, and then converted to a template. We can however edit the hardware resources of the template. The primary benefit of using a template to clone VMs is that a template allows us to create full-clone and linked-clone VMs.

In order to create VMs from a template, we need to create the template first. We can do this by converting a configured VM into a template. This option can be accessed by selecting the VM to be converted and then right-clicking and selecting **Convert to template** to open the dialog box:

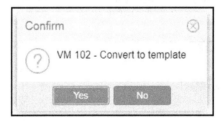

In this example, we are going to convert one of our VMs, **102 (centos1)**, into a template. Click on **Yes** to convert the VM into a template. As mentioned earlier, after the VM is converted to a template, the VM itself is no longer usable. Another noticeable difference is that the icon in the Proxmox dashboard is unique for KVM templates, as shown in the following screenshot:

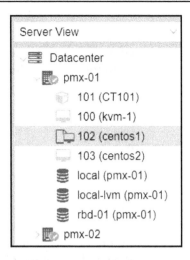

With the template, we can now clone VMs that will be identical to the template. The procedure to clone is the same whether it is a VM or a KVM template. To create a new VM or deploy multiple VMs from the template, right-click on the template to open the context menu and then click on the **Clone** option. This will open the cloning dialog box, as shown in the following screenshot:

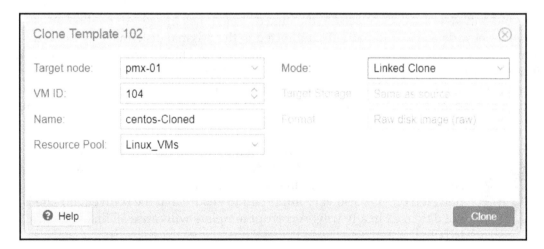

## Target node

This is a drop-down menu to select which node we want the cloned VM to be created on. It could be the same node or any other node in the cluster with sufficient resources.

## Mode

There are two cloning modes in Proxmox 5.0:

- **Full Clone**
- **Linked Clone**

**Full Clone** creates an identical copy of the VM, including the virtual disk image. This is a truly isolated VM since it is not dependent on the source template or VM in any way. Even if we delete the source template or VM, the newly deployed VM will still function without any issue. A **Full Clone** consumes as much storage space as the original VM since the virtual disk is also cloned. Full clones are useful when allocated resources are identical for all deployed VMs but the guest operating system may or may not be different.

A **Linked Clone** creates a duplicate of the original VM minus the original virtual disk image. This creates an additional blank disk image that is referenced to the original virtual disk, and only new data gets placed in the linked cloned disk image. All read requests, except for new data, are automatically redirected to the original disk image. A **Linked Clone** is heavily dependent on the source template or VM. This clone mode is useful when all cloned VMs will have the exact same hardware and software configuration, including guest operating system. A **Linked Clone** consumes much less storage space since the original or base image is never duplicated but only referenced by the new **Linked Clone** VM.

Although we cannot power up the template, we can still make resource changes such as CPU, and RAM. But it is not a recommended practice since any hardware change may cause issues when a cloned VM is powered on. It is also very important to ensure that the source template is not damaged in any way. A corrupt template will cause all linked clones to fail.

# Advanced configuration options for VMs

We will now look at some of the advanced configuration options we can use to extend the capability of KVM virtual machines.

# Configuring a sound device

In this section, we are going to see how to add sound support to a VM. Proxmox by default does not add audio hardware to a VM. In order for the VM operating system to start the sound service, some arguments must be added to the VM configuration file through CLI. As of Proxmox VE 4.1 it is not possible to add a sound interface through GUI. The following steps will add a sound device to a VM:

1. Log in to the Proxmox node through SSH or directly in the console.
2. Navigate to the VM configuration directory
   `/etc/pve/nodes/<node_name>/qemu-server/<vm_id>.conf`.
3. Open the VM configuration file with your favorite editor and add the following argument:

   For Windows 10 and later VMs:

   ```
   args: -device intel-had,id=sound5,bus=pci.0,
   addr=0x18 -device hda-micro,id=sound5-codec0,
   bus=sound5.0,cad=0 -device had-duplex,
   id=sound5-codec1,bus=sound5.0,cad=1
   ```

   For Windows XP VMs:

   ```
   args: -device AC97,addr=0x18
   ```

4. Save the configuration file and exit the editor.
5. Power-cycle the VM to activate the sound device.

# Configuring PCI passthrough

In Proxmox it is possible to passthrough PCI devices directly into a VM. In this section, we are going to see how to configure and verify PCI passthrough. The following steps are to enable and configure PCI passthrough in Proxmox:

1. Log in to the Proxmox node through SSH or directly in the console.
2. Open the grub configuration file using an editor:

   ```
   # nano /etc/default/grub
   ```

3. Change `GRUB_CMDLINE_LINUX_DEFAULT="quiet"` to the following:

   - For Intel CPUs:

     `GRUB_CMDLINE_LINUX_DEFAULT="quiet intel_iommu=on"`

   - For AMD CPUs:

     `GRUB_CMDLINE_LINUX_DEFAULT="quiet amd_iommu=on"`

4. Save the changes and exit the editor.
5. Run the following command to update grub:

   ```
   # update-grub
   ```

6. Only if using an AMD CPU, add the following line in the configuration file `/etc/modprobe.d/kvm_iommu_map_guest.conf`:

   ```
   options kvm allow_unsafe_assigned_interrupt=1
   ```

7. Ensure the following modules are loaded in `/etc/modules`:

   - `vfio_iommu_type1`
   - `vfio_virqfd`
   - `vfio_pci`
   - `vfio`

8. Reboot the Proxmox node.
9. Locate the PCI device address in the form of `xx:xx.x` using the following command:

   ```
   # lspci
   ```

10. Enter the following line with the PCI device ID in the VM configuration file:

    ```
    machine: q35
    hostpsi0: 01:00.0,pcie=1
    ```

11. Power-cycle the VM.
12. Install necessary drivers for the PCI device in the VM operating system.

# Configuring GPU passthrough

In this section, we are going to see how to configure a video adapter to be used directly in a VM. The GPU to be added to the VM must not be bound to the host node. To ensure that the device is not being used by the host, take the following steps:

1. We have to find out the vendor and device ID of the GPU device to use passthrough. To pinpoint the device, we can run the #lspci command. The device should be the one showing up as a VGA compatible controller. The following screenshot shows our VGA device with ID 00:02.0:

```
00:01.1 IDE interface: Intel Corporation 82371SB PIIX3 IDE [Natoma/Triton II]
00:01.2 USB controller: Intel Corporation 82371SB PIIX3 USB [Natoma/Triton II]
00:01.3 Bridge: Intel Corporation 82371AB/EB/MB PIIX4 ACPI (rev 03)
00:02.0 VGA compatible controller: Cirrus Logic GD 5446
00:03.0 Unclassified device [00ff]: Red Hat, Inc Virtio memory balloon
00:0a.0 SCSI storage controller: Red Hat, Inc Virtio block device
```

2. To find out the device and vendor ID, run the command again using the following format:

    **#lspci -n -s 00:02**

3. The command will produce a set of numbers. The device and vendor IDs are the last two sets of numbers. The following is the set of numbers for our example node:

    **# df00:02.0 0300:   1013:00b8**

4. Take note of the device ID then create a file /etc/modprobe.d/vfio.conf to explicitly define it as the GPU passthrough vfio device and to prevent VGA arbitration to opt-out devices. Enter the following line in the vfio.conf file:

    ```
    options vfio-pci ids=1013:00b8  disable_vga
    ```

5. We now have to blacklist the default VGA drivers so they are not loaded during boot, as follows:

    ```
    # echo "blacklist nvidia" >> /etc/modprobe.d/blacklist.conf
    # echo "blacklist radeon" >> /etc/modprobe.d/blacklist.conf
    # echo "blacklist nouveau" >> /etc/modprobe.d/blacklist.conf
    ```

When trying to add GPU passthrough for a VM, it is important to keep in mind that not all GPU devices are capable of being passthrough devices. Try different configurations.

At this stage, we are now ready to configure the VM itself to use GPU passthrough. The recommended way to configure is to use **Open Virtual Machine Firmware (OVMF)** PCI passthrough. OVMF is a project to enable VMs to use **Unified Extensible Firmware Interface (UEFI)** BIOS. To enable features of OVMF, the guest operating system must support UEFI. The following steps will help find out if the GPU device is UEFI compatible:

1. Log in to the node with the GPU device through SSH.

2. Run the following commands to download and compile a tool to download the GPU device's ROM content:

   ```
   # git clone https://github.com/awilliam/rom-parser
   # cd rom-parser
   # make
   ```

3. Run the following sets of command to download the ROM content of the GPU device in a temporary directory:

   ```
   # cd /sys/bus/pci/devices/0000:01:00.0/
   # echo 1 > rom
   # cat rom > /home/rom-parser/image.rom
   # echo 0 > rom
   ```

4. Run the following command to test the downloaded ROM with the ROM parser we have downloaded and compiled to figure out if the GPU device is UEFI compatible:

   ```
   # cd /home/rom-parser
   # ./rom-parser /tmp/image.rom
   ```

5. The command will display information similar to the following:

   ```
   Valid ROM signature found @0h, PCIR offset 60h
   PCIR: type 3, vendor 102b, device: 0532, class: 030000
   PCIR: revision 0, vendor revision: 2139
   EFI: Signature Valid
   Last image
   ```

If the PCIR is `type 3` then the GPU device is UEFI/OVMF compatible.

The VM configuration should look like the following after selecting OVMF BIOS and adding the `hostpci` line. Make the necessary changes and then power-cycle to activate the new configuration:

```
bios: ovmf
scsihw: virtio-scsi-pci
machine: q35
hostpci0: 02:00,pcie=1,x-vga=on
...................
...................
```

When using NVIDIA GPU devices, software such as GeForce Experience may cause the virtual machine to crash. In such cases, add the following line to `/etc/modprobe.d/kvm.conf`. The issue may occur when using software such as PassMark PerformanceTest and SiSoftware Sandra:

```
options kvm ignore_msrs=1
```

# Preparing for hotplug

In this section, we are going to see how to configure the hotplugging option in Proxmox virtual machines. Using the hotplugging feature, we can add and remove devices or resources on a VM without restarting or power-cycling it. As of Proxmox 5.0, we can use the hotplug option for the following resources:

- Disk
- Network interface
- CPU
- Memory
- USB

As of Proxmox 5.0, we can only increase CPU and memory but cannot decrease it. Both the disk and network interface can be equally hotplugged and unplugged. The following table shows which device types are supported on different operating systems:

| Device | Kernel | Hotplug/unplug | OS |
|--------|--------|----------------|-----|
| Disk | All | Both | All versions of Linux/Windows |
| NIC | All | Both | All versions of Linux/Windows |

| CPU | Greater than 3.10 | Hotplug only for Windows and both for Linux | All versions of Linux, Windows Server 2008 and greater |
| --- | --- | --- | --- |
| Memory | Greater than 3.10 | Hotplug only for Windows and both for Linux | All versions of Linux, Windows Server 2008 and greater |

While the main configuration to enable hotplugging for Proxmox should be done through CLI, we can enable or disable a hotplug device through the `Datacenter` I **Node** I **VM** I **Options** tab menu, as shown in the following screenshot:

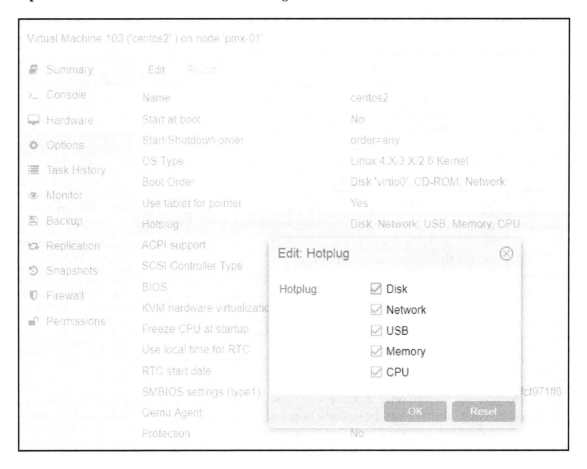

We need to prepare a Linux-based VM first before hotplug can be used. Two modules must be loaded inside the Linux guest OS to enable hotplug. We can load the modules using the following command:

```
# modprobe acpiphp
# modprobe pci_hotplug
```

To automatically load the modules during boot, we can add them into /etc/modules.

If the Linux guest OS is based on Kernel less than 4.7, then we need to create a new udev rule file in the /lib/udev/rules.d/80-hotplug-cpu-mem.rules file and add the following lines:

```
SUBSYSTEM=="cpu",ACTION=="add",TEST=="online",ATTR{online}=="0",
ATTR=={online}="1"
SUBSYSTEM=="memory",ACTION=="add",TEST=="state",
ATTR{state}=="offline",ATTR=={state}="online"
```

For Linux guest OS based on kernel 4.7 or newer, we do not need to add the udev rules for memory hotplug, but it is still required for CPU. We need to add the following kernel parameter during boot:

```
memhp_default_state=online
```

The following steps are to add the kernel parameter during boot to enable memory hotplug:

1. Run the following command from a Linux guest OS SSH:

   ```
   #gksudo gedit /etc/default/grub
   ```

2. Locate the line starting with GRUB_CMDLINE_LINUX_DEFAULT and type in the kernel parameter at the end of the line. The line now should appear as follows:

   ```
   GRUB_CMDLINE_LINUX_DEFAULT="quiet splash memhp_default_state=online"
   ```

3. Save the file and exit the editor.
4. Run the following command to update the grub boot loader:

   ```
   # sudo update-grub
   ```

5. The Proxmox node needs to be power-cycled to activate the modules, rules, and kernel parameter.
6. After reboot, run the following command to verify which kernel parameters successfully loaded during boot:

   ```
   # cat /proc/cmdline
   ```

# Configuring VMs with hotplug

For CPU and memory hotplug, we also have to make sure that the NUMA option is enabled for the VM. The NUMA option can be found under the `Datacenter` I **Node** I **VM** I **Hardware** I **Processors** menu. Click on **Edit** to open the CPU dialog box:

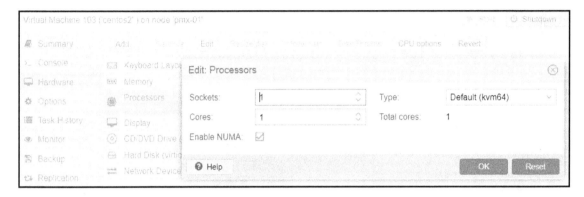

There is no additional configuration necessary to hotplug a virtual disk image or virtual network interface.

## Hotplugging vCPUs

To add a virtual CPU or vCPU, go to the `Datacenter` I **Node** I **VM** I **Hardware** menu. Then, select **Processors** and click on **Edit** to open the dialog box. Simply type in the number of cores or use the up and down option in the text to choose the desired number of cores or vCPUs. Click on **OK** to accept the changes. We can also add a new CPU from this dialog box. We can also add vCPUs by running the following command from the Proxmox node CLI:

```
# qm set <vm_id> -vcpus 2
```

Since our example VM already has one CPU, the previous command will add an additional CPU, making it a total of two CPUs for the VM.

## Hotplugging memory

To open the dialog box to edit allocated memory for a VM, go to the `Datacenter` I **Node** I **VM** I **Hardware** menu. Select **Memory** and then click on **Edit** to open the memory dialog box:

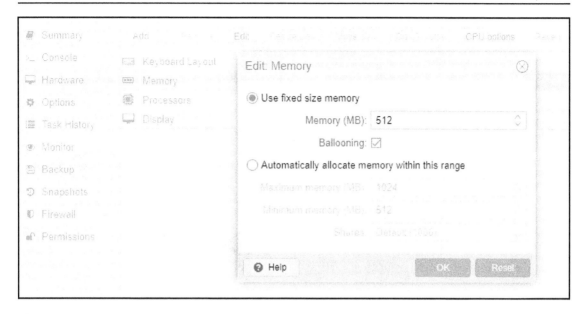

Change the amount of memory to be allocated and then click on **OK** to accept the changes. Ensure that the NUMA option is enabled in the **Processors** dialog box as mentioned in the previous section.

# Hotplugging disks/vNICs

To hotplug a new disk or network interface, go to the `Datacenter` I **Node** I **VM** I **Hardware** menu and then select an item from the **Add** drop-down menu. The dialog boxes to add these resources are similar to the dialog box for the VM creation process we have seen in an earlier section in this chapter. The **Add** drop-down menu is as shown in the following screenshot:

Although CPU and memory hotplug works for both Linux and Windows, ensure you run several tests before implementing them in a production environment. The CPU/memory hotplug can create an unstable situation for the VM, causing it to freeze and require a complete reboot.

# Migrating KVM virtual machines

Proxmox migration allows KVM virtual machines to be moved to a Proxmox node in both offline and online or live modes. The most common scenario of VM migration is when a Proxmox node needs a reboot due to a major kernel update or other patches. Other scenarios may include hardware failures, node replacement, software issues and so on. Without the live migration option, each reboot would be very difficult for an administrator as all the running VMs would have to be stopped first before reboot occurs. This will cause major downtime in a mission-critical virtual environment.

With the live migration option, a running VM can be moved to another node without downtime. During a live migration, the VM does not experience any major slowdown. After the node reboots, simply migrate VMs back to the original node. Any offline VMs can also be moved with ease.

Proxmox takes a very minimalistic approach to the migration process. To access the migration dialog box, right-click on the VM to be migrated to open the context menu and then select **Migration** or click on the **Migrate** button in the upper-right corner to open the dialog box. The following screenshot shows the migrate dialog box:

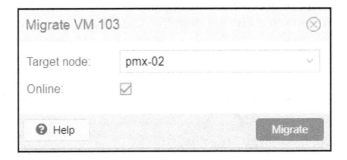

From the dialog, simply select the destination node and then, depending on online or offline migration, click on the checkbox. Then hit the **Migrate** button to get the migration process started. Depending on the size of virtual drive and allocated memory of the VM, the entire migration process time can vary. Live/online migration also migrates the virtual memory content of the VM. The bigger the memory, the longer it will take to migrate. In the previous example, we were live migrating VM ID #103 to node pmx-02.

# Summary

In this chapter, we looked at KVM virtual machines and how to create, clone, and migrate when need be. We also looked at some advanced configuration, such as adding a sound device and enabling PCI/GPU passthrough for a KVM VM. By leveraging this cloning technique, we can scale a virtual cluster effortlessly when deploying identical virtual machines. Optional and non-production setup of a nested virtual environment was also explained.

A KVM virtual machine is best practice for all non-Linux operating systems and also when total resource isolation between VMs is mandatory.

In the next chapter, we are going to look at LXC containers in greater detail. We will learn why a Proxmox administrator would choose them over KVM virtual machines.

# 7
# LXC Virtual Machines

From Proxmox VE 4.0, the OpenVZ container technology was replaced in favor of LXC container. In this chapter, we will see the features and benefits of using an LXC container and learn how to create and manage containers in Proxmox. We will cover some of the following topics:

- Exploring LXC containers
- Understanding container templates
- Creating an LXC container
- Managing an LXC container
- Migrating an LXC container
- Accessing an LXC container
- Unprivileged versus privileged containers
- Converting an OpenVZ container to an LXC container

## Exploring LXC virtual machines

Containers are a different form of the virtual machine that is completely dependent on the operating system of the host node. They are kernel-based virtualizations that share the host operating system, thereby reducing the overhead that a KVM virtual machine has. Due to the lower overhead, the virtual machine density per node can be tighter and more containers can be hosted than KVM virtual machines. This comes at a price of less virtual machine isolation. Since containers are dependent on the underlying operating system, there can only be Linux-based containers. No Windows operating system can be containerized. Unlike KVM virtual machines, we cannot clone a container or turn a container into a template. Each container is a virtual instance that runs separately.

LXC is just another type of container technology. OpenVZ is another container technology, which had been used by Proxmox until version 4.0. There are two major differences between the LXC and OpenVZ container technologies:

- LXC is available in the Linux kernel and doesn't need a separate kernel as in the case of OpenVZ
- OpenVZ supports live migration whereas LXC does not

The following are a few advantages of using LXC containers:

- Extremely fast deployment
- Higher density of virtual machine per node
- Smaller backup files
- Nested LXC containers with almost no overhead
- Ability to directly access data inside the container filesystem from the host node

In Proxmox, LXC containers are identified by a unique icon in the GUI dashboard. The following screenshot shows the icon of an LXC container with ID #101:

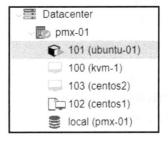

# Understanding container templates

Unlike KVM virtual machines, which can be installed from ISO images, LXC containers can only be deployed using container templates. Container templates are not the same as the templates we created for KVM in the previous chapter. LXC templates of various operating systems and an application-specific container can be directly downloaded from the Proxmox repository. To view a list of available templates already downloaded, we need to select an attached storage that can store container templates and click on the **Content** tab, as shown in the following screenshot:

In the preceding screenshot, we can see that we have a Ubuntu container template that is already downloaded to our local storage. To view a list of available LXC templates and to download them from the Proxmox repository, we need to click on the **Templates** menu to open the dialog box:

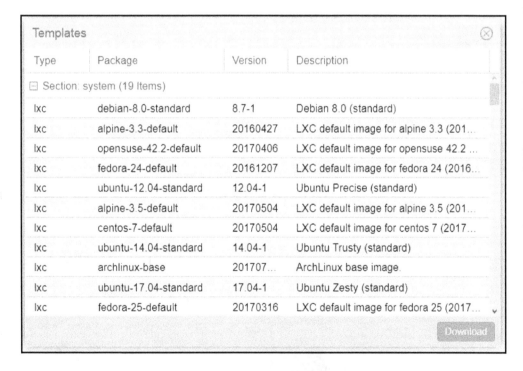

There are over 100 templates available to be downloaded from this dialog box. If you are not able to see the complete list and it only shows the **Section: system** templates, then run the following command from the CLI to update the template list:

```
# pveam update
```

To download a template, simply select it and click on the **Download** button. The downloaded template will now be available in the storage. The default location to store the containers templates for local storage is as follows:

```
/mnt/pve/<storage>/template/cache
```

# Creating an LXC container

After ensuring that we have the desired template for the container, it is now time to create one. We can click on the **Create CT** button in the top-right corner of the Proxmox GUI to open the container-creation dialog box, as shown in the following screenshot:

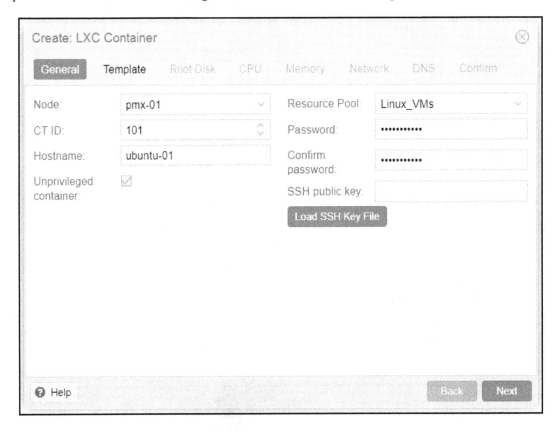

# General tab

The **General** tab of the dialog box is used to assign identification information such and create a root password for the container.

# Node

This is a drop-down list used to select which Proxmox node the container is going to be created in. In our example, we will create the container in node pmx-01.

# CT ID

This is a textbox used to enter the numeric ID of the container. We can also use the up and down arrows in the box to assign the IDs. If we assign an ID that already exists in the cluster, the box will show a red border around the textbox. For our example container, we are using ID #101.

# Hostname

This is a textbox used to enter the hostname of the container. The **Hostname** does not need to be FQDN.

# Unprivileged container

Unprivileged containers are when the container is created and run as a user as opposed to root. This is the safest way to use a container because if the container security gets compromised and the intruder breaks out of the container, they will find themselves as a *nobody* user with extremely limited privileges. Unprivileged containers do not need to be owned by the user since they are run in user namespaces. This is a kernel feature that allows the mapping of the UID of a physical host into a namespace inside where a user with UID 0 can exist. Unprivileged containers can also be run as root. By assigning a specific UID and GID to root, we can create unprivileged containers throughout the system and run them as root.

Privileged containers are when they are created and run by the root user only. These containers are not secure because all the processes are still run as root. All containers created through the Proxmox GUI or PCT tools are privileged containers.

Enable this option to create unprivileged containers.

If total security or virtual machine full isolation is the primary concern for an environment, it is best to use a KVM virtual machine, because KVM is a fully independent virtual machine without any dependency on the host operating system or sharing resources.

## Resource Pool

This is a drop-down list menu used to select a previously created pool. It is only necessary if we want to assign the container to a specific pool.

## The Template tab

This tab is to select a template the container is going to be based on. Select **Storage** from the drop-down menu where the template is stored, and then from the **Template** drop-down list, select the template, as shown in the following screenshot:

# The Root Disk tab

This tab is used to define the disk storage space the container can use. The following screenshot shows the dialog box with the configuration for our example container with the local storage selected:

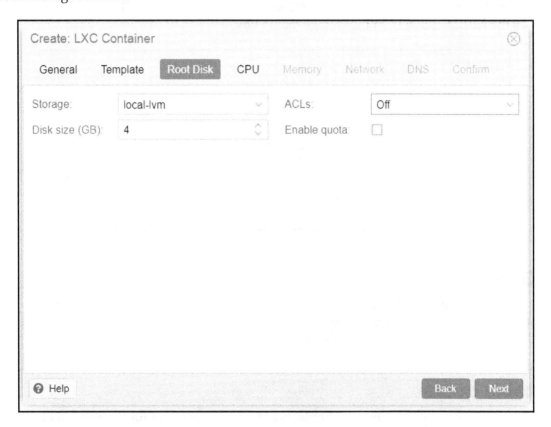

# Storage

LXC containers can be stored in all storage types without any modification with only one exception for the Ceph RBD storage. **KRBD** must be enabled for the RBD storage in order to store an LXC container. The inclusion of this option now allows leveraging the Ceph distributed storage to be used with the LXC container platform. The following screenshot shows the **KRBD** option from the storage dialog box:

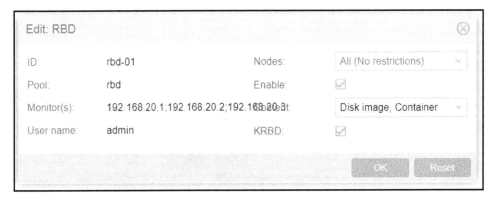

# ACLs

**Access control lists** or **ACLs** allow us to set more fine-tuned file ownership than the traditional Linux user or group access models. By default, Proxmox creates LXC containers with ACLs. To create a container without ACLs, select Off from the drop-down.

# Enable quota

Enabling this option allows us to set limits inside an LXC container for the amount of disk space each container user can use. However, this option currently only works on container storage images based on the ext4 filesystem. It also does not work on unprivileged containers.

# The CPU tab

This tab allows configuration of a virtual **CPU** for a container. The following screenshot shows the dialog box with the available CPU options:

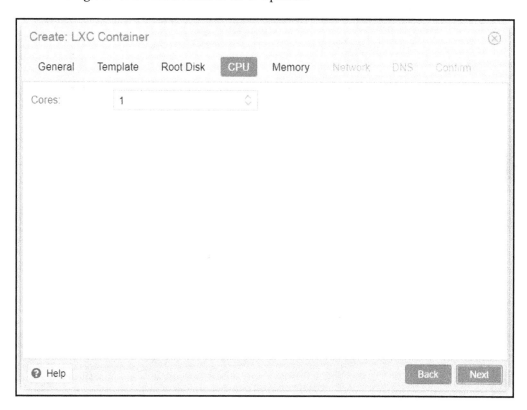

# Cores

Unlike KVM virtual machines, we can only allocate CPU cores and not CPU sockets. We can type in a value or select from the up and down arrows how many cores the container can use. For our example container, we have allocated 1 CPU core.

# The Memory tab

This tab is used to define the allocated memory and swap the size for the container. It is common practice to allocate an equal amount of swap size as the memory. Keep in mind that for LXC containers, this swap allocation actually gets allocated to the host node swap since the container does not have its own kernel running. This size can be adjusted for a container at a later time without restarting the container. The following screenshot shows the **Memory** tab dialog box with 512 MB of **Memory** and 512 MB of **Swap** space allocated:

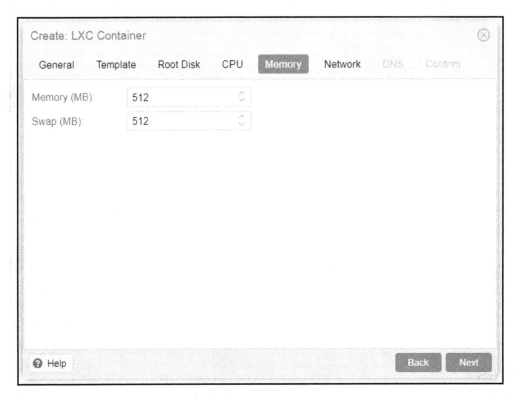

# The Network tab

This tab allows the network configuration of the container. The same dialog box is used to edit or add a new network interface for the container. The following screenshot shows the dialog box for our example container:

## Name

This is a textbox to define a name for the network interface.

## MAC address

By default, all MAC addresses for virtual network interfaces are automatically assigned. By typing a **MAC address** in this textbox, we can specify a particular MAC address for the interface. This may be necessary when a specific MAC address is required by an application in the container.

# Bridge

This is a drop-down list used to select a virtual bridge that the interface will be connected to.

# The VLAN Tag

This is used to set a VLAN ID on the virtual interface.

# Rate limit

With this option, we can set a limit on how much bandwidth the container can use. The unit is megabytes per second. By default, there is no limit.

# Firewall

To enable the Proxmox firewall for the network interface, this option needs to be checked. Without this option, no firewall rules will be applied to the interface. We will take a look at the Proxmox firewall in detail in `Chapter 9`, *The Proxmox VE Firewall*.

# IPv4/IPv6

We can set both IPv4 and IPv6 on the virtual network interface. We can also manually set IP addresses or enable DHCP for automatic IP assignment. The IP must be entered along with CIDR. Proxmox also supports dynamic IPv6 assignment using stateless configuration, such as SLAAC. To learn about **Stateless Auto Configuration** or **SLAAC**, refer to `https:// tools.ietf.org/html/rfc4862`.

# The DNS tab

This tab is used to configure the DNS information for the LXC container. Enter the domain name to be used by the container and IP address(es) of the DNS server(s). The following screenshot shows the DNS domain and DNS server information for our example container:

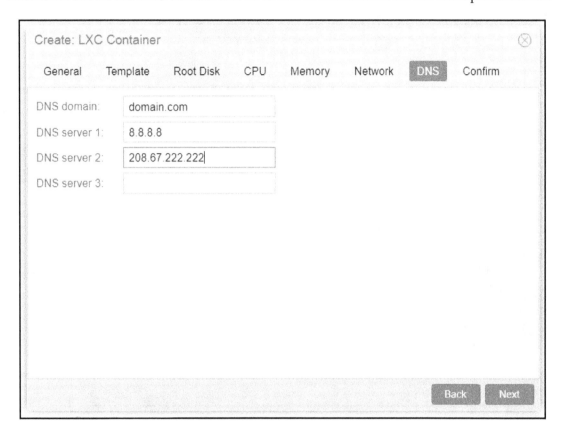

# The Confirm tab

This tab is to ensure the accuracy of the new container configuration. If any changes need to be made, we can simply click on a tab to go back without losing values already entered or selected. Click on **Finish** to create a container. The following screenshot shows our new example container powered on and running:

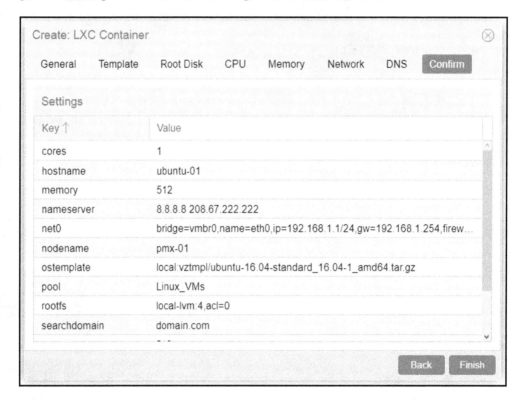

# Managing an LXC container

In Proxmox, each LXC container has two configuration files. One defines the raw resource allocation while the other, used by Proxmox, is used to define a container. The Proxmox container configuration file can be found at the following location:

```
/etc/pve/local/lxc/<container_id>.conf
```

For our example container ID #101, the following are the contents of this configuration file:

```
arch: amd64
cores: 1
hostname: ubuntu-01
memory: 512
nameserver: 8.8.8.8 208.67.222.222
net0: name=eth0,bridge=vmbr0,firewall=1,gw=192.168.1.254,hwaddr=C6:5B:9C:CB:4C:D4,ip=192.168$
ostype: ubuntu
rootfs: local-lvm:vm-101-disk-1,acl=0,size=4G
searchdomain: domain.com
swap: 512
unprivileged: 1
```

The raw container configuration file can be found at the following location:

```
/var/lib/lxc/<container_id>/config
```

The following is the content of the resource allocation configuration file for our example container:

```
  GNU nano 2.7.4                      File: /var/lib/lxc/101/config

lxc.arch = amd64
lxc.include = /usr/share/lxc/config/ubuntu.common.conf
lxc.include = /usr/share/lxc/config/ubuntu.userns.conf
lxc.monitor.unshare = 1
lxc.id_map = u 0 100000 65536
lxc.id_map = g 0 100000 65536
lxc.tty = 2
lxc.environment = TERM=linux
lxc.utsname = ubuntu-01
lxc.cgroup.memory.limit_in_bytes = 536870912
lxc.cgroup.memory.memsw.limit_in_bytes = 1073741824
lxc.cgroup.cpu.shares = 1024
lxc.rootfs = /var/lib/lxc/101/rootfs
lxc.network.type = veth
lxc.network.veth.pair = veth101i0
lxc.network.hwaddr = C6:5B:9C:CB:4C:D4
lxc.network.name = eth0
lxc.cgroup.cpuset.cpus = 1
```

There is another directory for the root filesystem that is a mount point for the allocated storage space inside the container. The location of the directory is `/var/lib/lxc/<container_id>/rootfs/`.

But in Proxmox, this directory is not used to store container data. For local storage, the container virtual disk image is created in `/var/lib/vz/images/<container_id>/`.

For shared storage, the container virtual disk image is created in `/mnt/pve/<storage>/images/container_id/`.

We can adjust allocated resources for a container in real time without power-cycling the container. This feature is known as hotplug for KVM virtual machines. However, for LXC containers, this feature is built into the container technology without needing any additional modification. There are three ways in which we can adjust allocated resources for a container:

- The Proxmox GUI
- The command line
- Editing a configuration file

# Adjusting resources using the GUI

Using the Proxmox GUI to change resource allocation is the preferred way to adjust the container resource. Any changes made get committed to the container instantly without needing to power-cycle it. For day-to-day operations, the GUI provides almost all the resource options to be changed with a few clicks.

To change a particular resource, we need to select a container from the left-hand navigation bar, and then we need to select the resource to be changed. For example, if you want to increase the allocated CPU cores to 2 from 1, you need to select the **Cores** line item and then click on **Edit** to open the **CPU Core** dialog box. The following screenshot shows the **Resources** currently allocated to the example container #101:

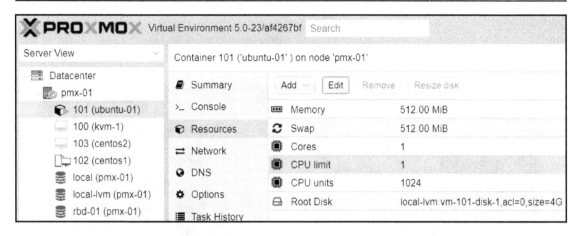

To increase allocated storage space, we need to select the **Root Disk** line item under **Resources** and then click on the **Resize disk** button to open the dialog box:

As of Proxmox 5.0, we can only increase the size of the allocated storage but cannot decrease it. We can type in a value in GB or use the up and down arrows to adjust size. It is important to note here that the value we will select here is not the total size of the allocated space. This value adds on top of the already allocated space. For example, in our example container #101, the allocated space is currently at 4 GB. So if we want to increase that to a total size of 6 GB, we will type in 2 in the dialog box, which will increase the size by 2 GB. Click on the Resize disk button in the dialog box to finalize the value.

We can verify that the disk space has indeed increased by running the `#df -H` command from inside the container. The following screenshot shows the command output, which shows that the size of the root mount point has increased to 6.3 GB:

```
root@ubuntu-01:~# df -H
Filesystem                       Size  Used Avail Use% Mounted on
/dev/mapper/pve-vm--101--disk--1  6.3G  665M  5.3G  12% /
none                             504k     0  504k   0% /dev
udev                             2.1G     0  2.1G   0% /dev/tty
tmpfs                            2.1G     0  2.1G   0% /dev/shm
tmpfs                            2.1G  8.6M  2.0G   1% /run
tmpfs                            5.3M     0  5.3M   0% /run/lock
tmpfs                            2.1G     0  2.1G   0% /sys/fs/cgroup
tmpfs                            402M     0  402M   0% /run/user/0
root@ubuntu-01:~#
```

# Adjusting resources using the CLI

LXC comes with a vast number of command-line commands to manage containers. It is not possible to cover all the commands in this book. The good news for Proxmox users is that there are some tools or commands provided by Proxmox to make managing containers an easier task through the CLI. The `pct` command is a script created by Proxmox developers that wraps `lxc` commands. To see the available Proxmox commands for containers, we can run the following command:

```
# pct help
```

We can also get details of all the `pct` commands from the Proxmox wiki at https://pve.proxmox.com/wiki/Manual:_pct.conf.

Resource changes made using these commands get committed to the container immediately without the need to restart the container. If the Proxmox GUI becomes inaccessible, we can manage a container entirely using the CLI. The `format` command used to change container resources is as follows:

```
# pct set <ct_id> [options]
```

For example, if we want to change the IP address of the container #101, the command will be as follows:

```
# pct set 101 -net0 name=eth0,bridge=vmbr0,ip=192.168.1.17/24
```

We can verify that the new network configuration has been applied to the container by checking the network configuration file of the container in /etc/network/interfaces as follows:

```
auto lo
iface lo inet loopback

auto eth0
iface eth0 inet static
        address 192.168.1.17
        netmask 255.255.255.0
```

It is very important to note here that the gateway address is now missing from the network configuration. The reason for this is that when we entered the previous command to change the IP address, we did not mention the gateway. The pct set command will replace the previous configuration for a resource is changed. If we want to include the gateway address, the entire command will be as follows:

```
# pct set 101 -net0
name=eth0,bridge=vmbr0,ip=192.168.1.17/24,gw=192.168.1.254
```

To adjust the allocated memory of the container in real time, we can use the following command:

```
# pct set <ct_id> -memory <int_value>
```

To change the CPU limit of the container, we can use the following command. The value 0 disables any CPU limit:

```
# pct set <ct_id> -cpulimit <0 - 128>
```

The following command changes the hostname of the container:

```
# pct set <ct_id> -hostname <string>
```

To increase the size of the root filesystem of the container, we can use the following command:

```
# pct set <ct_id> -rootfs size=<int_value for GB>
```

At times, due to an incomplete backup, a container may become locked and will be unable to start or stop. The following command will unlock the container from the CLI:

```
# pct set <ct_id> -unlock
```

The following command will show a list of LXC containers in the node:

```
# pct list
```

The following commands will start or stop an LXC container from the CLI:

```
# pct start <ct_id>
# pct stop <ct_id>
```

LXC commands are a very useful tool should the Proxmox GUI become inaccessible for any reason and any container needs to be managed right away.

# Adjusting resources using direct modification

Although modifying a configuration file to change resources of a container is possible, it is not recommended for day-to-day operations. Any manual modification made to the files does not get passed right away until the container is restarted, thus causing downtime. However, there are some situations when manually editing the configuration file is necessary. The number of configuration options can then be changed through the GUI, and the pct tools are geared toward standard containers. LXC containers have a large number of configuration options, which cannot be changed through the GUI or pct tools. Only by editing the configuration files and restarting the containers can these options be applied. To learn more about the advanced configuration options, refer to the following link:

```
http://manpages.ubuntu.com/manpages/precise/man5/lxc.conf.5.html
```

# Migrating an LXC container

As of Proxmox VE 5.0, live migration of LXC containers is not possible. The container must be turned off before it can be moved. This is not a limitation of Proxmox but rather the LXC technology itself. To migrate a container, right-click on **Container** to open the **Context** menu, and then select **Migrate** or click on the **Migrate** button in the top-right corner of the GUI to open the **Migration** dialog box:

Select a destination node from the **Target node** drop-down list. Check the **Restart Mode** box to auto-restart the container after the migration is complete. Click on the **Migrate** button to initiate the migration. The migration process will auto-stop the container, migrate it to the destination node, and then auto-start it at the end of the process.

Live migration is under heavy development by LXC, so we should expect it in the mainstream LXC package in the near future. To some of us, the lack of this feature may be a huge deal breaker, especially in a container-dominant environment with many container instances.

# Accessing an LXC container

There are several ways in which we can access an LXC container:

- The noVNC console
- SSH
- Direct shell through the CLI

# The noVNC console

We can access and view the container directly from the GUI using the noVNC console. It is almost visual remote access to the instance. The console is identical to a KVM virtual machine. If we try to access the container using the console after a long period of inactivity, it may appear as just a cursor and no login option:

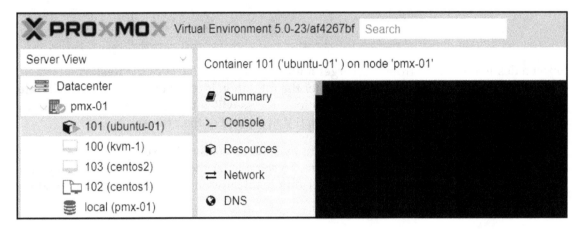

By simply pressing the *Enter* key, we can make the login prompt appear, as shown in the following screenshot:

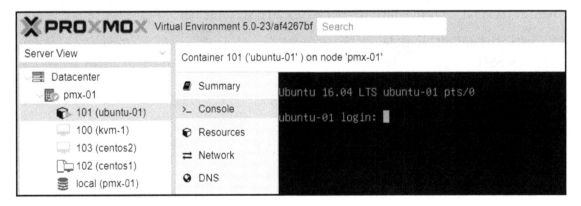

# Direct shell through the CLI

One of the best features of an LXC container is the ability to directly access the container shell through the CLI of the host node. The Proxmox command to access the LXC container shell is as follows:

```
# pct enter <ct_id>
```

This gives us the direct shell prompt of the container, as shown in the following screenshot:

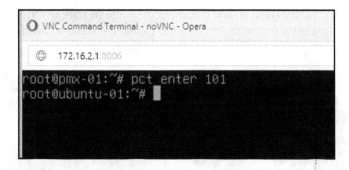

In the previous example, we are accessing the LXC container ubuntu-01 from the Proxmox node pmx-01. Note that no password was asked to be entered into the container from the Proxmox node. Since a container is running as root, we can perform any tasks inside the container. Once done, we can simply type exit to go back to the Proxmox node from the container.

We can also run various commands inside an LXC container without actually entering the container. The following Proxmox command format is used to execute commands inside a container:

```
# pct exec <ct_id> -- <command>
```

By following the previous format, if we want to create a directory inside the container and verify that it has been created, our command will be as follows:

```
root@pmx-01:~# pct exec 101 mkdir /home/test
root@pmx-01:~# pct exec 101 ls /home
test
root@pmx-01:~#
```

If we try to execute a command with additional arguments using the following, we will see a parsing error:

```
root@pmx-01:~# pct exec 101 df -H
Unknown option: h
400 unable to parse option
pct exec <vmid> [<extra-args>]
root@pmx-01:~#
```

In the previous example, we tried to see the storage usage in megabytes inside a container using an additional option argument, -H. In such cases, we have to modify the pct command by adding -- after the container ID, as shown in the following screenshot:

```
root@pmx-01:~# pct exec 101 -- df -H
Filesystem                      Size  Used Avail Use% Mounted on
/dev/mapper/pve-vm--101--disk--1  6.3G  665M  5.3G  12% /
none                            504k     0  504k   0% /dev
udev                            2.1G     0  2.1G   0% /dev/tty
tmpfs                           2.1G     0  2.1G   0% /dev/shm
tmpfs                           2.1G  8.6M  2.0G   1% /run
tmpfs                           5.3M     0  5.3M   0% /run/lock
tmpfs                           2.1G     0  2.1G   0% /sys/fs/cgroup
root@pmx-01:~#
```

In the preceding screenshot, we can see that the command to check the storage space has been executed successfully inside the container.

# Converting OpenVZ to LXC

This section is for container users who are still using Proxmox 3.x or earlier with OpenVZ container technology. Since OpenVZ has been completely replaced in Proxmox VE 4.0 and later versions, all OpenVZ containers must be converted to LXCs in order to make them usable. The full conversion can be performed through the Proxmox GUI. The simple process of this conversion can be summarized as follows:

1. Write down the OpenVZ container network information.
2. Power off the OpenVZ container, and then perform a full backup.
3. Restore the OpenVZ container on Proxmox 4.0 or later.
4. Reconfigure the network based on information collected in *step 1*.

Do not upgrade to Proxmox VE 4.0 or later before making a full backup of the existing OpenVZ containers. Otherwise, these containers will not start.

The reason it is important to write down the network configuration in *step 1* is that when OpenVZ containers are restored in Proxmox 4.0 or later, the network interfaces are stripped off and need to be reattached and reconfigured.

We can also perform the conversion using the CLI without the Proxmox GUI. After collecting the network information of the OpenVZ containers, we can power off the containers and commit a full backup using the following command:

```
# vzctl stop <ct_id> && vzdump <ct_id> -storage <storage_id>
```

Restore the container in Proxmox 4 or later using the following command:

```
# pct restore <ct_id> <storage>/dump/<backup_file>.tar
```

# Summary

In this chapter, we learned about LXC containers, how to create and manage them, and the difference between unprivileged and privileged containers. We also learned how to convert OpenVZ containers to LXC containers and use them in Proxmox VE 4.0 or later versions. Despite not having the live migration ability, an LXC container is still a better choice of containerization than OpenVZ and works very well in a Proxmox environment.

In the next chapter, we will see some advanced features of network components in a Proxmox cluster. We will learn the benefits of a virtual network, what Open vSwitch is, and why we should use it in a virtual environment.

# 8
# Network of Virtual Networks

In this chapter, we are going to take an in-depth look at how we can create a virtualized network within a virtual environment. We will learn what the network building blocks are that make up the Proxmox hypervisor and how it manages both internal and external network connectivity. We will examine several network diagrams to see how Proxmox can be utilized to create an entire colony of virtual machines connected with virtual networks. We will also take a look at the Open vSwitch implementation in Proxmox along with the network configuration file, network bonding, VLAN, and so on. We can create dozens of virtual machines at will, but without a planned network model, we will fail to run an efficient virtual environment. If we compare virtual machines with bricks as building blocks, then it is the virtual network that acts as mortar to create anything from a hut to a cathedral.

In this chapter, we will cover the following topics:

- Defining virtual networks
- Networking components of Proxmox, such as bridge, vNIC, VLAN, and bonding
- The Proxmox network configuration file
- Open vSwitch implementation
- Adding network components to a VM
- Sample virtual networks
- Multi-tenant virtual environments

# Exploring virtual networks

A virtual network is a software-defined network where all links and components may or may not have direct interaction with physical hardware. In most cases, direct interaction with physical hardware is made by the hypervisor or host controller. All links between virtual machines, virtual switches, virtual bridges, and virtual network interfaces are made completely virtually. The following are the two types of network virtualization:

- **External network virtualization**: This consists of several local networks operating as one virtual network. Physical LANs can be in the same location or spread over multiple locations. Usually, external virtualization is a cloud network service-based model that multiple companies can use to connect their multi-site virtual environment for a service fee. External network virtualization can be easily achieved by combining several internal virtual networks into a single virtualized network using a WAN, or the internet using technology such as VPN.

- **Internal network virtualization**: This usually happens locally within a hypervisor between virtual machines. Do not confuse this with the local area network. Here, internal network virtualization refers to the network connectivity between VMs, bridges, vNICs, and so on, which do not necessarily have to utilize the external LAN. This provides company IT staff with total control over virtual network operations. Network issues can be diagnosed faster; customization of expansion or contraction can happen without delay. Internal virtualization heavily uses virtual components, such as virtual bridges and vNIC, to form a virtual network.

> For in-depth information on external and internal network virtualizations, refer to `http://en.wikipedia.org/wiki/Network_virtualization`. In particular, follow the *References* and *Further reading* book list at the bottom of the wiki page.

In this chapter, we will take a look at the internal network virtualization in the Proxmox hypervisor and how to manage and configure it. We will also take a look at some network diagrams of internal and external virtual network combinations later in the book in Chapter 12, *Proxmox Production-Level Setup*.

# Physical networks versus virtual networks

We will now see the difference between a physical network and a virtual network. The following diagram represents a physical network without any virtualization platform:

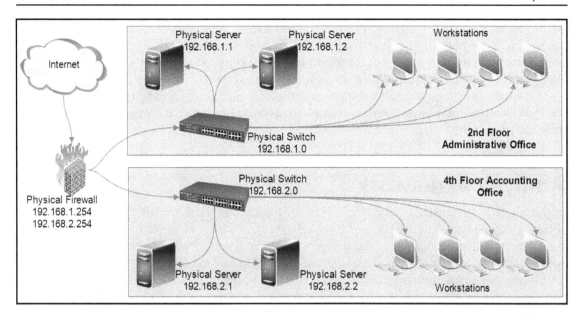

The following diagram represents virtualization as the main infrastructure:

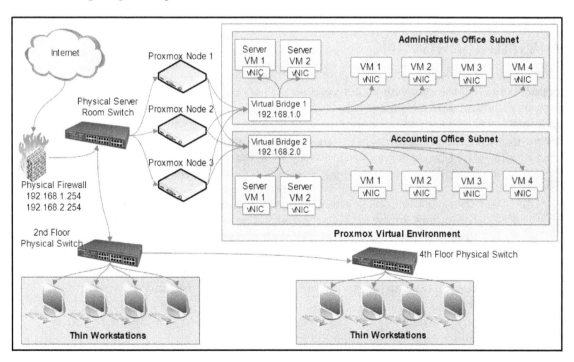

Before we dive into virtual network building blocks, we need to understand how networks are set up in the preceding diagrams. Both the diagrams represent the same office setup where the main administrative department is on the second floor, and the accounting department is on the fourth floor of the building. It is apparent from the diagrams that a physical network is less complex than a virtual network, but by leveraging virtualization, we can cut costs, increase efficiency, reduce hardware maintenance complexity, and increase portability.

# A physical network

In the physical network diagram, there is no virtualization platform set up. The network is set up with physical devices, such as firewalls, switches, servers, and full desktops. Each department has its own servers and network segments. A centralized management for the whole company does not exist. This is a costly solution due to all the physical hardware. If redundancy is a requirement, it will incur twice the cost since we will need identical physical servers. All the connectivity in this network is done with physical cable links. Backups in this setup are quite challenging since all the physical servers in the two departments have to be backed up on a per-device basis.

# A virtual network

The virtual network diagram represents how Proxmox can handle a setup with multiple departments. All the connections between servers and users' virtual machines happen virtually without a physical network device. Using virtual bridges and vNICs, both the administrative and accounting departments can coexist on the same Proxmox cluster. Since all computing happens in the hypervisor, end users can have thin workstations to minimize cost significantly. Users can connect to their virtual machines with remote protocols, such as SPICE, VNC, or RDP.

 Thin workstations or clients are very underpowered, cheap, and basic computers for the end user, providing just the essentials to connect to dedicated server resources. Since all processing happens in a virtual environment, thin workstations do not need to be very powerful. The main purpose of a thin workstation is to allow the user to connect peripherals, such as the monitor, keyboard, mouse, and network cable. A thin workstation can be purchased under $200. There are a lot of environments where Raspberry Pi 3 is being used as a thin workstation due to its price and reliability.

In this setup, all servers and user machines are virtualized. If there is a need for a new server, it is just a matter of creating a virtual server with vNIC with a few clicks. In such a scenario, all virtual machines can simply be migrated to another available Proxmox node, and everything is up and running in minutes. Both the departments in our example are separated by two virtual bridges.

Through the use of the Proxmox GUI, all management can be done from one location, including backup and restore. Virtual servers can be migrated over network links, which can be spread over large or small physical distances. Although a virtual network setup is much more robust and feature-rich, it has a much lower budgetary requirement. New departments can be added by creating new virtual bridges for separate subnets and using virtual LANs or VLANs on existing physical network switches.

# Networking components in Proxmox

We will now take a look at the networking components of Proxmox, which allow virtual machines to communicate with or be segmented from other internal machines as well as the internet.

## Virtual Network Interface Cards

A **Virtual Network Interface Card (vNIC)** is a software-defined representation of a **Media Access Control (MAC)** interface of physical network interfaces. It is basically a virtual network card for a virtual machine. Multiple vNICs can share a physical network interface of a host node. In a way, networking starts with vNIC when a virtual machine sends data to other virtual machines or networking devices within a virtual environment or physical environment. In the following screenshot, the example virtual machine has a virtual network interface named net0 assigned with the virtio driver and configured with the bridge vmbr0:

| | | |
|---|---|---|
| 🖥 Hardware | ▦ Memory | 128.00 MiB/512.00 MiB |
| ⚙ Options | ▣ Processors | 1 (1 sockets, 1 cores) |
| ☰ Task History | 🖥 Display | Default |
| | ◉ CD/DVD Drive (ide2) | none,media=cdrom |
| 👁 Monitor | 🖫 Hard Disk (virtio0) | local-lvm:vm-100-disk-1,size=1G |
| 🗎 Backup | ⇄ Network Device (net0) | virtio=CA:35:61:2A:34:CD,bridge=vmbr0 |

The `virtio` is a Linux kernel driver used to virtualize virtual network interfaces and virtual disk devices. This is the default vNIC for new virtual machines in Proxmox. When `virtio` drivers are used inside a guest virtual machine operating system, the VM is fully aware that it is located inside a virtual environment. Thus the OS does not need to emulate a physical device. Any emulation adds extra overhead, robbing performance. The `virtio` has now become the virtualization standard for network and disk devices in a virtual environment.

Proxmox has four models of virtual network interfaces: Intel e1000, VirtIO, Realtek RTL8139, and VMware `vmxnet3`. Out of these four models, VirtIO provides the maximum network performance for a VM. All Linux-based operating systems come equipped with VirtIO drivers. For Windows, the VirtIO interface driver can be downloaded from `http://www.linux-kvm.org/page/WindowsGuestDrivers/Download_Drivers`.

For Mac OS, the VirtIO interface driver can be downloaded from `https://github.com/pmj/virtio-net-osx`.

# Adding/removing vNIC

To add a new virtual network interface for a VM, we can open the network device dialog using the **Add** button from the **Hardware** tab of the VM:

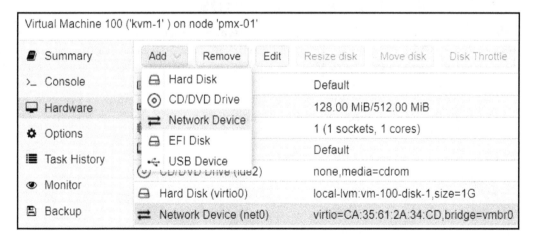

The dialog box for creating vNICs is similar to the network dialog box that we learned about in `Chapter 6`, *KVM Virtual Machines,* in the *Creating a KVM* section. To remove a vNIC, simply select the network device and click on the **Remove** button.

If the **Hotplug** option for the network interface is enabled for the VM, we can add or remove the network interface without powering down the VM. The following screenshot shows the **Hotplug** option for KVM VMs:

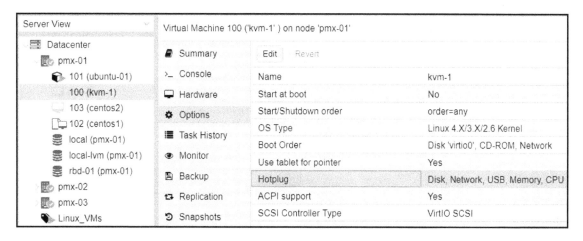

# A virtual bridge

Just as a real-world bridge connects two sides of a river, a virtual bridge connects a Proxmox virtual network to a physical network. A virtual bridge is like a physical network switch where all virtual machines connect to and can be configured using the **Spanning Tree Protocol** (**STP**). A virtual bridge is a great way to create separate subnets. All VMs in the same subnet can connect to their respective bridges. Proxmox creates one virtual bridge by default during the installation process. Each Proxmox node can support up to 4,094 bridges. When the same bridge configuration is entered on all nodes, the bridge can be used from any nodes in the cluster, thus making live migration possible without network connectivity interruption. The default naming format of a bridge is vmbrX, where X represents an integer between 0 to 4,094.

Proxmox will allow a bridge to be created and not be connected to a physical NIC. This allows an isolated environment, that has no access to the physical or any other network on the LAN. Using Open vSwitch, however, we can configure one bridge with multiple VLANs, such as a real physical switch. We will take a look at the Open vSwitch implementation later in this chapter.

We can change a virtual bridge of a VM in real time without needing to power-cycle it. For example, if a VM is configured with a virtual bridge, vmbr0, and we want to change the bridge to vmbr10 later, we can do so without turning off the VM.

# Adding a virtual bridge through the GUI

We can add a new virtual bridge through the Proxmox GUI or CLI. Virtual bridges are created at the node level. So select the node which will have the bridge and then click on **Network** to see the list of existing configured virtual bridges and physical network interfaces installed in that node. The following figure shows the **Network** option for our node pmx-01 in our example cluster:

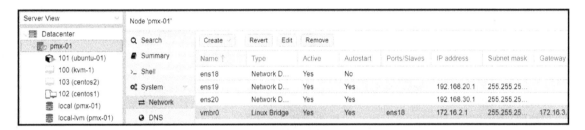

Note that if the GUI is used to create a bridge, then the node will need to be restarted to apply the configuration. This is because a new network interface configuration through the GUI gets written in /etc/network/interfaces.new, and only by rebooting does the new configuration get permanently written in /etc/network/interface. The following screenshot shows the pending change information after creating a new bridge named vmbr1:

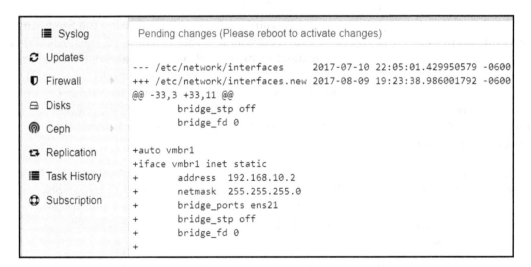

To revert the changes before a reboot is done, we can simply click on the **Revert changes** button.

To create a new bridge through the GUI, we need to click on **Create** under **Network,** and then we need to select the Linux **Bridge** option to open the bridge creation dialog box, as shown in the following screenshot:

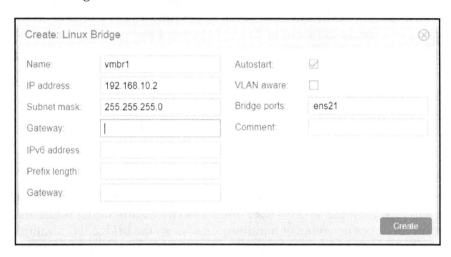

## Name

In the **Name** textbox, type in the name of the new bridge to be created. The naming format must be vmbrX where X can be any integer from 0 to 4,094. For our example bridge, we are naming it vmbr1.

## IP information

We can configure both IPv4 and IPv6 for the bridge. However, the **Gateway** entry must remain *blank* since we already have a default bridge configured with the gateway. There can only be one bridge configured with the gateway per node. If we try to create another bridge with a gateway address, the bridge creation process will abort with an error:

## Bridge ports

The **Bridge ports** textbox is to type in the physical network interface of the host to which this bridge will be connected. There is no drop-down menu to choose a physical network interface from. The name of the interface needs to be typed in. If the virtual network traffic is not going to go out of the node but will remain isolated among the virtual machines within the node, then we can leave the port's textbox blank.

 It is important to note here that we can only configure one virtual bridge per physical network interface. One physical interface can never be shared among multiple bridges.

## VLAN-aware

The VLAN-aware checkbox is a new addition that allows Proxmox to act as a trunk in a switch that will pipe multiple VLANs over one connection. Although it is not important to enable it, however, it is a new way of handling VLANs on the bridge. For example, if we need to implement 10 VLANs, we will need to create 10 virtual bridges in the traditional Linux bridge way. However, using the VLAN-aware option, we can create one bridge and just add the VLAN ID to it, thus saving a lot of time typing out multiple bridge configurations.

The following shows a basic example configuration of a traditional Linux virtual bridge for 10 VLANs:

```
auto vlan0
iface vlan0 inet manual
        vlan_raw_device eth0

auto vmbr0
iface vmbr0 inet manual
        bridge_ports vlan0
        bridge_stp off
        bridge_fd 0
..........
..........

auto vlan10
iface vlan10 inet manual
        vlan_raw_device eth0

auto vmbr10
iface vmbr10 inet manual
        bridge_ports vlan10
```

```
bridge_stp off
bridge_fd 0
```

In the preceding configuration, we can see that there are a lot of bridge instances in the traditional Linux form. However, using the VLAN-aware option, we can reduce the entire configuration to just a few lines. The following is an example configuration of a VLAN-aware bridge for 10 VLANs:

```
auto vmbr0
iface vmbr0 inet manual
        bridge_vlan_aware yes
        bridge_ports eth0
        bridge_vids 1-10
        bridge_pvid 1
        bridge_stp off
        bridge_fd 0
```

For a traditional Linux bridge, we have used additional lines of configuration to create a VLAN port first, and then we pass that port as a bridge port for the bridge. The configuration option is `vlan_raw_device <physical_port>`. Although there is more than one way to create a VLAN-backed bridge, this is the preferred method of configuration.

The advantage of using the traditional Linux method is that each VLAN gets its own virtual bridge, thus isolating the network traffic further. For instance, when reconfiguring a bridge of a particular VLAN ID, only that bridge and all the VMs connected to that bridge are affected. For the VLAN-aware mode, when there is a misconfiguration, it can interrupt network connectivity for all the VMs connected to the bridge. The VLAN-aware mode provides similar functionalities as Open vSwitch but without the extra package. We will learn about Open vSwitch later in this chapter.

When using the VLAN-aware bridge, we have to tag each virtual interface with the VLAN ID, as shown in the following screenshot:

When using traditional mode without the VLAN-aware option, we have to select the VLAN tagged bridge itself instead of entering the **VLAN Tag** for the virtual network interface.

# Adding a virtual bridge through CLI

Perform the following steps to create a virtual bridge in Proxmox through the CLI:

1. Log in to the Proxmox node through the console.
2. Open the interface file `/etc/network/interfaces` using an editor.
3. Add the configuration lines using the following format at the end of the file:

```
auto <bridge_name>
iface <bridge_name> inet static
       address 192.168.10.1
       netmask 255.255.255.0
       bridge_ports ens21
       bridge_stp off
       bridge_fd 0
```

4. Save the file and exit the editor.
5. Activate the bridge from the CLI using the following command:

```
# ifup <bridge_name>
```

The new virtual bridge should now be activated and running. If virtual machines are to be migrated to other nodes, then the configuration must be duplicated in all the nodes.

# Extra bridge options

There are two extra bridge options that are usually used with the virtual bridge configuration.

## bridge_stp

This option allows multiple bridges to communicate with each other for network discovery and loop avoidance. This is useful to eliminate data cycles to provide optimal packet routing because with *STP* on, bridges can talk to each other and figure out how they are connected, and then provide the best routing possible for the data packet transmission. STP also allows fault tolerance since it checks the network topology if a bridge fails. To turn on the STP option, just modify the bridge configuration, as follows:

```
bridge_stp on
```

STP increases bandwidth efficiency while posing security issues. Do not use STP when a virtual subnet requires isolation from the other virtual subnet in the same cluster and you do not want the bridges to talk to each other. It is a useful option when working inside the virtual environment of a company, where data can flow freely between departments' subnets.

 STP is turned off by default.

STP does not have any authentication and assumes all network interfaces to be trustworthy. When a bridge inquires about the network topology from another bridge, information is freely shared without any authentication. Thus, a user in the bridge can potentially gather data of the entire network topology and other bridges in the network. This leads to a dangerous situation when bridging between the internal environment and the internet.

## bridge_fd

**FD** refers to **forwarding delay**. The `bridge_fd` option sets the delay before the interface will be ready. During the delay, the bridge tries to discover other bridges and checks that there are no network loops if STP is on. By default, the forwarding delay is set to 0, as shown in the following code:

```
bridge_fd 0
```

In most cases, the default value of 0 is enough. In a very complex virtual environment with several dozen bridges, increasing this number to 3 or 4 might help. Without this delay, the bridge will start transmitting data packets regardless of whether the other destination bridge is available or not. Increasing the delay time allows the source bridge to check all the bridges and not transmit any data if the destination bridge is down, thus preventing unnecessary network bandwidth consumption.

> There are many more `bridge_` options to be used in a network configuration file, such as `bridge_hello`, `bridge_maxage`, and `bridge_bridgeprio`. Bridge options are Linux specific and beyond the scope of this book. For in-depth information on bridges, visit `http://www.linuxfoundation.org/collaborate/workgroups/networking/bridge`.

# Virtual LAN

A VLAN is a logical local area network within a physical local area network. It can be compared with partitions within a physical disk storage. A physical network interface can be partitioned to transport data for multiple separate subnets. This partition is achieved using a VLAN ID. For details on VLANs or the IEEE 802.1q standard, refer to `http://en.wikipedia.org/wiki/IEEE_802.1Q`.

Once VLAN data leaves the virtual environment, a physical network switch with the VLAN feature tags each data with an ID and then directs the data to its proper destination. Each subnet should have the same VLAN ID on the virtual environment and on the physical network switch. VLAN helps reduce the broadcast traffic of multiple domains on the same network. By segmenting a large network into smaller VLANs, broadcasts can be sent only to relevant VLANs without interrupting other data traffic on the network.

VLAN also provides an added security layer on a multi-domain network since a user can no longer just plug into the network and capture just about any data of any domain on the network. Network segmentation is usually done with a layer 3 device such as a router. However, by using a VLAN, significant cost savings can be achieved with the existing layer 2 devices on the network, such as a managed switch or smart switch. There are seven layers defined by the **Open Systems Interconnection** (**OSI**) model by which network communication takes place. For in-depth details on OSI, refer to `http://en.wikipedia.org/wiki/OSI_model`.

# Adding a VLAN

VLAN can be set up on both the virtual machines and on bridges. If the VLAN traffic leaves a virtual environment, it is important for each switch and physical network device to be VLAN-aware and tagged properly. Tagging VMs with the VLAN ID is very straightforward through the Proxmox GUI. Just enter the VLAN ID during the addition of a network interface to a VM or edit the already added vNICs. The following screenshot shows a virtual interface for a VM after it was tagged with a VLAN ID:

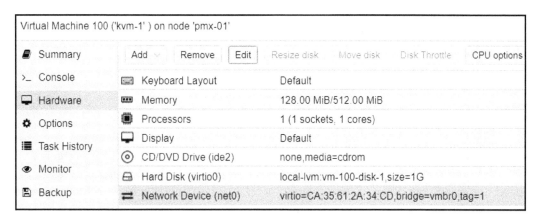

In the previous example, we have tagged the interface for VLAN ID 1. This tagging works when the bridge has the VLAN-aware option enabled, or when Open vSwitch has been implemented. When each virtual bridge is configured with a separate VLAN ID, then instead of assigning a tag ID, we will configure the interface to use the bridge for that VLAN. In the following screenshot, we have configured the network interface to use the bridge `vmbr1` instead of tagging:

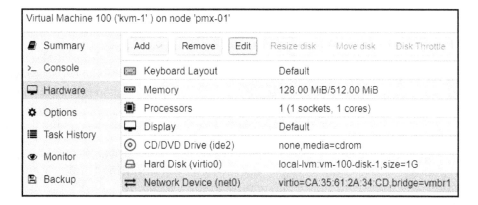

We can also configure a VLAN for bonded network interfaces. For this, instead of assigning a physical interface as a VLAN raw device, we need to create a new bonded interface and then use that for the VLAN raw device, as shown in the following example configuration:

```
auto bond0
iface bond0 inet manual
    slaves eth0 eth1

auto vlan1
iface vlan1 inet manual
    vlan_raw_device bond0

auto vmbr1
iface vmbr1 inet manual
    bridge_ports vlan1
    bridge_stp off
    bridge_fd 0
```

In the previous example, we created a bonded interface using the physical ports `eth0` and `eth1`. Then, we created a VLAN interface `vlan1` using the bonded interface as the raw device. The new virtual bridge `vmbr1` was created from `vlan1`. Notice that nowhere have we used the VLAN tag. Instead, we created the VLAN raw device based on the desired tag. The name of the bridge is not important here, but the name of the VLAN interface is. If we have to create a bridge for VLAN ID 9, then our configuration will look like this:

```
auto vlan9
iface vlan9 inet manual
    vlan_raw_device bond0

auto vmbr9
iface vmbr9 inet manual
    bridge_ports vlan9
    bridge_stp off
    bridge_fd 0
```

Besides the tagged virtual bridge and virtual network interface, in order to make the VLAN work, we also have to configure a physical switch. Without a VLAN, the capable switch network traffic will not be able to traverse between nodes or go outside the local network. Traffic will be limited to inside the node only. Each physical switch comes with its own GUI for switch configuration, but the basic idea of the VLAN configuration remains the same for all.

The VLAN configuration is done on a physical switch by configuring trunks or general ports. The option is usually found by navigating to the **Switching** | **VLAN** menu of the GUI. The following screenshot is an example of the VLAN setting on the Netgear GS748T smart switch:

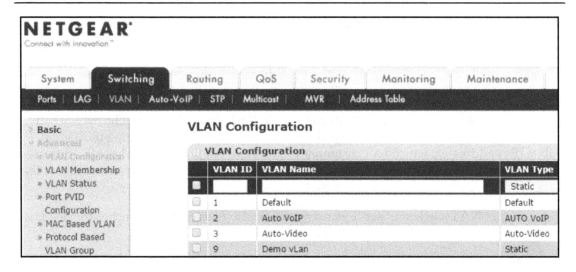

In the previous example, a demo VLAN with **ID #9** was set up for the bridge, vmbr9. Next, we have to configure the ports that are part of VLAN 9 under the VLAN Membership menu, as shown in the following screenshot, where we have tagged ports 2, 3, 4, and 5 for VLAN 9:

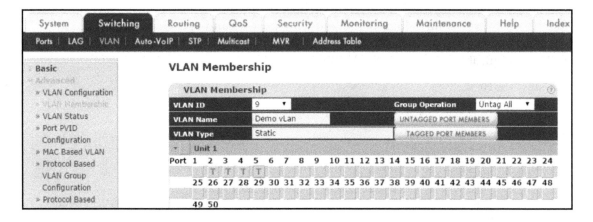

 A good practice to identify which VLAN belongs to which bridge is to use the same number for both the interfaces. For example, a bridge vmbr10 will have the VLAN ID 10. Without some order, in the beginning, bridges and VLANs will quickly get out of control as the network grows over time.

# Network Address Translation/Translator

**Network Address Translation/Translator** (**NAT**) is a method of remapping one IP address space into another by modifying the network address information in the IP datagram packet headers while they are in transit across a traffic routing device.

NAT secures a device by not directly exposing it to the internet or to a public network. It also allows more physical devices to be able to communicate without having individual public IPv4 addresses, which will cost money, and there is a limited supply of IP addresses on the internet. NAT is usually configured in the router or firewall of a network, where the policy is created for local-to-global and global-to-local IP address mapping.

 NAT is relevant for IPv4 networks. An IPv6 network diminishes the need to use NAT because IPv6 addressing is always public.

## Adding NAT/masquerading

NAT is a way to hide internal network IP addresses from the external network, such as the internet. Any outgoing traffic uses the main host IP address instead of using its own local IP address. Add the last three lines of the following post-up and post-down settings to the `/etc/network/interfaces` configuration file. Only add these lines under the virtual bridge configuration that needs the NAT option:

```
auto vmbr0
iface vmbr0 inet static
address 192.168.145.1
netmask 255.255.255.0
    bridge_ports none
    bridge_stp off
    bridge_fd 0
    post-up echo 1 > /proc/sys/net/ipv4/ip_forward
    post-up iptables -t nat -A POSTROUTING -s '192.168.145.0/24' -o eth0
    -j MASQUERADE
    post-down iptables -t nat -D POSTROUTING -s '192.168.145.0/24' -o eth0
    -j MASQUERADE
```

It is recommended that all NAT configurations be handled by a dedicated physical or virtual firewall. Most firewalls have an out-of-the-box NAT option. Also, using virtualized firewalls, we can create truly isolated virtual networks for multiple clients on the same Proxmox cluster. Having a virtual firewall provides the client control over their own filtering while keeping their network hidden from the other client networks in the cluster.

# Network bonding

**Network bonding** or **Teaming** or **Link Aggregation** (**LAG**) is a concept where multiple interfaces are combined to increase the throughput, set up network redundancy, and balance network load. This concept is heavily used in high-demand environments where downtime and slow network I/O are not acceptable. The Proxmox GUI provides excellent features to create and manage to bonding within the cluster node. Bonding modes supported by Proxmox are `balance-rr`, `active-backup`, `balance-xor`, broadcast, **Link Aggregation Control Protocol** (**LACP**) or `802.3ad`, `balance-tlb`, and `balance-alb`. The following table lists the various bonding modes as well as their policies and descriptions:

| Bonding mode | Policy | Description |
| --- | --- | --- |
| `balance-rr` or `Mode 0` | Round robin | Packet transmission takes place sequentially from the first participating network interface to the last. This provides load balancing and fault tolerance. |
| `active-backup` or `Mode 1` | Active backup | Only one participating network interface is active. The next interface becomes active when the previous active interface fails. This only provides fault tolerance. |

| `balance-xor` or `Mode 2` | XOR | This mode selects the same participating interface for each destination MAC address. Transmission takes place based on bonded network interfaces of the MAC address XOR'd with the destination MAC address. This provides both load balancing and fault tolerance. |
|---|---|---|
| `broadcast` or `Mode 3` | Broadcast | Transmission takes place on all participating bonded network interfaces. This provides fault tolerance only. |
| `802.3ad` or `Mode 4` | Dynamic link aggregation | All participating network interfaces in the aggregated group share the same speed and duplex settings. All interfaces are utilized according to the `802.3ad` specification. A network switch with `802.3ad` or the LACP feature is required. This provides fault tolerance. |
| `balance-tlb` or `Mode 5` | Adaptive transmit load balancing | Outgoing packets are distributed according to the current load on each participating interface. Incoming packets are received on the current interface, and if the same interface fails, then the next available interface takes over. This provides fault tolerance and load balancing for only outbound packets. |

| balance-alb<br>or<br>Mode 6 | Adaptive load balancing | This is the same as balance-tlb with the inclusion of load balancing for incoming packets on all interfaces. This provides fault tolerance and load balancing for both incoming and outgoing traffic. |
|---|---|---|

# Adding a bonding interface

We will now see how to add network bonding to our cluster. There are several types of bonding options available. However, only balance-rr, active-backup, and LACP (802.3ad) are the most widely used. The balance-rr option provides the round robin method to increase the overall interface bandwidth with failover. The balance-rr option does not require any special network switch. Just about any switch can be used to make this work. The major drawback of balance-rr is a waste of data packets. LACP is known as the industry-standard bonding.

In this book, we will only take a look at the LACP bonding protocol. However, to give you an idea of what balance-rr bonding looks like, the following diagram shows balance-rr bonding between Proxmox nodes and Ceph distributed storage clusters. In this example, the Proxmox public network is on 192.168.10.0/24, while the storage backend is on a private 192.168.201.0/24 subnet. Separate switches are used for the Ceph storage network to increase redundancy. Each Proxmox node has three 1-gigabit NICs. One is used from the main cluster of server virtual machines, and the remaining two are used for balance-rr bonding. This type of bonding is a very economical way to provide network redundancy:

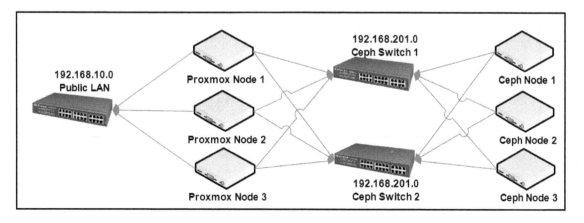

LACP can combine multiple interfaces to increase the total throughput but not the actual connection. For example, an LACP bonding of four 1-gigabit network interfaces will still have a total connection speed of 1-gigabit, but it will be able to respond to more simultaneous requests closer to the 1-gigabit speed.

 To know more about link aggregation/bonding/teaming, refer to `http://` `en.wikipedia.org/wiki/Link_Aggregation_Control_Protocol#Link_` `Aggregation_Control_Protocol`.

For LACP to work, it is very important to know whether the physical switch supports this feature. A quick visit to a switch manufacturer's website will give us the information about whether the LACP feature is supported. Some manufacturers will list this feature as 802.3ad.

Like virtual bridges, we can also configure a network bond through the Proxmox GUI or CLI. A bond created through the GUI will only be activated after the node reboots, whereas a bond added through the CLI by editing the network configuration file directly can also be activated through the CLI. We can open the bond interface creation dialog box from the **Hardware** tab of the node. The following screenshot shows the dialog box for a bonded interface, bond0, in our example Proxmox node:

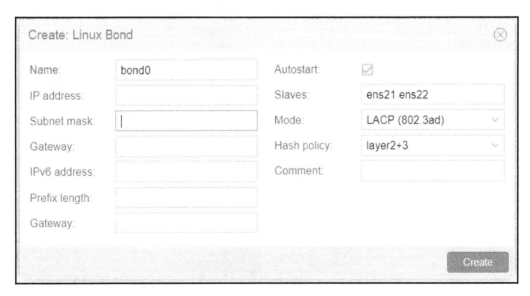

In the previous example, we used physical interfaces, `ens21` and `ens22`, for our bonded interface, `bond0`. We have not used any IP information since this bonded interface will not be directly connected, but we will create VLAN interfaces and virtual bridges based on the bond interface. For bond mode, we are using LACP with the `layer 2+3` hash policy. There are three hash policies to choose from the drop-down list:

- **layer2**
- **layer2+3**
- **layer3+4**

To maximize the performance and stability of the network connectivity, it is important to know the difference between the policies.

## The layer 2 hash policy

If no policy is selected, then Proxmox uses the layer 2 policy by default. This policy generates the transmission hash based on the MAC addresses of the network interface. This policy puts all the network traffic on a single slave interface in the bonded LACP.

## The layer 2+3 hash policy

This policy creates the transmission hash based on the combined MAC and IP addresses. These are also the layer 2 and layer 3 protocols of the network layer. This policy also sends the network traffic to a destination on the same slave interface. However, it provides more balanced network transmission than just using the layer 2 policy. For best performance and stability, use this policy.

## The layer 3+4 hash policy

This policy creates the transmission hash based on the upper network layer whenever it is available. The combination of layer 3 and 4 allows multiple network traffic or connections spanning over multiple slave interfaces in the bonded LACP. However, one connection will not span over multiple slave interfaces. For non-IP network traffic, this policy uses the layer 2 hash policy. Do keep in mind that the layer 3+4 policy is not fully LACP or 802.3ad compliant.

To create the bonding interface through the CLI, the following lines need to be added to the configuration file. In our example, we are adding the physical interface ports, `ens21` and `ens22,` to the bonding interface:

```
auto ens21
iface ens21 inet manual
auto ens22
iface ens22 inet manual

# bonding interfaces
auto bond0
iface bond0 inet manual
    slaves ens21 ens22
    bond_miimon 100
    bond_mode 802.3ad
```

We are going to add the following lines of code to create a virtual bridge using the bonded port:

```
auto vmbr1
iface vmbr1 inet static
    address 192.168.10.1
    netmask 255.255.255.0
    bridge_ports bond0
    bridge_stp off
    bridge_fd 0
```

Activate the bridge by rebooting the node or from the CLI by stopping and restarting the bridge. Use the following commands:

```
# ifup bond0
# ifdown vmbr1
# ifup vmbr1
```

After configuring Proxmox nodes with LACP bonding, we now have to set up LACP on a physical switch. Each switch comes with its own documentation on how to configure LACP link aggregation. In this section, we are going to take a look at the Netgear GS748T smart switch LACP feature. The option to enable LACP can be found by navigating to **Switching | LAG** in the Netgear GUI. First, we have to enable LACP for each link group. The following screenshot shows LACP enabled for group 1 to 3 through the **LAG Configuration** menu:

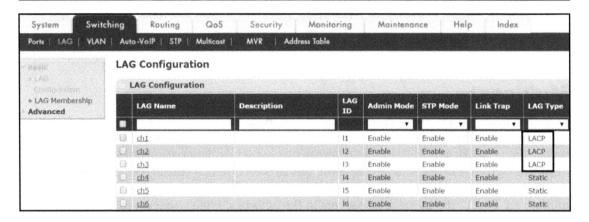

After the link groups are enabled, we will assign switch ports to each groups. In our example, we are assigning port 1 and 2 to group 1 named `ch1`, port 3 and 4 to a group named `ch2`, and port 5 and 6 to a group named `ch3`. The following screenshot shows ports enabled for group 1:

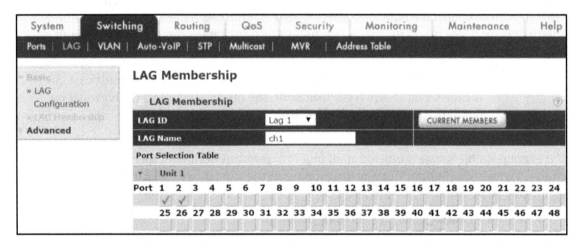

Bonding can also be used with a VLAN. Refer to the *Virtual LAN* section in this chapter to learn how to integrate bonding with a VLAN.

# Multicast

From Proxmox VE 4.0 and later, multicast is now required for proper cluster communication. In simple words, multicast delivers a single transmission to multiple server nodes in a network simultaneously, whereas unicast sends data packets to a single destination from a single source. The more nodes there are in a cluster, the more separate unicast packets need to be sent by it. Using multicast, this extra amount of traffic is vastly minimized. Due to the increase of packets in the network when using unicast, implementing it in a cluster with five or more nodes should be avoided. In order for multicast to work, the physical switch in the network must be multicast and IGMP snoop capable.

**IGMP snooping** is simply a process where the physical switch listens or snoops for an IGMP conversation between the nodes and the switch. This allows the switch to maintain a table or map to determine how and where to direct multicast requests. After enabling IGMP snoop, it takes a few hours for the switch to establish the table after gathering enough data for all multicast-enabled switch ports.

> Keep in mind that Open vSwitch currently does not handle multicast. So for the Open vSwitch environment, the multicast querier router must be configured on the physical switch.

If it is not possible to use multicast at all in a Proxmox environment, then unicast is the only choice. To test whether multicast is functioning in the cluster, we can run the following command on all the Proxmox nodes:

```
# omping <remote_node_ip> <local_node_ip>
```

If multicast is functioning fully, the output will show multicast responses:

```
root@pmx-01:~# omping -c 5 172.16.2.1 172.16.2.2
172.16.2.2 : waiting for response msg
172.16.2.2 : joined (S,G) = (*, 232.43.211.234), pinging
172.16.2.2 :   unicast, seq=1, size=69 bytes, dist=0, time=0.103ms
172.16.2.2 : multicast, seq=1, size=69 bytes, dist=0, time=0.289ms
172.16.2.2 :   unicast, seq=2, size=69 bytes, dist=0, time=0.186ms
172.16.2.2 : multicast, seq=2, size=69 bytes, dist=0, time=0.206ms
172.16.2.2 :   unicast, seq=3, size=69 bytes, dist=0, time=0.170ms
172.16.2.2 : multicast, seq=3, size=69 bytes, dist=0, time=0.194ms
172.16.2.2 :   unicast, seq=4, size=69 bytes, dist=0, time=0.236ms
172.16.2.2 : multicast, seq=4, size=69 bytes, dist=0, time=0.270ms
172.16.2.2 :   unicast, seq=5, size=69 bytes, dist=0, time=0.318ms
172.16.2.2 : multicast, seq=5, size=69 bytes, dist=0, time=0.346ms
172.16.2.2 : given amount of query messages was sent

172.16.2.2 :   unicast, xmt/rcv/%loss = 5/5/0%, min/avg/max/std-dev = 0.103/0.203/0.318/0.080
172.16.2.2 : multicast, xmt/rcv/%loss = 5/5/0%, min/avg/max/std-dev = 0.194/0.261/0.346/0.062
root@pmx-01:~#
```

If you only see an error message `waiting for response msg`, that means the command `omping` is only running on one node. Only by running it on multiple nodes simultaneously can we generate multicast traffic. Unsuccessful multicast responses will show packet loss for the node. The documentation of each physical switch should show whether the switch is multicast capable. However, nowadays, almost all smart and managed switches have the multicast feature. It is, however, disabled on all ports and must be enabled for proper Proxmox cluster communication.

# Configuring multicast on Netgear

In this section, we will see how to configure multicast for the Netgear smart switch GS748T. To configure multicast, navigate to **Switching** | **Multicast**. First, we are going to enable the IGMP snooping status through the **IGMP Snooping Configuration** option, as shown in the following screenshot:

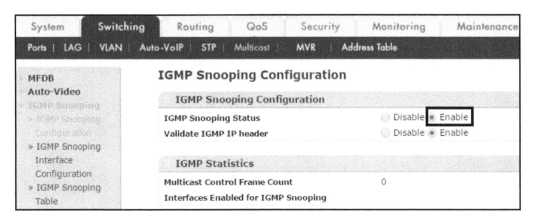

Next, we have to **Enable** admin mode for the interface that will be used for IGMP snooping. We can enable it from the **IGMP Snooping Configuration** interface option. As shown in the following screenshot, in our example switch, we are enabling IGMP snooping for switch ports 1 to 6, which is where Proxmox nodes are connected:

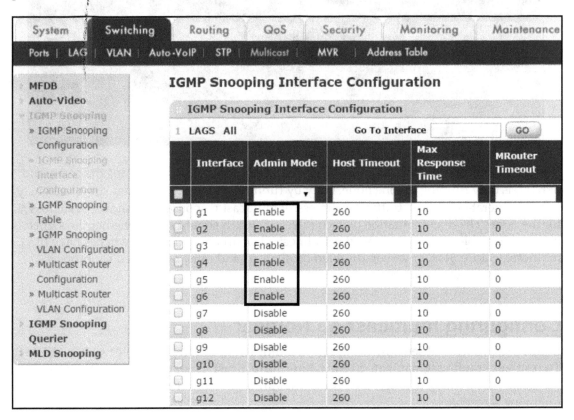

The last configuration to be made is to enable multicast traffic for switch ports from the **Multicast Router Configuration** option. In our example, we are enabling multicast on ports 1 to 6, as shown in the following screenshot:

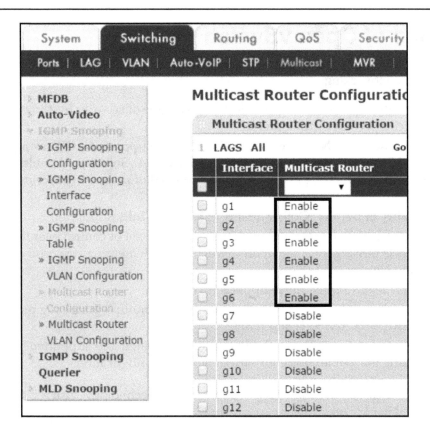

# Open vSwitch

Licensed under the open source Apache 2.0, Open vSwitch is a multi-layered, enterprise-grade virtual switch born specifically to be used in modern virtual networks of a virtual environment. This is similar to a virtual bridge of Linux but has more capabilities and robust features. A question often asked is why one should choose Open vSwitch over time- and industry-proven traditional Linux bridge and networking. Once we understand the features and advantages Open vSwitch provides for a virtual network, the answer becomes obvious.

# Features of Open vSwitch

The following are some of the features that make Open vSwitch a better option than standard Linux networking:

- **Security**: Open vSwitch provides a high degree of security by allowing you to set policies per VM virtual interface.
- **LACP and VLAN-aware**: Open vSwitch fully supports LACP link aggregation and VLAN tagging. We can configure one Open vSwitch with multiple VLAN tags, thus reducing the management overhead of many virtual bridges per VLAN tag.
- **Quality of Service**: QoS or quality of service is fully supported.
- **Network monitoring**: We can get an extreme level of control over network packets passing through Open vSwitch by implementing powerful monitoring using Netflow and sFlow.
- **IPv6**: Open vSwitch fully supports IPv6.
- **Tunneling protocol**: This has full support for multiple tunneling protocols, such as GRE, VXLAN, STT, and IPSEC.
- **Proxmox support**: Open vSwitch is fully integrated and supported by Proxmox, making it a viable choice for virtual network configuration.

 For complete details on the Open vSwitch technology, visit the official site at http://www.openvswitch.org/.

It is possible to build a Proxmox cluster entirely with the traditional Linux bridge without using Open vSwitch at all. But for a large environment, Open vSwitch does make great sense since it can lessen tedious virtual network management while providing excellent visibility over network traffic. In a multi-tenant environment, taking control over what is going on in the network is very important.

Open vSwitch is not installed in Proxmox by default. It must be manually installed and configured. On a clean installed Proxmox node, we have to configure the network as usual, so the node can have internet connectivity. Then, run the following command to install Open vSwitch:

```
# apt-get install openvswitch-switch
```

Even if Open vSwitch is not installed, the Proxmox GUI will show the menu options for the Open vSwitch bridge and interface under the **Create** tab of the **Network** menu of the node.

An important thing to remember when using Open vSwitch is never to mix traditional Linux components; for example, bridge, bond, and VLAN should never be mixed with Open vSwitch components. We must not create an Open vSwitch bridge based on a Linux bond and vice versa.

There are three components that we can use with Open vSwitch:

- Open vSwitch bridge
- Open vSwitch bond
- Open vSwitch IntPort

# Adding an Open vSwitch bridge

The Open vSwitch bridge is similar to the Linux bridge except that it is enough to configure one Open vSwitch bridge, such as a physical switch, where we can pass several VLANs. We do not need to create separate bridges for each VLAN, like Linux bridges. Configuring an Open vSwitch bridge is a little more complicated than a Linux bridge. We need to configure the port first before creating the actual bridge. In our example, we are going to configure the port, eth1, which is what our Open vSwitch bridge, vmbr1, is going to be based on. For this, we need to add the following lines of code to /etc/network/interfaces:

```
allow-vmbr1 ens21
iface ens21 inet manual
    ovs_type OVSPort
    ovs_bridge vmbr1

auto vmbr1
allow-ovs vmbr1
iface vmbr1 inet static
    address 192.168.0.171
    netmask 255.255.255.0
    ovs_type OVSBridge
    ovs_ports ens21
```

Unlike a Linux bridge, where VLANs are passed through bridge tagging, in Open vSwitch, we can pass VLANs through ports directly. VLAN trunks are configured as additional Open vSwitch options in the configuration, as shown in the following example, where we are passing VLAN 2, 3, and 4:

```
allow-vmbr2 ens21
iface ens21 inet manual
    ovs_type OVSPort
    ovs_bridge vmbr2
    ovs_options trunks=2,3,4
```

We can also create the Open vSwitch bridge through the Proxmox GUI. However, we need to keep in mind that any network configuration performed through the GUI is not activated until a node is restarted.

We can open the Open vSwitch bridge-creation dialog box from the network tab of a node. The following screenshot shows the Open vSwitch bridge-creation dialog box with the necessary information:

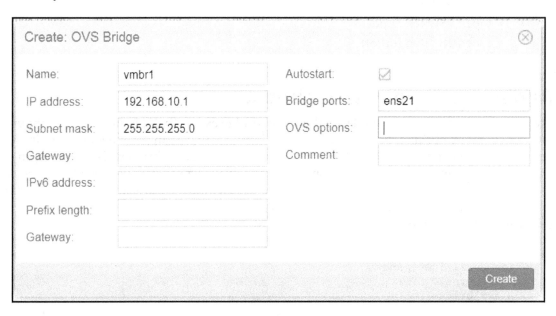

In the OVS options, we can include additional options for the bridge.

## Adding the Open vSwitch bond

Like the Linux bridge, we can create various Open vSwitch bond interfaces. In this example, we are going to create the LACP bonded interface for Open vSwitch. The following configuration parameters are used to create a bond interface using the interface to create an Open vSwitch bridge:

```
allow-vmbr1 bond0
iface bond0 inet manual
    ovs_type OVSBond
    ovs_bridge vmbr1
    ovs_bonds ens21 ens22
    pre-up (ifconfig ens21 mtu 8996 && ifconfig ens22 mtu 8996)
    ovs_options bond_mode=balance-tcp lacp=active trunks=2,3,4
```

```
    mtu 8996

auto vmbr1
iface vmbr1 inet manual
    ovs_type OVSBridge
    ovs_ports bond0
    mtu 8996
```

In the previous example, a new parameter is added called **pre-up**. This is used to configure jumbo packets. The default `mtu` for all the interfaces is 1,500. When configuring jumbo packets, using the value of 8,996 is safer instead of 9,000 since some additional bytes are added on top of the configured MTU for which a data packet may get discarded if the MTU goes beyond 9,000.

We can configure the same Open vSwitch bond through the Proxmox GUI using the bond-creation dialog box, as shown in the following screenshot:

The Open vSwitch bridge must be created before creating the Open vSwitch bond. We can select the OVS bridge from the drop-down menu of the dialog box. It is not possible to add extra parameters, such as configuring the desired MTU through the Proxmox GUI. So before we restart the node, we can add the parameter to `/etc/network/interfaces.new` so that the configuration gets committed to `/etc/network/interfaces` during the node reboot.

# Adding Open vSwitch IntPort

In Open vSwitch, it is possible to give the host or physical node access to a VLAN through the configured Open vSwitch bridge. This is done by creating an Open vSwitch component called **IntPort**. In simple words, an IntPort splits a VLAN, which we can configure to assign the IP information. This is useful to give the Proxmox node access to a VLAN. For example, our example Proxmox node `pmx-01` is currently configured to use the Linux bridge, `vmbr0`. If we want to use Open vSwitch instead, we will have to create an Open vSwitch IntPort to give the node access to the Open vSwitch bridge utilizing the VLAN. The following parameters need to be added to the network configuration. `ens18` is our main physical network interface for the node:

```
auto vmbr0
allow-ovs vmbr0
iface vmbr0 inet manual
    ovs_type OVSBridge
    ovs_ports ens18 vlan1

allow-vmbr0 vlan1
iface vlan1 inet static
    ovs_type OVSIntPort
    ovs_bridge vmbr0
    ovs_options tag=50
    ovs_extra set interface ${IFACE} external-ids:iface-id=$(hostname -s)-
${IFACE}-vif
    address 172.16.2.1
    netmask 255.255.255.0
    gateway 172.16.2.254
    mtu 1500
```

Note that in the port configuration, we have added both `ens18` and IntPort interface `vlan1`:

```
ovs_ports ens18 vlan1
```

 Even though we have specified the Open vSwitch bridge through `ovs_bridge vmbr0` for the IntPort, we still have to specify it in the Open vSwitch bridge definition or else the interface will never be started.

# CLI for Open vSwitch

Besides the option to create and edit Open vSwitch devices through the Proxmox GUI, Open vSwitch comes loaded with command-line options to manage and gather information of a particular bridge, bond, or interface. There are four types of commands in Open vSwitch:

- `ovs-appctl`: This is used to query and control the Open vSwitch daemon
- `ovs-vsctl`: This is used to manage the Open vSwitch configuration database
- `ovs-ofctl`: This is a tool used to monitor and manage the OpenFlow switch
- `ovs-dpctl`: This is used to manage Open vSwitch data paths

It is beyond the scope of this book to go into details of all the available commands of Open vSwitch. In this section, we will only take a look at the commands that may prove to be very helpful while managing a Proxmox cluster:

- To see a list of configured Open vSwitch bridges, ports, and interfaces, use the following commands:

  ```
  # ovs-vsctl list br
  # ovs-vsctl list port
  # ovs-vsctl list interface
  ```

- To see a list of all the interfaces in Open vSwitch, run the following command:

  ```
  # ovs-vsctl show
  ```

- To modify options at runtime without rebooting node:

  ```
  # ovs-vsctl set <interface_type> <interface_name> <option>
  ```

- For example, if we want to add more VLAN IDs to our Open vSwitch bonded interface, run the following command:

  ```
  # ovs-vsctl set port bond0 trunks=2,3,4,5,6,7
  ```

- We have to mention all the existing VLAN IDs along with the new ones. Otherwise, the trunk configuration will get replaced with only the new ones while the old configuration will get replaced. We also have to add the new IDs to the `/etc/network/interfaces` file.

- To snoop and display traffic to and from the Open vSwitch bridge, run the following command:

    ```
    # ovs-ofctl snoop <bridge_name>
    ```

- To see the status of each of Open vSwitch components, run this command:

    ```
    # ovs-ofct lshow <name>
    ```

- To dump OpenFlow flows, including hidden ones, run this command:

    ```
    # ovs-appctl bridge/dump-flows <bridge_name>
    ```

- To print the version of Open vSwitch, run the following command:

    ```
    # ovs-appctl version
    ```

For a complete list of the available Open vSwitch commands, visit the following link:

```
http://www.pica8.com/document/v2.3/pdf/ovs-commands-reference.pdf
```

# Practicing Open vSwitch

If you are using Open vSwitch for the first time, it may seem slightly complex at first. But with practice and exposure, it really gets easier to create and manage a complex virtual network fully powered by Open vSwitch. In this section, you are given the task to create a network configuration for a Proxmox node using all the network components that we've learned so far. The full configuration is given in the following section but try to create it on your own first.

## Configuration requirements

The Proxmox node has three physical network interface ports—eth0, eth1, and eth2—and one InfiniBand interface, ib0.

We have to configure an LACP bonded Open vSwitch interface with two of the physical ports. The bridge needs to be configured as a trunk for VLAN 11, 12, 13, and 14. All VMs tagged as interfaces will connect to this bridge. The third physical interface will have to be configured for backup purposes on a separate subnet without the VLAN.

The `infiniband` interface has to be configured to be used with Ceph on a separate subnet. The node must use VLAN 12 for all host-related communication utilizing the Open vSwitch bridge.

## Solutions

The following is the full network configuration for the given requirements:

```
auto lo
iface lo inet loopback

# LACP Bonded Open vSwitch Interface
allow-vmbr0 bond0
iface bond0 inet manual
    ovs_bridge vmbr0
    ovs_type OVSBond
    ovs_bonds eth0 eth1
    pre-up (ifconfig eth0 mtu 8996 && ifconfig eth1 mtu 8996)
    ovs_options bond_mode=balance-tcp lacp=active other_config:lacp-
time=fast trunks=11,12,13,14
    mtu 8996

# Creating Open vSwitch bridge
auto vmbr0
allow-ovs vmbr0
iface vmbr0 inet manual
    ovs_type OVSBridge
    ovs_ports bond0 vlan12
    mtu 8996

# Creating IntPort for physical node
allow-vmbr0 vlan12
iface vlan12 inet static
    ovs_type OVSIntPort
    ovs_bridge vmbr0
    ovs_options tag=12
    ovs_extra set interface ${IFACE} external-ids:iface-id=$(hostname -s)-
${IFACE}-vif
    address 172.16.0.171
    netmask 255.255.252.0
    gateway 172.16.3.254
    mtu 1500

# Creating Infiniband interface
auto ib0
iface ib0 inet static
    address 192.168.0.171
```

```
        netmask 255.255.255.0
        pre-up modprobe ib_ipoib
        pre-up echo connected > /sys/class/net/ib0/mode
        mtu 65520

    # Creating dedicated interface for backup
    auto eth2
    iface eth2 inet static
        address 192.168.10.171
        netmask 255.255.255.0
```

# Sample virtual networks

At this stage, we have covered components of virtual networks within the Proxmox cluster environment. We know the components Proxmox uses to hold everything together.

We are going to take a look at a few virtual environment scenarios to solidify our understanding of networking in a Proxmox virtual environment. These are scenario-based network diagrams and some of them are taken from a real production environment.

# Network #1 – Proxmox in its simplest form

This is a small-scale Proxmox cluster with three nodes and two subnets within the virtual environment. Each Proxmox node has two NICs, and both the bridges vmbr0 and vmbr1 are attached to eth0 and eth1, respectively. Each bridge has three virtual machines attached to it. Outside the virtual environment, there is a physical switch, which connects Proxmox nodes, and an admin console for all management work. This is Proxmox in its simplest form in a production environment. This type of network can be used as a learning platform or in a very small business environment with less demanding workload. Internet connectivity is provided to the second subnet directly from the firewall with a second NIC, as shown in the following diagram:

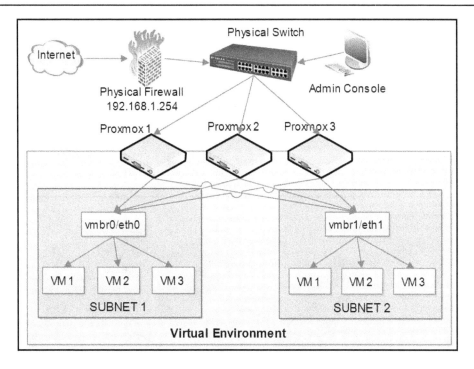

# Network #2 – the multi-tenant environment

This network setup is almost the same as the previous network with the added benefit of a fully multi-tenant virtual platform. In a physical firewall, we can only add a very small number of NICs to provide internet connectivity to isolated subnets. Using a virtualized firewall, we can add as many firewalls or vNICs as we want. This setup is especially useful when multiple, isolated client subnets need to be hosted and each subnet requires its own firewall control for filtering purposes. In this example, vmbr0 is directly served by the physical firewall. The bridges vmbr1 and vmbr200 have their own virtualized firewalls. The firewalls also act as bridges between bridges. For example, the firewall for the subnet 2 has two vNICs. One of these setups was WAN, where vmbr0 acts as an internet provider. The second vNIC is LAN facing, which serves the subnet 2.

This is a common scenario for infrastructure service providers who host virtual networks for multiple clients. Since multiple companies can access their virtual networks remotely, it puts extra workload on the physical firewall. Single-point firewall failure should be avoided at all costs by creating a cluster of physical firewalls to provide load balancing and failover firewall service.

Never use a virtualized firewall on the same cluster to connect to the internet directly. Always use separate physical hardware as the main firewall to act as a barrier between the internet and internal network.

For firewall virtualization, pfsense is a great choice to set up. It is easy to set up, yet extremely powerful and customizable. Get pfsense and more information from the official link at https://www.pfsense.org/.

The following diagram is an example of a multi-tenant virtual environment:

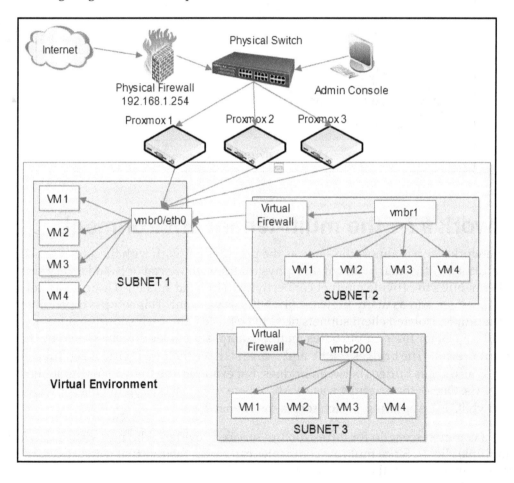

# Network #3 – academic institution

This network diagram is an example of an academic institution network. The following diagram shows network connectivity between the admin office, library, and a remote campus. There are two physical firewalls providing internet connectivity redundancies. The main virtual network consists of the database server, file server, accounting server, and library catalog server. The database server and the file server are connected with the bridge vmbr0. The accounting server is connected with the bridge vmbr10 and VLAN ID 10. The library server is connected with the bridge vmbr20 and VLAN ID 20. The main switch is set up with VLAN 10 and 20. The library switch is set up with VLAN 20. In this setup, accounting server data goes straight to the admin office and the library catalog server data goes to the library building without causing additional stress to the network. Remote campus students and staff can access the main campus network through VPN, thus eliminating the need to set up a separate virtual environment.

Of course, the following diagram is a very simplified form of the actual network topology of an academic institution. But the basics of using VLANs and bridges are the same for any network size:

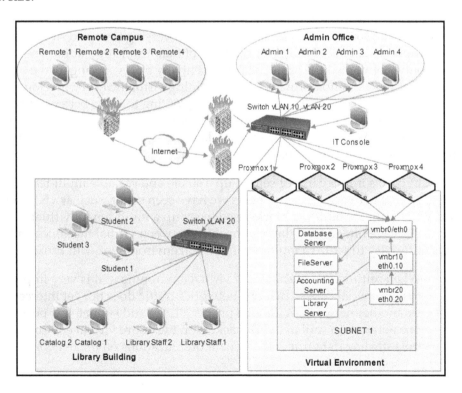

# A multi-tenant virtual environment

Multi-tenancy is a very frequently used word in the world of cloud computing, where a virtual environment is regularly used by different clients from different organizations set up with fully isolated networks. Multi-tenancy is an integral part for a service provider who provides **Infrastructure as a Service (IaaS)** to many clients.

 To know more about cloud computing, visit
`http://en.wikipedia.org/wiki/Cloud_computing`.

In this type of setup, the service provider hosts or *rents out* computing time and storage space to their clients. Because of the standard monthly subscription or SLA-based payment method required for this type of service, multi-tenancy quickly gained popularity. Basically, a multi-tenant virtual environment is where several isolated networks coexist on the same platform without interfering with one another. Almost all public datacenters are multi-tenancy platforms.

Multi-tenancy is not new in the world of information. The first multi-tenant environment appeared back in the 1960s, when companies rented processing time and storage space on mainframe computers to reduce the giant expenses of mainframe operation. The virtual environment only augmented the same idea exponentially by leveraging all the virtualization features Proxmox provides. By combining virtualization with cloud computing, multi-tenancy is able to get a very strong footing to serve better and serve more customers without increasing financial overheads. Prior to virtualization, the physical space and power requirements to host customers in an IaaS environment meant it was rare and cost prohibitive, thus not many people enjoyed its benefit.

The Proxmox hypervisor is capable of setting up a stable and scalable multi-tenant virtual environment. All the networking components we have seen so far, such as vNIC, virtual bridge, and VLAN, are the building blocks used to set up a multi-tenant virtual environment. Once we understand the relationships between virtual machines and virtual bridges, it is fairly easy to set up a multi-tenant virtual environment with Proxmox.

 When setting up a multi-tenant virtual environment, it is very important to take special care so that one network's traffic does not get intercepted by another network. Without a proper VLAN and subnet, it is possible for one network to sniff network packets on the entire virtual environment, thus stealing data from other tenant organizations on the network.

# A multi-tenant network diagram

The following is an example of a network diagram of a typical cloud service provider who provides IaaS to their clients. The entire client network is virtualized within the service provider's virtual environment:

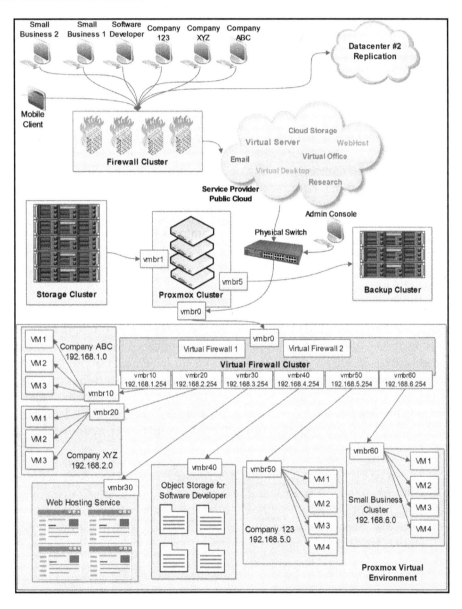

On the client side, they only have simple desktop computers and mobile devices to access their virtual cloud resources, such as desktop, storage, and processing power. Clients access these resources through virtual means, such as **Virtual Network Computing** (**VNC**), **SPICE**, or **Remote Desktop Protocol** (**RDP**).

Virtual networks are isolated with separate subnets. VLANs are set up (not shown in the diagram) to reduce mass broadcast traffic. All virtual machine data is stored on a separate storage cluster with full redundancy. A backup cluster does a regular backup of all virtual machines, and granular file backup with histories are done with a third-party backup software. A virtual firewall cluster is set up in between the virtual environment and the host Ethernet interface to provide internet connectivity to all client virtual machines. Each virtualized firewall has several vNICs to connect to each subnet.

Since the firewall is virtualized, we can add any number of virtual network interfaces without worrying about running out of physical slots. A virtualized clustered firewall provides maximum uptime. Each company network in this example has its own virtual bridge, which only talks to that company's virtual machines and firewall interface, eliminating any chance of packet sniffing by other company networks.

**Packet sniffing** is a process when data packets passing through a network interface are captured and analyzed. Packet sniffer software can be placed in a subnet to capture data. This is a common practice of someone with malicious intentions to capture sensitive unencrypted data passing through, such as usernames and passwords in clear text.

This environment is serving multiple clients or organizations, so uptime is a big concern. To eliminate this issue, the entire virtual environment is replicated to another datacenter to ensure 99.9 percent uptime. The previous diagram is an overly simplified version of what really goes on inside a very busy Proxmox virtual environment. Studying this diagram will give a clear understanding of virtual network mechanics. From the previous diagram, we can see that this network environment heavily uses virtual bridges. So, it is imperative to understand the role of bridges and plan out a draft diagram before actually setting up this level of a complex virtual network.

When working with a complex virtual network, always keep a network diagram handy and update it whenever you make any changes. An up-to-date network diagram will help greatly to have total control over a virtual network. Especially when any issue arises, it is easy to pinpoint the cause of the issue with a diagram.

# Summary

We were very busy in this lively chapter. We looked at the differences between physical and virtual networks. We learned about the network components that make up a Proxmox-based virtual network. We also learned about Open vSwitch and its components to create a really complex virtual network. We even got to analyze a few network diagrams from the basic to the advanced to get a better understanding of how the Proxmox virtual network really comes to life.

Proxmox provides all the tools we need to build any level of virtual network. It is up to the network administrator's imagination, the company's budget, and the need to foresee how all pieces should come together to form a well-designed and efficient virtual network. The best part is that any mistake is easily correctable in a virtual environment. We can always go back and change things until we are satisfied. For this very reason, a virtual network is always evolving. Over time, a virtual network becomes an extension of the network administrator's mental picture of the network. The configurations and design of a virtual network infrastructure can give us a window into how that administrator thinks and the logic they used to construct the environment.

In the next chapter, we are going to learn all about the built-in Proxmox firewall and learn how to protect from the whole cluster down to a single virtual machine.

# 9
# The Proxmox VE Firewall

The Proxmox VE firewall is a security feature that allows easy and effective protection of a virtual environment for both internal and external network traffic. By leveraging this firewall, we can protect VMs, host nodes, or the entire cluster by creating firewall rules. By creating rules at the virtual machine level, we can provide total isolation for VM-to-VM network traffic, including VM-to-external traffic. Prior to the Proxmox VE firewall, security and isolation were not possible at the hypervisor level. Keep in mind that the built-in Proxmox firewall should not be a substitute for a VM-level firewall. We must still apply a firewall policy inside a guest VM, but the hypervisor-level firewall provides an added layer of protection should the VM operating system firewall be misconfigured or not configured at all. This also creates added management overhead because network administrators or managers must now open or close ports or apply firewall policies at the hypervisor level. In this chapter, we will cover the following topics related to the Proxmox VE firewall:

- Exploring the Proxmox VE firewall
- Configuring the cluster firewall rules
- Configuring the host firewall rules
- Configuring the VM firewall rules
- Integrating a Suricata IPS
- Enabling the IPv6 firewall
- Firewall CLI commands

# Exploring the Proxmox VE firewall

The Proxmox VE firewall leverages iptables of each Proxmox node for protection. The iptables is an application that allows you to manage rules tables for the Linux kernel firewall. All firewall rules and configurations are stored in the Proxmox cluster filesystem, thus allowing a distributed firewall system in the Proxmox cluster. The pre-firewall service provided by Proxmox for each node reads the rules and configurations from the cluster filesystem and automatically adjusts the local iptables. Rules can be fully created and maintained by the Proxmox GUI or CLI. The Proxmox firewall can be used in place of a virtualized firewall in the cluster.

> Although the Proxmox firewall provides excellent protection, it is highly recommended that you have a physical firewall for the entire network. This firewall is also known as an **edge firewall** since it sits at the main entry point to the internet. The internet connection should not be directly connected to Proxmox nodes. A virtualized firewall should not be used as a physical firewall substitute.

# Components of the Proxmox firewall

There are several components that make up the Proxmox VE firewall. In order to effectively implement a firewall in a Proxmox cluster, it is important to know the components and their functions.

## Zones

The Proxmox firewall protection area is divided into the following three logical zones:

- **Datacenter**: Rules in this zone define traffic to and from all hosts and guests
- **Host**: Rules in this zone define traffic to and from a cluster and Proxmox nodes
- **VM**: Rules in this zone define traffic to and from each VM

All rules in the Datacenter and host zones are cascaded. This means that a rule created in the Datacenter zone will be applied to all hosts or nodes and all the VMs, while rules created in a host zone will be applied to all VMs in that host or Proxmox node. Care must be taken when creating rules in the host zone for particular VMs, because when the VM is migrated to a different node, these rules in the previous node will not apply to the new node for the VM. These host-level rules must be created in the new host, and only then will they be applied to the VMs. Rules created for a VM apply to that VM only. There is no rule cascading for the VM zone. The following diagram is a depiction of how Proxmox firewall policies are laid out:

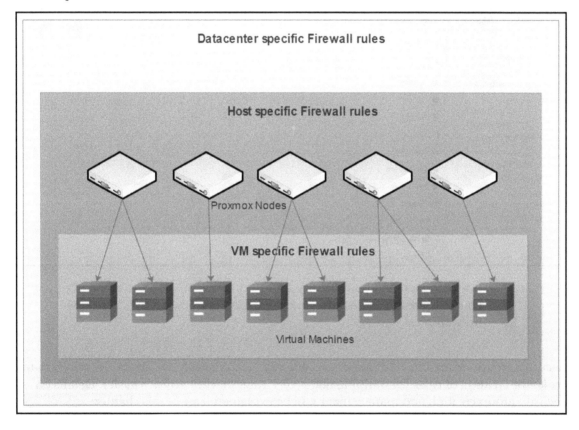

# Security groups

This allows the grouping of several firewall rules into one rule. This is very helpful when the same multiple rules apply to several VMs. For example, we can create a **Security Group** named `webserver` and add multiple rules to open ports, such as `21`, `22`, `80`, `443`, and so on. Then, we can apply these security groups to any VMs used as a `webserver`. Similarly, we can create a **Security Group** to open ports for servers for emails only. The following screenshot shows an example of a `webserver` **Security Group** with rules to open ports for **FTP, SSH, HTTP,** and **HTTPS**:

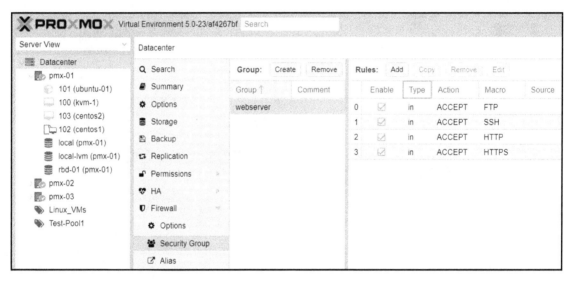

 It should be noted that security groups are only created in `Datacenter` zones. There are no security group creation options in the host or VM firewall zone.

Security groups created in a `Datacenter` zone can be applied to any zones. Security groups make the creation of rules for multiple nodes or virtual machines much easier. Details on security group creation and management will be explained later in this chapter.

# IPSet

Sometimes, it is necessary to create firewall rules to restrict or allow traffic solely based on IP addresses. An **IPSet** allows us to create firewall rules that may apply to multiple IP addresses or IP subnets. For example, we can create an **IPSet** to allow access to the Proxmox GUI from only a few limited IP addresses. The following screenshot shows an example of an **IPSet** to allow the `proxmoxgui` access from only three IP addresses:

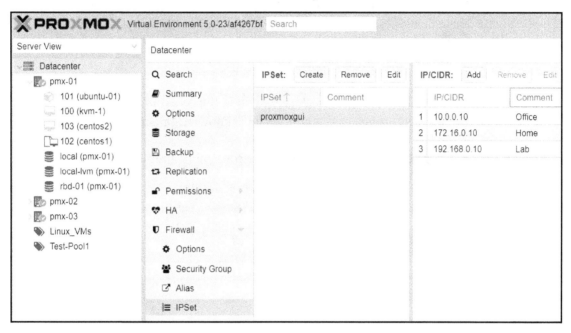

We can create rules based on individual IPs or the entire subnet using the CIDR format in the rules.

An **IPSet** can be created in both the `Datacenter` and VM zones as the option dialog boxes are also identical. An **IPSet** created in `Datacenter` zones can be applied to any hosts and VMs in the cluster. But the **IPSet** created under a VM zone is applicable to that VM only.

Another good example of **IPSet** usage is to create blacklists and whitelists of IP addresses in `Datacenter` zones. A whitelist will allow the defined traffic while a blacklist will block access to the defined IPs. Details on **IPSet** creation and management will be explained later in this chapter.

# Rules

Rules are the heart of a Proxmox firewall configuration. Rules define the flow and type of traffic that will be allowed or denied in the zones. There are two directions in which network traffic can flow:

- **in**: This refers to traffic inbound from anywhere to any zones except when specific IP addresses or ports are mentioned
- **out**: This refers to traffic outbound from any zones to anywhere except when specific IP addresses or ports are mentioned

There are three types of action that a firewall rule can be applied to:

- **ACCEPT**: This allows traffic packets matching the constraints in the rule
- **REJECT**: Packets are rejected, and then an acknowledgment of the rejection is sent to the sender
- **DENY**: Drops traffic packets matching the constraints in the rule without sending any acknowledgment to the sender

A typical rule will contain the direction of traffic, the action to apply to the traffic, and which port or protocol the rule affects. The following screenshot shows rules to block traffic on port 80 and allow it on port 443 for an example VM in our cluster:

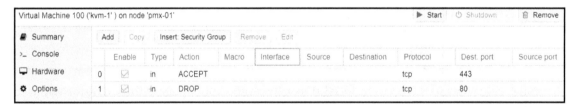

# Protocols

In a Proxmox firewall, we can create rules based on various network protocols, such as TCP, UDP, ICMP, and so on. Depending on application requirements, different protocol selections may be necessary. For example, if we want to allow ping for a zone, we need to create a rule with the ICMP protocol. Predefined protocols are available for selection through the rules dialog box, as shown in the following screenshot:

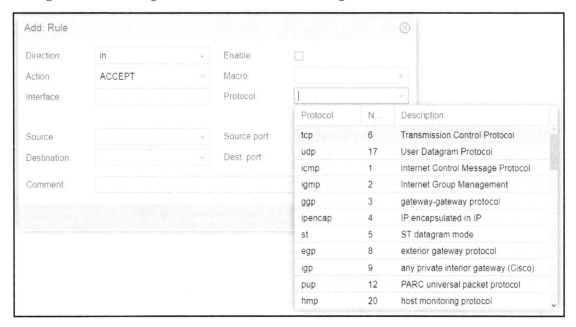

# Macros

Macros are various precreated port configurations for most known services, such as HTTP, HTTPS, SSH, FTP, Telnet, MySQL, NTP, VNC, and so on. Keep in mind when using the FTP macro that it will only work in FTP passive mode. Each macro has a predefined protocol and port number. So, when selecting a **Macro**, we do not have to define a protocol or port number. In fact, when a **Macro** is selected through the drop-down menu, the Proxmox dialog box automatically disables the protocol and port textboxes, as shown in the following screenshot:

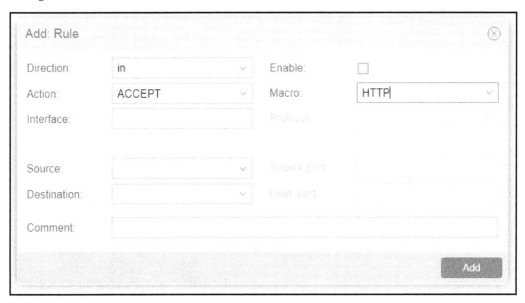

If we need to enter a custom port for any rule, then selecting the **Macro** will not work. We have to manually define the port number and a proper protocol for the rule.

The following screenshot shows the **Macro** drop-down menu in the firewall **Rule** dialog box:

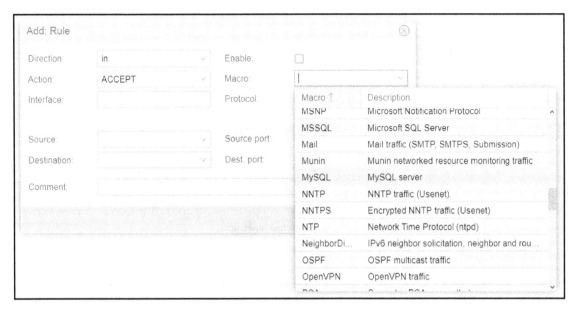

The firewall feature can be accessed through the **Firewall** tab of all three zones, Datacenter, host, and nodes, and virtual machines of both KVM and LXC.

# The pve-firewall and pvefw-logger services

There are two services that enable the Proxmox firewall:

- pve-firewall: This is the main service to run a firewall and it updates iptables rules
- pvefw-logger: This is responsible for logging all firewall traffic when logging is enabled

The pve-firewall service is started automatically when a node is rebooted. We can also manually start, stop, and restart the service using the following commands:

```
# pve-firewall start
# pve-firewall stop
# pve-firewall restart
```

To check the status of a firewall service, we can use the following command:

```
# pve-firewall status
```

When there are no issues in the firewall's operation, the output of the status command will appear as follows:

```
Status: enabled/running
```

# Configuration files of a firewall

Although the Proxmox firewall can be managed entirely from the Proxmox GUI, at times accessing the rules from the CLI may be necessary, especially when a cluster is locked out due to the misconfiguration of firewall rules. All firewall configurations and rules follow the same naming format, with the .fw extension. The firewall configuration and rule files are stored in two different directories for all three zones:

```
/etc/pve/firewall/cluster.fw
```

This is the data center configuration and zone rule file. All other data center-wide firewall information, such as security groups and IPSets, are also stored in this single file. We can enable or disable the data center-wide firewall by editing this configuration file:

```
/etc/pve/nodes/<node_name>/host.fw
```

**CAUTION!**
Do not enable the data center-wide firewall before reading the *Configuring the data center-specific firewall* section later in this chapter.

This is the configuration and rules file for a Proxmox node or host:

```
/etc/pve/firewall/<vm_id>.fw
```

Each virtual machine, whether it is KVM or LXC, has a separate firewall configuration file with its VM ID stored in the same directory the data center firewall file is stored.

When new rules are created or edited through the Proxmox GUI, these are the files that get changed. Whether the changes are made through the GUI or CLI, all rules take effect immediately. There are no reboots or restarting of a firewall service required.

# Configuring the data center-specific firewall

As mentioned earlier, data center-specific firewall rules affect all resources, such as clusters, nodes, and virtual machines. Any rules created in this zone are cascaded to both hosts and VMs. This zone is also used to fully lock down a cluster to drop all incoming traffic and then only open what is required. In a freshly installed Proxmox cluster, the data center-wide firewall option is disabled.

**CAUTION!**
Extra attention should always be used when creating data center-specific firewall rules to prevent full cluster lockout.

# Configuring the Datacenter firewall through the GUI

The following screenshot shows the **Firewall** option for the `Datacenter` zone through the `Options` tab by navigating to `Datacenter` | **Firewall** | **Options**:

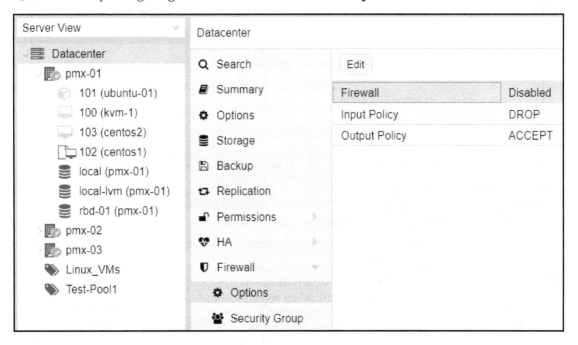

As we can see in the preceding screenshot, by default the Proxmox firewall for the Datacenter zone is disabled with **Input Policy** set to **DROP** and **Output Policy** set to **ACCEPT**. If we did enable this firewall option right now, then all inbound access will be denied. You will have to be on the console to access the node. Before we enable this option, we must create two rules to allow the GUI on port 8006 and the SSH console on port 22.

# Creating the Datacenter firewall rules

To open the rule creation dialog box, we need to click on **Add** by navigating to the Datacenter | **Firewall** menu. For the first rule, we are going to allow the Proxmox GUI on port 8006, as shown in the following screenshot:

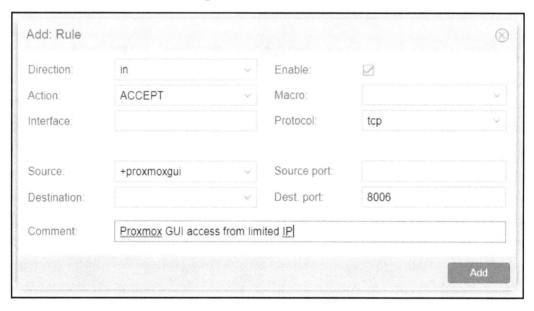

The dialog box for rules is identical for all three zones, so it is important to know the details of the option items in this dialog box. The following table summarizes the purpose of the text and drop-down list available in the rules dialog box:

| Items | Functions |
|---|---|
| **Direction** | This is a drop-down list used to select the direction of the traffic for the rule, and it is a required field. |
| **Action** | This is a drop-down list used to select actions that need to be taken, such as **ACCEPT**, **DROP**, or **REJECT** incoming or outgoing traffic. This is a required field. |

| Interface | This is a textbox used to define the interface to apply this rule to. This does not apply to the `Datacenter` zone. It is useful to define this for a VM with multiple interfaces. |
|---|---|
| **Source** | This is a drop-down list used to select a preconfigured IPSet or textbox to type in the IP address where the traffic originates from. We can also define a subnet in the CIDR format. When left blank, it accepts traffic from all the source IP addresses. In our previous example screenshot, we have selected IP set to allow a GUI connection from specific hosts only. |
| **Destination** | This is a drop-down list used to select a preconfigured IPSet or textbox to type in the IP address of the destination device in the cluster. When left blank, it accepts traffic from all the destination IP addresses. |
| **Enable** | This is a checkbox used to enable or disable the rule. |
| **Macro** | This is a drop-down list used to select preconfigured macros. We can also type the macro name, which filters the list of macros. |
| **Protocol** | This is a drop-down list used to select protocols. We can also type the protocol name, which filters the list of protocols. |
| **Source port** | This is a textbox used to define the originating port number for the incoming traffic. When left blank, it accepts traffic from any ports. We can also define the port ranges, separated by a colon ( : ), in this field. This source port field is also used for the outgoing traffic when the traffic originates internally from a VM, node, or cluster. |
| **Dest. Port** | This is a textbox used to define the destination port of the incoming traffic. When left blank, it accepts traffic from any port. We can also define port ranges, separated by a colon ( : ), in this field. |
| **Comment** | This is a textbox used to write descriptions or any notes regarding the rule. |

To allow the SSH console traffic, we are going to create a rule with the **SSH** macro. The following screenshot shows the firewall feature of the `Datacenter` zone with two rules created to allow access to the Proxmox GUI and SSH:

The Proxmox GUI can only be accessed from one IP address, which is `172.16.0.3`, whereas SSH can be accessed from any IP address. Remember that all data center rules are cascaded down to hosts and VMs. In this scenario, SSH is open for all hosts and VMs in the cluster. In certain situations, we may need to block SSH for certain VMs in order to increase the security. If we keep the previous rule as it is, we will need to create a separate VM-level rule to drop SSH traffic for all VMs. However, this can become a tedious task since some VMs may require SSH access and there can be dozens of VMs. A revised advanced rule to allow SSH access to only Proxmox nodes would be to create an IPSet in `Datacenter` with IP addresses for Proxmox nodes only, and then assign the IPSet as the **Destination** for the rule.

# Creating the Datacenter IPSet

The following screenshot shows the IPSet named `proxmox_nodes` with IP addresses for three nodes in our example cluster:

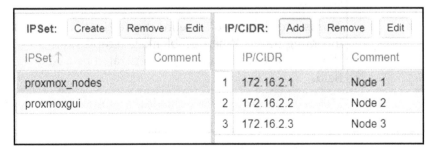

From the IPSet management page, we need to create the IPSet itself first, and then add IPs from the right-hand side **IP/CIDR** option. IP addresses can be added separately or defined in an entire block using the CIDR value. The IPSet's name can only be alphanumeric, with two special characters: – and _. But when Proxmox displays the IPset in the drop-down list, it adds + as a prefix. This is not part of the IPset's name. If a string is entered as capital letters, it automatically gets changed to lowercase. The following screenshot shows the rules dialog box, where we selected an IPSet for Proxmox nodes in **Destination** to allow SSH only for Proxmox nodes:

This revised rule will ensure that SSH is only enabled for Proxmox nodes and not VMs. As we can see, in the previous example, when creating rules in the `Datacenter` zone, it is very important to think about the cascading effect of the `Datacenter` rules and how it can affect nodes and VMs. It is best to use the `Datacenter` zone rules for cluster-related traffic and not VMs in any nodes.

After we have created rules to allow SSH and the Proxmox GUI, we are ready to enable the `Datacenter`-wide **Firewall** through the **Options** menu. The following screenshot shows the menu with the **Firewall** now **Enabled**:

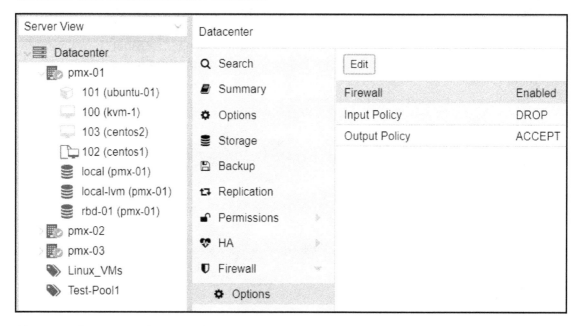

The preceding screenshot shows a policy that will drop all incoming traffic, but outgoing traffic will be permitted. To have a fully locked down and secured cluster, both policies should be set to **DROP**. The reason to set the **Output Policy** to **DROP** is to prevent malicious traffic leaving the network in the case of malware infection or there being any compromised devices within the internal network. Alternatively, in a multitenant environment, outgoing traffic should be firewalled. This way, we can control the type of traffic that can leave a VM. An example of traffic that should be denied would be ICMP or ping traffic, which will allow one VM to discover other devices in the network.

If both the inbound and outbound firewall rules are set to **DENY** or **DROP**, you will likely have to configure all the allowed traffic, even updates and common traffic. If you are implementing **DROP** for the **Input Policy** in an already established Proxmox cluster, make sure that you first create all the necessary rules for all VMs and nodes before enabling the `Datacenter`-wide firewall. Failure to do so will cause all VMs and nodes to drop connectivity.

# Creating aliases

Aliases make it simple to see what devices or group of devices are affected by a rule. We can create aliases to identify an IP address or a network. They are similar to an IPSet, but one alias only points to one IP address or network, whereas an IPSet holds multiple IP addresses or networks. For example, in a scenario where we have a Proxmox network as `172.16.2.0/24` and Ceph public network as `192.168.20.0/24`, we can create two aliases using the alias creation dialog box by clicking on **Add** from the **Alias** menu, as shown in the following screenshot:

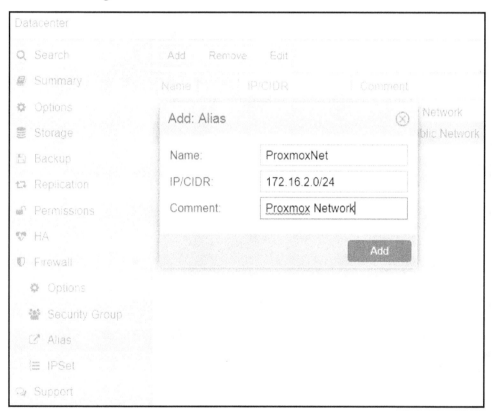

In the preceding screenshot, we created an alias named `ProxmoxNet` to identify the network `172.16.2.0/24`. Using the same dialog box, we will create another alias named `CephNet` for the IP subnet `192.168.20.0/24`. The following screenshot shows the **Alias** window with both aliases created:

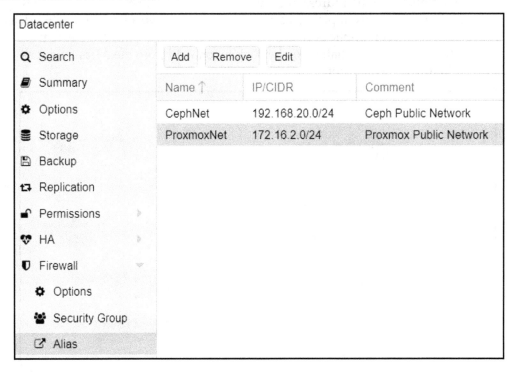

The advantage of having an alias is that whenever we create rules, we can use these aliases instead of typing in the entire IP address. This is especially useful when using IPv6. Since IPv6 addresses are quite long, we can create an alias to call the IP address in a rule whenever we need them.

This is also another way to identify a numeric IP address with text. Aliases are accessible through the drop-down list for both **Source** and **Destination** from the rules dialog box. The following screenshot shows the rule creation dialog box with the aliases in the drop-down list for **Source**:

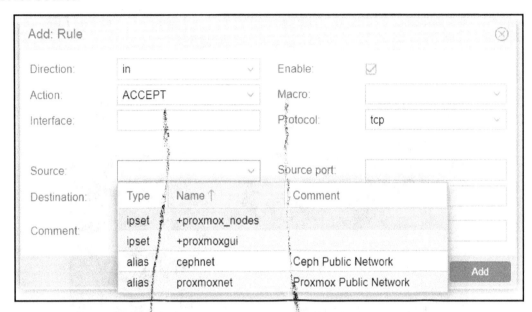

Aliases created in the Datacenter zone are useable throughout the cluster in both the host and VM zones.

# Configuring the Datacenter firewall through the CLI

The Proxmox firewall can also be managed entirely through the CLI by editing the firewall configuration and rules files directly. The content of the configuration and rule files are laid out in a very specific format. The following screenshot shows the /etc/pve/firewall/cluster.fw file of the Datacenter zone after adding rules from the previous section:

```
[OPTIONS]

enable: 1

[ALIASES]

CephNet 192.168.20.0/24 # Ceph Public Network
ProxmoxNet 172.16.2.0/24 # Proxmox Public Network

[IPSET proxmox_nodes]

172.16.2.1 # Node 1
172.16.2.2 # Node 2
172.16.2.3 # Node 3

[IPSET proxmoxgui]

10.0.0.10 # Office
172.16.0.10 # Home
192.168.0.10 # Lab

[RULES]

IN SSH(ACCEPT) -dest +proxmox_nodes # Allow SSH
IN ACCEPT -p tcp -dport 8006 # Proxmox GUI access from limited IP

[group webserver]

IN FTP(ACCEPT)
IN SSH(ACCEPT)
IN HTTP(ACCEPT)
IN HTTPS(ACCEPT)
```

As we can see, in the preceding screenshot, there are four segments in the firewall configuration file for the `Datacenter` zone. They are as follows:

```
[OPTIONS]
. . . . . . . .
[ALIASES]
. . . . . . . .
[IPSET <name>]
. . . . . . . .
[RULES]
. . . . . . . .
[group <name>]
. . . . . . . .
```

# [OPTIONS]

This area is used to enable or disable a `Datacenter`-wide firewall. Currently, our example cluster has the default input/output policy, which is set to drop all incoming traffic while allowing all outgoing traffic. If we were to change the input policy to accept all incoming traffic, then the [OPTIONS] segment would appear as follows:

```
[OPTIONS]
policy_in: ACCEPT
enable: 1
```

If due to firewall rules misconfiguration we locked ourselves out, we can disable the `Datacenter`-wide firewall using the following option on the console:

```
enable: 0
```

# [ALIASES]

This segment shows all the aliases created in the `Datacenter` zone. It shows the name of the alias and IP address or the network the alias belongs to. Each line is used for a separate alias entry.

# [IPSET <name>]

This segment clumps all IPSets created under the `Datacenter` zone. It shows the name of the IPSet and the IP addresses added in the set. In our example, we have two IPSets named `proxmox_nodes` and `proxmoxgui`.

# [RULES]

This segment contains all the firewall rules, one on each line. To disable any rule, we simply need to put a | in front of the rule and save the configuration file. In the preceding screenshot, the rule to allow ping is disabled in this way.

# [group <name>]

This segment clumps all the security groups created in the `Datacenter` zone. It shows the name of the security group and the rule added to the group. In the preceding screenshot, we can see that we created a security group named `webserver` and added macro rules in order to allow `HTTPS`, `HTTP`, `SSH`, and `FTP` traffic. We can also manually add rules in this segment by defining a protocol and port. For example, if we want to allow the TCP traffic to port `565` only from IP address `10.0.0.2`, we will add the following line of code to the `webserver` security group:

```
IN ACCEPT -source 10.0.0.2 -p tcp -dport 565
```

# Configuring a host-specific firewall

Any rules created in the host zone only apply to the node where the rule itself was created and the VMs in that host node. Rules for one node do not get replicated to the other nodes, although the rule files are stored in the Proxmox cluster filesystem. There are no options to create IPSet or security groups in the host-specific firewall option. We can only create firewall rules.

# Creating host firewall rules

Creating new rules for the host zone is identical to the rule creation process that we have already discussed in the *Configuring the data center-specific firewall* section earlier in this chapter. Besides creating rules from scratch, we can also assign predefined rules in the form of a security group to a node. We cannot create a new security group under the host **Firewall** menu, but we can assign it some predefined rules. For example, earlier in this chapter, we created a security group named `webserver`. If a Proxmox node is only going to host VMs used for web servers, then we can assign the security group `webserver` to that node, and all the rules will be cascaded into all the VMs in the host. Thus, we would save a lot of time by not having to create separate rules for each VM.

To open the dialog box to assign a security group, click on **Insert: Security Group** from the `Datacenter` | **Node** option. The following screenshot shows the dialog box with `webserver` selected from the **Security Group** drop-down list:

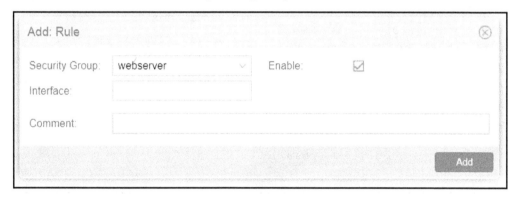

We have to ensure that we enable the rule by clicking on the checkbox, and then we need to click on **Add** to assign the security group. The following screenshot shows the rule added to the `pmx-01` node:

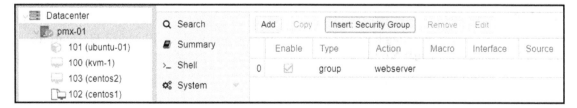

# Options for the host zone firewall

The Proxmox node firewall has several items under the **Options** tab. Most of the items can be left at their default values, as shown in the following screenshot. However, an understanding of this item will aid in combating security through the cluster. The following screenshot shows the **Option** items with default values for an unmodified Proxmox node:

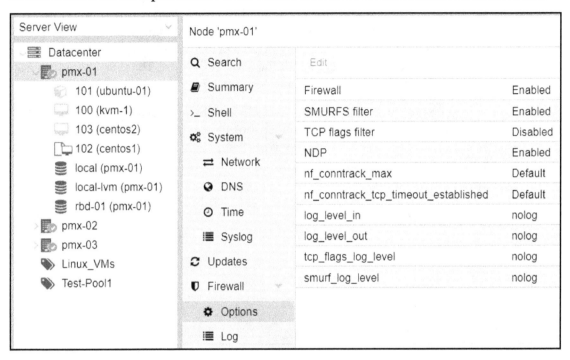

To change the settings of any option item, we need to select the line item, and then click on the **Edit** button.

## Enable a firewall

By default, all Proxmox nodes have the **Firewall** option enabled. To disable a **Firewall** for the node completely, select **No** for this option.

# The SMURFS filter

By default, the **SMURFS filter** is **Enabled**. By nature, Smurf is a **distributed denial-of-service (DDoS)** attack. In this attack, an attacker sends a very large number of ICMP data packets with the victim's spoofed IP address as the source, and it is broadcast to a network using the broadcast address. Generally, all network devices answer an ICMP ping. During a Smurf attack, the victim's device gets flooded by ICMP responses. If there are a large number of devices on the network, then the flooding becomes extreme, making the victimized device unresponsive. This is why this filter should remain enabled at all times.

# The TCP flags filter

In simple terms, TCP flags are control bits that indicate how TCP packets should be handled by the client. These control bits or indicators reside in the TCP header. There are a total of nine control bits with one bit for each flag. The full description of how exactly these TCP flags work is beyond the scope of this book since TCP is a vast subject of various complexities. Here, we will only see what those TCP flags are and how the Proxmox firewall handles TCP flag filtering. The following table is a summary of the TCP flags and their functions:

| TCP flag | Function |
|---|---|
| URG—1 bit | This indicates that the TCP packet is urgent. |
| ACK—1 bit | This indicates the acknowledgment field. After the initial SYN for all packets, they are usually followed by this flag. |
| PSD—1 bit | This flag asks for the buffer data to be pushed as soon as possible to the receiving side of the client application. |
| RST—1 bit | This flag indicates the TCP connection reset. |
| SYN—1 bit | This flag indicates a synchronized sequence number before initiating a TCP connection. Only the first packet that is sent from a source usually has this flag. |
| FIN—1 bit | This flag indicates the end of TCP packets. |

TCP flags are useful to detect and pinpoint oddly-behaved TCP packets and determine a possible intrusion. Arguments for TCP flag filtering are added to the firewall rules right after the -p syntax, as shown in the following code:

```
[RULES]
IN DROP -p tcp -tcp-flags SYN,ACK SYN -dport
```

 As of Proxmox VE 5.0, there are no options used to manually add TCP flags to filter through the GUI. We can add them through the CLI but this makes the rule disappear from the GUI.

By default, TCP flag filtering is disabled in the Proxmox VE. We can enable it to let the Proxmox firewall automatically filter odd packets with out-of-sync bits. All data packets traversing through the network have a uniform SYN behavior. Odd packets usually indicate that they are from a bad source.

## NDP

**Neighbor Discovery Protocol** (**NDP**), is an IPv6-specific option. Unlike IPv4, IPv6 does not use the ARP protocol, but uses **NDP** instead. **NDP** is also used for IPv6 auto configuration and advertising router data packets. By default, this option is enabled for both host- and VM-specific Proxmox firewalls. If you are not going to use IPv6 at all and have no future plans to do so, this option can be disabled.

## nf_conntrack_max

This value defines the maximum size of a netfilter connection tracking table. This table keeps a record of all live connections and deletes them when a connection is closed. By default, the size of this table is 65,536 bytes. While for most of the nodes, this is perfectly fine, for high-volume connection servers, such as DNS or web server, this table may become full quickly. For a Proxmox node, which holds lots of high-traffic VMs, this value needs to be increased. We can check the current value of nf_conntrack_max using the following command:

```
# sysctl -a | grep nf_conntrack_max
```

The following command will show you the number of current live connections in the node:

```
# sysctl -a | grep nf_conntrack_count
```

The following screenshot shows the connection count for our example node pmx-01:

```
root@pmx-01:~# sysctl -a | grep nf_conntrack_count
sysctl: reading key "net.ipv6.conf.all.stable_secret"
sysctl: reading key "net.ipv6.conf.default.stable_secret"
sysctl: reading key "net.ipv6.conf.ens18.stable_secret"
sysctl: reading key "net.ipv6.conf.ens19.stable_secret"
sysctl: reading key "net.ipv6.conf.ens20.stable_secret"
sysctl: reading key "net.ipv6.conf.lo.stable_secret"
sysctl: reading key "net.ipv6.conf.vmbr0.stable_secret"
net.netfilter.nf_conntrack_count = 79
root@pmx-01:~#
```

Note that if the tracking table is full due to many live connections, then the node will drop all new connection packets.

## nf_conntrack_tcp_timeout_established

This node only keeps track of the netfilter connections if they live. Dead connections are deleted automatically from the table. This deletion happens based on the set timeout period. The longer the timeout period, the longer the record of the connection will stay in the tracking table. The value of this option is in seconds. By default, the value is set to 4,32,000 seconds or 12 hours. We can check the current value using the following command:

```
# sysctl -a | grep nf_conntrack_tcp_timeout_established
```

By reducing this value, we can keep the tracking table lean which is faster for a high-traffic node. It should be noted here that lowering this value might also break long running idle TCP connections.

## log_level_in/out

A firewall is only as good as its logging capability. It is only by going through the log that we can see what is being blocked and what is not. Proxmox comes with a custom service named `pvefw-logger`, which is based on the netfilter logging daemon. The sole purpose of this service is to log a connection activity based on the set firewall rules. Through the firewall's **Options** tab, we can set logging at various levels of verbosity. There are eight levels of logging available for the iptable-based firewall. The following table shows the iptable logging levels and their availability in the Proxmox firewall:

| Log Level | Type | |
|-----------|------|--|
| Level 0 | Emergency | Available in Proxmox |
| Level 1 | Alert | Available in Proxmox |
| Level 2 | Critical | Available in Proxmox |
| Level 3 | Error | Available in Proxmox |
| Level 4 | Warning | Available in Proxmox |
| Level 5 | Notice | Not available in Proxmox |
| Level 6 | Info | Available in Proxmox |
| Level 7 | Debug | Available in Proxmox |

In addition to these levels, Proxmox also has the `nolog` option. This disables all logging for a resource. The log level info is used the most, as it logs all the good and bad connections. This way, we can see exactly what is being blocked and allowed. However, the info log level also creates many log entries in a very short period of time. As a good rule of thumb, always select some form of logging when enabling a firewall.

## tcp_flags_log_level

Similar to the standard log level, we can also enable different log levels for the TCP flags. If the **TCP flags filter** is not enabled, this will not produce any log entries. When enabled, we will see the **TCP flags filter** logged in the log window.

### smurf_log_level

Like the TCP flags log, this also shows log entries for Smurf attacks. This also follows various log levels.

# Configuring the host firewall through the CLI

We can also configure and manage the host zone firewall through the CLI. The firewall configuration file for the host is in /etc/pve/local/host.fw. The following screenshot shows the content of the host.fw file:

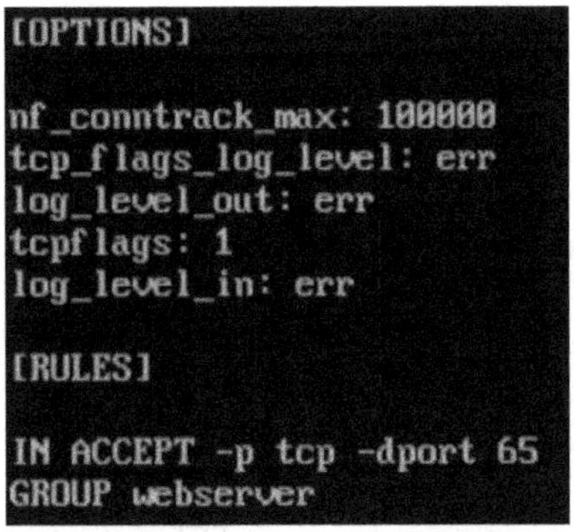

```
[OPTIONS]

nf_conntrack_max: 100000
tcp_flags_log_level: err
log_level_out: err
tcpflags: 1
log_level_in: err

[RULES]

IN ACCEPT -p tcp -dport 65
GROUP webserver
```

As we can see in the preceding screenshot, there are only two segments in the firewall configuration file for the host zone. They are as follows:

```
[OPTIONS]
 . . . . . . . .
[RULES]
 . . . . . . . .
```

The functions of these segments are exactly the same as the segments in the *Configuring the Datacenter firewall through the CLI* section earlier in this chapter. Note that there are no segments for security group or IPSet. This is because these features are not present in the host firewall zone.

# Configuring a VM-specific firewall

Rules created for a VM only apply to that particular virtual machine. Even when the virtual machine is moved to a different node, the firewall rule follows the VM throughout the cluster. There are no rules cascading from this zone. Under the VM firewall feature, we can create rules, aliases, and IPSets, but we cannot create a security group. The firewall management is the same for both the KVM virtual machines and LXC containers. We can go to the firewall feature of a VM by navigating to the VM | **Firewall** menu:

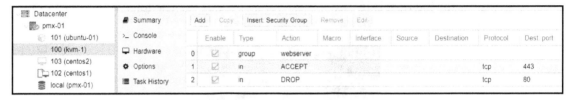

# Creating VM firewall rules

Creating new rules for a VM is identical to the rule creation process that we have already seen in the *Configuring the Datacenter firewall through the CLI* section earlier in this chapter. Besides creating rules from scratch, we can also assign predefined rules in the form of a security group to a VM. The preceding screenshot shows that our example VM has three firewall rules to allow standard web server and HTTPS traffic, but drop all HTTP or port 80 traffic.

# Creating aliases

An alias for a VM zone serves the same purpose as the alias for the Datacenter zone. The alias creation process is also identical to the *Configuring the Datacenter firewall through the CLI* section that we have seen earlier in this chapter. Aliases created under a VM stay with that particular VM only. An alias for one VM can be used in another VM.

# Creating IPSets

Like aliases for a VM, an IPSet created under a VM also stays with that particular VM. The IPSet creation process is identical to the IPSet for the Datacenter zone we have already seen in the *Configuring the Datacenter firewall through the CLI* section earlier in this chapter.

# Options for a VM zone firewall

All the option items under the VM zone **Options** menu are the same as items for the `Datacenter` and host zone already described, except for the **DHCP** and **MAC** filters. The following screenshot shows the **Options** items for our example VM `100 (kvm-1)`:

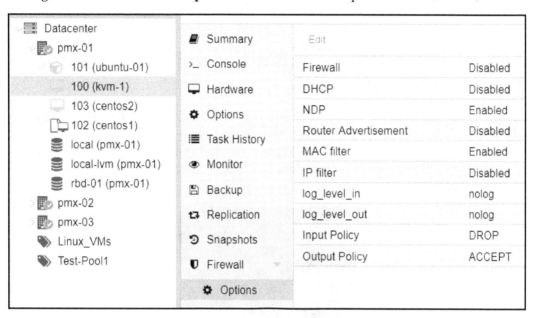

## Enable DHCP

This option is used for a VM that is configured as a DHCP server. A DHCP server uses the UDP ports `67` and `68` to complete IP requests from clients. Instead of manually opening these ports, we can enable this option to let all DHCP-related pass to and from the VM. By default, **DHCP** is **Disabled**.

## The MAC filter

When this option is **Enabled**, it prevents the VM user spoofing their own MAC address of the virtual network interface and sending out traffic. This filter will drop the packets from the spoofed MAC address. By default, this option is **Enabled**.

## Input/output policy

These options are to enable default firewall behavior for the virtual network interface. For example, if you select the policy to **DROP**, by default it will block all traffic. We will have to add rules to open required ports. By default, the **Input Policy** is to **DROP** all incoming traffic.

# Configuring a VM-specific firewall through the CLI

As with other firewall zones in Proxmox, we can also configure and manage a virtual machine-specific firewall through the CLI. The configuration file for each VM is in `/etc/pve/firewall/<vm_id>.fw`. All segments in the configuration file are the same as the `Datacenter` or host zone configuration. The following screenshot shows the content of a firewall configuration file for VM `100` (`kvm-1`):

# Integrating a Suricata IDS/IPS

The security protection of the Proxmox VE firewall can be further enhanced by configuring an intrusion detection and prevention system such as Suricata. It is a high-performance IDS/IPS engine that is able to protect a virtual machine by rejecting traffic that may be possible intrusions. Currently, Snort and Suricata are two open source mainstream IDS/IPS available, although there are a few others. One of the primary advantages of Suricata is that it is multithreaded, whereas Snort is single-threaded. Suricata is under rapid deployment and has gained popularity in a short amount of time.

By default, Suricata is not installed on a Proxmox node. It needs to be manually installed and configured. As of Proxmox VE 5.0, Suricata can only be used to protect a virtual machine and not any Proxmox host nodes.

 Do not try to manually download the Suricata package from any other source other than the Proxmox repository and install it on the Proxmox node. It may break the system. Always use the `apt-get` installer in Proxmox to install Suricata.

If you are new to Suricata, then visit the official Suricata site that will help you gain some knowledge of Suricata as an IDS/IPS:

`http://suricata-ids.org/`

# Installing/configuring Suricata

We can install Suricata in a Proxmox node using the following command:

```
# apt-get install suricata
```

After Suricata is installed, we have to load the netfilter queue subsystem's `nfnetlink_queue` module using the following command:

```
# modprobe nfnetlink
```

To ensure that this module gets loaded automatically whenever the node is rebooted, we need to add it to the `/etc/modules` file. The installer installs all the necessary files for Suricata, including Oinkmaster rules. All IDS/IPS engines are heavily dependent on rules. These rules are precompiled and prepackaged in rule files. Oinkmaster is a script that allows us to easily update and manage rules. It is mainly used by Snort but is also supported by Suricata. Without these rules, Suricata will not perform anything. Visit the official Snort site for information on rules at `https://www.snort.org/`.

There are no options to enable Suricata for a VM through the GUI. So, we have to manually enable it through the CLI by editing the VM firewall configuration file in `/etc/pve/firewall/<vm_id>.fw`. We need to add the following lines to the `[OPTIONS]` segment of the configuration file:

```
ips: 1
ips_queues: 0
```

The `ips_queues` option binds to a specific CPU queue of the virtual machine due to its multithreaded nature. Available queues that Suricata should listen to are defined in `/etc/default/suricata`, as follows:

```
NFQUEUE=0
```

The value is usually set based on the number of CPUs. For example, to use four CPU cores for Suricata, we can use the value 3 for `NFQUEUE`. The default value 0 indicates that we only use the first CPU, which is CPU 0.

Suricata will only work when listening on `NFQUEUE`. This is configured by default when Suricata is installed on a Proxmox node. All traffic that is only accepted by the Proxmox firewall gets passed to Suricata for inspection. All other dropped or rejected traffic does not get passed to Suricata. The Suricata configuration files are in `/etc/suricata/suricata-debian.yaml`. The default configuration should work in most cases.

It is easier to write your own custom rules for Suricata than it is for Snort. You can refer to the excellent documentation on how to learn to write your own rules for Suricata at the following link:

`https://redmine.openinfosecfoundation.org/projects/suricata/wiki/Suricata_Rules`

We can start the Suricata service by running the following command:

```
# systemctl start suricata
```

The following screenshot shows the command to check the status of the Suricata service and displays the status information:

```
root@pmx-01:~# systemctl status suricata
● suricata.service - Suricata IDS/IDP daemon
   Loaded: loaded (/lib/systemd/system/suricata.service; disabled; vendor preset: enabled)
   Active: active (running) since Sat 2017-08-19 09:37:17 MDT; 10min ago
     Docs: man:suricata(8)
           man:suricatasc(8)
           https://redmine.openinfosecfoundation.org/projects/suricata/wiki
 Main PID: 3912 (Suricata-Main)
    Tasks: 8 (limit: 4915)
   CGroup: /system.slice/suricata.service
           └─3912 /usr/bin/suricata -D --af-packet -c /etc/suricata/suricata.yaml --pidfile /var/run/suricata.pid
```

# Limitations of Suricata in Proxmox

As mentioned earlier, there are no GUI options for Suricata in Proxmox. All configurations are done through the CLI. Without a proper knowledge of IDS/IPS rules, it is very difficult to create rules based on their own environments. Suricata cannot be used to protect any Proxmox nodes, only virtual machines. This limitation may be due to the fact that IDS/IPS can frequently consume a large amount of CPU resources. While for a dedicated firewall appliance, this may or may not be an issue, for a hypervisor, where the CPU is shared between the hypervisor itself and hosted virtual machines, this could be fatal due to CPU overconsumption.

There are no dedicated log view options for Suricata as there are for the Proxmox firewall through the GUI. All Suricata logs are stored in the /var/log/Suricata directory by default. However, we can pass Suricata IPS logs to syslog by changing the configuration file in /etc/pve/suricata/suricata-debian.yaml. We have to make the following changes in order to pass the Suricata logs to syslog:

```
# a line based alerts log similar to fast.log into syslog
syslog:
enabled: yes
identity: "Suricata"
level: Info
```

There are a few more options available to log the output in the same configuration file. Some Proxmox users try to pass Suricata logs to a third-party solution using Logstash and Kibana from Elastic (www.elastic.co). Suricata or any other IPS is a complex task to manage on a day-to-day basis. Suricata is still in infancy in Proxmox. Over time, it may be integrated with the GUI for easier management. But for now, using a dedicated firewall appliance, such as pfSense, Untangle, ClearOS, or any other open source firewall may be a better option to integrate Suricata in a network. Suricata is fully supported in pfSense with a large amount of manageable features, all through the pfSense GUI dashboard. Implementing an IDS/IPS system in a network is not optional but should be made mandatory to protect it from any sort of intrusion.

# Summary

In this chapter, we learned about one of the most powerful features of Proxmox, the built-in firewall. We learned what it is and how to implement it to protect the entire cluster, Proxmox host nodes, and virtual machines. We learned how to manage the firewall rules and configuration using both the GUI and CLI. Proxmox adds security where it is needed the most. By leveraging a flexible and granular firewall protection at the hypervisor level, we are now able to have a better-secured cluster. This is not to say that firewall policies are not needed internally in each VM, but having a firewall built into the hypervisor offers an extra layer of protection from an infrastructural point of view.

In the next chapter, we are going to learn about the Proxmox VE High Availability feature for VMs, which has been completely redesigned from the ground up. The new changes brought higher stability while making the management and configuration a much simpler task.

# 10
# Proxmox High Availability

In this chapter, we are going to see one of the most prominent features that make Proxmox an enterprise-class hypervisor. Proxmox VE **High Availability** (**HA**) allows the cluster to move or migrate virtual machines from a faulty node to a healthy node without any user interaction. We will take a look at the following topics:

- Understanding HA
- Requirements for HA
- Configuring Proxmox HA
- Configuring the Proxmox HA simulator

## Understanding HA

HA is a combination of components and configurations that allows continuous operation of a computational environment. Basically, it means that even when unattended server hardware goes bad in a live environment, HA can manage the remaining servers on its own and keep a virtual environment running by automatically moving or migrating virtual machines from one node to another, while minimizing downtime as little as possible. It should be noted here that Proxmox HA does not provide *zero* downtime migration of VMs. When a node with VM goes down hard, for obvious reason the VM becomes fully inaccessible. What Proxmox HA does when that happens is, it automatically moves the VM configuration files to member nodes and starts. A properly configured HA should require very little actual user interaction during a hardware failure. Without HA in place, all nodes will require constant monitoring by a network manager in order to manually move virtual machines to healthy nodes when a node goes bad.

In a small environment, manually moving VMs is not a major issue, but in a large environment with hundreds of virtual machines and nodes, constant monitoring can be very time consuming. Although there can be monitoring software in place to automatically alert administrators for any node failure, without HA, the administrator will have to manually move or migrate any virtual machine from a faulty node. This can cause longer downtime due to the network staff's response time. That's where the Proxmox HA feature comes in. HA takes operator intervention out of the equation by simply moving or migrating virtual machines to a node as soon as server hardware failure occurs.

# HA in Proxmox

To set up functional HA in Proxmox, it is important to have all the virtual machines on shared storage. It is crucial to understand that Proxmox HA only handles Proxmox nodes and virtual machines within the Proxmox cluster. These HA features are not to be confused with shared storage redundancy, which Proxmox can utilize for its HA deployment. High availability in shared storage is just as important as Proxmox VMs' HA. A third-party shared storage can provide its own HA features. So both the Proxmox cluster and shared storage will need to be configured to provide a truly highly available environment. It is beyond the scope of this book to go into the details of high-availability storage.

There can be levels of redundancy in a Proxmox computing node, such as the use of RAID, redundant power supplies, aggregated network links, or bonds. HA in Proxmox is not a replacement for any of these layers. It just facilitates redundancy features for virtual machines to keep running during a node failure. Proxmox uses a software stack called HA-manager to provide fully automated high availability from Proxmox virtual environments.

It should be noted that in a Proxmox node, a reboot due to an applied update will cause all HA-enabled virtual machines to shut down and move to the next available Proxmox node and restart. In such a situation, it may be necessary to manually live-migrate virtual machines first before rebooting the node. But by using a service such as Kernel Care from CloudLinux, we can mitigate reboots due to update because Kernel Care applies security updates without ever needing to reboot a node. Find out more about this service from `https://www.cloudlinux.com/all-products/product-overview/kernelcare`.

# How Proxmox HA works

When a node becomes unresponsive for various reasons, Proxmox HA waits for 60 seconds before fencing the faulty node. Fencing prevents cluster services from coming online during that time. Then, HA moves the VM to the next available node in the HA member group. As of Proxmox VE 5.0, LXC containers cannot be live-migrated. So, HA will stop all LXC containers and then move them to the next node. Even if the node with VMs is still powered up but loses network connectivity, Proxmox VA will try to move all VMs out of the node to a different node.

Once the faulty node comes back online, however, HA will not automatically move the VMs back to the original node. This must be done manually. But a VM can only be moved manually if HA is disabled for that VM. So we have to disable HA first and then move to the original node and enable HA on the VM again. As we can see, Proxmox HA likes to manage everything on its own, although it adds little annoyances to manually performing certain functions. HA is focused on maintaining uptime, which it does suitably. Later in this chapter, we will see how to configure HA for virtual machines.

# Requirements for HA setup

In Proxmox 4.0, the HA feature has been completely redesigned from the ground up, making it much simpler to configure and use. There are a few requirements that the virtual environment must meet before configuring Proxmox HA. They are as follows:

- At least three nodes
- Shared storage
- Fencing

# At least three nodes

HA must be configured in a cluster with a minimum of three nodes because with three nodes or more, achieving a quorum is possible. Quorum is the minimum number of votes required for Proxmox cluster operation. This minimum number is the total vote by a majority of the nodes. For example, in a cluster of three Proxmox nodes, a minimum vote of two Proxmox nodes is required to form a quorum. In a cluster with eight nodes, a minimum vote of five Proxmox nodes is required to form a quorum. With just two nodes, the ratio of votes will always be 1:1, so no quorum is possible.

# Shared storage

During a node failure, VM configuration files are moved to the next member node in the HA and auto started. Note that this migration applies to the configuration files only and not the virtual disk image. A VM cannot be started by HA when the disk image is not stored on shared storage. When a VM is stored locally, then HA will only move the configuration file and will be unable to move the disk image. This will produce error when HA tries to auto start the VM.

 Do not try to enable HA for any locally stored VM. The HA will forcefully move the VM configuration file and not move the location of the disk image.

# Fencing

Fencing is a concept of isolating a node or its resources during node failure so that other nodes cannot access the same resources, putting them at risk of data corruption. In Proxmox, fencing prevents multiple nodes from running on the same virtual machine or cluster-specific services. Fencing ensures data integrity during a node failure by preventing all nodes from running on the same virtual machine or cluster services at the same time.

As of Proxmox VE 5.0, a separate *fencing* device used to configure Proxmox HA is no longer required. Fencing now uses a hardware-based watchdog or a Linux softdog. A Linux softdog is a software version of a traditional watchdog. Most modern server BIOSes have the watchdog functionality, but it is normally disabled. When enabled, this will reboot server nodes after a certain period of inactivity. Proxmox HA will always check whether there is a hardware watchdog, and if not, it will automatically use a softdog. The use of a softdog now allows HA to be implemented in a nested virtual environment. This is helpful to set up a virtualized Proxmox environment to learn and test Proxmox HA without effecting changes on the main systems.

# BIOS power-on feature

Before we set up fencing and Proxmox HA, we have to make sure that nodes can boot immediately after a power cycle or power loss. Usually, this feature is disabled. The following screenshot shows this BIOS feature:

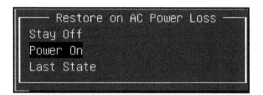

 It is important that the BIOS power on functionality be tested and verified. To do so, unplug the power cord, then plug it back again to see whether the node powers up. Without this feature enabled, the node will not be able to auto boot or power cycle using Proxmox HA fencing.

# Configuring Proxmox HA

Thanks to the new version of HA in Proxmox, all configuration of Proxmox HA can be done from the GUI. The HA feature is available by navigating to `Datacenter` | **HA**. This is the menu where we will perform all HA-related configuration and management. The following screenshot shows the Proxmox HA management interface:

# The HA menu

The HA menu is divided into two parts and two submenus where we can perform all configuration and management tasks.

# Status

The **Status** shows the cluster-wide quorum formation for the HA to function properly and the status of member nodes configured in HA. A clean-installed Proxmox cluster will show only one line item for a healthy quorum. Once the new member nodes are added to the HA configuration, this status menu will show running states of all the nodes and the virtual machines that have HA enabled.

# The Resources menu

This is the menu where we enable HA for a virtual machine or container. Click on **Add** to open the VM resource dialog box. The following screenshot shows that we are configuring our example VM 100 with the HA feature:

**Max. Restart** and **Max. Relocate** are two new options added to the HA resource-adding dialog box. The value for **Max. Restart** is the number of times Proxmox HA will try to restart services and/or the VM after migrating should any failure occur. The **Max. Relocate** value is to define the number of times HA will try to relocate VM services to another node before quitting.

**Request State** is a drop-down menu to define what action HA should take after the VM is migrated to another node during a failure. We can select **started** to start the VM after migration, **stopped** to migrate the VM but not start, and **disabled** to disable the HA feature for the VM. This is useful when we want to temporarily disable the resource and we may use it in future.

After adding a VM into HA, we may see a number of error messages showing failure to enable HA on that VM. The following screenshot shows some example errors we may encounter after adding VM 100 into the HA:

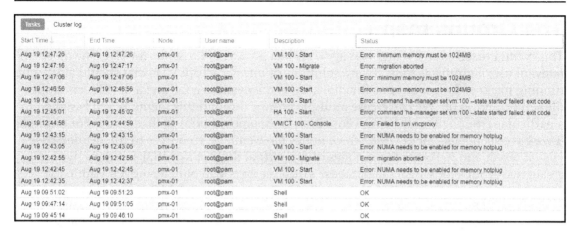

| Start Time ↓ | End Time | Node | User name | Description | Status |
|---|---|---|---|---|---|
| Aug 19 12:47:26 | Aug 19 12:47:26 | pmx-01 | root@pam | VM 100 - Start | Error: minimum memory must be 1024MB |
| Aug 19 12:47:16 | Aug 19 12:47:17 | pmx-01 | root@pam | VM 100 - Migrate | Error: migration aborted |
| Aug 19 12:47:06 | Aug 19 12:47:06 | pmx-01 | root@pam | VM 100 - Start | Error: minimum memory must be 1024MB |
| Aug 19 12:46:56 | Aug 19 12:46:56 | pmx-01 | root@pam | VM 100 - Start | Error: minimum memory must be 1024MB |
| Aug 19 12:45:53 | Aug 19 12:45:54 | pmx-01 | root@pam | HA 100 - Start | Error: command 'ha-manager set vm:100 --state started' failed: exit code .. |
| Aug 19 12:45:01 | Aug 19 12:45:02 | pmx-01 | root@pam | HA 100 - Start | Error: command 'ha-manager set vm:100 --state started' failed: exit code .. |
| Aug 19 12:44:58 | Aug 19 12:44:59 | pmx-01 | root@pam | VM/CT 100 - Console | Error: Failed to run vncproxy |
| Aug 19 12:43:15 | Aug 19 12:43:15 | pmx-01 | root@pam | VM 100 - Start | Error: NUMA needs to be enabled for memory hotplug |
| Aug 19 12:43:05 | Aug 19 12:43:05 | pmx-01 | root@pam | VM 100 - Start | Error: NUMA needs to be enabled for memory hotplug |
| Aug 19 12:42:55 | Aug 19 12:42:56 | pmx-01 | root@pam | VM 100 - Migrate | Error: migration aborted |
| Aug 19 12:42:45 | Aug 19 12:42:45 | pmx-01 | root@pam | VM 100 - Start | Error: NUMA needs to be enabled for memory hotplug |
| Aug 19 12:42:35 | Aug 19 12:42:37 | pmx-01 | root@pam | VM 100 - Start | Error: NUMA needs to be enabled for memory hotplug |
| Aug 19 09:51:02 | Aug 19 09:51:23 | pmx-01 | root@pam | Shell | OK |
| Aug 19 09:47:14 | Aug 19 09:51:05 | pmx-01 | root@pam | Shell | OK |
| Aug 19 09:45:14 | Aug 19 09:46:10 | pmx-01 | root@pam | Shell | OK |

From the errors we can see that to enable HA for a VM, there are certain criteria that need to be met. For example, NUMA must be enabled and the VM memory allocation must be at least 1024 MB. The following screenshot shows the **Resources** menu with the example vm 100 assigned to the HA group after we enabled NUMA and allocated 1024 MB of memory:

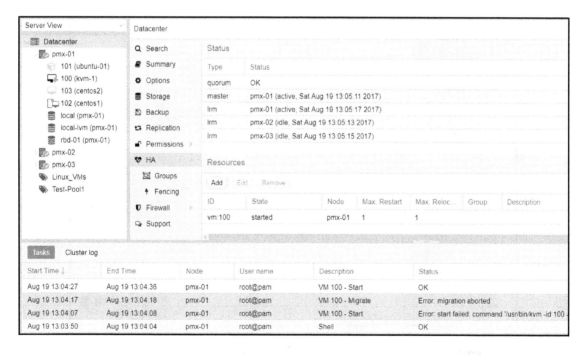

# The Groups menu

This menu is used to create and manage different groups of Proxmox for HA. The most relevant use of groups is for software solutions or infrastructure VMs that should always be running together for continuous functionality in the event of a failure: a domain controller, file server, and so on. We can create multiple groups through this menu. A VM assigned to a particular group will only be moved within the member nodes in that group. For example, if we have six nodes, out of which three nodes have enough resources to run the database virtual server and the other three nodes to run virtual desktops or VDI solutions, we can create two groups for which the database virtual servers will only be moved within the nodes that we have assigned for that group. This ensures that a VM is moved to a correct node that will be able to run the VMs. To open the group-creation dialog box, simply click on **Create** in the **Groups** submenu. The following screenshot shows the groups dialog box for our example group named Pmx_HA_Test:

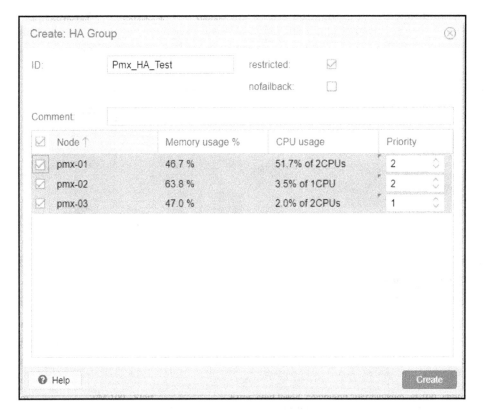

The following are the items available in the **HA Group** dialog box.

# ID

This is a textbox used to enter a name for the **HA Group**. The **ID** string can be alphanumeric text with only underscore (_) as the special character.

 Note that once we create a group, we cannot change the group name. We will have to delete the group and create a new one with a proper ID if we need to change the group name.

# Node

This is a list of all the Proxmox nodes in the cluster. We can select multiple nodes in the list. In order to create the group, we need to select at least one node. Unlike the **ID** textbox, we can change the assigned member nodes for the group even after the group has been created.

# The restricted checkbox

This is a checkbox used to allow VMs to be moved by Proxmox HA only within the available member nodes in the HA group. If there are no available member nodes, then the VMs will be stopped automatically. This option is not enabled by default.

# The nofailback checkbox

This is also a checkbox used to prevent the group from automatic failback when a new node joins the cluster. This is not enabled by default. Unless there is a strict requirement, this option should not be enabled. One scenario of using this is when an administrator is trying to diagnose a node or network failure. By enabling this option, we can prevent recovered VMs or services from moving back into the original node.

The following screenshot shows the **Groups** submenu interface with our example group created:

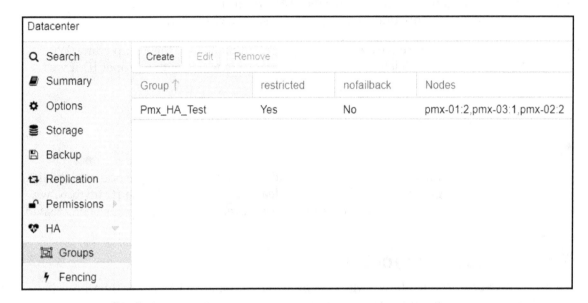

At first glance, using groups may seem like just another layer of complexity, but proper use of groups really can help us create a highly complex automated *administrator*. Groups allow us to create multiple layers of failover, bind certain services to specific nodes, and distribute VMs to specific nodes to name a few. Let's look at the following scenario to better understand how groups can be used in a complex environment.

For this scenario, let's assume that this is a three-node Proxmox cluster where node #1 is powerful enough to run all VMs, whereas node #2 is powerful enough to run half and node #3 only a handful of VMs. In this scenario, creating just one group will try to move all VMs to one of the nodes, resulting in half of the VMs remaining powered off due to shortage of resources. But if we create two groups, one to move half of the VMs to node #2 and another group to move the remaining VMs to node #3, we can easily create an HA strategy to handle node failure automatically.

Another scenario is to use groups to create different HAs for different VM groups. For example, we can have an HA group only to handle SQL database cluster VMs whereas another group will handle all VMs functioning as file servers. Due to the differing workloads of database and file servers, it may be more efficient to run them on specific groups of Proxmox nodes.

# The Fencing menu

As of Proxmox 5.0, there is no use for this menu. It only displays the fencing device being used by Proxmox HA. Proxmox uses a hardware watchdog and software Linux watchdog for fencing. The following screenshot shows the **Fencing** menu interface:

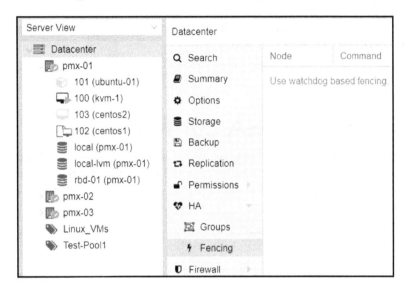

At this point, we've created a Proxmox HA group and added a VM to the group to be managed by HA. Our VM is currently in the pmx-01 node and is ready to be managed by Proxmox HA. The following screenshot shows the **Status** menu of HA:

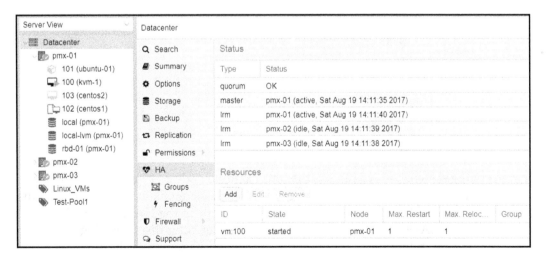

As we can see, in the preceding screenshot, the **Status** menu shows the current state of the entire HA feature. For our example cluster, it shows the following vital information:

- Cluster quorum is established
- The master node pmx-01 of the HA group is active and the timestamp of the last heartbeat has been checked
- All the three member nodes of the HA group are active and the timestamp of the last heartbeat has been checked
- The VM service for 100 has been started on the first node, pmx-01

# Testing Proxmox HA configuration

To test whether the HA is really working, we will disconnect network connectivity for the node pmx-01 and observe the **Status** window for HA changes. The **Status** window displays the status of resources in real time. The following screenshot shows the **HA** status after interrupting network connectivity:

In the preceding screenshot, we can see that our example node pm4-1 is no longer connected to the cluster, and HA does not get any acknowledgement from the node. After 60 seconds, Proxmox HA promotes the next available node in the HA group as the master and migrates any HA-enabled VM. In our example cluster, after disconnecting node pmx-01, the HA migrating the VM is as shown in the following screenshot:

After the VM resources are fenced, in the next stage, the VM is fully stopped. Since the node itself is down, the VM cannot be live-migrated because the memory state of the running VM cannot be retrieved from the down node. After the VM is stopped, it is moved to the next available node in the HA group and started automatically. The following screenshot shows that the VM has now moved to node pmx-02 and has been started:

After the failed node comes back online, the VM will continue to run on the node it was migrated to by HA. From the **Status** interface we can see that the second node pmx-02 is now active while the other two nodes are idle:

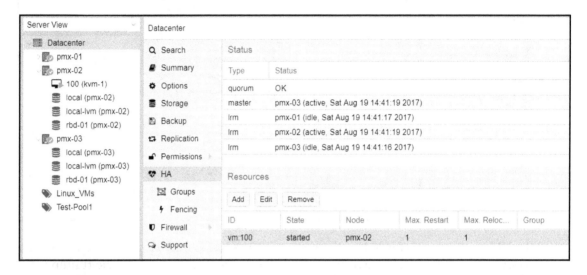

It is possible that Proxmox HA will produce an error during the automatic VM move for various reasons. After any error, Proxmox HA will make several attempts with the *restart* and *relocate* policy to recover from the error. If all attempts fail, Proxmox HA puts the resource in the error state and will not perform any automated tasks for it. For this reason, even after the error has been addressed and fixed, HA will not automatically start the VM. We will manually have to start it. This is one of the unintended side effects of enabling Proxmox HA where it may not behave as expected after an error has occurred.

If the VM is automatically moved after a node failure and then restarted on a new node, this completes the entire process of the Proxmox HA configuration.

# The Proxmox HA simulator

Although Proxmox HA has become far easier to configure and manage, it is still a complex topic to grasp. With the use of software-based watchdogs, it is entirely possible to configure, test, and learn Proxmox HA in a virtualized environment before implementing it in a production cluster. There is also a simulator for Proxmox HA that we can use to see HA in action without setting up any clusters. The simulator allows us to see the HA configuration in action and see how the states change at different stages.

# Configuring the Proxmox HA simulator

The Proxmox HA simulator is not shipped with the distribution and needs to be manually installed. Along with the simulator package, we also need xorg and xuath because the simulator requires X11 redirection, which is also known as X11 forwarding. We can use the following commands to install the packages:

```
# apt-get install pve-ha-simulator
# apt-get install xorg
# apt-get install xauth
```

We can access the simulator from both Linux and Windows operating systems. If we log in from Linux, use the standard SSH command with the -Y option, as shown in the following command:

```
# ssh root@<pmx_node> -Y
```

For Windows, we can use an advanced terminal, such as MobaXterm, which can be downloaded from the following link:

http://mobaxterm.mobatek.net/

After we access the Proxmox node through Linux or Windows, we need to create a directory, which will be used as the working data directory for the simulator. After the directory is created, we can run the simulator, pointing it to the working directory. The following screenshot shows the SSH console with the directory created and simulator started using the MobaXterm program:

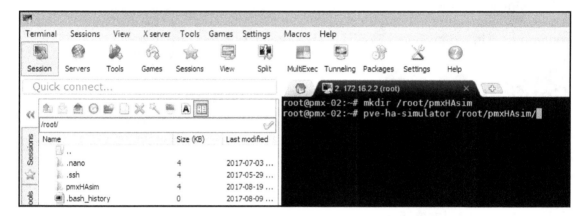

After the command is executed, the Proxmox HA simulator is started in a graphical interface, as shown in the following screenshot:

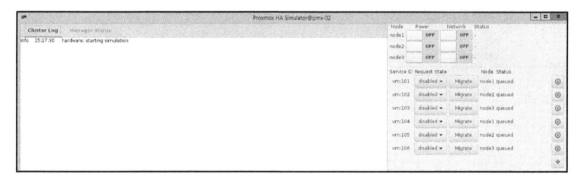

As we can see, in the preceding screenshot, the simulator provides a three-node HA setup with two VMs per node. We can simulate a node or network failure using the **Power** or **Network** buttons and watch HA in action. Before HA takes action, we have to enable it for each VM. We will see that as various HA states change, the configuration entries of the HA also change in real time. This simulator will aid in understanding Proxmox HA better through practice. The cluster log shows line-by-line info as you try and test different HA scenarios.

# Summary

In this chapter, we learned about the different aspects of the recently redesigned and enhanced Proxmox HA feature and how it can benefit a virtual environment. By leveraging HA, we can automate the response to a failure by auto-migrating VMs, thus reducing downtime during node power failure or network failure. We explained the requirements the infrastructure must meet in order to implement a fully functional HA feature. We walked through the process of HA configuration and finally tested HA by simulating device failure. We also learned how to install and use the Proxmox HA simulator to see HA in action without setting up any clusters.

Due to the nature of Proxmox HA, it is highly recommended you test this feature to its full extent before diving into implementing it for production clusters. HA can limit user interaction during some operations. The need for HA should be evaluated and, if used, it should be thoroughly tested before being implemented in a production environment. It is also quite important to group and size the HA solution properly. If the nodes cannot handle the load of virtual machines that HA requires, the entire solution could be at risk when a failure occurs, compounding the issue.

In the next chapter, we are going to see the effectiveness of a good network monitoring system and how to implement one to monitor a Proxmox environment.

# 11
# Monitoring the Proxmox Cluster

Monitoring a network environment of any size is mandatory to ensure healthy operation and timely responses to any issues. In this chapter, we will see how to monitor and configure notifications, so that when something goes wrong in the cluster, we know about it right away and can take necessary actions. We will cover the following topics in this chapter:

- An introduction to monitoring
- Proxmox built-in monitoring
- Zabbix as a monitoring solution
- Configuring the disk health notification
- Configuring SNMP in Proxmox
- Monitoring the Proxmox cluster with Zabbix

## An introduction to monitoring

In a network of any size, it is only a matter of time before an issue arises due to intentional or unintentional circumstances. The root cause of an issue could be hardware failures, software issues, human errors, or just about any other environmental factor that causes loss of network or data. Network monitoring is a practice in which an administrator checks the pulse of the network components in a network environment.

There is no system to monitor everything. A good monitoring system is usually put together with various tools and some types of notification options to send alerts automatically. The Proxmox cluster is a sum of switches, network cables, physical nodes acting as hosts, and virtual machines. A monitoring system should be able to monitor all of these components and automatically send notifications via a medium, such as an email or SMS, to responsible parties. There are wide ranges of network monitoring tools available today, such as Icinga, Zabbix, Nagios, OpenNMS, Pandora FMS, and Zenoss. There are many more options, both paid and open source. In this chapter, we will see how to use Zabbix to monitor the Proxmox cluster. Zabbix has a user-friendly GUI, graphing ability, and many more features out of the box. It is very easy to learn, for novice and network professionals alike. Once Zabbix is installed, all the configuration and monitoring can be done through the GUI.

A monitoring node should be a standalone reliable machine. For learning and testing purposes, it can be set up as a virtual machine. However, to monitor a production-level cluster, a separate node outside the main cluster is an ideal solution. This will ensure that even if the internal network is down, the monitoring system can still send out notifications.

# Proxmox built-in monitoring

Proxmox has limited monitoring capabilities built into the GUI to monitor the health of a cluster and gather real-time data on various resources. A visually appealing representation of data makes it easily understandable while gathering particular data through just a few clicks. Each separate entity comes with its own status page to monitor various aspects of the cluster.

## Datacenter Status

From this **Status** page, we can gather critical data at a glance, such as whether a node is online or offline, total cluster storage, number of virtual machines, and so on. The following screenshot shows the **Status** page of a production cluster. The **Status** page can be accessed through the Datacenter | **Summary** menu:

As shown in the previous screenshot, from the `Datacenter` | **Summary** page we can see the entire cluster status at a glance. The **Health** shows the current state of the Proxmox cluster. It shows the name of the cluster, the quorum presence, and the total number of online and offline Proxmox member nodes. When there is a cluster-related issue, we can quickly check the cluster status here.

The **Guests** section shows the total number of KVM and LXC virtual machines **Running** and **Stopped** in the cluster.

The **Resources** section shows the amount of cluster-wide available resources, such as **CPU**, **Memory**, and **Storage** space. It also shows resources used as a percentage. The **CPU** and **Memory** count is the total CPU cores and memory of all Proxmox nodes in the cluster. The **Storage** is the total of all attached storage, including the local storage of all nodes and any shared storage node attached to the cluster.

The **Nodes** section shows a list of all cluster nodes. We can sort this list by clicking on any heading, such as **Server Address**, **CPU usage**, and so on. In the previous screenshot, the list was sorted by **Server Address** in ascending order.

# Node Status

The **Status** page shows node-specific data only. Proxmox comes with built-in RRD-based graphs to show the historical resource usage and performance data up to 1 year previously. Using this tool, we can analyze the performance trend of a resource over a period of time. All consumption and performance data is under the **Summary** tab menu for both Proxmox nodes and virtual machines. We can view data on a per hour, day, week, and year basis. The following screenshot shows the **Summary** page of the node `pmx-01` with the drop-down list to select data for a period:

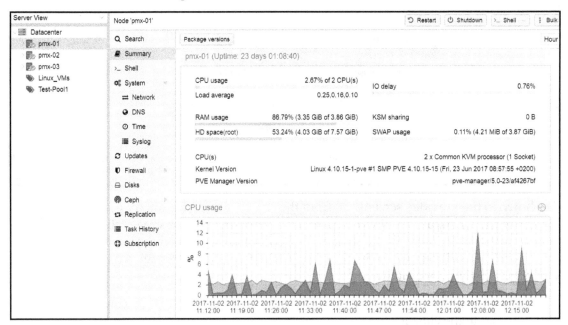

There are also ways to display a list of all the nodes and virtual machines in the cluster and sort them by consumption to get quick information on the highest or lowest resource consuming entity. We can see the list by navigating to `Datacenter` I **Search**. The following screenshot shows the list of Proxmox nodes and virtual machines of a production cluster, sorted by the highest memory consuming entity:

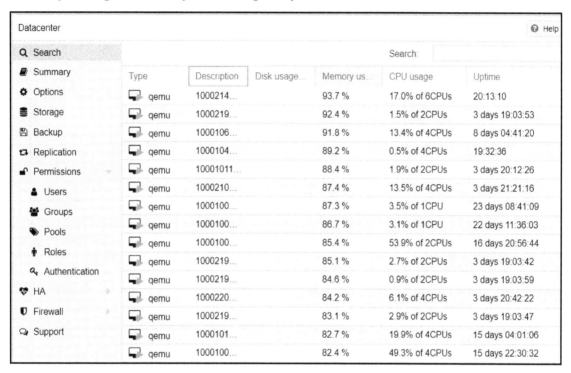

| Type | Description | Disk usage... | Memory us... | CPU usage | Uptime |
|------|-------------|---------------|--------------|-----------|--------|
| qemu | 1000214... | | 93.7 % | 17.0% of 6CPUs | 20:13:10 |
| qemu | 1000219... | | 92.4 % | 1.5% of 2CPUs | 3 days 19:03:53 |
| qemu | 1000106... | | 91.8 % | 13.4% of 4CPUs | 8 days 04:41:20 |
| qemu | 1000104... | | 89.2 % | 0.5% of 4CPUs | 19:32:36 |
| qemu | 10001011... | | 88.4 % | 1.9% of 2CPUs | 3 days 20:12:26 |
| qemu | 1000210... | | 87.4 % | 13.5% of 4CPUs | 3 days 21:21:16 |
| qemu | 1000100... | | 87.3 % | 3.5% of 1CPU | 23 days 08:41:09 |
| qemu | 1000100... | | 86.7 % | 3.1% of 1CPU | 22 days 11:36:03 |
| qemu | 1000100... | | 85.4 % | 53.9% of 2CPUs | 16 days 20:56:44 |
| qemu | 1000219... | | 85.1 % | 2.7% of 2CPUs | 3 days 19:03:42 |
| qemu | 1000219... | | 84.6 % | 0.9% of 2CPUs | 3 days 19:03:59 |
| qemu | 1000220... | | 84.2 % | 6.1% of 4CPUs | 3 days 20:42:22 |
| qemu | 1000219... | | 83.1 % | 2.9% of 2CPUs | 3 days 19:03:47 |
| qemu | 1000101... | | 82.7 % | 19.9% of 4CPUs | 15 days 04:01:06 |
| qemu | 1000100... | | 82.4 % | 49.3% of 4CPUs | 15 days 22:30:32 |

We can sort this list by **Type**, **Description**, **Disk usage %**, **Memory usage %**, **CPU usage**, and **Uptime** by clicking on the column header. There is no historical data in this list. It only shows the resource consumption in real time.

We can leverage S.M.A.R.T. for disk drives to receive automated emails about the Proxmox node when there are any major issues occurring in any disk drives in the node. For this, we will need to install S.M.A.R.T. monitor tools, using the following command:

```
# apt-get install smartmontools
```

Make sure that you install this in all the Proxmox nodes in the cluster. There is no other configuration needed to receive the email, except ensuring that the correct email address is entered for the root user in Proxmox.

We can check the correctness of the email address from the user details dialog box in the `Datacenter` | **Users** menu, as shown in the following screenshot:

Whenever there is a major issue in any disk drive in the Proxmox node, it will send out an automated email with the name of the node where the issue originated and the nature of the failures or issues for the disk drive. The email also shows the details of the drive itself, such as the serial number and the device ID of the drive. The following screenshot shows a sample of an email received from the node `pm4-1` with the sector error for the device `/dev/sda`, with the serial number `V1FA516P`:

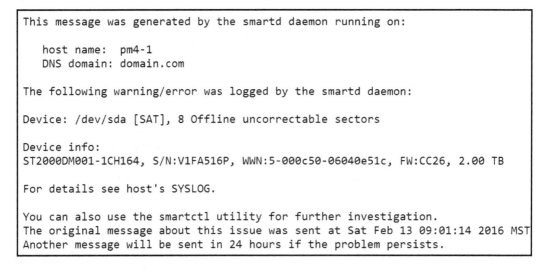

If the same error continues to occur, the Proxmox node will send this email every 24 hours. Based on the information provided in the email, we can pinpoint the drive and replace it if necessary.

As we can see, Proxmox really does not have a robust monitoring system, and it's very unlikely it ever will. Its strength lies in being a great hypervisor and not a monitoring system. However, we can easily fill the gap using a third-party monitoring system, such as Zabbix.

# Zabbix as a monitoring solution

Zabbix was released in 2004 and is a robust web-based network monitoring tool capable of monitoring many hundreds of hosts and running thousands of checks per host at any set time. Zabbix is completely open source and does not have enterprise or paid versions. Zabbix takes just a few minutes to install, even by a beginner, and it can be fully configured through a web-based interface. The following screenshot shows the Zabbix 3.0 dashboard after logging in through the web GUI:

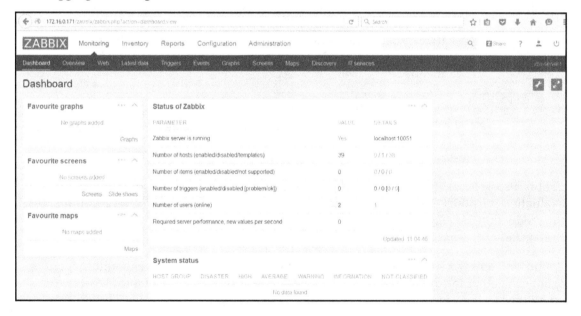

Zabbix has a very active community and many downloadable templates used to monitor a variety of devices or equipment. It is also comparatively easier to create our own custom Zabbix template for nonstandard devices. More details on Zabbix can be found on the official Zabbix site at `http://www.zabbix.com/`.

Why give preference to Zabbix over mainstream monitoring systems, such as Nagios or Icinga, or any other solutions currently available? The reason is that Zabbix offers simplicity, without sacrificing any of the features that make a great monitoring system. Zabbix is fully managed through the GUI, without requiring you to edit any script file through the CLI. This eases the burden of device configuration through the script file, such as in the case of a Nagios-based monitoring system. Whether it is a small network environment or a large one spread across regions, Zabbix is up to the challenge.

# Installing Zabbix

In this section, we will see how to install Zabbix and configure it to monitor the Proxmox cluster and network devices. We are going to install the Zabbix version 3.0 on CentOS 7. Zabbix can be installed very easily on other major distributions, such as Debian or Ubuntu.

For stability and performance when monitoring a large production environment, using CentOS as the base operating system is highly recommended.

Always make sure that you set up a separate node or a virtual machine to offer maximum performance. A fully configured Zabbix with thousands of items will run frequent checks, which is resource heavy. Using Zabbix in a node or VM, which serves other roles, will greatly affect the performance.

Zabbix also provides preinstalled and preconfigured downloadable appliances for evaluation purposes. It is useful for learning and testing purposes but is not recommended for production use. Zabbix appliances can be downloaded from `http://www.zabbix.com/download.php`.

Zabbix will still work without a Zabbix agent installed on the host to be monitored, but an agent can gather much more data from the host. There are agents available for all major operating systems, including Linux, Windows, FreeBSD, AIX, Solaris, and HP-UX. For devices where an agent installation is not possible, such as a managed switch or other network equipment, Zabbix is able to monitor them through SNMP. After the Zabbix server installation is completed, install Zabbix agents on hosts to be monitored.

A Zabbix agent can capture much more data than SNMP. Use an agent over SNMP whenever possible. This reduces the complexity of configuring SNMP while creating a lot more custom checks. Agents are a great option for Proxmox host nodes.

The Zabbix official documentation has excellent instructions to install Zabbix on various Linux distributions.

> Refer to the documentation for instructions on how to install the Zabbix 3.0 server and agent at
> `https://www.zabbix.com/documentation/3.0/manual/installation/install_from_packages`.

After the installation is complete, the Zabbix server can be accessed through: `http://<node_ip>/zabbix`.

By default, the **Username** and **Password** to log in to the Zabbix web GUI are **Admin** and **zabbix**, where the username is case sensitive. It is highly recommended that you change the password right after logging in. Go to **Administration** | **Users**, then click on the **Admin** (Zabbix administrator) member, or click on the **User profile** icon in top-right corner of the GUI, to change the administrative password, as shown in the following screenshot:

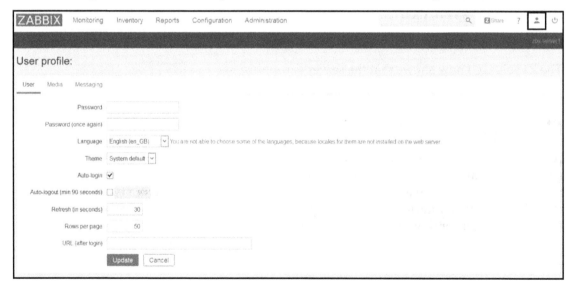

If you are using CentOS 7 for the Zabbix server, after accessing the Zabbix GUI you may notice that the status informs that the Zabbix server is not running, even though the Zabbix service is running, as shown in the following screenshot:

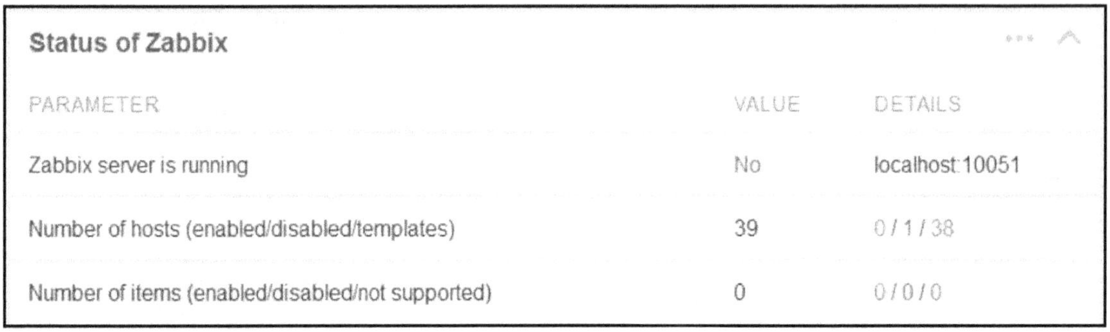

| Status of Zabbix | | ••• ∧ |
| --- | --- | --- |
| PARAMETER | VALUE | DETAILS |
| Zabbix server is running | No | localhost:10051 |
| Number of hosts (enabled/disabled/templates) | 39 | 0 / 1 / 38 |
| Number of items (enabled/disabled/not supported) | 0 | 0 / 0 / 0 |

This is due to the `httpd_can_connect_network` argument in the SELinux firewall configuration. The argument needs to be enabled in order to let Zabbix access the network. Run the following command to check whether it is off or disabled:

> **# getsebool httpd_can_network_connect**

If the result shows off, then enable it by running the following command:

> **# setsebool httpd_can_network_connect on**

The Zabbix GUI now shows that the server is running.

# Configuring Zabbix

After the Zabbix server is installed and functioning, we have to set up emails so that we get automated emails whenever there is an issue. Zabbix 3.0 is able to send emails through SMTP. We can configure it by navigating to the **Administration** | **Media types** menu and changing the SMTP information under **Email**. After the email is configured, it is now time to add some hosts or devices to start monitoring.

# Configuring a host to monitor

In this section, we will see how to add a host, whether it is a Proxmox node or a virtual machine, to the Zabbix monitoring server. This procedure is the same for adding any host with a Zabbix agent installed. By default, the Zabbix server is added to the monitoring host. We are now going to add our example Proxmox node pmx-01 to Zabbix in order to be monitored. The following steps show how to add the host to Zabbix:

1. Go to **Configuration** ǀ **Hosts** and click on **Create Host**.
2. Type in the **Host name** and **Visible name**. The **Host name** must match the hostname entered in the host Zabbix agent configuration file. We will configure the agent after we add the host in the Zabbix server. The **Visible name** can be anything.
3. Select an appropriate **Group**. Since we are adding a Proxmox host node, we need to select **Hypervisors** as the **Group**.
4. If we are adding a host with the agent installed, we type in the IP address of the host in the **Agent interfaces**. By default, the agent listens on port 10050. If we are using a different port, we type in the port here. Make sure that you open the ports in the firewall if the host is behind any firewall. The following screenshot shows the **Host** configuration page after adding the necessary information:

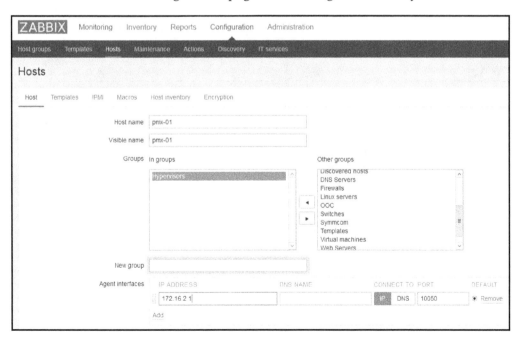

5. Click on the **Templates** tab to add a template to the host. In Zabbix, templates are preconfigured groups of checks. By assigning a template to a host, we apply multiple checks at once instead of manually adding each check.

6. Type a template name in the **Link new templates** textbox, or select one by clicking on the **Select** button. The textbox is a self-search box, so the value does not need to be the exact name of the template. For example, we have typed in Linux, which pulled up two possible templates. We are going to select **Template OS Linux**, as shown in the following screenshot:

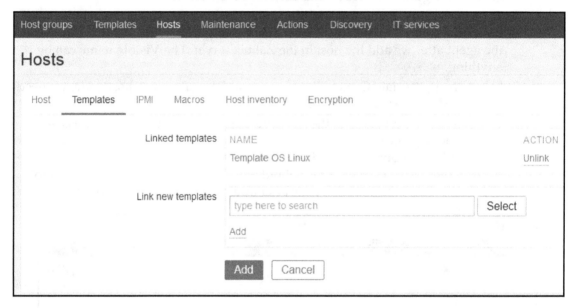

7. We can also assign an SNMP device using the same template page. Refer to the *Configuring SNMP in Proxmox* section later in this chapter for how to install and configure SNMP in Proxmox nodes.

8. Click on **Add** to assign the template to the host.

9. Click on **Host inventory**, and then select **Automatic** so that the Zabbix agent can pull relevant information about the host, such as the host brand, serial number, OS installed, and so on. We can also manually enter data, such as longitude, latitude, hardware, and software installed in the node. This is helpful to build an inventory list.

10. Click on **Save** to finish adding the host.

The following steps need to be performed to configure the Zabbix agent in a host:

1. Open the Zabbix agent configuration file in the `/etc/zabbix/zabbix_agentd.conf` file of the host.

2. Make the changes for the following option lines:

   ```
   Server=172.16.2.172 //IP of Zabbix Server
   ServerActive=172.16.2.171:10051 //IP_Server:Server_Port
   Hostname=pmx-01
   //must be same as Hostname typed in Zabbix Server for the host
   ```

3. Save and exit the editor. Run the following command to restart the Zabbix agent in the host:

   ```
   # service zabbix-agent restart
   ```

Within a minute or so of adding the host, the Zabbix server will run auto checks and will discover that the host now has a live agent. The following screenshot shows the node after adding it to the Zabbix monitoring:

From the list, we can also see that the template added **32** items, **15** triggers, and **5** graphs to the host. Items are what are being checked by Zabbix and triggers are what initiate certain actions, such as sending automatic notifications for any event. The template has two discovery items, which automatically gather information of installed and configured disk drives and partitions in the node. The following screenshot shows the **Triggers** page for the host pmx-01:

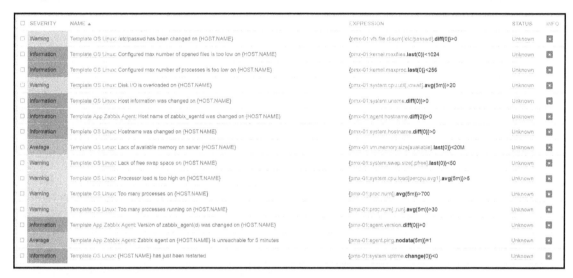

| | SEVERITY | NAME ▲ | EXPRESSION | STATUS | INFO |
|---|---|---|---|---|---|
| | Warning | Template OS Linux: /etc/passwd has been changed on {HOST.NAME} | {pmx-01:vfs.file.cksum[/etc/passwd].**diff(0)**}>0 | Unknown | ✕ |
| | Information | Template OS Linux: Configured max number of opened files is too low on {HOST.NAME} | {pmx-01:kernel.maxfiles.**last(0)**}<1024 | Unknown | ✕ |
| | Information | Template OS Linux: Configured max number of processes is too low on {HOST.NAME} | {pmx-01:kernel.maxproc.**last(0)**}<256 | Unknown | ✕ |
| | Warning | Template OS Linux: Disk I/O is overloaded on {HOST.NAME} | {pmx-01:system.cpu.util[,iowait].**avg(5m)**}>20 | Unknown | ✕ |
| | Information | Template OS Linux: Host information was changed on {HOST.NAME} | {pmx-01:system.uname.**diff(0)**}>0 | Unknown | ✕ |
| | Information | Template App Zabbix Agent: Host name of zabbix_agentd was changed on {HOST.NAME} | {pmx-01:agent.hostname.**diff(0)**}>0 | Unknown | ✕ |
| | Information | Template OS Linux: Hostname was changed on {HOST.NAME} | {pmx-01:system.hostname.**diff(0)**}>0 | Unknown | ✕ |
| | Average | Template OS Linux: Lack of available memory on server {HOST.NAME} | {pmx-01:vm.memory.size[available].**last(0)**}<20M | Unknown | ✕ |
| | Warning | Template OS Linux: Lack of free swap space on {HOST.NAME} | {pmx-01:system.swap.size[,pfree].**last(0)**}<50 | Unknown | ✕ |
| | Warning | Template OS Linux: Processor load is too high on {HOST.NAME} | {pmx-01:system.cpu.load[percpu,avg1].**avg(5m)**}>5 | Unknown | ✕ |
| | Warning | Template OS Linux: Too many processes on {HOST.NAME} | {pmx-01:proc.num[,,avg(5m)**}>700 | Unknown | ✕ |
| | Warning | Template OS Linux: Too many processes running on {HOST.NAME} | {pmx-01:proc.num[,,run].**avg(5m)**}>30 | Unknown | ✕ |
| | Information | Template App Zabbix Agent: Version of zabbix_agent(d) was changed on {HOST.NAME} | {pmx-01:agent.version.**diff(0)**}>0 | Unknown | ✕ |
| | Average | Template App Zabbix Agent: Zabbix agent on {HOST.NAME} is unreachable for 5 minutes | {pmx-01:agent.ping.**nodata(5m)**}=1 | Unknown | ✕ |
| | Information | Template OS Linux: {HOST.NAME} has just been restarted | {pmx-01:system.uptime.**change(0)**}<0 | Unknown | ✕ |

The expression column in the **Triggers** page shows when an event is triggered. For example, the expression {pmx-01:system.cpu.util[,iowait].avg(5m)}>20 for disk I/O overload will trigger a warning when the I/O wait exceeds 20 for 5 minutes in the host. Another example trigger is {pmx-01:proc.num[].avg(5m)}>300, which may trigger when the number of running processes exceeds 300 for 5 minutes. Modern servers can run many more processes at once. So, for a node or host that hosts many virtual machines, this process limit of 300 may not be enough, and will trigger a warning frequently. We can change the trigger, for example, to 900, to increase the limit.

 To learn more about triggers, refer to https://www.zabbix.com/documentation/3.0/manual/config/triggers/expression.

We can also add each virtual machine as a host and then monitor it through Zabbix. For this, we need to install the Zabbix agent inside the virtual machine, and add it as a host in Zabbix. To group all virtual machines together, we need to create a group named Virtual Machine in Zabbix and assign all VMs to be monitored in that group.

# Displaying data using a graph

Zabbix comes with an excellent graphing ability out of the box, without any manual configuration. As soon as data is pulled from a resource, the graphing utility starts plotting using the raw data. Almost all the built-in templates in Zabbix have some graphing items predefined. We can get graphs of monitored items by navigating to **Monitoring** | **Graphs** in the Zabbix GUI. The following screenshot shows the graph of the **CPU load** over a period of 15 minutes for a host:

We can also create our own graph items, through a few clicks, for any host or device being monitored. For example, let's create a graph to visualize data for the CPU iowait overtime. For this, we need to go to **Configuration** | **Hosts**, and then click on the node. Once inside the node, click on the **Graphs** menu to open the graph editor page, as shown in the following screenshot:

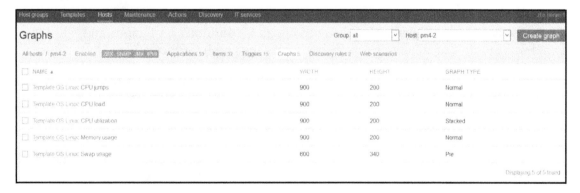

In the preceding screenshot, we can see that there are five graph items that have already been created. We are going to add a new item to the pm4-2:CPU iowait time. Click on the **Create graph** button to open a new graph item page. Type in an easily understandable name for the graph item. We are going to name it CPU IOWait time. From the **Items** box at the bottom of this, click on **Add** to open a list of available items to choose from. We are going to select pm4-2:CPU iowait time for this example. We can configure the color and type of the graph being created. Click on the **Add** button when you are satisfied with the configuration. The following screenshot shows the graph creation page for our example of pm4-2:CPU iowait time:

To see the newly created graph item, we need to go to **Monitoring** | **Graphs** and select the item for the node. The following screenshot shows the graph for the gathered CPU IOWait time over a period of 15 minutes:

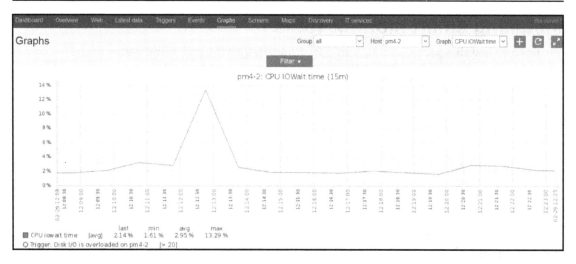

In the preceding screenshot, we can see that the CPU IOwait time is shown in green, and if there are any trigger events due to the CPU IOwait time being greater than 20%, they will be shown in yellow.

# Configuring the disk health notification

In the *Proxmox built-in monitoring* section, we saw how we can leverage S.M.A.R.T. to receive automated emails if there are any issues for any disk drives. In this section, we are going to accomplish the same thing, but with Zabbix, and with an additional feature: graphing. A great use case of a graph for a disk drive is monitoring data for temperature. High temperature is a bad thing for all spinning drives. Using the Zabbix graph, we can see the exact temperature trend of the storage cluster, down to a single drive, and take action accordingly. Zabbix can also send automated emails when there are any issues in any of the drives, such as read or write issues, due to a bad sector or any other S.M.A.R.T. event.

Almost all HDDs and SSDs nowadays have the S.M.A.R.T. ability, which can gather valuable data on the disk drive's health. Using the S.M.A.R.T. monitoring tool, we can avoid premature drive failure by detecting potential problems early on. We can configure each Proxmox node to send email alerts when any problem is detected in any attached drives.

 If drives are connected to RAID controllers and configured as some form of arrays, then the S.M.A.R.T. tool will not be able to retrieve the drive's health data.

# Installing smart monitor tools

We need to install `smartmontools` in our storage using the following command:

```
#apt-get install smartmontools
```

Retrieve a list of all the attached drives using the following command:

```
# fdisk -l
```

Verify that each attached drive has the S.M.A.R.T. feature, and that it is turned on, using the following command:

```
#smartctl -a /dev/sdX
```

If the drive has the S.M.A.R.T. feature and it is enabled, it will appear as shown in the following screenshot:

```
smartctl 6.4 2014-10-07 r4002 [x86_64-linux-4.2.8-1-pve] (local build)
Copyright (C) 2002-14, Bruce Allen, Christian Franke, www.smartmontools.org

ATA device successfully opened

Use 'smartctl -a' (or '-x') to print SMART (and more) information
```

If the feature is available but disabled for any reason, we can enable it using the following command:

```
#smartctl -s on -a /dev/sdX
```

# Configuring the Zabbix agent

Adding the disk drive monitoring into Zabbix is a two-step process. In the first step, we need to add arguments in the Zabbix agent configuration file, and then add the drive items in the Zabbix server for each host. These special arguments are known as user parameters. They work similar to a script, where we can define commands to be run on the host, and then the Zabbix agent passes the data to the Zabbix server.

In this example, we are going to add user parameters to pull data for the serial number and drive temperature. The following two lines need to be added at the end of the agent configuration file in `/etc/zabbix/zabbix_agentd.conf`:

```
UserParameter=hdd.temp[*],smartctl -A /dev/$1 | grep -E -i '^[ ]*($2)[ ]' | cut -c88-90
UserParameter=hdd.serial[*],smartctl -i /dev/$1 | grep 'Serial Number' |cut -c19-
```

After adding the lines, we need to restart the Zabbix agent using the following command:

```
# service zabbix_agentd restart
```

# Creating a Zabbix item in the GUI

After the user parameters are added, we need to create new items in the Zabbix server for the host. First, we will add an item to gather data for the drive temperature. Go to **Configuration** | **Hosts** | **Items**, and then click on **Create item** to open a new item page. The following screenshot shows the page with the necessary configuration:

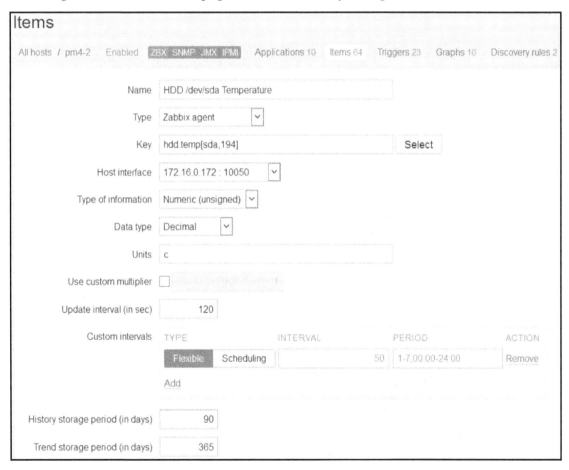

The name of the item can be any text string. Since we are pulling data through the user parameters of the Zabbix agent, we need to select the agent as **Type**. The **Key** textbox is the most important thing here, as this is where we define what data we are pulling. The key entered, as shown in the preceding screenshot, tells Zabbix to pull the drive temperature for the sda device. The numeric value of 194 in the key is for the temperature information. Each smart monitor attribute has a unique numeric ID. For example, if we want to gather data for an uncorrectable sector count, the code would be 197.

To view a complete list of smart monitor attribute codes, refer to https://en.wikipedia.org/wiki/S.M.A.R.T.#Known_ATA_S.M.A.R.T._at tributes.

**Type of information** is a drop-down list used to select the nature of data being collected. Since the temperature is a numeric value, we will select the **Numeric (unsigned)** type. To increase the temperature accuracy, we need to select **Decimal** as the **Data type**.

**Update interval (in sec)** is a textbox used to enter seconds, which needs careful attention. This is the interval at which Zabbix will run checks for each item. By default, Zabbix uses an interval of 30 seconds. When adding high-volume checks, such as a disk drive's data, with more disk drives present in a node, the volume of checks will increase exponentially. For example, if we want to gather drive data for a Ceph node with 12 drives, Zabbix will run checks every 30 seconds for all the 12 drives, and that will add up to hundreds of checks per hour. To reduce the check bottleneck, we can set it to a higher interval. In our example, we are using 2 minutes, or 120 seconds, for a drive check. Click on **Add** to finish creating the item.

We need to create separate new items for each drive that needs to be monitored. Change the device ID for each item, such as sdb, sdc, and so on.

# Creating a trigger in the GUI

After the item is created, we now need to create a trigger so that Zabbix can send auto notification emails if the temperature goes beyond a threshold. To create a trigger, go to **Configuration** | **Hosts** | **Triggers**, and click on the **Create trigger** button. The following screenshot shows the new trigger creation page with the necessary information entered:

# Triggers

All hosts / pm4-2    Enabled    ZBX SNMP JMX IPMI    Applications 10    Items 65    Triggers 23    Graphs 16

Trigger    Dependencies

Name    HDD Over Temperature /dev/sda

Expression    {pm4-2:hdd.temp[sda,194].last()}>40    Add

Expression constructor

Multiple PROBLEM events generation    ☐

Description

URL

Severity    Not classified    Information    Warning    Average    High    Disaster

Enabled    ☑

Add    Cancel

Type in a **Name** to identify the trigger, and then enter an **Expression** for the trigger. The **Expression** is used to set a threshold beyond which Zabbix will trigger an event, such as sending an email. In our example, shown in the preceding screenshot, our **Expression** shows that if the last temperature gathered is greater than 40 degrees Celsius, Zabbix will send an alert email.

In order to identify the importance of the trigger, we need to select the **Severity** level. For example, we have selected **Warning** as the severity of the trigger. Select the appropriate severity depending on the trigger. This creates color coded information throughout Zabbix to identify how serious the issue is. Click on **Add** to finish creating the trigger. Like triggers, each drive will need a separate trigger item.

## Creating graphs in the GUI

Following the instructions to display data using a graph, as discussed earlier in this chapter, we are now going to create a new graph item to show the drive temperature data visually. Unlike triggers and items, we do not need to create separate graph items. We can configure one graph item to show multiple drive data by simply adding the drive items in the same graph item. The following screenshot shows the drive temperature graph for a Ceph node with seven disk drives over a 6 hour period:

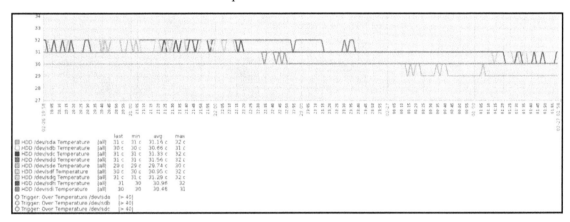

# Configuring SNMP in Proxmox

**Simple Network Management Protocol** (**SNMP**) is a network management protocol used to monitor a wide variety of network devices. It is especially useful when a full network monitoring agent installation is not possible, such as with switches, routers, printers, IP-based devices, and so on. Almost all network monitoring programs support some level of SNMP.

If the choice of monitoring a package does not have any agents, SNMP is the best option to monitor those devices. SNMP is fully configurable in Linux distributions, and since Proxmox is based on Debian, it inherits all the benefits of SNMP.

To learn more about SNMP, refer
to `https://en.wikipedia.org/wiki/Simple_Network_Management_Proto col`.

There are a couple of components of SNMP worth mentioning here, since we will be using them to configure SNMP. They are as follows:

- **Object Identifier (OID)**
- **Management Information Base (MIB)**

# Object Identifiers

OIDs are objects that SNMP query to gather information from a device. An object can be a network interface status, disk storage usage, device name, and so on. These object identifiers are extremely structured in a hierarchical tree manner. Each OID is specifically numbered. For example, the OID of the object that gathers the device name is `1.3.6.1.2.1.1.5.0`. OIDs always have numerical values. OIDs can be compared with IP addresses, where numeric values are used to identify a device in a network.

Each dot in an OID represents segmentation of the network element. We can think of an OID like an address of a location. Let's take the following address:

`Wasim Ahmed 111 Server Street, 4th Floor Calgary, AB 111-222 Canada`

If we put this address in OID format, it will look like the following:

`Canada.AB.Calgary.111-222.Server Street.111.4th Floor.Wasim Ahmed`

Putting this in a formula will look like the following:

`Country.Province.City.Postal code.Street name.Street number.Unit number.Contact name`

Just like the address example, the OIDs also follow a strict hierarchy, as shown here:

*1 = ISO 1.3 = Organization 1.3.6 = US Department of Defense 1.3.6.1 = Internet 1.3.6.1.2 = IETF*

*Management 1.3.6.1.2.X = Management-related OIDs*

To look up management-related OIDs, refer to http://www.alvestrand.no/objectid/1.3.6.1.2.1.html.

# Management Information Base

There are databases where objects are stored. MIB acts as a translator and allows an SNMP server to query an object using a textual OID instead of numeric. For example, to retrieve a device name through SNMP queries, we can use the OID 1.3.6.1.2.1.1.5.0 or the OID SNMPv2-MIB::sysName.0. Both of them will give you the exact same result. But the textual OID is easier to understand than just a numeric OID. We can compare MIB to OID as being similar to a domain name to an IP address. Some manufacturers provide their own MIB since they do not exist in the standard MIB. It is important to know the MIBs when configuring unsupported devices for monitoring tools. There are a number of MIBs ready to be downloaded. Proxmox does not install any MIB by default. It has to be manually installed.

For more details on MIBs, refer to https://en.wikipedia.org/wiki/Management_information_base.

There are three versions of SNMP currently available. Before implementing an SNMP infrastructure, it is important to know which version to use. The three versions are as follows:

- **SNMP version 1**: This is the oldest SNMP version, which only supports 32-bit counters and has no security at all. A community string is sent as plain text in this SNMP.
- **SNMP version 2**: This has all the features of version 1, with added features to support 64-bit counters. Most of the devices nowadays support version 2.
- **SNMP version 3**: This has all the features of version 1 and 2, with the added benefits of security. Both encryption and authentication are added to counters. If security is the biggest concern, this is the SNMP version that should be used.

SNMP is not installed by default in Proxmox. The following steps show how to install SNMP in Proxmox and how to configure it.

Run the following command to install SNMP on Proxmox nodes:

```
# apt-get install snmpd snmp
```

Add the following repository in the /etc/apt/sources.list of the Proxmox node. This is used to add a repository to install SNMP MIBs:

```
deb http://http.us.debian.org/debian/stretch main non-free
```

Run the following commands to install SNMP MIBs:

```
# apt-get update
# apt-get install snmp-mibs-downloader
```

Open the SNMP /etc/snmp/snmpd.conf configuration file using an editor.

Ensure that the following line is uncommented. We can specify the node IP address. SNMP listens on port 161. Change it here if required:

```
agentAddress udp:127.0.0.1:161
```

Add the following line to the SNMP configuration file:

```
rocommunity <secret_string> <IP/CIDR>
```

In our example, we have added the following line:

```
rocommunity SecretSNMP 172.16.0.0/24
```

Save the file and restart SNMP using the following command:

```
#service snmpd restart
```

# Adding an SNMP device in Zabbix

Adding an SNMP device in Zabbix is a similar process to adding a host, except that we have to select **SNMP interfaces** instead of **Agent interfaces**, as shown in the following screenshot:

By default, SNMP devices listen on port 161. Zabbix comes with prebuilt SNMP templates, which can gather a vast amount of data for devices where agent installation is not possible or desired. A common example of an SNMP device is a network switch. Zabbix has excellent support for switch monitoring through the SNMP template.

In this example, we will add a Netgear 48 port switch using the SNMP interface. Go to **Configuration** | **Hosts** and click on the **Create host** button to open a new host creation page. Besides using the SNMP interface in the host creation page, we need to select the SNMP device template and type in the SNMP v2 community string under **MACRO**, as shown in the following screenshot:

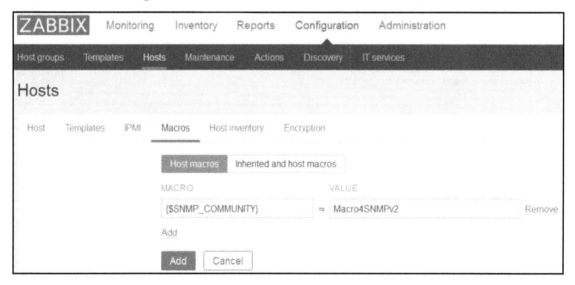

The {$SNMP_COMMUNITY} macro is used to pass a community secret string, which is used by the SNMP version 2. The value of this **MACRO** must match the **VALUE** entered in the monitored device itself.

After the host or device is added, Zabbix will start checks on the switch in a few minutes and start gathering data. The SNMP device template has auto discovery configured, which will automatically scan the switch for the number of ports and show data for both incoming and outgoing traffic on each port. The template also has a graph item configured to show you the visual data of each port. The following screenshot shows the graph of incoming and outgoing traffic usage for port 1 of the Netgear 48 port switch over a 1-hour period:

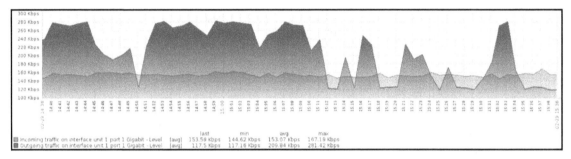

Like the switch, we can add just about any network device with the SNMP capability for Zabbix to monitor at all times.

# Monitoring the Ceph cluster with the Proxmox GUI

As of Proxmox VE 5.0, we can monitor and manage the Ceph storage cluster through the Proxmox GUI. Under the Ceph tabbed menu of each node, you will see a great amount of data, such as the health status of the Ceph cluster, the number of OSDs, mons, pools, Ceph configurations, and so on. Refer to Chapter 5, *Installing and Configuring Ceph*, for information on Ceph management through the Proxmox GUI.

The **Ceph** | **Status** page of the Proxmox GUI shows all relevant information about the Ceph cluster. Data such as **Health**, **Monitors**, **OSDs** status, and so on, are presented in real time. This is critical to maintaining a healthy Ceph cluster. Whenever an issue arises within Ceph, we can quickly pinpoint where the issue is through this **Status** page. The following screenshot shows the Ceph status of our example cluster:

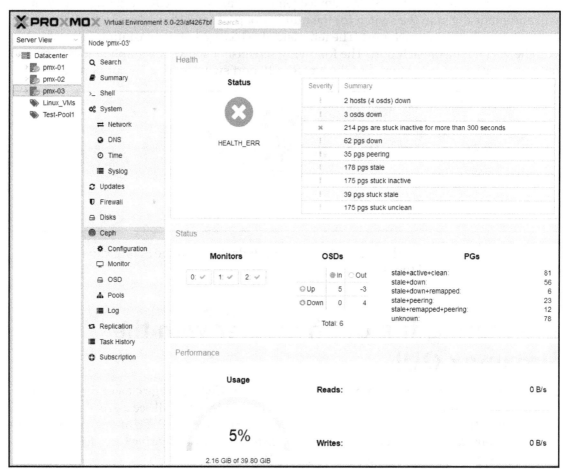

In the previous screenshot, we can clearly see that the Ceph cluster has errors due to some OSDs being out and down. Ceph **placement groups** (**PGs**) have some defined states that show the current condition of the PGs: conditions such as **stale+active**, **stale+down**, **active+clean**, and so on, to name a few. Understanding these various states is very important to manage a fully functional Ceph cluster.

To learn more about the PG states visit the official Ceph documentation at `http://docs.ceph.com/docs/master/rados/operations/pg-states/`.

# Monitoring a Ceph cluster with third-party options

In this section, we will see how to implement a third-party solution to monitor the Ceph cluster. There are several options that can be used to monitor a Ceph cluster graphically, which are as follows:

- **Calamari**: `https://ceph.com/category/calamari/`
- **Kraken dash**: `https://github.com/krakendash/krakendash`
- **The Ceph dashboard**: `https://github.com/Crapworks/ceph-dash`

All three options are viable options used to monitor the Ceph cluster, but due to the simplicity and effectiveness of Ceph dashboard, we are going to see how to install the Ceph dashboard in this chapter. This is the only free monitoring dashboard, and it is read-only, without any management ability. This is also safer, since an unauthorized user cannot make Ceph changes. The Ceph Calamari and Kraken dashboards are both equally challenging to install and configure.

The Ceph dashboard can be installed on any Ceph node or Proxmox+Ceph node in the cluster. As long as it can read the `ceph.conf` file, it will function just fine. The Ceph dashboard does not require a web server or any other services to function. We can download the Ceph dashboard package from Git. By default, Git is not installed in the Proxmox node. We can install it using the following command:

```
# apt-get install git
```

Next, we need to clone the Ceph dashboard GitHub repository, using the following command:

```
# git clone https://github.com/Crapworks/ceph-dash
```

After the download is complete, we need to add the IP address of the node where the dashboard will be located. We need to make changes in the following line in the `ceph-dash.py` file:

```
app.run(host='ip_address',debug=True)
```

To start the dashboard after making the changes, simply run the following command:

```
# <dashboard_directory>/ceph-dash.py
```

We can access the dashboard by pointing to the node, such as at the following link:

```
http://ip_address:5000
```

The following screenshot shows the status of our example cluster using the Ceph dashboard:

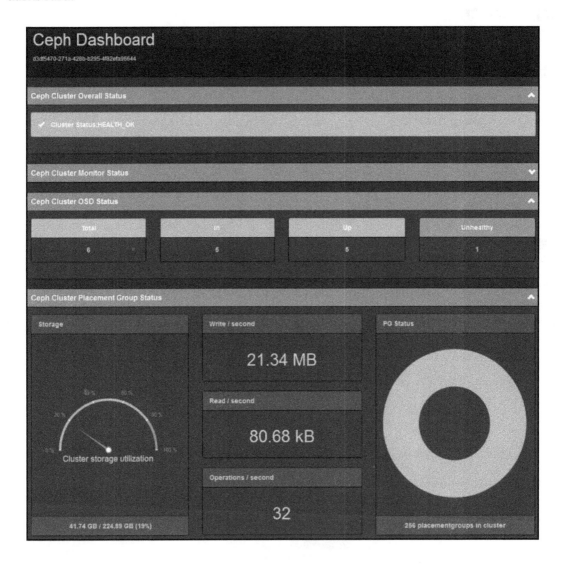

The Ceph dashboard displays the following information on a Ceph cluster:

- The Ceph cluster key
- The overall health status
- The monitor status
- The OSD status
- The PG status
- The storage utilization percentage
- The total available space and used space
- Read/write speed per second
- Operations per second

Refer to `Chapter 5`, *Installing and Configuring Ceph*, for information on Ceph components, such as mon, OSD, PG, and so on. All the data is automatically updated at regular intervals. When faults within the cluster occur, the dashboard will show related information in a color coded format. Using port forwarding in the firewall, we can also monitor a Ceph cluster remotely.

# Summary

In this chapter, we saw how we can monitor a Proxmox cluster network using powerful monitoring systems, such as Zabbix. The only monitoring option available as a mainstream choice, but it does have many advantages over other solutions. The out-of-the-box features, such as graphing, templates, SNMP, auto notification, and so on, are just the tip of the iceberg of what Zabbix has to offer. Whether it is a small environment or a large cloud service provider spanning multiple regions, Zabbix can monitor them all. A good network administrator will try a few solutions and find the one that suits their environment best.

In the next chapter, we will see some complex production-level virtual network environments leveraging Proxmox as a hypervisor. We will take a look at a scenario-based network diagram to gain knowledge of what Proxmox can do.

# 12
# Proxmox Production-Level Setup

So far in this book, we have seen the internal workings of Proxmox. We now know how to properly set up a fully functional Proxmox cluster. We discussed Ceph—a robust and redundant shared storage system—and how we can connect it with Proxmox. We also saw what a virtual network is and how it works with the Proxmox cluster.

In this chapter, we are going to see which components play a crucial part in making a Proxmox cluster production-ready, with multilayer redundancy, good performance, and stability. We are going to cover the following topics:

- Definition of production level
- Key components of a production-level setup
- Entry-level and advanced-level hardware requirements

Throughout this chapter, you will notice that we have used user-built hardware configurations instead of ready-made branded servers. The purpose of this is to show you what sort of node configuration is possible using off-the-shelf commodity hardware to cut costs while setting up a stable Proxmox cluster. The example configurations shown in this chapter are not theoretical scenarios, but are taken from various live clusters in service. Use the information in this chapter purely as a guideline so that you can select the proper hardware for your environment at any budget.

# Defining the production level

Production level is a scenario where a company's cluster environment is fully functional and actively serving its users or clients on a regular basis. It is no longer considered as a platform to learn Proxmox or a test platform to test different things on. A production-level setup requires much advanced planning and preparation, because once the setup is complete and the cluster has been brought online, it cannot be taken offline completely at a moment's notice when users are dependent on it. A properly planned production-level setup can save hours, or days, of headache. If you are still learning Proxmox, you might want to set aside hardware to practice on so that you can hone your skillset before attempting a production-level setup. In this section, we are going to cover some of the key components or characteristics of a production-level environment.

# Key components

The following key components should be kept in mind while planning for a production-level cluster setup, due to stability and performance requirements:

- Stable and scalable hardware
- Redundancy
- Current load versus future growth
- Budget
- Simplicity
- Hardware inventory tracking

# Stable and scalable hardware

Stable hardware means minimum downtime. Without quality hardware, it is not unusual to have randomized hardware failure in a cluster environment, causing massive, unnecessary downtime. It is very important to select a hardware brand with a good reputation and support behind it. For example, Intel's server class components are well known for their superb stability and support. It is true that you pay more for Intel products, but sometimes the stability outweighs the higher cost per hardware. AMD is also an excellent choice, but statistically, AMD-based hardware has more stability issues.

For budget-conscious enterprise environments, we can mix both Intel- and AMD-based hardware in the same cluster. Since Proxmox provides a full migration option, we can have Intel nodes serving full time, while AMD nodes act only as failover. This reduces cost without compromising stability. Throughout this chapter, we are going to stay primarily with Intel-based hardware. At the end of this chapter, we will see some proven AMD-based clusters to give you some idea of how viable AMD is in a Proxmox cluster environment.

When choosing between Intel and AMD, apart from stability, the following two criteria are also deciding factors:

- Energy cost
- Heat generation

Intel CPUs use less energy and run much cooler than their AMD counterparts. Increased heat generation in AMD servers means an increased requirement for cooling, and thus, increased utility bills. By design, AMD CPUs use a much higher wattage per CPU, which is the direct cause of high heat generation.

Another deciding factor for hardware is scalability and availability. Hardware components used in server nodes must be easily available when they need to be replaced. Using difficult-to-find components, even if they cost much less, only prolongs downtime when something needs to be replaced. A common practice is to use identical hardware for groups of servers based on their workload. This makes hardware management easier and also allows in-hand stock buildup to quickly replace a node when needed. This is extremely difficult in an environment where a cluster has been put together using all sorts of different brands, models, and configurations.

# Redundancy

The need to have redundancy in different layers in a production environment cannot be stressed enough. There must be redundancy in different levels of components.

## Node level

Node-level redundancy usually includes redundant power supply, network cards, RAID, and so on. This redundancy is confined to the node itself. With redundant power supply, the node can be connected to two different power sources, thus ensuring continuous operation during power failure.

Always use mirrored SSD drives as the operating system drive. This will ensure that the operating system itself will run uninterrupted, even if a drive fails entirely.

## Utility level

In order for the cluster nodes to keep running during power loss, we need to provide some sort of backup power, whether by means of a UPS, a generator, or a large battery bank.

## Network level

Network-level redundancy includes network infrastructure, such as switches and cables. By using multiple switches and multiple network paths, we can ensure that network connectivity will not be interrupted during a switch or cable failure. Layer three managed switches, such as stackable switches, are the correct components to create truly redundant network paths.

## HVAC level

Proper cooling equipment, with backup systems for continued cooling in the event the HVAC system goes down, is often overlooked. Depending on the number of server nodes, switches, and so on, each network environment creates enormous amounts of heat. If there is no redundancy in place, a failure of the cooling system can result in the failure of extreme-heat-generating components. Whether it is air or liquid cooled, there must be a contingency in the cooling system to prevent any damage. Damage of components also means loss of connectivity and increased cost.

## Storage level

Storage plays an important role for any virtual environment and deserves the same level of redundancy attention as the rest of the cluster. There is no point in implementing redundancy in all Proxmox host nodes, networks, and power supplies, then putting virtual disk images on a single NAS storage without any redundancy. If the single node storage fails, even though it is considered shared storage, all VMs stored on it will be completely unusable. In a production environment, use of enterprise-grade storage systems such as Ceph and Gluster is critical. This type of storage has redundancy built into the firmware/operating system. We still need to ensure that these storage nodes have node, utility, network, and HVAC-level redundancy in place.

# Current load versus future growth

When designing a cluster, you should always think of future growth, at least the growth for the foreseeable future. An enterprise cluster must be able to grow with the company and adapt to increased workloads and computational requirements. At the very least, plan in such a way that you do not exceed your resources within a few months of your deployment. Both the Proxmox and Ceph clusters have the ability to grow at any time and to any size. This provides the ability to simply add new hardware nodes to expand cluster size and increase the resources required by the virtual machines.

When provisioning your node memory configuration, take failover load into account. You will likely need to have 50 percent capacity available for a single node failure. If two nodes of a three-node cluster were to fail, you would want each machine to utilize only 33 percent of the available memory. For example, let's say all six nodes in a Proxmox cluster have 64 GB memory, and 60 GB is consumed at all times by all the virtual machines. If node 1 fails, you will not be able to migrate all virtual machines from node 1 to the other five nodes, because there is not enough memory to go around. We could just add another spare node and migrate all the virtual machines. However, we have to make sure that there are enough power outlets to even plug in the new node.

# Budget

Budgetary concerns always play a role in decision making, no matter what kind of network environment we are dealing with. The truth is that a setup can be adaptable to just about any budget with some clever and creative planning. Administrators often need to work with very small IT budgets. Hopefully, this chapter will help you to find that missing thread to connect a budget with proper hardware components. By using commodity equipment over complete brand servers, we can easily set up a full Proxmox cluster on a very lean budget. Proxmox works very well on quality commodity hardware components.

# Simplicity

Simplicity is often overlooked in a network environment. A lot of times, it just happens naturally. If we are not mindful about simplicity, we can very quickly make a network unnecessarily complex. By mixing hardware RAID with software RAID, putting RAID within another RAID, or through multi-drive setup to protect OS, we can cause a cluster's performance to drop to an almost unusable or unstable state. Both Proxmox and Ceph can run on high-grade commodity hardware, as well as common server hardware. For example, just by selecting desktop-class i7 over server-class Xeon, we can slash costs in half while providing a very stable and simple cluster setup, unless the task specifically calls for a multi-Xeon setup.

# Tracking hardware inventory

An administrator should have access to key information about hardware being used in a network: information such as the brand, model, and serial number of a hardware component; when was it purchased; who the vendor was; when is it due for replacement; and so on. A proper tracking system can save a lot of time when any of this information needs to be retrieved. Each company is different, and thus, tracking systems could be different, but the responsibility of gathering this information falls solely on the network manager or administrator. If there is no system in place, then creating a simple spreadsheet can be enough to keep track of all hardware information.

# Hardware selection

Several factors affect what type of hardware to select, such as whether the cluster is going to support many virtual machines with fewer resources or serve few virtual machines with more resources. A cluster focused on many virtual machines needs to have a much higher processor core count, so our goal should be to put as many cores as possible per node. When a cluster is focused on few virtual machines, with a lot more users per virtual machine, we need to have a large memory. Thus, a system with a smaller core but a greater amount of memory is much more appropriate. Also, a cluster can focus on both types and create a hybrid cluster environment. A hybrid environment usually starts with an entry-level hardware setup and then matures into an advanced-level setup as the company grows and a larger budget is available. For example, a small company can start its cluster infrastructure with stable desktop-class hardware, and then gradually replace that with a server-class platform such as Xeon to accommodate company expansion.

# Sizing CPU and memory

A question often asked when it comes to creating virtual environments is how much CPU or memory will be needed in each node and how much to allocate per virtual machine. This is one of those questions that is very open-ended, because its answer varies greatly from environment to environment. However, there are a few pointers that need to be kept in mind to avoid over-allocation or under-allocation.

It is a fact that we will, and often do, run out of memory much sooner than CPU for a given Proxmox or any other host node. From the usage of each VM on the Proxmox nodes, we can determine the RAM and CPU requirements on that node. In this section, we are going to go over the factors that will help us to decide on CPU and memory needs.

# Single socket versus multi-socket

A multi-socket node will always have better performance than a single socket, regardless of the number of cores per CPU. They work efficiently in distributing VM workload. This is true for both Intel and AMD architectures. If the budget is available, a quad-socket node will provide the maximum performance of any socket configuration node.

# Hyper-threading – enable versus disable

One of the major differences between Intel and AMD is hyper-threading. All cores in AMD CPUs are true cores, whereas all Intel CPUs have hyper-threading, which creates two virtual cores per physical core. Another question that is asked far too often is whether to enable or disable hyper-threading. From hundreds of reports and testing, it appears that it is better to leave it on for newer Intel servers. The fear of performance degradation due to hyper-threading is no longer valid, as it has gone through decades of development and all the initial issues have been resolved. It is also best to not count all hyper-threading cores as real cores, since they are still virtual. When counting the number of total cores available in a node, take a conservative approach and count slightly fewer than the total cores.

# Start small with VM resources

A virtual machine is completely different from a physical machine and it needs to be treated as such. They do not consume CPU and memory like a physical node does. The best practice is to always provision CPU and memory resources sparingly, and then increase them as you see the application's performance. This allows the VM to use allocated resources efficiently, which in turn makes all the VMs run efficiently in the node. By over-provisioning CPU and memory for all VMs in the node, we degrade node performance, because all VMs will be fighting to have more CPU time. Always start with one virtual CPU (vCPU) for most of the VMs. Start from two vCPUs for processor intensive VMs such as database servers, exchange servers, and so on. Monitor the VM's resource utilization and adjust accordingly. A quick way to see which VM is using the most CPU or memory is through the **Datacenter** or **Node Search** menu, which shows the list of all entities and is sortable.

When allocating vCPU for a single VM, never exceed the total number of cores in the node. This will degrade the performance of the entire node and all VMs in it.

Keep in mind that in a virtual environment, more CPU and memory for a virtual machine does not always mean better performance.

# Balancing node resources

Always ensure that each Proxmox node in a cluster has similar CPU and memory resources. If some nodes end up with more than the others, it will cause an issue when trying to move or migrate VMs from a high-resource node to a low-resource node. The node with less resources will not be able to handle all VMs, causing longer downtime during node failure. This issue can be mitigated by using a combination of a few high resource nodes and more low resource nodes.

# Ceph cluster production

As mentioned throughout this book, Ceph is a very resilient distributed storage system that pairs well with Proxmox to store virtual disk images. There are a few key factors that make a Ceph cluster a good choice for a production-level virtual environment.

# Forget about hardware RAID

When it comes to Ceph nodes and clusters, we can forget about hardware-based RAID. Instead, we have to think multi-node or clustered RAID. That is because of the distributed nature of Ceph and how data is dispersed in all the drives in the cluster regardless of which node the drive is in. With Ceph, we no longer need to worry about a device failure in a particular node. Ceph performs best when it is given access to each drive directly without any RAID in the middle. If we are to place drives in RAID per node, we will actually hurt Ceph immensely and take away everything that makes Ceph great. We can, however, still use the RAID interface card to implement JBOD configuration or to be able to connect many drives per node.

# Solid State Drive for Ceph Journal

Incoming data for the Ceph cluster gets written to a journal before it gets passed down to the OSDs themselves. So, a dedicated drive such as SSD will increase write speed greatly, since it can achieve an extreme write speed, much faster than a standard SATA or SAS drive. Even the fastest 15,000 rpm enterprise-grade disk drive does not come close to the performance of SSD. When selecting SSD for a Ceph journal, care must be taken in brand or model selection.

Not all SSDs will perform well for a Ceph journal. Currently, the only SSD that can withstand the rigorous load of Ceph while providing great write speed and power loss protection is the Intel DC S3700 or S3500. There are other SSDs that can also perform well, but the ones mentioned have a much longer lifespan. Their built-in power loss protection also prevents journal data corruption, which may lead to corrupt data in OSDs. Visit the following link for an article on how to test suitable SSD drives for Ceph and a list of possible SSDs for the Ceph cluster:
```
http://www.sebastien-han.fr/blog/2014/10/10/ceph-how-to-test-if-your-ssd-is-sui
table-as-a-journal-device/.
```

Instead of standard SATA SSDs, we can also use PCI-based SSDs, which can provide an extreme performance increase over that of standard SATA SSDs. If there is a drive bay limitation for dedicated SSDs, then this is a perfect choice. The following link specifies Intel PCI-E SSDs that can be considered as Ceph journal:
```
http://www.intel.com/content/www/us/en/solid-state-drives/solid-state-drives-75
0-series.html.
```

Ceph can still be used without the use of dedicated SSD journal drives. We can configure Ceph OSDs to store journals on the same spinning drive, but due to the low speed of mechanical drives, we will see high IO wait times in the Proxmox nodes. Use of enterprise-grade SATA or SAS drives will lessen this IO wait time, but not as much as a dedicated SSD.

> Never put a dedicated journal, whether SSD or HDD, on any sort of RAID. This will reduce journal performance, which in turn affects Ceph's overall performance.

# Network bandwidth

Having ample network bandwidth is crucial for Ceph or any other storage. The more bandwidth that is dedicated, the more VM's performance and latency will benefit. Note here that when a dedicated journal such as SSD is used, the requirement for network bandwidth will increase significantly, because more data will traverse the Ceph cluster for replication and distribution. For a Ceph cluster where SSD is used as a dedicated journal, a gigabit network should not be used for the Ceph cluster network. At the very least, 10 GB would be a good network. We can also use InfiniBand as an alternative network solution on a lower budget. If neither is possible, then multiple bonded gigabits would also work. On a single gigabit, the network will become a bottleneck, causing cluster-wide performance degradation.

Also, Ceph cluster sync should be on its own dedicated network, with the Ceph public facing network on another. Ceph uses the cluster network to commit all syncs between OSDs. This prevents unnecessary load on the public facing network.

# Liquid cooling

In this solution, computer equipment is cooled using liquid, as liquid is 1,000 times better at heat transfer than air. We can effectively remove heat directly from IT equipment and transfer it with great ease out of the facility. Liquid cooling takes away the hassle of running a large HVAC system, thus saving enormous costs and reducing noise significantly. Liquid cooling requires no internal fans, thus we can increase server density per rack tenfold. Liquid cooling is the future, as more and more IT facilities are realizing its full potential. By using liquid cooling, we can also decrease our energy consumption, reducing our carbon footprint enormously. There are different liquid cooling solutions available on the market.

# Total immersion in oil

IT equipment is totally submerged in mineral oil. Hot oil is pumped through a liquid-to-liquid heat exchanger, where the heat is carried away, using water, to an outside cooling tower. Water and oil never have full contact, only heat transfer. This is not only the most cost-effective liquid cooling solution today, but also the messiest, as servers are dipped in oil. It also requires more space, since all racks are laid on their backs. However, this extra space can easily be compensated for by increased density per node. Currently, **Green Revolution Cooling** pioneers this technology. Visit the following links for their official site and a great video showing the technology in action:

- Official website: `http://www.grcooling.com/`
- YouTube video: `https://www.youtube.com/watch?v=U5zoIEjo1Zk`

There is another technology worth mentioning here that is similar to immersion, but the immersion is isolated in the server node itself. LiquidCool Solutions has a unique approach of filling up a sealed server chassis with mineral oil to remove heat.

Visit the following link for more info on this approach:

`http://www.liquidcoolsolutions.com`

# Total immersion in 3M Novec

Similar to oil immersion cooling, this is also a total immersion technology, where 3M Novec engineered fluid is used instead of mineral oil. The advantage of this option is zero mess. Unlike oil, this fluid does not stick to any equipment and does not require any heat exchanger or pump to move the fluid itself. This fluid has a boiling temperature of 60 degrees Celsius, at which it becomes vapor. When the vapor hits a cold coil on top of the container, it turns to liquid and drops back down to the tank. Only a pump is needed to circulate water through the coil, thus it needs only half of the equipment needed for oil-based cooling.

Visit the following link for a video presentation of the technology:

`https://www.youtube.com/watch?v=a6ErbZtpL88`

# Direct contact liquid cooling

Heat is removed directly from the heat source, such as the CPU and memory, using a cold plate and liquid coolant such as water or any other coolant agent. Since no equipment is immersed, this technology can be used with existing infrastructure with major modification, while still increasing density per node and reducing energy consumption. This is not a unique technology, as this type of liquid cooling solution had been in use for several years. Consumer class liquid cooling solutions use this off-the-shelf technology. Asetek is known for desktop liquid cooling solutions for desktop users.

Visit their official site through the following link:

```
http://www.asetek.com/
```

Another direct contact liquid cooling solution provider worth mentioning here is from CoolIT Systems. They also take the cold plate approach to cool equipment through liquid cooling. Some of their solutions can be implemented directly in the rack as a standard mounted cooling unit, without the need to have a water facility or cooling tower.

Visit the following link for more information on their solution:

```
http://www.coolitsystems.com/
```

# Real-world Proxmox scenarios

Equipped with all the knowledge we have gathered from the previous chapters in this book, we are now ready to put all the pieces together to form a complex virtual environment for just about any scenario that we are going to be called for. A set of scenarios to build networks using Proxmox for various industries is given in the next section. At the end of the chapter, you will find network diagrams of each scenario given in the first part of the chapter.

Some scenarios have been taken from real-life production environments, while some are theoretical, to show how complex networks are possible with Proxmox. You can take these network models and use them as they are or modify them to make them even better.

We hope that through these network scenarios and models, you will start seeing Proxmox from a whole new point of view and be fully prepared to face any level of virtual infrastructure you are challenged with.

While analyzing these scenarios, keep in mind that the solutions and diagrams provided in this chapter are some of the many ways the network infrastructure could be set up. To fit the diagrams within the confinement of the book, some non-vital components might have been omitted. All network and identification information used in the network diagrams is fictional.

The network diagrams show the relationship between components within infrastructure, such as virtual environment, cluster of nodes, and overall network connectivity. They also represent how virtual network components such as bridges relate to each other, network segmentation, and so on.

# Scenario 1 – an academic institution

This scenario is for a typical academic institution with multiple networks, multiple campuses, and multiple building setups, along with both private and public networks.

Key requirements are as follows:

- Network isolation to protect sensitive data.
- Ability to have centralized management for network infrastructure.
- Professors should be on separate Wi-Fi, accessible only by them. This Wi-Fi should give professors the ability to log in to the main campus server to retrieve their files for lectures.
- Students should have on-campus Wi-Fi access and wired internet connection to their dormitories. These subnets must be separated from the main campus network.
- The library should be on a separate subnet with its own server.
- Classrooms, admin offices, and professors should be on the main isolated network. Professors should have the ability to retrieve their files from file servers in classroom computers during lectures.

This is a scenario for a typical academic institution campus network. Thanks to Proxmox, we can have all the main server equipment and the virtual environment in one place to have centralized management. There are five subnets in this network:

| Subnet | Network description |
|---|---|
| 10.170.10.0 | Wired network for dormitory. Firewall provides DHCP. This subnet does not need to go through the main network. |
| 10.180.10.0 | Student and public Wi-Fi on campus. Firewall provides DHCP. This subnet does not need to go through the main network. |
| 10.160.10.0 | Main administrative and professor network. Private Wi-Fi for professors is an extension of this network, to allow professors to retrieve their files wirelessly. All classrooms are also on this network to provide in-class access to files for professors. |
| 10.110.10.0 | Storage cluster. |
| 10.190.10.0 | Library subnet. DHCP provided by virtualized library server. This server is for the library only. Separate LAN (eth2) is used to connect the virtual machine with the library building. |

The following diagram shows typical network flow of academic institution:

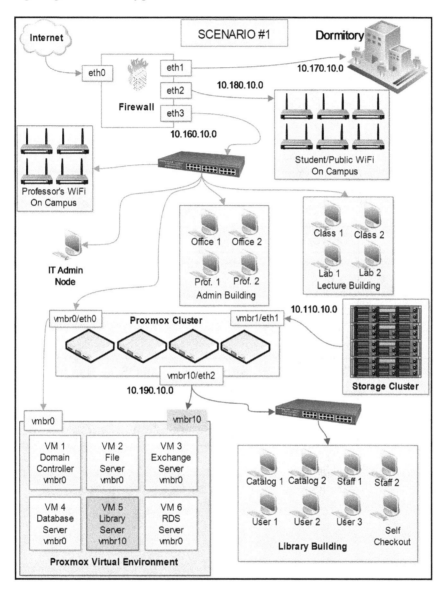

# Scenario 2 – multi-tier storage cluster with a Proxmox cluster

Key requirements are as follows:

- Need separate storage clusters for SSD, Hybrid HDD, and HDD
- Storage clusters should be on separate subnets
- Storage should be distributed with high availability and high scalability

For this scenario, each Proxmox node must have at least four network interface cards: three to connect to three storage cluster subnets and one to connect the virtual environment. This example is for six virtual machines to have access to three differently performing **storages**. The following are the three Ceph clusters and their performance categories:

| Subnet | Network description |
|---|---|
| 192.168.10.0:6789 | CEPH cluster #1 with SSDs for all OSDs. This subnet is connected with Proxmox nodes through eth1. This storage is used by VM6. |
| 192.168.20.0:6790 | CEPH cluster #2 with hybrid HDDs for all OSDs. This subnet is connected with Proxmox nodes through eth2. This storage is used by VM5. |
| 192.168.30.0:6791 | CEPH cluster #3 with HDDs for all OSDs. This subnet is connected with Proxmox nodes through eth3. This storage is used by VM1, VM2, VM3, and VM4. |
| 10.160.10.0 | This is the main subnet for all virtual machines. |

Multi-tiered infrastructure is very typical for data centers where there is a different level of SLA-based clients with various requirements for storage performance:

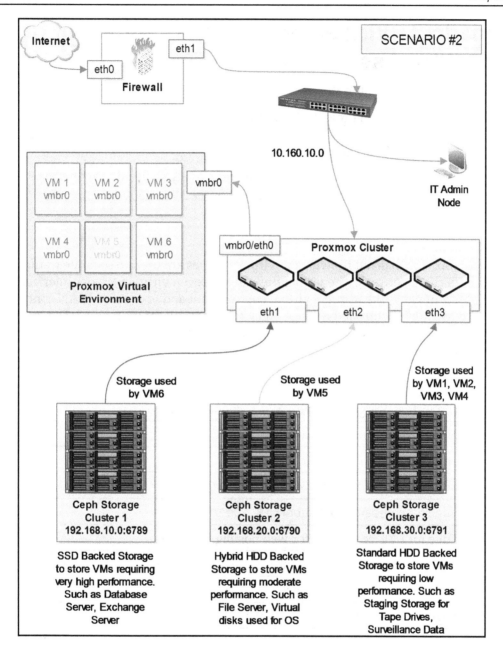

# Scenario 3 - Virtual infrastructure for a multi-tenant cloud service provider

Key requirements are as follows:

- There should be a firewall cluster for edge firewalls
- Each client network must be fully isolated from others
- A separate storage cluster for backup is required
- Client users must be able to access their company's virtual desktops via RDP
- There must be a bandwidth control ability for client networks' internet connectivity
- Replicate all data to another data center

In this scenario, a virtualized firewall and virtual bridges are used to separate traffic between each client network. The virtual firewall has seven virtual network interfaces to connect six client networks within a virtual environment and to provide WAN connectivity. Internet bandwidth is controlled through the virtual firewall for each vNIC. The virtual firewall is connected to WAN through the main virtual bridge, vmbr0. The Proxmox cluster has nine virtual bridges:

| Subnet | Network description |
|--------|---------------------|
| vmbr0 | Main virtual bridge to provide WAN connection to virtual firewall |
| vmbr1 | Connects main storage cluster |
| vmbr5 | Connects storage cluster for backup |
| vmbr10 | Bridge for company ABC subnet 10.10.10.0 |
| vmbr20 | Bridge for company XYZ subnet 10.20.20.0 |
| vmbr30 | Bridge for LXC containers for web hosting instances |
| vmbr40 | Bridge for object storage instances to be used by software developers |
| vmbr50 | Bridge for company 123 subnet 10.50.50.0 |
| vmbr60 | Bridge for a small business's virtual cluster |

Each bridge connects the client company's virtual machines together and creates isolated internal networks for respective clients:

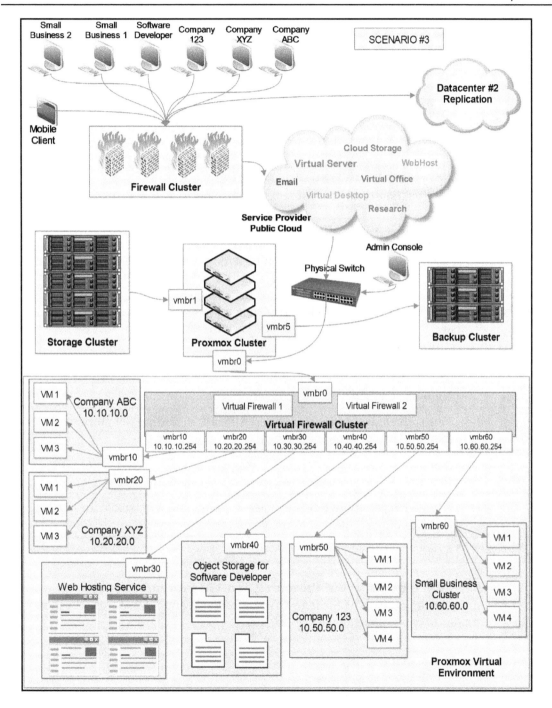

# Scenario 4 – nested virtual environment for a software development company

Key requirements are as follows:

- Developers must have nested virtual environments to test software
- Outsourced developers should have access to nested virtual environments using RDP
- Developers must have the ability to create or delete virtual clusters
- Nested virtual environments must be fully isolated from main company network

In this scenario, a nested Proxmox virtual cluster is created inside the main cluster for a software development company, mainly for software testing purposes. Since virtual clusters can be created and taken down at any time, it reduces cost and time setting up the entire hardware and setup process. A virtual firewall is used to direct traffic between nested and main virtual environments. All developers access their nested virtual machines through RDP port forwarding. Outsourced developers also need to connect to nested virtual environments using RDP. The main firewall does port forwarding to the virtual firewall. Then, the virtual firewall does port forwarding to nested virtual machines. Four subnets are used in this example:

| Subnet | Network description |
| --- | --- |
| 10.160.10.0 | This is the main company subnet. All staff, including developers, are on this subnet. |
| 10.160.20.0 | Main storage cluster subnet. It is connected to the main cluster with vmbr1. |
| 10.170.10.0 | Nested cluster subnet. It is isolated from the main cluster with vmbr2, which is only connected to the virtual firewall. |
| 10.170.20.0 | Nested storage cluster subnet. |

Virtual machines **VM Proxmox 1**, **VM Proxmox 2**, and **VM Proxmox 3** are used to create a nested Proxmox cluster, while **VM Storage 1**, **VM Storage 2**, and **VM Storage 3** virtual machines are used to create a nested storage cluster:

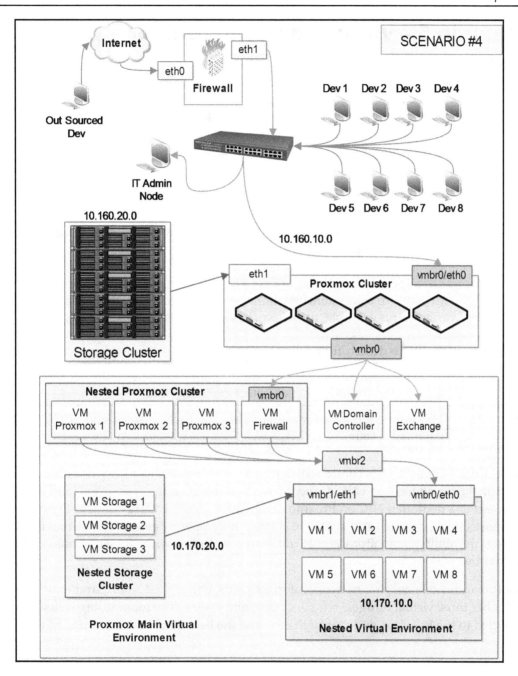

# Scenario 5 – virtual infrastructure for a public library

Key requirements are as follows:

- Catalog consoles should be on a separate subnet along with the main admin subnet
- Public Wi-Fi and consoles for public internet usage should be on the same separate subnet
- Need kiosks for self check-in/check-out of books and media
- Need online access to the library catalog
- Public internet traffic must be monitored for any **Internet Usage Policy** violation
- Public computers should have printer access

This is a typical scenario for a public library network system. Since a public library is a public place with access to computers for public usage, it is very important to isolate sensitive networks. In this example, the network is isolated using two subnets:

| Subnet | Network description |
|---|---|
| `10.16.10.0` | Main network for library staff and protected consoles only, such as catalog, kiosks, staff printers, and self check-in/check-out. |
| `10.20.10.0` | This public subnet is for public Wi-Fi, internet consoles, and printers, with a payment system. |

The network `10.20.10.0` is controlled, managed, and isolated using a virtual firewall, VM5. The virtual firewall has two vNICs, one for WAN connection through `vmbr3` and the other to connect to a dedicated NIC on Proxmox node through `vmbr4`. The `eth2` of Proxmox node is connected to a separate LAN switch to connect only public devices. The virtual firewall provides the ability to monitor internet traffic to keep in line with any violations of **Library Internet Usage** Policy.

Each Proxmox node has four network interface cards, `eth0`, `eth1`, `eth2`, and `eth3`, and the cluster has three virtual bridges, `vmbr0`, `vmbr2`, and `vmbr4`. The main storage cluster is connected to the Proxmox node through eth1 and the backup cluster is connected to `eth3`:

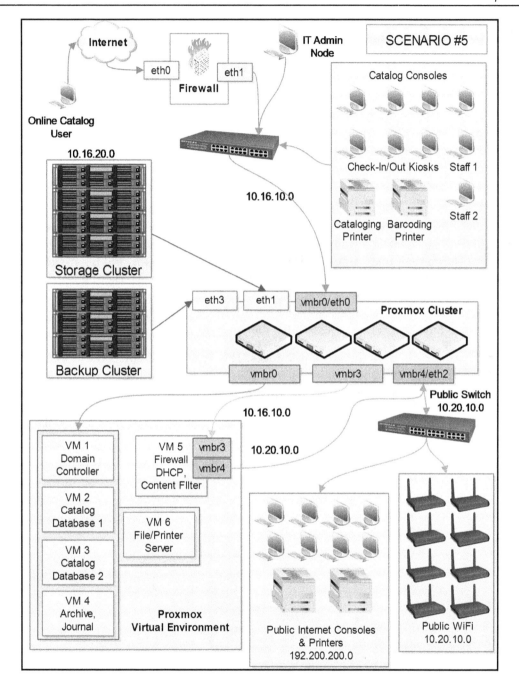

# Scenario 6 – multi-floor office virtual infrastructure with virtual desktops

Key requirements are as follows:

- All staff members should be on virtual desktops
- Redundant internet connectivity
- Each department should have their own remote desktop server
- Accounting department network traffic should only be directed to their department

This is a common scenario for an office building where departments are on different floors of the building. Since the accounting department requires data isolation, we are going to use a VLAN to isolate their data. Administrative offices, the copy room, and the main server room are on the 4th floor. The HR department is on the 5th floor, Marketing is on the 6th, and the accounting department is on the 7th floor. The 5th, 6th, and 7th floors have their own LAN switches. So, we could easily use VLAN for another floor if it was required. We only need to set up VLAN on the switch for the 4th floor.

Each Proxmox node has two network interfaces. The eth1 is to connect the storage cluster and eth0 is to connect all virtual machines to their departments. The vlan0.10 is used to separate Accounting traffic, which is only directed to the 7th floor.

All department staff use virtual desktops through RDP. Each department's virtual server acts as a remote desktop server and the department's main server:

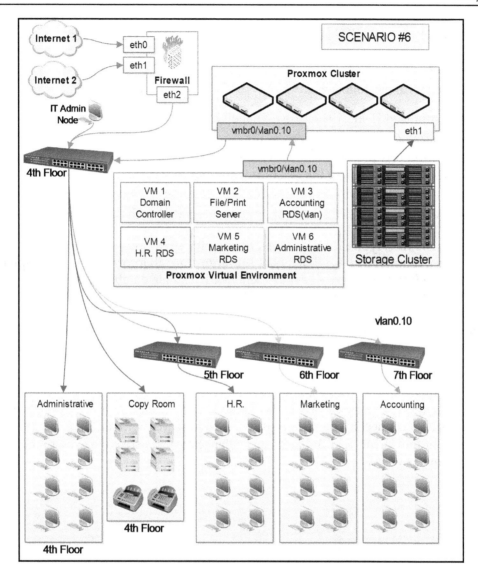

# Scenario 7 – virtual infrastructure for the hotel industry

Key requirements are as follows:

- Centralized IT infrastructure management.
- Dedicated secured Wi-Fi access for guests.
- Secured private Wi-Fi access in the restaurant and bar for menu tablets only. The Wi-Fi needs to talk to the restaurant and bar server.
- All staff must have remote desktops for day-to-day work.
- A video surveillance system should be integrated with the virtual environment.

This is a scenario for a typical hotel establishment with an in-house restaurant. This example uses a central virtualized database server to store all information. Although it is an unconventional way to connect all departments with a single database (including a surveillance system), it is possible to use an all-in-one single solution to reduce cost and management overhead. In a typical scenario, separate software is used to handle different departments without data portability. In this example, unified management software connects all departments with a single database and a customized user interface for each department.

Secured non-filtered Wi-Fi connectivity is provided for all guests. DHCP is provided directly by the firewall. Secured private Wi-Fi is set up for restaurant menu tablets only. All menu tablets only connect to the restaurant/bar virtual server, with an IP of 10.190.1.5. All department thin clients and IP-based surveillance cameras are connected to the main network subnet 10.190.1.0:

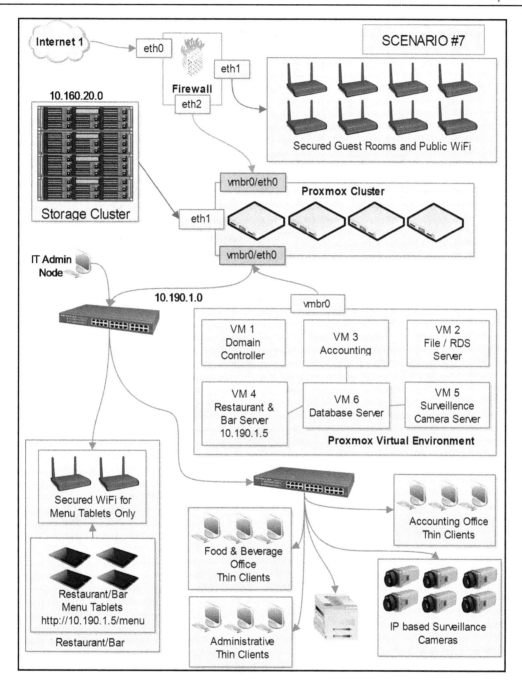

# Scenario 8 – virtual infrastructure for geological survey organization

Key requirements are as follows:

- Field surveyors should submit their work orders from their mobile devices through a VPN connection
- There must be a fail-over infrastructure in the multi-site network topology

In this scenario, a geographical survey company has a main office and branch office connected by 1+ GBps hard-link network connectivity. Each office has an identical infrastructure set up. All surveyors use mobile devices, such as tablets, for their survey work. The survey software automatically detects which office IP is live and sends data to the infrastructure of that office. All data is replicated at the block level in real time between the two offices.

If the infrastructure of one office becomes unavailable, staff can simply continue to work using the infrastructure from the other office:

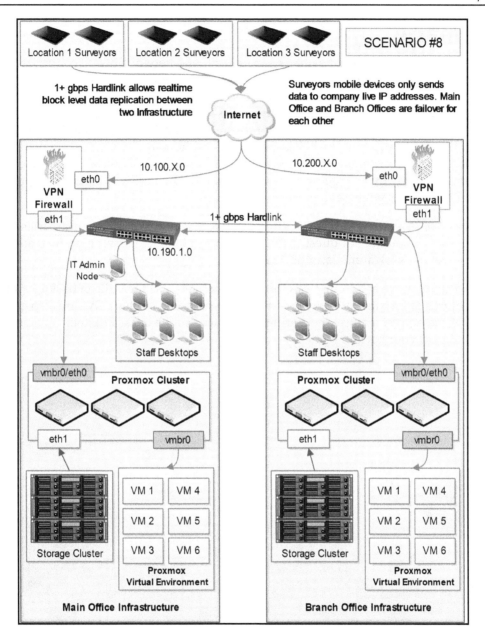

SCENARIO #8

Location 1 Surveyors    Location 2 Surveyors    Location 3 Surveyors

1+ gbps Hardlink allows realtime block level data replication between two Infrastructure

Internet

Surveyors mobile devices only sends data to company live IP addresses. Main Office and Branch Offices are failover for each other

10.100.X.0    eth0    VPN Firewall    eth1

10.200.X.0    eth0    VPN Firewall    eth1

1+ gbps Hardlink

10.190.1.0

IT Admin Node

Staff Desktops    Staff Desktops

vmbr0/eth0    Proxmox Cluster    Proxmox Cluster    vmbr0/eth0

eth1    vmbr0    eth1    vmbr0

Storage Cluster    VM 1    VM 4    Storage Cluster    VM 1    VM 4
                   VM 2    VM 5                     VM 2    VM 5
                   VM 3    VM 6                     VM 3    VM 6

Proxmox Virtual Environment    Proxmox Virtual Environment

**Main Office Infrastructure**    **Branch Office Infrastructure**

# Summary

Virtual environments are very flexible, so there is no one-network-fits-all configuration. Each network will be unique. The components and requirements described in this chapter are mere guidelines to show how to take the correct approach to plan for a production-level Proxmox setup. We saw some of the requirements of a production-level setup, and we covered how to allocate CPU and memory resources properly for both the Proxmox host node and the virtual machine itself. We also discussed how to give Ceph storage the best chance of providing redundancy along with performance. Finally, we saw how to cool equipment efficiently by leveraging liquid cooling, thus increasing Proxmox computing node density per rack while saving energy.

We also saw some real-world scenarios of Proxmox in action in different industries. We hope this will aid you in your quest to find that perfect balance between performance and budget that all network administrators crave.

In the next chapter, we are going to see how to effectively use the built-in backup and restore features of Proxmox to be part of a disaster planning strategy. We are also going to learn about the newest feature, replication, introduced in the latest Proxmox 5.0 release, and how this can aid your backup strategy.

# 13
# Back Up and Restore Virtual Machines

A good backup strategy is the last line of defense against disasters such as hardware failure, environmental damage, accidental deletions, or misconfigurations. In a virtual environment, a backup strategy can turn into a daunting task because of the number of virtual machines that need to be backed up. In a busy production environment, a new virtual machine can come and go anytime. Without a proper backup plan, the entire backup task can become difficult to manage. Gone are the days when we had only a little server hardware to deal with and backing it up was an easy task. In today's virtual environments, a backup solution has to deal with several dozen, or possibly several hundred, virtual machines.

Depending on the business requirement, an administrator may have to back up all the virtual machines regularly, instead of just the files inside VMs. Backing up an entire virtual machine takes up a very large amount of space after a while, depending on how many previous backups we have. A granular file backup helps you quickly back up user data but provides no protection against entire VM corruption or loss.

Along with a backup strategy, a restore plan is equally important, because a backup is only useful when we can successfully restore data in a timely and proper manner after a disaster. In this chapter, we will cover the following topics:

- Exploring Proxmox backup options
- Configuring backups
- Configuring snapshots
- Restoring VMs
- VM replication
- Backing up a configuration file

# Proxmox backup options

As of Proxmox VE 5.0, there are two backup options included out of the box:

- **Full backup**: This backs up the entire virtual machine
- **Snapshots**: This freezes the state of a VM at a point in time

Proxmox 5.0 can only do a full backup and cannot do any granular file backup from inside a virtual machine. Proxmox also does not use any backup agents for guest VMs.

# A full backup

A full backup is a complete, compressed backup of a virtual machine, including its configuration file. We can take this backup and restore it locally to the same cluster or to an entirely different Proxmox cluster. We can potentially set up a full backup every day, or on a different schedule of up to one week. Since a full backup commits the complete backup of the entire virtual machine, including all the virtual disk images in it, it is the slowest backup option. It is also the safest, since the final backup file is not dependent on the original VM. Two of the most important components of a full backup are backup modes and compression level.

# Full backup modes

Various backup modes offer different data assurance and speed. There are three types of modes available for a full backup.

### Snapshot

Snapshots for a full backup are not the same as snapshots for virtual machines, where they freeze the state of the VM in a point in time. A snapshot for a full backup is when it is committed without powering off or temporarily suspending the VM. This is also known as a **live backup**. Since a backup occurs while the VM is running, there is no downtime for this mode, but it also has the longest backup time. On rare occasions, files in use can cause backup errors due to file locks.

## Suspend

In this mode, a backup occurs after temporarily suspending or freezing the VM. There is no need to completely power off the VM; thus, the downtime is moderate during a backup. After a backup is completed, the VM resumes regular operation. This mode has a much lower chance of errors during a backup since a VM is suspended.

## Stop

In this mode, running VMs are automatically powered off or stopped and then powered on after the backup has been completed. This provides the maximum assurance of zero errors in the backup, since the VM is not running at all. This is also the fastest backup mode.

# Backup compression

In Proxmox, we can commit a backup with different compression levels. The higher the level, the less space is used to store backup files, but it also consumes higher CPU resources to perform compression. There are three compression levels in a Proxmox backup.

## None

When this level is selected, no compression occurs for the backup task. While this will take the least amount of CPUs during a backup task, do keep in mind that it will take a significantly large amount of space to store backup files. Proxmox virtual disk images are sparsed, which means that an allocated disk image only uses some of the actual data space. The rest of the allocation is sparsed, or filled with zeros.

A backup with no compression will save the disk image without compressing the empty spaces. This will cause the backup file to take as much room as the disk image itself.

> Use this option with care and ensure that the backup storage has enough storage space to hold uncompressed backup files.

## LZO

This is the default compression level in Proxmox. LZO provides a balance between speed and compression. It also has the fastest decompression rate, making the restoration of a VM much faster.

## GZIP

This level provides a much higher compression ratio but also takes a longer time to back up. Due to an increased compression rate, this level consumes a lot more CPU and memory resources. We need to ensure that backup nodes have sufficient processing ability before we enable this level.

# Snapshots

Snapshots freeze or capture the state of a virtual machine at a point in time. This is not a full backup of a VM, since the snapshots are fully dependent on the original VM. We cannot move snapshots elsewhere for safekeeping. Snapshots are used to roll back to a previous state. Since snapshots do not back up the entire virtual machine with disk images, they are the fastest backup option to quickly save the state of the VM. In Proxmox, we can take snapshots of a running VM; in which case, the content of the running memory also gets saved. This way, we can revert to the earlier VM exactly as it was running when a snapshot was taken.

A good use case of this backup is when testing software or applying updates. We can take snapshots of a VM prior to installing any software or applying updates. So, if something goes wrong after the installation, we can simply revert to the previous state in a matter of minutes instead of reinstalling the entire virtual machine. This is much faster and cleaner than uninstalling the tested software itself.

A full backup should never be substituted with snapshots. Always include a full backup in a primary disaster recovery strategy.

As of Proxmox VE 5.0, there is no snapshot scheduling option. All snapshots must be performed manually. For this reason, snapshots are not widely used as a means of main backup planning. Two of the most used scenarios for snapshots are to save the state of a VM before applying updates/patches or installing software for testing, and to save very mission critical VM states in between full backups. In an environment with several dozen virtual machines, manual snapshots can become a time-consuming task. It is possible to set up snapshot scheduling using `bash`, `cron`, and `qm`, but these methods can be flawed and they are known to be somewhat unstable; therefore, they are not recommended for a production environment.

If a full backup is performed on a virtual machine that has snapshots applied, the snapshots do not get placed in the backup file. A full backup task ignores all the snapshot images. Also, when a virtual machine is deleted, all the snapshots belonging to the virtual machine also get deleted.

# Configuring backup storage

A sound backup strategy has a dedicated shared storage for the backup images instead of local storage or storage that is used for the disk images themselves. This way, we can centralize the backup location and restore them even in the event of a Proxmox node failure. If the backup is stored locally on the same node, during hardware failures, that node may become completely inaccessible, causing a VM restoration delay.

One of the most popular options for a backup storage node is NFS. In an enterprise or mission-critical environment, a cluster with built-in redundancy dedicated to backups is a recommended practice. In smaller environments, good redundancy can still be achieved using storage options, such as Gluster or DRBD. With the addition of ZFS and Gluster in Proxmox VE, it is now a viable option to turn a Proxmox node into a backup using ZFS and still manage the node through the Proxmox GUI. Unfortunately, we cannot store backup files on the Ceph RBD storage.

For a single backup storage node, FreeNAS is a great option without cluster redundancy. Regardless of which storage system is used, the primary goal is to store a backup on a separate node instead of the computing node. Refer to `Chapter 4`, *Storage Systems*, for information on how to attach various storage systems to Proxmox. Once a storage is set up and attached to Proxmox, we need to ensure that the content type for the storage is configured in order to store backup files and backup rotation quantity. There are two options in the storage dialog box to select the content type and to define the backup rotation quantity. The following screenshot shows the storage dialog box for an NFS storage in our example cluster:

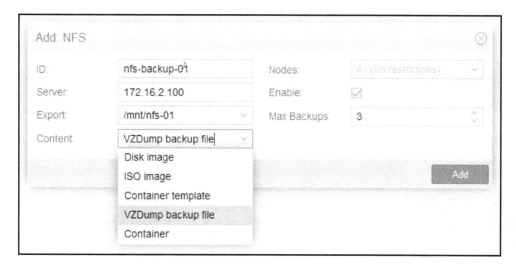

In the preceding screenshot, we selected the **VZDump backup file** from the drop-down list and typed 3 in the **Max Backups**, or backup rotation, quantity tab. This means that the storage will allow you to store backup files and three recent backups will always be kept. Older backups will automatically be deleted. This will only happen automatically when the backup is handled by a backup schedule.

When performing manual backups, this quantity value will actually prevent committing manual backups if there are already three backups stored in the storage for a VM. In such cases, we will have to manually delete older backups or increase the quantity value to accommodate new manual backups. We can delete backup files for the VM through the **Backup** tab menu of the VM or directly from the storage device in the content tab. We need to select the backup file that we need to delete and then click on **Remove**. The following screenshot shows the backup menu for a VM:

| | Backup now  Restore  Remove  Show Configuration | | |
|---|---|---|---|
| 🗐 Summary | | | |
| >_ Console | Name ↑ | Format | Size |
| 🖵 Hardware | vzdump-qemu-10001041-2016_05_22-04_59_45.vma.lzo | vma.lzo | 616.84 GiB |
| ⚙ Options | vzdump-qemu-10001041-2016_05_29-09_30_33.vma.lzo | vma.lzo | 730.40 GiB |
| ☰ Task History | | | |
| 👁 Monitor | | | |
| 🖺 Backup | | | |
| ↻ Replication | | | |
| ⟲ Snapshots | | | |

Make sure that you set appropriate values for **Max Backups**, because higher values will keep more backup files, consuming a lot more space in the storage node. Too many backup files and not enough space will cause new backup tasks to fail. We can also set up two storage nodes and use one to store frequent backups, for example, weekly, while the other one can be used to store longer interval backups, for example, biannually.

Depending on the backup strategy and business requirement, there may be a need to keep certain periods of backup history. Proxmox allows both automatic and manual deletion of any backups outside the required history range. Automatic deletion is performed through the value of **Max Backups** in the backup dialog box. We can enter any number between 0 to 365 as **Max backups**. For example, our NFS storage has a **Max Backups** of 3. This means that during a full backup, Proxmox will keep the three newest backups of each virtual machine and delete anything older.

If we were to commit daily backups, we could potentially keep 365 days', or 1 year's, worth of backups at any given time. If we did a backup every other day, then it would be 2 years' worth of backups.

# Show VM configuration from backup

**Show Configuration** is a new feature added from Proxmox 5.0. Previously, we could not see the configuration of a VM that was backed up without restoring it completely. This is useful when the VM does not exist any more and only a backup is available. The option is under the **Backup** menu, named **Show Configuration**, as shown in the following screenshot:

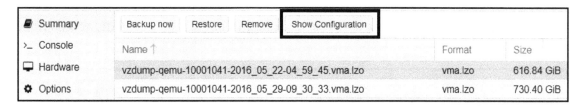

To view the configuration, select a backup file, then click on **Show Configuration**. This will open a dialog box with the full configuration of the VM this backup file belongs to. The following screenshot shows the configuration of the VM #101:

```
Configuration                                                                    ⊗

arch: amd64
cores: 1
cpulimit: 1
hostname: ubuntu-01
memory: 512
nameserver: 8.8.8.8 208.67.222.222
net0: name=eth0,bridge=vmbr0,firewall=1,gw=192.168.1.254,hwaddr=C6:5B:9C:CB:4C:D4,ip=192.168.1.1/24,type=veth
ostype: ubuntu
rootfs: local-lvm:vm-101-disk-1,acl=0,size=6G
searchdomain: domain.com
swap: 512
unprivileged: 1
```

# Configuring full backup

All full backups are in the `.tar` format, containing both the configuration file and virtual disk image file. The backup files are all you need to restore a virtual machine on any nodes and on any storage. Full backup files are named based on the following formats for both KVM and LXC virtual machines:

```
vzdump-lxc-<ct_id>-YYYY_MM_DD-HH_MM_SS.tar
vzdump-lxc-<ct_id>-YYYY_MM_DD-HH_MM_SS.tar.lzo
vzdump-lxc-<ct_id>-YYYY_MM_DD-HH_MM_SS.tar.gz

vzdump-qemu-<vm_id>-YYYY_MM_DD-HH_MM_SS.vma
vzdump-qemu-<vm_id>-YYYY_MM_DD-HH_MM_SS.vma.lzo
vzdump-qemu-<vm_id>-YYYY_MM_DD-HH_MM_SS.vma.fz
```

The following screenshot shows a list of backup files in a backup storage node, as seen from the Proxmox GUI:

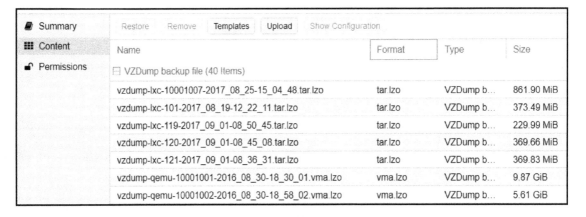

| Name | Format | Type | Size |
| --- | --- | --- | --- |
| ⊟ VZDump backup file (40 Items) | | | |
| vzdump-lxc-10001007-2017_08_25-15_04_48.tar.lzo | tar.lzo | VZDump b... | 861.90 MiB |
| vzdump-lxc-101-2017_08_19-12_22_11.tar.lzo | tar.lzo | VZDump b... | 373.49 MiB |
| vzdump-lxc-119-2017_09_01-08_50_45.tar.lzo | tar.lzo | VZDump b... | 229.99 MiB |
| vzdump-lxc-120-2017_09_01-08_45_08.tar.lzo | tar.lzo | VZDump b... | 369.66 MiB |
| vzdump-lxc-121-2017_09_01-08_36_31.tar.lzo | tar.lzo | VZDump b... | 369.83 MiB |
| vzdump-qemu-10001001-2016_08_30-18_30_01.vma.lzo | vma.lzo | VZDump b... | 9.87 GiB |
| vzdump-qemu-10001002-2016_08_30-18_58_02.vma.lzo | vma.lzo | VZDump b... | 5.61 GiB |

The backup list is sortable by the **Format**, **Type**, or **Size** of backup files. From the same page, we can also delete or restore backup files.

# Creating a schedule for backup

In Proxmox, we can schedule automated backup tasks or commit manual backups for each virtual machine. Whether scheduled or manual, the backup process is the same for both KVM and LXC virtual machines. Schedules can be created from the **Backup** option under the Datacenter tabbed menu. We will see each option box in detail in the following sections. The **Backup** option shows a list of already created backup schedules, along with options to **Add**, **Remove**, and **Edit** tasks. The schedule dialog box is the same for adding, removing, and editing backup tasks. We can click on **Add** to open the dialog box, as shown in the following screenshot:

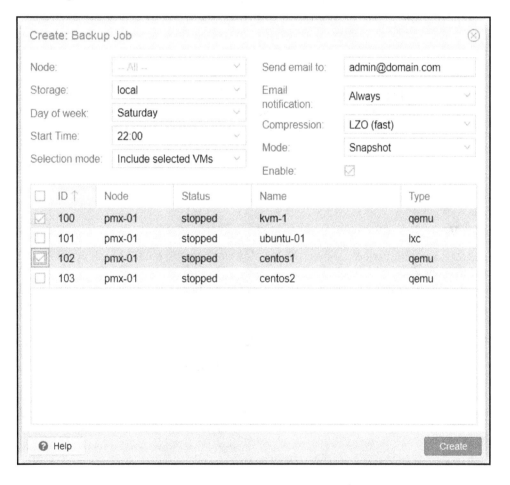

In the preceding screenshot, we created a backup task to perform twice a week for selected virtual machines. The dialog box has several components, which need to be defined in order to schedule a backup task.

# Node

This is a drop-down list used to select a Proxmox node to show only the virtual machines in that node. This also sets the task to apply to that node only. For example, if we select a particular node and a VM in it to commit a backup, and we later move that VM to another node, no backup task will be performed since the VM is no longer in the original node. By default, all nodes are selected. In our example, we have selected all nodes.

# Storage

This is a drop-down list used to select a backup storage destination where all full backups will be stored. Typically, an NFS server is used for backup storage. They are easy to set up and do not require a lot of upfront investment due to their lower performance requirements. Backup servers are much leaner than computing nodes since they do not have to run any virtual machines. Some storage nodes, such as ZFS, do need a lot of memory to operate adequately.

# Day of week

This is a drop-down list used to select which day or days the backup task applies to. We can select multiple days in this list. In order to create a daily backup task, all days need to be selected. As of Proxmox VE 5.0, we can only create daily or weekly backup schedules.

# Start Time

Unlike **Day of week**, only one time slot can be selected. Multiple selections of times, to backup different times of the day, are not possible.

> If the backup needs to run multiple times a day, create a separate task for each time slot.

# Selection mode

This is a drop-down list used to define how VMs are selected for backups. There are three options available to select from:

- The **All** mode will select all the virtual machines within the whole Proxmox cluster or node, depending on the selection in the **Node** drop-down list
- The **Exclude selected VMs** mode will back up all VMs except the ones selected
- The **Include selected VMs** mode will back up only the ones selected

# Send email to

Enter a valid email address here so that the Proxmox backup task can send an email upon backup task completion, or if there was an issue during backup. The email includes the entire log of the backup tasks.

 It is highly recommended that you enter an email address here so that an administrator or backup operator can receive backup task feedback emails. This will allow you to find out if there was an issue during backup or how much time it actually took, to see if any performance issues occurred during backup.

# Email notification

This is a drop-down list used to define when the backup task should send automated emails. We can select this option to always send an email or to only send an email when there is an error or a failure.

# Compression

This is a drop-down list used to select the compression level for the backup task. Refer to the *Backup compression* section earlier in this chapter to see the differences between the various compression levels. By default, the **LZO (fast)** compression method is selected.

# Mode

This is a drop-down list used to define the backup mode for the task. Refer to the *Full backup modes* section earlier in this chapter to see the differences between backup modes. By default, all running virtual machine backups occur with the snapshot option.

# Enable

This is a checkbox used to enable or disable a backup task. This was newly added in the recent Proxmox version. With this option, we can disable a backup task temporarily instead of deleting and creating from scratch, as was the case in previous Proxmox versions. The following screenshot shows the **Backup** option with our newly created backup task listed:

# Creating a manual backup

A manual backup can be performed on a particular virtual machine at any time through the Proxmox GUI. The manual backup option is accessible through the **Backup** tabbed menu of the virtual machine. From the same **Backup** menu, we can back up, restore, and delete backup files.

To open the backup creation dialog box, we select the VM we are going to back up, then click on the **Backup now** button. The manual backup dialog box is extremely simple. We only need to select the destination **Storage** node, the backup **Mode**, and the **Compression** level, as shown in the following screenshot:

# Creating snapshots

A snapshot are a great way to preserve the state of a virtual machine. It is much faster than a full backup, since it does not copy all the data. A snapshot is not really a backup, in a way, and does not perform granular level backup. It captures the state at a point in time and allows rollback to that previous state. A snapshot can be really helpful when used in between full backups. The **Take Snapshot** option can be found under the **Snapshots** tabbed menu of the virtual machine. A newly installed VM without any snapshots will appear under the **Snapshots** menu, as shown in the following screenshot:

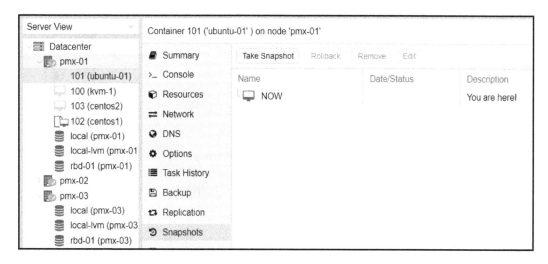

The actual snapshot creation process is very straightforward. Click on **Take Snapshot** to open the dialog box, and then just enter a **Name**, select or deselect the RAM content, and type in some **Description**. The **Name** textbox does not allow any spaces and the name must start with a letter of the alphabet. The following screenshot shows the snapshots creation dialog box for our example VM #100:

Keep in mind that when creating snapshot of an LXC container, the option to **Include RAM** is not present. When selecting this option for KVMs, the bigger the RAM allocation is for the virtual machine, the longer it will take to create a snapshot, but it is still much faster than a full backup.

The snapshot feature is available for both KVM and LXC virtual machines. The following screenshot shows the **Snapshots** option with our newly created snapshot:

If we want to go back to the snapshot image, we just select the snapshot we want to go back to and click on **Rollback**. Simply click **Yes** when prompted to confirm the rollback.

Keep in mind that when you roll back to the earlier virtual machine state, it will erase all the changes that happened to the virtual machine between the time of rolling back and the snapshot being rolled back to.

# Restoring a virtual machine

Like backup, we can also restore virtual machines through the Proxmox GUI. VMs can be restored through the **Backup** menu tab of the VM or by selecting a backup file through the storage content list. If **Restore** is selected through the VM **Backup** option, then the **VM ID** cannot be changed. To understand this better, let's take a look at the following example:

In the preceding screenshot, we are under the **Backup** option for VM #100. Since the **Backup** option shows a list of all backup files stored in that backup storage node, we can see the backup file for VM #100. If we select the backup file and then click on **Restore**, we will not be able to restore the VM #100 on its own. Instead, it will actually replace VM #100. The following screenshot shows the **Restore** dialog box where the destination **VM ID** is not definable:

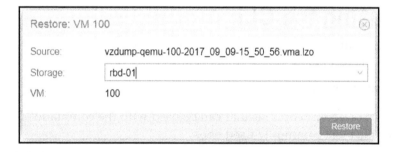

If we select the backup file for VM #100 from the storage content list and then click on **Restore**, we will be able to define a **VM ID** in the **Restore** dialog box, as shown in the following screenshot:

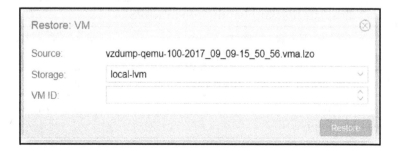

Defining the **VM ID** during restore is needed when we want to restore a VM while the VM's same ID stays intact. If the same **VM ID** is kept, then the existing virtual machine in the cluster with the same ID will be deleted and restored from the backup version. If we use a different ID before restoring it, then we will have an exact copy of the original VM with a different VM ID.

> One important thing to remember is that a full backup created for a virtual machine with the `.qcow2` or `.vmdk` image format can only be restored to local, CephFS, or NFS-like storages. But a virtual machine with the `.raw` image format can be restored on just about any storage system. RBD and LVM storages do not support image types such as `.qcow2` or `.vmdk`.

# Backup/restore through the CLI

In Proxmox, the entire backup and restore process can be managed from the command line if the GUI becomes inaccessible.

## Backup using the CLI

The command to commit a backup for both KVM and LXC virtual machines is the same. The following is the command format for a backup:

```
# vzdump <vmid> <options>
```

There is a long list of `vzdump` options that can be used with the command. The following are just a few of the most commonly used ones:

| Options | Description |
|---|---|
| `-all` | The default value is 0. This option will back up all available virtual machines in a Proxmox node. |
| `-bwlimit` | This adjusts the backup bandwidth in KBPS. |
| `-compress` | The default value is LZO. This sets the compression type or disables compression. The available options are 0, 1, `gzip`, and `lzo`. |
| `-mailto` | This is the email address used to send a backup report. |
| `-maxfiles` | This contains an integer number. This sets the maximum number of backup files to be kept. |

| -mod | The default value is stop. This sets the backup mode. The available options are snapshot, stop, and suspend. |
|---|---|
| -remove | The default value is 1. This removes older backups if the value entered is more than in -maxfiles. |
| -lockwait | This is the maximum time in minutes to wait for a global lock. The default value is 180. |
| -storage | This is the storage ID of the destination backup storage. |
| -tmpdir | This specifies a temporary directory to store files during backup. This is optional. |

# Restore using the CLI

Although the same command can be used to perform a backup for both KVM and LXC, there are two separate commands available to restore the KVM and LXC virtual machines:

- qm restore: To restore KVM-based VMs
- pct restore: To restore LXC containers

The following command format will restore KVM VMs through the command line:

```
#qmrestore <backup_file> <new/old_vmid> <options>
```

Based on the previous command, if we want to restore our example KVM #100 from a backup onto local storage, it will appear as follows:

```
#qmrestore /var/lib/vz/dump/vzdump-qemu-110-2017_08_13-20_24_26.vma.lzo 110
-storage local
```

The following options can be used with the `qmrestore` command:

| Options | Description |
|---------|-------------|
| `-force <int>` | The Boolean value is 0 or 1. This option allows for overwriting the existing VM. Use this option with caution. |
| `-unique <int>` | The Boolean value is 0 or 1. This assigns a unique, random Ethernet address to the virtual network interface. |
| `-pool <string>` | This is the name of the pool to add the VM to. |
| `-storage <string>` | This is the storage ID of the destination storage where the VM disk image will be restored. |

The following command format will restore LXC containers through the command line:

```
#pct restore <ct_id> <backupfile> <options>
```

Based on the previous command, if we want to restore our example container #101 onto local storage, it will appear as follows:

```
#pct restore 101 /var/lib/vz/dump/vzdump-
lxc-101-2017_08_25-18_49_04.tar.lzo -storage local
```

The following options can be used with the `pct restore` command:

| Options | Description |
|---------|-------------|
| `-force <int>` | The default value is 0 or 1. This option allows overwriting the existing VM. Use this option with caution. |
| `-cpulimit <int>` | The value range is from 0 to 128 with the default value as 0. This defines the number of CPUs or CPU time. Value 0 defines no CPU limit. |
| `-cpuunits <int>` | The value range is from 0 to 500,000, with the default value as 1,024. This defines the CPU weight of the VM in relation to other VMs. |
| `-console <int>` | The default value is 1. This defines the number of consoles to be attached to the container. |
| `-force <int>` | The Boolean value is 0 or 1. This allows overwriting of the existing container with the restored one. |

| `-hostname <string>` | This sets the hostname of the container after a restore. |
|---|---|
| `-memory <int>` | The default value is `512`. This defines the amount of memory allocated for the container. |
| `-swap <int>` | The default value is `512`. This defines the amount of swap space for the container. |
| `-password <string>` | This sets the root password in the container after a restore. |
| `-storage <string>` | This defines the destination storage ID where the container will be restored. |

# Unlocking a VM after a backup error

Any backup process can be interrupted before it is finished due to various issues, such as backup storage node failure, loss of network connectivity, very large virtual disk images, and so on. Prior to starting the actual backup process, Proxmox puts a global lock on the VM so that multiple backup tasks cannot be run on the same node. If the backup is not finished successfully, this lock sometimes remains in place and is not automatically removed. If we try to start/stop the VM, we may see an error message that informs us that the VM is locked.

In such cases, we need to manually unlock the VM to resume the normal operation. The unlocking cannot be done from the Proxmox GUI, but only through the CLI. The command will need to be run in the node where the VM is. The following command will unlock a locked VM in a Proxmox node:

```
# qm unlock <vm_id>
```

# Virtual machine replication

Virtual machine replication is a brand new feature that has been added from the Proxmox VE 5.0 release. This is a very useful feature for a single-node Proxmox environment where VM disk images reside locally on the same computer node the VMs actually run from. With this option, VMs can be replicated to a different node in real time should the primary node go down for any number of reasons. In such a scenario, the second node with a replica of the VMs can be brought online, thus minimizing downtime significantly.

It is very important to note here that this replication will only work when the VM disk image is stored on a local ZFS storage.

The storage must be attached to a Proxmox cluster using the **ZFS** storage plugin, as shown in the following screenshot:

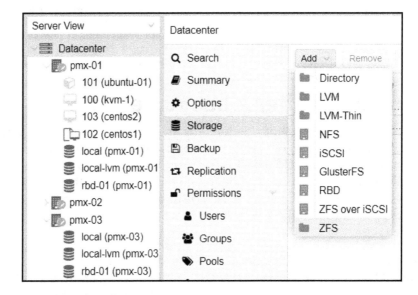

The replication simply will not work when the disk image is on any other storage. Even if the disk image is stored on a ZFS storage with NFS share, replication will not work. In such a scenario, when trying to create replication, the following error message will be displayed:

ZFS is needed because the replication uses ZFS snapshots to perform replication, minimizing network traffic. A new command line tool, `pvesr`, has been added to perform all replication tasks. When we manage replication through the GUI, it just leverages the `pvesr` command.

It should be noted here that the replication feature is presented as a technology preview in Proxmox 5.0, but from our extensive lab testing, it has proven very stable. If you have a single-node Proxmox deployment and want to use replication as a primary backup strategy, then doing tests to familiarize yourself with the replication process is highly recommended.

# Creating a replication task through the GUI

The replication menu is accessible from `Datacenter`-, node-, and VM-specific menus. The only difference is each replication menu shows the specific entity-related replication tasks. For example, the `Datacenter`-specific replication menu shows all replication tasks within the cluster, whereas the node-specific replication menu shows replication tasks for that node only.

To access the replication dialog box through the Proxmox GUI, select a VM you want to replicate; then, from the **Replication** option, click on **Add**, as shown in the following screenshot:

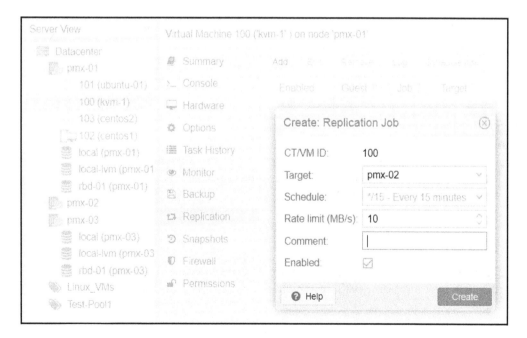

Since we are creating a replicated version of the VM, we cannot define any manual ID for the VM. The replicated VM is going to be an exact copy of the existing VM, including the same ID and identical configuration.

# Target

This is a drop-down list to select which Proxmox node the VM is going to be replicated to. Note that the destination node must also have ZFS storage set up. If the source VM is on ZFS but the destination node has no ZFS storage, we cannot create the replication task. We will see an error message, as shown in the earlier section. It is possible to replicate a VM to multiple nodes, thus increasing redundancy. We can achieve this by creating multiple tasks for the VM, but we can never replicate a VM to the same storage or same node the VM is in.

# Schedule

Here, we define how frequently the VM will be replicated. Initially, when a replication task is started, the process will replicate the entire VM; after that, it will only replicate incrementally on set intervals. The drop-down list has some predefined schedules, which can be also customized, simply by typing the value. For example, if we want to replicate the VM every 5 minutes, we can simply type */5 in the schedule textbox, since there is no predefined schedule for 5 minutes. Note that frequent replication will increase bandwidth consumption, depending on how much data is changing in the VM.

# Rate limit (MB/s)

We can limit the amount of bandwidth that can be consumed during the replication process. By default, it is set to unlimited bandwidth. When replicating multiple VMs on the node, it may be very helpful to limit the rate so the running VMs can be used without any issue. The rate limit is defined in MBps.

# Enabled

To enable the replication task, this option needs to be checked. This is useful when disabling the replication task temporarily. To enable it again, simply select the task and click on the **Edit** button.

# Creating a replication task through the CLI

In order to create a replication task through the CLI, it is very important to know that each replication task created must have a cluster-wide unique ID. When the tasks are created through the GUI, the ID gets created and assigned automatically. But when they are created through the CLI, we have to manually assign the ID. This unique job ID is node-specific only. For example, if the first node has a replication task using a job ID from 0 to 10, another node can also have unique job ID of the same sequence. The format of this ID is:

```
<vmid>-<integer job number>
```

We are going to use the pvesr command to create a replication task. The following is the command-line format to create a task:

```
# pvesr create-local-job <vmid>-<job number> <destination_node> --schedule
"<frequency>" --rate <limit in MB/s>
```

Using the command-line format, if we want to create a replication task for VM #100 to replicate to node pmx-02 every 5 minutes with a rate limit of 20 MBps, we will enter the following command:

```
# pvesr create-local-job 100-0 pmx-02 --schedule "*/5" --rate 20
```

If we want to create another task for VM #102 to node pmx-02 every 30 minutes without a rate limit, we will enter the following command:

```
# pvesr create-local-job 102-1 pmx-02 --schedule "*/30"
```

Note that we have entered a unique ID of 1 for this task, for VM #102.

Once the task is created, we can also edit it through the CLI. The following command format is to update an already created replication task:

```
# pvesr update <vmid>-<job number> --schedule "<frequency>"
```

To change the schedule of replication 100-0 to half an hour, we would enter the following command:

```
# pvesr update 100-0 --schedule "*/30"
```

To see a list of all replication tasks, use the following command format:

```
# pvesr list
```

To disable or enable a replication task, use the following command format:

```
# pvesr <disable/enable> <vmid>-<job number>
```

# Replication process

The replication process will start automatically, at set intervals, without any user interaction. If the replication task is created for a VM for the first time, it will initially send an entire copy of the VM to the destination node. Once the initial transfer is done, then the replication process will only send new data that has changed incrementally.

Also, after the initial transfer, we are now fully ready with VM redundancy. In the event the node with the running VM goes down, we can simply turn on the replicated VM on the second node while we fix the issue on the primary node. This can significantly decrease the downtime for a small environment without shared storage. Depending on what replication interval has been used, users will only lose data since the last sync. So if the scheduled task is set to run every 5 minutes, then the replicated VM will only lose the last 5 minutes.

Replication depends on SSH, so it is important that nodes can connect to each other with proper SSH keys. If there is a problem with SSH connectivity, you may see a replication error like the following:

You may have to find the cause of the SSH issue, but in most cases it can be fixed using the following command:

```
# ssh-copy-id <proxmox_Node>
```

To run a replication task manually at any time, select the replication task, then click on the **Schedule now** button on the **Task** page.

# Backup configuration file

The backup configuration file in Proxmox allows more advanced options to be used. For example, if we want to limit the backup speed so that the backup task does not consume all of the available network bandwidth, we can limit it with the bwlimit option. As of Proxmox VE 5.0, the configuration file cannot be edited from the GUI. It has to be done from the CLI, using an editor. The backup configuration file can be found in /etc/vzdump.conf. The following is the default vzdump.conf file on a new Proxmox cluster:

```
# tmpdir: DIR
# dumpdir: DIR
# storage: STORAGE_ID
# mode: snapshot|suspend|stop
# bwlimit: KBPS
# ionice: PRI
# lockwait: MINUTES
# stopwait: MINUTES
# size: MB
# stdexcludes: BOOLEAN
# mailto: ADDRESSLIST
# maxfiles: N
# script: FILENAME
# exclude-path: PATHLIST
# pigz: N:
```

All the options are commented in the file by default because Proxmox has a set of default options already encoded in the operating system. Changing the vzdump.conf file overwrites the default settings and allows us to customize the Proxmox backup.

# The bwlimit option

The most common edit in vzdump.conf is to adjust the backup speed. This is usually done in the case of remotely stored backups and interface saturation if the backup interface is the same as that used for the VM production traffic. The value must be defined in **kilobytes per second (KBps)**. For example, to limit backup to 200 MBps, make the following adjustment:

```
bwlimit: 200000
```

# The lockwait option

The Proxmox backup uses a global lock file to prevent multiple instances running simultaneously. More instances put an extra load on the server. The default lock wait in Proxmox is 180 minutes. Depending on different virtual environments and numbers of virtual machines, the lock wait time may need to be increased. If the limit needs to be 10 hours or 600 minutes, adjust the option as follows:

```
lockwait: 600
```

The lock prevents the VM from migrating or shutting down while the backup task is running.

# The stopwait option

This is the maximum time in minutes the backup will wait until a VM is stopped. A use case scenario is a VM that takes much longer to shut down, for example, an exchange server or a database server. If a VM is not stopped within the allocated time, backup is skipped for that VM.

# The stdexcludes option

This is a Boolean option to enable or disable exclusion of standard files, such as temporary files, log files, or hidden OS system files. By default, this option is enabled.

# The mailto option

This is a comma-separated value to define email address to which the backup notifications will be sent after a successful backup or failure.

# The script option

It is possible to create backup scripts and hook them with a backup task. This script is basically a set instruction that can be called upon during the entire backup tasks to accomplish various backup-related tasks, such as starting/stopping a backup, shutting down/suspending a VM, and so on. We can add customized scripts as follows:

```
script: /etc/pve/script/my-script.pl
```

# The exclude-path option

To exclude certain folders from backing up, use the `exclude-path` option. All paths must be entered on one line, without breaks. Keep in mind that this option is only for LXC containers:

```
exclude-path: "/log/.+" "/var/cache/.+"
```

The previous example will exclude all the files and directories under `/log` and `/var/cache`. To manually exclude other directories from being backed up, simply use the following format:

```
exclude-path: "/<directory_tree>/.+"
```

# The pigz option

In simple terms, `pigz` allows multiple threads on multiple cores during the `.gzip` compression backup. The standard `.gzip` backup process uses a single core, which is why the backup is slower. Using the `pigz` package, we can notify the backup process to use multiple cores, thus speeding up the backup and restore process. `pigz` is basically a `.gzip`, but with multi-core support. It is not installed in Proxmox by default. We can install it using the following command:

```
# apt-get install pigz
```

In order to enable `pigz` for backup, we need to select the `.gzip` compression level for the backup task in GUI. Then, the following `pigz` option in the backup configuration file enables the `pigz` feature:

```
pigz: 1
```

By default, this value is `0` and is used to disable `pigz`. A value of `1` uses half of the total core in the node, while any value greater than `1` creates a number of threads based on the value. The value should not exceed the maximum number of CPU cores in the node.

 It is worth noting here that `pigz` is not faster than or superior to the LZO compression level, but when using the maximum compression, such as `.gzip`, the use of `pigz` will significantly reduce the backup time while compressing backup at the maximum level.

# Summary

In this chapter, we looked at the backup and restore features in Proxmox, how to configure them, and how to use them to create a good data disaster recovery plan. We also looked at the new VM replication feature to replicate a VM across nodes for safekeeping when using local storage.

There are no substitutes for backing up data in order to mitigate any disasters where data may be at risk. As much as backing up is important, the ability to restore is also equally important, since backup files will not mean anything if a restore is not possible in times of need. Although Proxmox does not provide everything you need for backing up, such as a granular file backup, the ability to back up a virtual machine is very helpful. The backup features in the Proxmox platform have proven to be reliable in production environments and during actual disaster scenarios.

In the next chapter, we are going to take a look at the necessity for an up-to-date Proxmox cluster and how to apply new releases or patches regularly.

# 14
# Updating/Upgrading Proxmox

There is no such thing as a perfect piece of software. All software matures as it progresses through time by getting new features and finding and fixing hidden bugs. By releasing regular updates and upgrades, the developers can ensure that their software does not become obsolete due to the rapid evolution of technology. In this chapter, we will see how to update and upgrade a Proxmox node. We will cover the following topics:

- Introducing Proxmox updates
- Updating Proxmox through the GUI
- Updating Proxmox through the CLI
- Updating after subscription change
- Rebooting dilemma after updates

## Introducing Proxmox updates

Proxmox updates keep a node up to date with the latest stable packages, patch security vulnerabilities, and introduce new features. Each node checks for the latest updates and alerts administrators through emails if there are any available updates. It is vital to keep all Proxmox nodes up to date, especially when security patches are released. Proxmox developers are very prompt in closing vulnerabilities through updates in a timely manner.

The number and nature of updates vary depending on your Proxmox subscription level. For example, a Proxmox free version without a subscription receives the most up-to-date stable updates, while a node with a subscription receives updates that are not so cutting edge and go through an additional layer of testing. Delaying the new package releases for subscription levels creates a buffer to address any issues that may not have been identified during the initial release.

This is not to say that a node without a subscription is not as stable as a paid version. Both offer a very high level of stability and performance. The only difference is that the delay allows subscribed updates to receive bug fixes which may not have been noticed during the initial release of the update in the free version of Proxmox.

A Proxmox node can be updated through both the GUI and CLI. There is no strict recommendation on which one to use. But it is best to perform at the console or through server IPMI. The reason is, if you are using Open vSwitch as the networking option and if the Openv Switch package has been updated in the release, it may interrupt network connectivity.

# Updating Proxmox through the GUI

In this section, we will see how to update a Proxmox node through the GUI. Proxmox checks for daily updates and displays relevant packages for which updates are available based on subscription levels. The **Updates** menu in the Proxmox GUI can be accessed by selecting the node and clicking on the **Updates** menu. The following screenshot shows the available update packages for our example node, pmx-01:

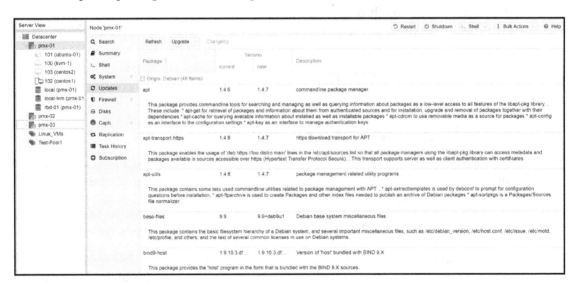

In the preceding screenshot, we can see that the node `pmx-01` has **48** updates available. The **Updates** feature shows the name of the package, the current version installed, the new available version, and a description of the package. To start the update or upgrade process, we simply need to click on **Upgrade**. It will open the node shell on the default console, such as noVNC, and will start the update process. Depending on the packages being updated, it may be necessary to act on some prompts. The following screenshot shows a typical prompt waiting for a response during the update process:

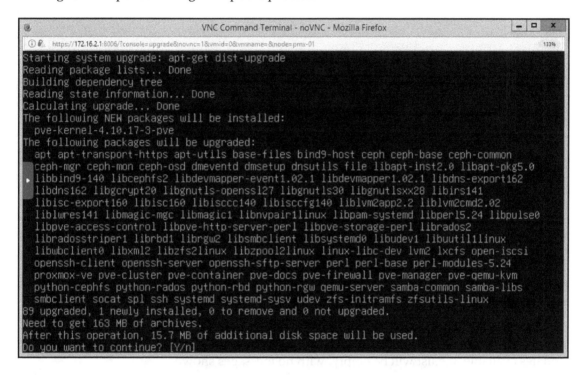

If the package list is old and has not been refreshed, it will notify that the package database is out of date, as shown in the following screenshot:

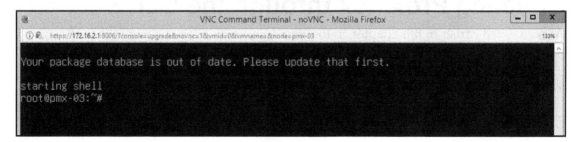

We can update the package list by clicking on **Refresh** through the GUI. To restart the update process, click on the **Upgrade** button on the GUI again. The following screenshot shows the updated interface in the GUI after clicking on **Refresh**:

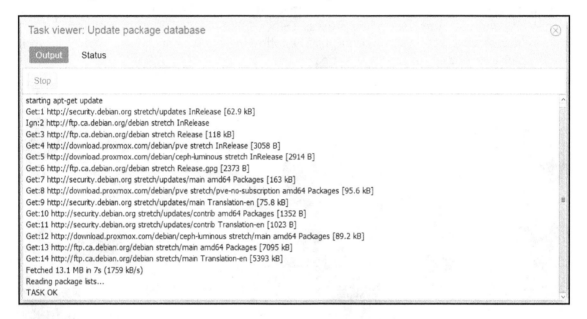

The package database task window shows the list of the repositories being read and the size of each package list being downloaded. We can stop the package database update by clicking on **Stop**.

Proxmox downloads or refreshes the updated package list daily and sends an email to the root email address. The Proxmox GUI update menu visually displays the list. If there are no updates available, the list will be empty, with no messages shown.

# Updating Proxmox through the CLI

As mentioned earlier in this chapter, in the recent Proxmox release, a bug in the software resulted in upgrading through the GUI having some issues. The GUI is basically a frontend of the behind-the-scene commands that are run through Proxmox scripts. Still, updating or upgrading Proxmox through the CLI seems to be the safest path.

There are no special Proxmox-specific commands to update a Proxmox node. The standard `apt-get` for all Debian-based distributions is used for the updating process. Log in to the Proxmox node directly on the node or through SSH, and then run the following command to update the list of new packages:

```
# apt-get update
```

After the package database is up to date, we can start the update process using the following command:

```
# apt-get dist-upgrade
```

# Difference between upgrade and dist-upgrade

Besides the `dist-upgrade` command, there is another option available for upgrade:

```
# apt-get upgrade
```

This is also the standard Debian-based Linux distribution command. However, there is a big difference between these two commands.

The `apt-get upgrade` command will only update the already installed packages without installing any new ones or making significant changes to the packages, such as removing them. This also will not satisfy any dependency issues. If any packages require dependencies to be resolved, this command will simply leave them alone. The main benefit of this package is that it will very rarely break the system. On the downside, it also will not update or patch everything that is necessary to bring a node up to date.

The `apt-get dist-upgrade` command, on the other hand, will upgrade all the packages and remove any unneeded packages dictated by the package maintainer. This command will also intelligently satisfy almost all the required dependencies for a package being updated or marked for a new installation.

Based on the previous explanation of these two update commands, we can see that both of these commands have advantages and disadvantages. But to keep a Proxmox node up to date, the `apt-get dist-upgrade` command seems to be the right way to go. Proxmox is not just another Linux distribution, but a highly specialized hypervisor. So packages that are included in a distribution are carefully chosen by Proxmox developers. Also, there is no mention of the `apt-get upgrade` command anywhere in the Proxmox wiki.

# Recovering from the grub2 update issue

Due to the latest grub2 update, there may be some instances, when updating a Proxmox node through the GUI, that cause issues by breaking packages. This is especially true for an earlier release, such as Proxmox 3.4. All the newer versions of Proxmox seem to have this issue fixed. To prevent this issue from happening, it is best to upgrade a node through SSH or the console by logging in directly on the node and not through the GUI. If the upgrade has already been applied through the GUI and there are unconfigured packages due to issues, perform the following steps to fix the issue:

1. Check package status:

   ```
   # pveversion -v
   ```

2. Before configuring grub, we need to know the device where Proxmox is installed. We can find the device by running the following command:

   ```
   # parted -l
   ```

3. If there are incorrect packages, run the following commands to kill the background dpkg process and configure all the packages, including the new grub2:

   ```
   # killall dpkg
   # dpkg --configure -a
   ```

4. Select the Proxmox device name when prompted during the grub2 installation.
5. Reboot the node.
6. It is also possible to manually install grub2 on the **Master Boot Record** (**MBR**). Run the following command to install grub2 on the boot device:

   ```
   # grub-install /dev/sdX
   ```

# Updating after a subscription change

The Proxmox subscription level for a node can be changed at any time by simply applying a subscription key through the GUI. Different subscription levels have different natures of package updates. If a node has started with no subscription, it can always be changed to any paid subscription at any given time. After the subscription level changes, it is important to update the node accordingly so that updates related to the subscription level can be applied. In this section, we will see how to update a node if the subscription level of the node changes at any time. For example, we are assuming that the node is on no subscription and we are adding a paid-level subscription. We can upload a subscription key through the **Subscription** tabbed menu for a node on the Proxmox GUI. But the modification that needs to be made to activate the repository for subscription needs to be done through the CLI. To disable the free subscription-level repository, we are going to comment out the following command in the `/etc/apt/sources.list` file:

```
# deb http://download.proxmox.com/debian stretch pve-no-subscription
```

After this, we need to uncomment the following line of code in `/etc/apt/sources.list.d/pve-enterprise.list` to enable the subscription-level repository:

```
# deb https://enterprise.proxmox.com/debian/pve stretch pve-enterprise
```

After these modifications are made, we can update the Proxmox GUI by following the steps in the *Updating Proxmox through the GUI* section in this chapter.

To update through the command line, we can follow the steps in the *Updating Proxmox through the CLI* section in this chapter.

The same enterprise repository works for all paid subscription levels, such as **Community**, **Basic**, **Standard**, and **Premium**. All paid subscriptions receive the same type of updates.

# Rebooting dilemma after Proxmox updates

After an update, all administrators face the question of whether the node should be rebooted or not. The Proxmox upgrade process is usually very informative and tells us whether the node really needs a reboot. Most of the updates do not require any reboot. They are simply packaged updates. But some upgrades, such as kernel releases, newer grubs, and security patches, will require a node reboot every time. The exact method of rebooting depends on the environment, number, and nature of the VMs stored per node. In this section, we will see the most widely used method, which is by no means the only method.

For minimal virtual machine downtime, we can live-migrate all the VMs from a node to a different node, and then migrate them back to the original node. As of Proxmox VE 5.0, there is a nice GUI feature addition to instruct all VM migrations with a menu instead of selecting and migrating one VM at a time. The feature is under the **Bulk Actions** drop-down menu in the top-right corner of the GUI, as shown in the following screenshot:

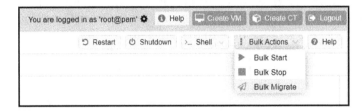

As you can see from the previous screenshot, we can also start or stop all virtual machines. The selected action will only take place on a selected node from the left-hand navigation pane of the GUI. If the Proxmox node requires a reboot after an update, we can select **Bulk Stop** from the **Bulk Actions** drop-down menu to shut down all VMs in the node, and then restart the node. After the node restarts, start all VMs by clicking on **Bulk Start** under the drop-down menu.

 Always check and read all major or minor Proxmox update releases before applying them to a node. This gives you a good idea of what is being updated and its importance. If the importance or seriousness is not critical, we can always put off the update to avoid any node reboots. You can refer to the Proxmox roadmap, which is a good place to find out new feature additions, bug fixes, or simply information on changes, at `http://pve.proxmox.com/wiki/Roadmap#Roadmap`.

The official Proxmox forum is also a great place to hang out to get information on issues due to updates. This is also a great place to learn about fixes posted by Proxmox developers if there are any issues with the released update.

Visit the official Proxmox forum at the following link:

`https://forum.proxmox.com`

# Applying update without reboot

Although there is no built-in feature in Proxmox that will allow us to update the host without ever needing a reboot, there is a third-party solution to achieve this and never have to reboot again after applying an update. A server reboot can be very disruptive for a busy virtual environment where downtime has a high price tag on it. A service named KernelCare from CloudLinux can solve this issue. More information about KernelCare can be found at `https://www.cloudlinux.com/all-products/product-overview/kernelcare`.

Simply put, what KernelCare does is applies security patches on the runtime kernel without needing to reboot a node. This allows a node to stay updated at all times. Due to the possible downtime, many administrators forego patching. With KernelCare, security updates are applied as they become available. This does not disrupt the normal functioning or services of the node in any way. The extremely affordable price and the easiness of the installation make KernelCare an effective solution for an environment of any size.

KernelCare also provides completely free trial licenses to try out the service before making a purchase. They can be installed in minutes by following the official documentation at `http://docs.kernelcare.com/index.html?installation.htm`.

# Summary

In this chapter, we learned about the importance of keeping Proxmox nodes up to date in a cluster and how to properly update and upgrade a node through both the GUI and CLI. We also covered when to reboot or not reboot a node after an upgrade.

In the next chapter, we are going to learn how to troubleshoot a Proxmox cluster when various issues arise. These issues have been taken from real-world Proxmox clusters serving live users.

# 15
# Proxmox Troubleshooting

In this chapter, we are going to learn about the common Proxmox issues found in a production environment and solutions to those issues. Once a Proxmox cluster is set up, it usually runs without issues. However, when issues arise, a system administrator's knowledge is tested. Learning how to properly troubleshoot can be made easier by learning about other people's resolutions. Throughout this chapter, we will gain some insight into Proxmox troubleshooting, so that hopefully, when these issues arise in our own Proxmox clusters, we will be able to identify and resolve problems quickly and with ease.

All the issues explained in this chapter are those that may be commonly faced by others. It is just not possible to explain all error possibilities, mainly due to all of the components that work in concert to make up a stable system. As you run your own cluster, you may face other issues that we have not documented here.

The issues are divided into the following sections:

- Proxmox nodes
- The main cluster
- Storage
- Network connectivity
- The KVM virtual machine
- LXC containers
- Backup/restore
- The VNC/SPICE console
- A firewall

# Proxmox node issues

This section contains issues related to the Proxmox node itself.

## Issue – fresh Proxmox install stuck with /dev to be a fully populated error during node reboot

This issue occurs when the OS tries to boot with a non-standard VGA driver. To prevent this issue, we need to add and modify some grub options. Restart the node, and then press the *E* key from the Proxmox boot menu. At the end of the Kernel boot line, add the following `nomodeset`, as shown in the following screenshot:

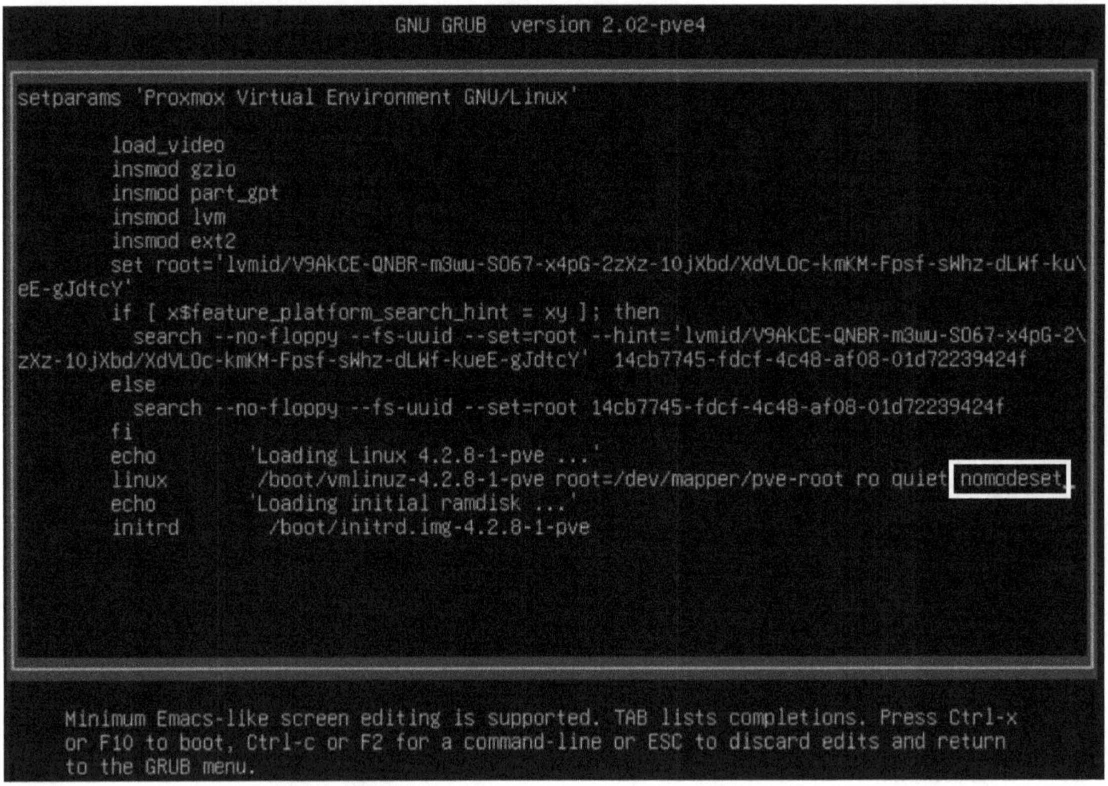

```
                          GNU GRUB  version 2.02-pve4


setparams 'Proxmox Virtual Environment GNU/Linux'

        load_video
        insmod gzio
        insmod part_gpt
        insmod lvm
        insmod ext2
        set root='lvmid/V9AkCE-QNBR-m3wu-SO67-x4pG-2zXz-10jXbd/XdVLOc-kmKM-Fpsf-sWhz-dLWf-ku\
eE-gJdtcY'
        if [ x$feature_platform_search_hint = xy ]; then
          search --no-floppy --fs-uuid --set=root  --hint='lvmid/V9AkCE-QNBR-m3wu-SO67-x4pG-2\
zXz-10jXbd/XdVLOc-kmKM-Fpsf-sWhz-dLWf-kueE-gJdtcY'  14cb7745-fdcf-4c48-af08-01d72239424f
        else
          search --no-floppy --fs-uuid --set=root 14cb7745-fdcf-4c48-af08-01d72239424f
        fi
        echo           'Loading Linux 4.2.8-1-pve ...'
        linux          /boot/vmlinuz-4.2.8-1-pve root=/dev/mapper/pve-root ro quiet nomodeset
        echo           'Loading initial ramdisk ...'
        initrd         /boot/initrd.img-4.2.8-1-pve




   Minimum Emacs-like screen editing is supported. TAB lists completions. Press Ctrl-x
   or F10 to boot, Ctrl-c or F2 for a command-line or ESC to discard edits and return
   to the GRUB menu.
```

Press *Ctrl* + *X* or *F10* to boot the node normally. To make this option permanent, make the following modifications in `/etc/default/grub`:

- Uncomment `GRUB_TERMINAL=console`
- Comment out `GRUB_GFXMODE=some_X,some_Y`

# Issue – rejoining a node to a Proxmox node with the same old IP address

If you are rejoining a Proxmox node back to the cluster with the same IP address, then the joining command must run with the `-force` option. Run the following command from the node that is being rejoined:

```
# pvecm add <any_proxmox_node_ip) -force
```

Without the additional `-force` option, the node will not be joined and an error message will be displayed informing you of the existence of a certificate. This also applies when a node is reinstalled completely with the same hostname and IP address.

# Issue – Proxmox installation completed but grub is in an endless loop after reboot

This is a common occurrence when Proxmox is installed on a node with newer UEFI BIOS. Simply disabling the UEFI mode will allow the system to boot. If this does not work, Proxmox should be installed manually over Debian Stretch.

To get information and instructions on how to install Proxmox when the ISO installer does not work, refer to the following:
`http://pve.proxmox.com/wiki/Install_Proxmox_VE_on_Debian_Stretch`

# Issue – LSI MegaRAID 9240-8i/9240-4i causes an error during booting of the Proxmox node

This issue can be prominent in the Supermicro motherboard with the LSI chipset for hot-swap bays. There are two ways in which we can use cards in the Proxmox mode:

## Downloading and updating the LSI driver

We can download and install the latest LSI drivers in Proxmox to activate the LSI cards by performing the following steps:

1. Run the following command to install the necessary program for compiling:

   ```
   # apt-get install build-essential
   ```

2. Run the following command to install header files for the currently installed kernel:

   ```
   # apt-get install pve-headers-<version>-pve
   ```

3. Download the LSI drivers from
   `http://www.avagotech.com/support/download-search`.

4. Extract the downloaded driver in `/usr/local/src`.

5. After extracting the driver, the directory may appear as follows:

   ```
   # /usr/local/src/megaraid_sas-v00.00.05.30
   ```

6. Enter the driver directory and rename `makefile` to `makefile.orig`. Then, copy `makefile.standalone` to `makefile`.

7. Compile the source using the following command:

   ```
   # make -C /usr/src/linux-headers-<version>/ M=$PWD modules
   ```

   It will show some text output and warnings, but they are safe to ignore. The driver will end up in the following directory:

   ```
   /usr/local/src/megaraid_sas-v00.00.05.30/megaraid_sas.ko
   ```

8. Remove or rename the existing driver file in the following directory:

   ```
   /lib/modules/<version>-pve/kernel/drivers/scsi/megaraid/
   megaraid_sas.ko
   ```

9. Copy the newly compiled driver to the previous directory, as follows:

   ```
   # cp /usr/local/src/megaraid_sas-v00.00.05.30/megaraid_sas.ko
   /lib/modules/<version>-pve/kernel/drivers/scsi/megaraid/
   megaraid_sas.ko
   ```

10. Back up the initial RAM disk by renaming it, as follows:

    ```
    # mv /boot/initrd.img-2.6.32-7-pve /boot/initrd.img-<version>
    -pve.bak
    ```

11. Run the following command to update `initramfs`:

    ```
    # update-initramfs -c -k 2.6.32-7-pve
    ```

12. Run the following command to update grub, and then reboot it:

    ```
    # update-grub
    ```

## Updating the Supermicro BIOS

We can also update the Supermicro BIOS to the latest firmware to use the LSI cards. Always check whether you have the latest firmware before updating it. For instructions on how to update the Supermicro BIOS firmware, refer to
`http://wahlnetwork.com/2013/06/03/the-easy-button-for-supermicro-bios-upgrades/`.

# Issue – the Upgrade button is disabled on the Proxmox GUI, which prevents the node upgrade

There are three common reasons why the **Upgrade** button could be disabled on the Proxmox GUI. Check the following alternatives to fix this issue:

1. If the node does not have a valid subscription, ensure that the `pve-no-subscription` repository is added. For Proxmox repository information, visit the link: `https://pve.proxmox.com/wiki/Package_repositories`.

2. Refresh the browser cache to reload the graphic interface.
3. A very basic mistake, but not unheard of, is to make sure that the root user is logged in to facilitate the upgrade. The **Upgrade** button is only visible when you log in with the root privilege.

# Issue – Proxmox cannot start due to the getpwnam error

Boot the Proxmox node in recovery mode using the Proxmox installation disk, or select the recovery option from Proxmox's boot menu at the beginning of the boot process. After the recovery shell is loaded, run the following commands from the command prompt and then reboot:

```
# apt-get update && apt-get dist-upgrade
```

# Issue – cannot log in to the GUI as root after reinstalling Proxmox on the same node

In order to log in to the Proxmox GUI as root, local loopback must be enabled in the network interface file. Look for the following two lines to make sure they are not commented out in /etc/network/interfaces:

```
auto lo
iface lo inet loopback
```

# The main cluster issues

This section contains issues related to the main Proxmox's cluster operations.

# Issue – Proxmox virtual machines are running, but the Proxmox GUI shows that everything is offline

This is usually caused by one of the three services, such as `pvedaemon`, `pvestatd`, or `pveproxy` crashing or stopping working for any number of reasons. Simply restarting them through SSH will fix this issue. One of the common causes of this issue is if any NFS shared storage gets stuck during an extended backup task. A node reboot will always fix this issue. But reboot is not always possible in a production node. Forcefully unmounting the NFS shared storage under `/mnt/pve/<share>`, then running the following commands will show everything normally again:

```
# service pvedaemon restart
# service pveproxy restart
# service pvestatd restart
```

# Issue – kernel panic when disconnecting USB devices, such as a keyboard, mouse, or UPS

There is no real solution to this issue yet, as the issue is not reproducible all the time. This issue has been seen on a variety of hardware with both standard and nonstandard Proxmox installations. However, almost all of the time, the issue does not cause the server to freeze permanently, thus the panic can just be ignored and you can go on as usual.

Kernel panic seems to mostly occur with kernels *2.6.32-26*, *2.6.32-27*, and *2.6.32-28*. It is nonexistent in kernel *3.2* and later. For the regular day-to-day operations of a cluster, this issue can be safely ignored unless it causes the node to freeze on occasions.

# Issue – virtual machines on Proxmox will not shut down if shutdown is initiated from the Proxmox GUI

This issue is not consistent and is not directly related to Proxmox. The **Shutdown** button on Proxmox's GUI only sends an ACPI signal to a virtual machine to initiate the shutdown process.

Once the VM receives an ACPI signal, it starts the shutdown process. However, if the VM has a number of processes running in the memory, it might take a while to end processes before shutdown. The ending of processes may take longer, which causes Proxmox to issue a timeout error. The issue may occur for both Windows and Linux. The workaround for this is to access the VM through a console or SPICE and then manually shut down the VM.

# Issue – kernel panic with HP NC360T (Intel 82571EB chipset) only in Proxmox VE 3.2

An immediate workaround is to use Broadcom for the network interface card. A permanent fix is to download E1000 drivers from the Intel website and compile a module from those sources. The E1000 driver can be downloaded from this link:

`http://www.intel.com/support/network/sb/cs-006120.htm`.

# Issue – the Proxmox cluster is out of quorum and cluster filesystem is in read-only mode

This occurs when a node falls out of quorum. To prevent an error occurring in the cluster configuration files, Proxmox puts the cluster filesystem in the read-only mode for the node in question. Run the following commands from the node with this issue. We have to stop the cluster service, start it in local mode, delete or move the existing `corosync.conf` file, and then restart the cluster. A new `corosync.conf` file will be synced with the node with a read-only issue. Perform the following steps to overcome this issue:

1. Stop the cluster in the node using the following command:

   ```
   # systemctl stop pve-cluster
   ```

2. Start the cluster filesystem in the local node using the following command:

   ```
   # /usr/bin/pmxcfs -l
   ```

3. Remove or back up the `corosync.conf` file using the following command:

   ```
   # mv /etc/pve/corosync.conf directory_path
   ```

4. Stop and start the cluster normally using the following commands:

   ```
   # systemctl stop pve-cluster
   # systemctl start pve-cluster
   ```

# Issue – VM will not respond to shutdown or restart

First check whether **High Availability (HA)** is enabled for the VM or not, as HA will prevent any manual action such as the VM shutdown, stop, restart, or start because the main purpose of HA is for actions to be taken without user interaction. In order to manually perform any task for a VM, we need to disable HA for the VM, perform a task, and then re-enable HA. Also, if anything inside the guest VM is preventing it from shutting down, it will not respond to the GUI shutdown or restart option. In such cases, it is best to shutdown or restart from within the guest VM.

# Issue – Proxmox GUI not responding after Firefox update

Due to a Firefox update, the Proxmox GUI may become non-responsive, even after successful login. In Firefox, on the address bar, type `about:config`.

On the search bar, type `touch` and find the following entry:

```
dom.w3c_touch_events.enabled
```

Change the value to `0` and try to log in to the GUI again.

# Issue – the Proxmox GUI is not showing RRD graphs

If a node or VM is running fine, but there are no RRD graphs on the **Status** page, it might be due to the stuck `pvestatd` service or corrupted RRD cache. Run the following commands to restart the `pvestatd` service and clear the RRD cache:

```
# rrdcache -P FLUSHALL
# systemctl restart pvestatd
```

# Storage issues

This section contains issues related to storage systems supported by Proxmox, such as local, NFS, Ceph, GlusterFS, and so on.

## Issue – deleting a damaged LVM from Proxmox with the error read failed from 0 to 4096

This error occurs when a LVM storage in Proxmox becomes partially or fully corrupted. In such cases the LVM may need to remove manually. This will remove the LVM which will cause data loss. Run the following command from the CLI to remove the LVM:

```
# dmsetup remove /dev/<volume_group>/<lvm_name>
```

## Issue – Proxmox cannot mount NFS share due to the timing out error

Some NFS servers, such as FreeNAS, do a reverse lookup for hostnames. In such cases accessing the NFS storage from Proxmox causes timing out error. We need to add Proxmox hostnames to the host files of the NFS server to prevent time out error:

```
# nano /etc/hosts
```

## Issue – how to delete leftover NFS shares in Proxmox or what to do when the NFS stale file handle error occurs?

When NFS shares are deleted from Proxmox storage, in some cases, it still remains mounted, which causes the NFS stale file handle error. Simply manually unmounting the share and removing the NFS mount point folder from the Proxmox directory fixes this issue. Run the following commands from the Proxmox node:

```
# umount -f /mnt/<nfs_share>
# rmdir /mnt/<nfs_share>
```

# Issue – Proxmox issues --mode session exit code 21 errors while trying to access the iSCSI target

Run the following command from the Proxmox node to fix the error:

```
# iscsiadm -m node -l ALL
```

# Issue – cannot read an iSCSI target even after it has been deleted from Proxmox storage

When trying to read the same iSCSI target after it has been deleted from Proxmox storage, an error occurs mentioning the target that has already been added to Proxmox. In these cases, the iSCSI daemon has to be restarted to clear the issue. Run the following command from all the Proxmox nodes:

```
# /etc/init.d/open-iscsi restart
```

# Issue – a Ceph node is removed from the Proxmox cluster, but OSDs still show up in PVE

This is a common occurrence when a Ceph node is taken offline without removing all the Ceph-related processes first. The OSDs in the node must be removed or moved to another node before taking the node offline. Run the following commands to remove OSDs:

```
# ceph osd out <osd.id>
# ceph osd crush remove osd <osd.id>
# ceph auth del osd.<id>
# ceph osd rm <osd.id>
```

# Issue – the no such block device error during creation of an OSD through the Proxmox GUI

When creating an OSD through the Proxmox GUI, sometimes this error occurs. This is not a common occurrence and is not reproducible at all times. Although there are no permanent fixes for this issue, it can be ignored. So, just retry to create an OSD. The issue seems to be isolated in Proxmox 4.x releases.

# Issue – the fstrim command does not trim unused blocks for the Ceph storage

To properly trim unused blocks for virtual disks stored on the Ceph storage, perform the following steps:

1. Use a `virtio` disk type for a virtual disk.
2. Enable the discard option through `<vm_id>.conf`. Add `discard=on` to the drive properties of `virtio0`, like the following:

```
# <rbd_storage>:<virtual_disk>,cache=writethrough,
size=50G,discard=on
```

# Issue – the RBD couldn't connect to cluster (500) error when connecting Ceph with Proxmox

Authentication failure is the most common cause for this error when Ceph RBD storage cannot connect to Proxmox. Proxmox requires a copy of the Ceph admin keyring to authenticate. The name of the keyring must match the storage ID assigned through the Proxmox GUI. Refer to `Chapter 5`, *Installing and Configuring Ceph*, for information on how to set up the Ceph cluster to be used as storage backend.

# Issue – changing the storage type from IDE to VirtIO after the VM has been set up and the OS has been installed

If IDE was used during the initial VM setup and needs to be changed to VirtIO later, this can be done through the Proxmox GUI without reinstalling the OS. The VM will need to be powered off first, and then the virtual disk needs to be removed through the Proxmox GUI. After clicking on **Remove**, the virtual disk will become unused, as shown in the following screenshot:

| | | |
|---|---|---|
| >_ Console | ⌨ Keyboard Layout | Default |
| 🖥 Hardware | ▦ Memory | 128.00 MiB/1.00 GiB |
| ⚙ Options | ▣ Processors | 1 (1 sockets, 1 cores) [numa=1] |
| ☰ Task History | 🖥 Display | Default |
| | ⊙ CD/DVD Drive (ide2) | none,media=cdrom |
| 👁 Monitor | ⇄ Network Device (net0) | virtio=CA:35:61:2A:34:CD,bridge=vmbr0 |
| 🖫 Backup | 🗄 Unused Disk 0 | local-lvm:vm-100-disk-1 |

Double-click on the unused virtual disk or navigate to **Add** | **Hard Disk** to add it back to the VM. Select **VirtIO** as **Bus/Device** from the dialog box. It is very important to keep in mind that following this procedure on a Windows VM, which has one single IDE disk image, will make the VM inaccessible. The reason is Windows does not come equipped with VirtIO driver, it needs to be manually loaded. To change the primary Windows disk image from IDE to VirtIO, add a second disk image of any size into the Windows guest VM, then boot into it. Load the VirtIO driver ISO file downloaded from `https://fedorapeople.org/groups/virt/virtio-win/direct-downloads/stable-virtio/virtio-win.iso`.

Go to **Control Panel** | **Device Manager** and update the disk drive detected using the driver from the loaded ISO image. Once the proper driver is loaded and the VirtIO disk drive is fully recognized, shutdown Windows. Then remove the disk image added for this purpose and follow the steps described earlier in this section.

# Issue – the pveceph configuration not initialized (500) error when you click on the Ceph tab in the Proxmox GUI

This error occurs when you click on the **Ceph** tab in the Proxmox GUI without initializing the Ceph storage. If Ceph is not going to be used along with Proxmox on the same cluster, then this error should simply be ignored. But if any Proxmox node is going to be used to manage Ceph through the Proxmox GUI, then simply copy the Ceph configuration file from `/etc/pve/ceph.conf` into `/etc/ceph/ceph.conf`, which will allow you to manage Ceph even if there is no OSD or mon in that node. Since Ceph configuration may change over time, it is recommended to create a symlink for the configuration file instead of a simple copy. The following command will create a symlink of the Ceph configuration file in the `/etc/ceph` directory:

```
# ln -s /etc/pve/ceph.conf /etc/ceph/ceph.conf
```

# Issue – the CephFS storage disappears after a Proxmox node reboots

CephFS needs to be mounted in order to make it available for storage service. If the mount point is not set in /etc/fstab, it will need to be remounted after each reboot. The following format is used to enter the CephFS in /etc/fstab:

```
id={user-ID}[,conf={path/to/conf.conf}] /mount/path  fuse.ceph defaults 0 0
id=admin,conf=/etc/ceph/conf.conf /mnt/<path>  fuse.ceph defaults 0 0
```

# Issue – VM cloning does not parse in the Ceph storage

When full cloning is performed on a virtual machine stored on Ceph storage, it looses parse on the virtual disk. For cloning, Proxmox uses the qemu-img method instead of rbd flattening. Until it is implemented in later versions of Proxmox, VM clones will lose parsing on Ceph storage.

# Issue – VM disk images stored on ZFS is extremely slow

If the VM disk images are stored on ZFS storage, which is configured as RAIDZ3, the VMs will suffer a big performance loss. Especially if the ZFS loses a drive and it goes into data rebalancing, the load on the storage will make the VM almost unusable. When using ZFS, the RAID10 will provide the best performance possible from ZFS storage. RAID10 will have paired vdevs where data will be mirrored and then will be stripped among multiple vdevs. One drawback of using RAID10 is it provides half of the disk capacity of the total number of drives. For example, if 20 2 TB drives are used in a RAID10 ZFS configuration, then the usable space will only be 20 TB. For a non-critical node such as backup storage, the use of RAIDZ3 could be a good choice, since it will provide the maximum capacity possible at the expense of performance.

# Network connectivity issues

This section contains issues related to virtual or physical network connectivity within Proxmox.

## Issue – no connectivity on Realtek RTL8111/8411 rev. 06 network interfaces

Some newer Realtek chipsets don't get compiled with the right drivers. This causes the interface to be up without any network traffic. In order to fix this issue, the older driver needs to be downloaded from the Realtek site and compiled manually. The driver can be downloaded from `http://www.realtek.com.tw/Downloads/`.

Since this driver is manually installed, during a kernel update it will get updated automatically. To prevent this and ensure that the driver builds itself automatically when a new kernel is installed, run the following commands and then reboot the node:

```
# apt-get install dkms build-essential pve-headers-4.10.15-pve
# mkdir /usr/src/r8168-8.037.00
# cat << EOF > /usr/src/r8168-8.037.00/dkms.conf
PACKAGE_NAME=r8168
PACKAGE_VERSION=8.037.00
MAKE[0]="'make'"
BUILT_MODULE_NAME[0]=r8168
BUILT_MODULE_LOCATION[0]="src/"
DEST_MODULE_LOCATION[0]="/kernel/updates/dkms"
AUTOINSTALL="YES"
EOF
# dkms add -m r8168 -v 8.037.00
# dkms build -m r8168 -v 8.037.00
# dkms install -m r8168 -v 8.037.00
# dkms status
```

# Issue – network performance is slower with the E1000 virtual network interfaces

The performance of the E1000 virtual network interfaces is about 30-35% less than VirtIO virtual network interfaces. Changing vNICs to VirtIO will increase the overall network bandwidth of a virtual machine. The VirtIO drivers are included in all major Linux flavors. For Windows machines, an ISO file with VirtIO drivers can be downloaded from `http://www.linux-kvm.org/page/WindowsGuestDrivers/Download_Drivers`.

# Issue – patch port for Open vSwitch in Proxmox not working

Currently, there are three Open vSwitch options that are fully supported through Proxmox, such as OVSBridge, OVSIntPort, and OVSBond. The OVSPatchPort option that is required for the patch port cannot be configured through the Proxmox GUI. Thus, even if we manually create a configuration in the network interface file, it still seems to be out of reach. An alternative solution where the patch port is required is to use an Open vSwitch fake bridge. A patch port allows us to create an extension of the main bridge. For example, if we are connecting two physical switches with each other, the ports where we will connect the network cable to becomes patch ports for these two switches. Fake bridges look and act like full Open vSwitch bridges but are tied to a particular VLAN. A fake bridge depends on an already configured main Open vSwitch bridge. Assuming that the main bridge is `vmbr0`, the content of the `/etc/network/interfaces` will look as follows for a fake bridge named `11` for VLAN ID #11:

```
auto vmbr11
allow-vmbr0 vmbr11
iface vmbr11 inet manual
  ovs_bridge vmbr0
  ovs_type OVSBridge
  ovs_options vmbr0 11
```

The entry option for a fake bridge is as follows:

```
ovs_options <main_bridge> <vlan_id>
```

We can now connect a VM to this bridge without assigning any VLAN ID to the virtual network interface.

# Issue – trying to add a node to a newly created Proxmox cluster when nodes do not form quorum

From Proxmox 4.0 and later, we now require the multicast feature. Without this, nodes will be unable to form quorum. So, when we add a new node to a cluster, if the process gets stuck at **Waiting for Quorum...**, we need to ensure that multicast is enabled on the switch. As soon as multicast is available, nodes will form quorum without any issues.

# Issue – implemented IPv6 but firewall rules do not get applied

All firewall rules are primarily applied to IPv4 traffic. In order to also apply these rules to IPv6, we need to ensure that the following entry is present in `/etc/network/interfaces`:

```
iface lo inet6 loopback
```

We also need to load the IPv6 driver into `/etc/modules` during boot. Simply add the following entry in `/etc/modules`:

```
ipv6
```

# KVM virtual machine issues

This section contains issues related to KVM virtual machines only.

# Issue – Windows 7/XP machine converted to Proxmox KVM hangs during boot

The Windows operating system can be unforgiving when you convert or migrate from one type of hardware to another. It is certainly possible to convert/migrate just about any Windows OS, as long as a proper procedure is followed. For in-depth information on the proper procedure to migrate Windows machines to a virtual machine, refer to http://pve.proxmox.com/wiki/Migration_of_servers_to_Proxmox_VE#mergeide.

# Issue – Windows 7 VM does not reboot, instead it shuts down, requiring a manual boot from Proxmox

This issue causes a Windows 7 virtual machine to shut down when a reboot is initiated from within the OS. A manual power-on through the Proxmox GUI is required to power up the VM. This is an issue caused by the installation of Windows itself, especially a VM that is configured with a standard video. Changing the display to SPICE solves the issue for this type of Windows 7 virtual machine. This is not a common occurrence and causes an issue in some Windows 7 VMs, while others run just fine. Following screenshot shows the display adapter selected as SPICE:

# Issue – the qemu-img command does not convert the .vmdk image files created with the .ova template in Proxmox VE 5.0

The .vmdk image files created with VMware's .ova template may present the following error messages during conversion with the qemu-img command:

```
# qemu-img convert -f vmdk disk1.vmdk -O qcow2 vm-101-disk-1.qcow2
qemu-img: 'image' uses a vmdk feature which is not supported by this qemu
version: VMDK version 3
qemu-img: Could not open 'disk1.vmdk': Could not open 'disk1.vmdk': Wrong
medium type
qemu-img: Could not open 'disk1.vmdk'
```

The .vmdk3 format is only supported in `pve-qemu-kvm 2.0` and later. Enter the following command to check the version installed in the Proxmox node:

```
# pveversion -v | grep pve-qemu-kvm
```

Look for the version number of `pve-qemu-kvm`. A .vmdk file can still be converted by following the instructions given at
`http://ask.xmodulo.com/convert-ova-to-qcow2-linux.html`.

# Issue – online migration of a virtual machine fails with a failed to sync data error

In order to migrate virtual machines online without powering them off, the virtual disk of the VM must be on a shared storage system. Any VM with a virtual disk on local storage cannot be migrated live. The error will look as follows:

```
Aug 12 19:54:37 starting migration of VM 134 to node 'pmx-02' (172.17.2.2)
Aug 12 19:54:37 copying disk images
Aug 12 19:54:37 ERROR: Failed to sync data - can't do online migration - VM
uses local disks
Aug 12 19:54:37 aborting phase 1 - cleanup resources
Aug 12 19:54:37 ERROR: migration aborted (duration 00:00:00): Failed to
sync data - can't do online migration - VM uses local disks
TASK ERROR: migration aborted
```

# Issue – no audio in Windows KVM

Sound devices must be added manually by adding the following line in a KVM virtual machine configuration file located in `/etc/pve/qemu-server/<vm_id>.conf`:

```
args: -device intel-hda,id=sound5,bus=pci.0,addr=0x18 -device hda-
micro,id=sound5-codec0,bus=sound5.0,cad=0 -device hda-duplex,id=sound5-
codec1,bus=sound5.0,cad=1
```

After saving the configuration file, the VM will need to be powered off and then powered on. Windows 7 and later will automatically install the necessary driver for the sound device.

# Issue – the VirtIO virtual disk is not available during the Windows Server installation

The VirtIO drivers are not included in the Windows Server installation. During the installation, the Windows setup will not see any VirtIO virtual disks attached to the virtual machine. A VirtIO driver must be downloaded and loaded during the installation in order to activate the VirtIO virtual disk with the Windows operating system. The ISO image of VirtIO drivers can be downloaded from

`http://www.linux-kvm.org/page/WindowsGuestDrivers/Download_Drivers`.

# LXC container issues

This section contains issues related to LXC containers only.

# Issue – a Proxmox node hangs when trying to stop or restart an LXC container

This has been an issue since the initial release of Proxmox VE 4.0. Due to a bug when shutdown, stop, or restart was initiated for LXC container from GUI, the node itself became unusable and all network connectivity was lost. The only way to come out of it was to reboot the entire node. In consecutive later releases, this issue has been addressed and patched by Proxmox developers. If you are in Proxmox 4.0, an immediate upgrade to 4.1 or later is highly recommended.

# Issue – the noVNC console only shows a cursor for LXC containers

Due to unknown reasons, the noVNC console may only show a cursor, as shown in the following screenshot, when trying to access an LXC container:

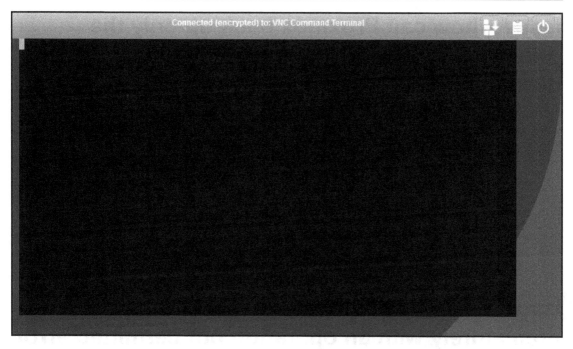

This does not mean that the container is frozen. Simply hit **Enter** to get to the login prompt.

# Backup/restore issues

This section contains issues related to backing up and restoring Proxmox.

## Issue – a Proxmox VM is locked after backup crashes unexpectedly

This is a common cause after a VM backup is interrupted or crashed. Simply unlocking the VM through SSH using the following command will fix this issue:

```
# qm unlock <vm_id>
```

# Issue – how can Proxmox back up only the primary OS virtual disk instead of all the virtual disks for a VM?

By default, a Proxmox backup will back up all the virtual disks assigned to a VM. If we want to exclude certain virtual disks from the backup process, we only need to add the `backup=no` option at the end of a virtual disk line item in `<vm_id>.conf`, as follows:

```
virtio0: rbd-hdd-01:vm-101-disk1,size=80G
virtio0: rbd-hdd-01:vm-101-disk2,size=200G,backup=no
```

In the previous example, the virtual machine has two virtual disks. The `disk1` is for the primary OS and `disk2` is for the secondary. By adding `backup=no`, Proxmox will skip this disk during the backup process and only back up the primary disk.

# Issue – backup of virtual machines stops prematurely with an operation not permitted error

This error usually looks like this from syslog of the Proxmox node:

```
ERROR: job failed with err -1 - Operation not permitted
INFO: aborting backup job
INFO: stopping kvm after backup task
ERROR: Backup of VM 101 failed - job failed with err -1 - Operation not
permitted
```

The primary cause of this issue is when the backup storage has less space than the total storage required for an assigned backup task. Verify the total storage space that is required for backing up the selected virtual machines.

# Issue – a backup task takes a very long time to complete, or it crashes when multiple nodes are backing up to the same backup storage

When multiple Proxmox nodes are backing up to the same backup storage simultaneously, it tends to take a very long time or the backup crashes. This is a common occurrence when backup traffic coexists with the main cluster traffic on a gigabit network and the backup node only has one network interface. By separating backups in multiple subnets over multiple network interfaces, we can prevent this issue.

# Issue – backup of virtual machines aborts a backup task prematurely

During a VM backup, the following error message appears in the backup log after it aborts a running backup task:

```
101: INFO: status: 1% (129309081/4294967296), sparse 0% (886784), duration
91, 33/33 MB/s
[...]
107: INFO: status: 80% (2706263244/4294967296), sparse 16% (698703462),
duration 1950, 5/4 MB/s
107: ERROR: interrupted by signal
107: INFO: aborting backup job
```

This error usually occurs when there is a version mismatch for the pve-qemu-kvm package in Proxmox. At the time of writing, the available pve-qemu-kvm package version is 2.9.0-4. Check for the version that is installed when you get this error during a backup. If you're using an older version, then upgrade to the latest version using the following command to fix the issue.

# Issue – backup storage has a lot of .dat files and .tmp folders using the storage space

Due to a backup crash or unfinished backups, there may be backup files leftover in the backup storage, such as the .dat files and .tmp folders. These files and folders can be easily deleted to reclaim storage space.

# VNC/SPICE console issues

This section contains issues related to the VNC and SPICE consoles in Proxmox.

## Issue – the mouse pointer is not shared with SPICE (virt-viewer) on Windows 8 VM

In order to have a seamless mouse point between the VM and host machine, SPICE guest tools must be installed inside the VM. The guest tools package contains full driver support for Windows 7 and Windows 2008 R2. However, the support for Windows 8 or 8.1 is close to nonexistent.

## Issue – remote viewer is unable to connect to a SPICE-enabled virtual machine on the Windows OS

This issue is caused by a firewall that blocks the SPICE port, which prevents SPICE-enabled virtual machines from being connected to SPICE. Open port 3128 from Windows firewall to allow remote viewer to connect to a SPICE virtual machine.

# Firewall issues

This section shows issues regarding the Proxmox firewall feature.

## Issue – rules are created and a firewall is enabled for vNIC, but rules do not get applied

On rare occasions, due to changes in the network interface or other reasons, the firewall service may get stuck. In such cases, we can restart the service using the following command:

```
# systemctl restart pve-firewall
```

If the previous command does not help, then check the syslog of the node to look for a clue. If nothing helps, then a reboot will clear any firewall issues. As of Proxmox VE 5.0, if a firewall becomes inactive, it does not fall back on a predefined set of protection; a firewall simply becomes nonexistent.

# Issue – a firewall is enabled for a VM and the necessary rules are created, but nothing is being filtered for that VM

This issue may occur when the firewall is not enabled in the virtual network interface of the VM. For each VM, a firewall needs to be enabled in two different places. The first one is under the **Firewall** tab menu, as shown in the following screenshot:

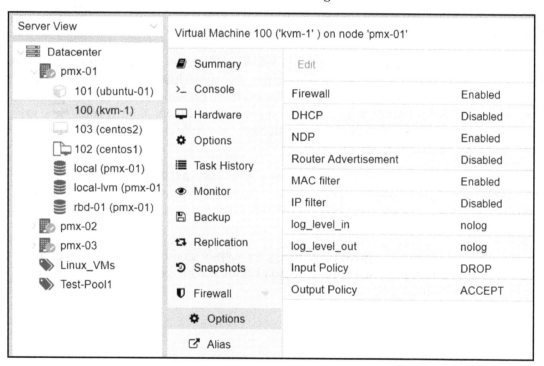

Another place where the firewall needs to be enabled is in the vNIC of the VM, as shown in the following screenshot:

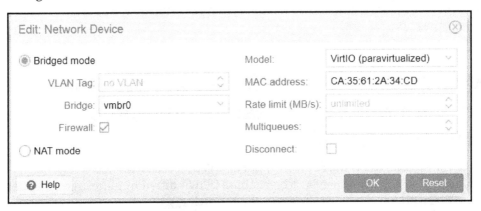

# Summary

We hope this troubleshooting chapter has provided you with some insight into some of the common issues that are most likely to surface in a Proxmox cluster. As mentioned earlier in this chapter, this is by no means a complete list of all the possible issues. If at all possible, always hold off major Proxmox upgrades for a production cluster. Give it some time to work out the bugs. This way, your cluster will have very little chance of going down due to any unforeseen bugs.

Purchasing a Proxmox subscription is the best way to ensure that there are fewer bugs in the repositories, since Proxmox Enterprise repositories go through an additional layer of scrutiny and testing. For information on Proxmox subscriptions, refer to `https://www.proxmox.com/proxmox-ve/pricing`.

The Proxmox forum is also a great place to ask for help or share issues with the community. There are many forum users who are ready to provide their expertise. Visit the forum at `http://forum.proxmox.com`.

# 16
# Rescuing Proxmox

Whether we want to accept it or not, a network environment is always at risk of something going wrong. Even if we take out the hardware and software from the equation, there is always the human factor. Sometimes all it takes is a small mistake that can snowball very rapidly to something major. A well thought out disaster plan can go a long way to combating a situation, or sometimes on the ball quick thinking can save the day.

As we approach the end of the book, in this concluding chapter we are going to see some situations where things went wrong and what do to do when the same happens to you in the virtual environment you are part of. Like Chapter 15, *Proxmox Troubleshooting*, these are not all-inclusive scenarios. You may, or will, come across other situations that are not covered in this chapter. As a good administrator, you can expand on this through your own documentation, but we hope we were able to put together some critical situations that you may face in your career and that the solutions provided here will prove extremely valuable.

This chapter is divided into the following categories of scenario:

- Recovering from OS drive failure
- Recovering from a quorum failure
- Recovering from a node failure
- Recovering from a network failure
- Recovering from Ceph failure

# Recovering from OS drive failure

OS drive failure is one of the critical failures when a node becomes fully inaccessible. Since Proxmox stores all cluster-related configuration files on **Proxmox Cluster file system (pmxcfs)**, no cluster data is lost even when the OS drive fails completely. Refer to Chapter 3, *Proxmox under the Hood*, to recap details on pmxcfs. There are mainly two types of OS drive failure:

- Physical drive failure
- OS data corruption

# Physical drive failure

This failure occurs when the physical drive itself becomes completely unusable or defective. In this scenario, the only option is to replace the damaged drive with a new one and install clean Proxmox VE on it. One way to prevent downtime due to physical drive failure is to use two physical drives for the OS in mirror mode. During Proxmox installation, we can select the **Advanced** option to create a ZFS mirror on two physical drives. This way when one drive becomes physically damaged, it does not cause any downtime since there is a second drive with all of the OS files. This same RAID-level redundancy can be achieved using a RAID card and by creating Raid 1 on two physical drives.

# OS data corruption

This failure occurs when no physical damage has occurred but critical files of the OS itself become corrupted, or some portion of the OS is accidentally deleted. In some cases, this can also occur due to an incomplete upgrade or due to the presence of bugs in the update or patch. File partition corruption can also cause severe unrecoverable OS data corruption. In most cases when there is a filesystem error or any data corruption, the OS boot process will drop in the maintenance shell or we can manually enter into Proxmox rescue mode by rebooting the node from Proxmox ISO CDROM and selecting **Rescue Boot**, as shown in the following screenshot:

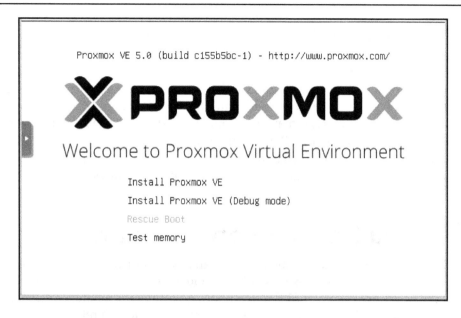

# Migrating VMs from a faulty node

Depending on the nature of the OS drive failure, the length of the downtime will vary. If the fix takes more than a tolerable amount of downtime, then it may be necessary to start the VMs previously served by the faulty node on different nodes in the cluster. When the VM disk images are stored on a shared storage node, then we can simply move the VM configuration file to a different node and turn them on. The following commands will move KVM and LXC VMs from one node to another within pmxcfs:

```
# mv  /etc/pve/nodes/<faulty_node>/lxc/<lxc_id>.conf
/etc/pve/nodes/<second_node>/lxc/<lxc_id>.conf
# mv  /etc/pve/nodes/<faulty_node>/qemu-server/<kvm_id>.conf
/etc/pve/nodes/<second_node>/qemu-server/<kvm_id>.conf
```

If the VM disk images are stored locally on the same OS drive, the previous method, however, will not work, because if the drive is physically damaged or corrupted, so will the VM disk images be. In other cases, where the VM disk images are stored locally on the same node but on different drives, the previous method will also not work since the VM disk images will need to be moved or the drives will need to be mounted on a different node first.

# Reinstalling Proxmox

If the Proxmox OS was not mirrored or if the OS is beyond repair, it may be necessary to reinstall Proxmox on a new or reformatted OS drive. If the node was part of a cluster, then after the OS reinstall, simply re-add the node into the cluster. If both IP address and hostname are the same as before, it may be necessary to add the node forcefully with the `-f` option in the `pvecm add` command. Reinstalling Proxmox and then re-adding to the cluster may be a faster solution in most cases than trying to fix an OS-related issue, but each use case will vary based on the environment and where disk images are stored.

# Recovering from a quorum failure

There are various reason why a Proxmox cluster can lose a quorum. For the cluster to operate correctly, a quorum must exist within the nodes. A quorum is established when the majority of the nodes are online. If 51% of the nodes go offline for whatever reason, a quorum will be lost, resulting in a cluster error. A Proxmox quorum relies on multicast. So if multicast gets disabled in the switch, the cluster can also lose a quorum. A manual misconfiguration in the cluster file can also cause loss of a quorum. When a quorum is lost, the following error messages will appear in log files under `/var/log/corosync`:

```
....................
corosync[9999]:  [QUORUM] Quorum provider: corosync_votequorum failed to
initialize.
corosync[9999]:  [SERV ] Service engine 'corosync_quorum' failed to load
for reason
    'configuration error: nodelist or quorum.expected_votes must be
configured!'
....................
```

The previous error may be because the hostname of the node could not be resolved. Adding all the nodes' hostnames and IP addresses to `/etc/hosts` may help establish a quorum. The following is the host's file content of our example node:

```
 GNU nano 2.7.4                                    File: /etc/hosts

127.0.0.1 localhost.localdomain localhost
172.16.2.3 pmx-03.domain.com pmx-03 pvelocalhost
172.16.2.1 pmx-01
172.16.2.2 pmx-02

# The following lines are desirable for IPv6 capable hosts

::1       ip6-localhost ip6-loopback
fe00::0 ip6-localnet
ff00::0 ip6-mcastprefix
ff02::1 ip6-allnodes
ff02::2 ip6-allrouters
ff02::3 ip6-allhosts
```

If the quorum is lost due to manual editing of the cluster configuration file, then we need to reverse the change by re-editing the `/etc/pve/corosync.conf` file or restoring it from a recent backup. Note that after a quorum is lost, the pmxcfs will become read-only and so will all the files in it, including `corosync.conf`. To be able to edit the file, we can run the following command to temporarily establish a quorum:

```
# pvecm expected 1
```

The previous command sets the total vote count to `1` and lets the cluster establish a quorum. Always make sure you edit the local copy of the cluster file and that the content of this configuration is the same on all nodes. Only then can a quorum be established. Any misconfiguration will cause split-brain, causing the full loss of a quorum.

It is of utmost importance to avoid any manual configuration of the `corosync.conf` file. If manual editing becomes necessary, then only commit changes when fully capable of doing so. If unsure of how the `corosync.conf` file works, it is best to avoid doing it yourself and seek help from the Proxmox forum or paid support.

After restoring the content of `corosync.conf` with a working configuration, restart the cluster using the following commands:

```
# systemctl restart pve-cluster
# systemctl restart corosync
```

If the quorum is lost or unable to be established due to a multicast error, then the first step is to check if the multicast is properly configured or exists on the network. We can use the following command format to check multicast between nodes:

```
# omping -c 10000 -i 0.001 -F -q <node1_ip> <node2_ip>
```

If the previous test fails, that means multicast does not exist and the quorum is failing.

# Recovering from a node failure

A Proxmox node can physically fail due to hardware component failure such as the motherboard, CPU, memory, power supply and so on, while the OS drive remains intact. In such a scenario, we can simply move the OS drive to a different node and power up. The new node does not need to be identical to the faulty one at all. Since the network interface may be different, we only will need to ensure the network configuration is set for the proper interface. Also, if the Proxmox OS has a paid subscription, the key will need to be reissued. Contact the seller where the subscription was purchased from or Proxmox directly to get the subscription key reissued.

The subscription key is bound to the hardware component, so the reissue of the key is required to bind the subscription key to the new hardware component. It is important to note that the CPU count will matter when moving the OS drive from one to another with a paid subscription. A Proxmox subscription key purchased for one CPU count will not work for multiple CPU nodes.

If the failed node had locally stored VM disk images on the same OS drive, the VM will just power up when the new node comes online with the moved OS drive from the failed node. If the disk images were stored locally on separate drives, then those drives will also need to be moved to a new node, and mount points must be reconfigured before the VM can be powered up.

# Recovering from a network failure

The extent of network failure can span over multiple layers, causing interruption between the Proxmox node and the user, or between the storage node and Proxmox nodes. The failure can occur due to physical network interface failure or an accidental network cable pull from nodes. The network failure can also occur due to heavy network traffic, which may be caused by but not limited to running a backup task on the same network path. In most production environments, server nodes usually contain more than one network interface for redundancy to reduce the loss of network connectivity to a minimum. The three most common scenarios for network connectivity interruptions are explained in the following sections.

# Loss of connectivity between Proxmox nodes

In this scenario, network connectivity is only interrupted between Proxmox nodes in a cluster. When over half of the Proxmox nodes in a cluster cannot communicate with each other, a quorum cannot be established. If multiple nodes lose network connectivity simultaneously, this usually indicates a network switch failure. This is a common scenario when a Proxmox cluster is on a dedicated management interface. So a loss of this connectivity only interrupts the quorum but not the VMs running on the nodes and users accessing it. When a quorum is lost, VMs in respective nodes function properly but from the GUI they may appear offline, including the nodes themselves, as shown in the following screenshot:

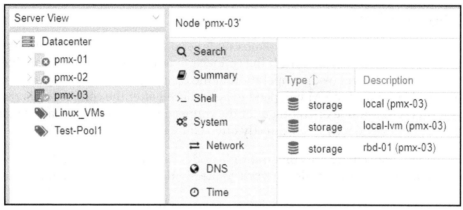

In the previous screenshot, the cluster lost a quorum so while accessing the GUI from node `pmx-03`, all other nodes appear offline even though they are running.

# Loss of connectivity between Proxmox nodes and users

In this scenario, when the connection between the user and Proxmox node is lost but the connection between Proxmox nodes and storage is unaffected, then the VM continues to run fine, except users cannot access the VMs. If a single interface is used for the Proxmox management and Proxmox public-side traffic, then a loss of connectivity on this interface will interrupt cluster communication and users will not be able to access their VMs running on this node. This will also prevent any console access through SSH. If another interface is used for shared storage and that interface did not lose connectivity, then the VM itself will keep running without interruption. Restoring connectivity will resume all usual operation of the node within moments.

Another scenario when a node itself can lose network connectivity is the use of Open vSwitch. In Proxmox 4.4, there was a situation when the node was updated and rebooted, but the node could not start the network interface due to an updated Open vSwitch package. The network service needed to be manually restarted. If the node is in a remote location without immediate access, and if there were other network interfaces in the node configured, that were not Open vSwitch-dependent, such as InfiniBand or standard Linux bridging on a different subnet, then we could still access the node from another node through a different network interface.

# Loss of connectivity between Proxmox and storage nodes

If the network connectivity between Proxmox nodes and storage nodes is lost, users will experience a frozen state in their VMs. If the connection is stored within a reasonable amount of time, the VM will resume operation. If the connection is not restored after an extended amount of time, the VM will need to be restarted after the connection is restored. The reason VMs can continue operating after the connection is restored is that VM data remains in the memory, which is not directly affected by the storage node.

Usually, network connectivity affecting multiple nodes can be traced down to a physical network switch, while a single node network connectivity loss is due to the node itself or a single network cable.

# Recovering from Ceph failure

Ceph is a very resilient, highly available storage system. Once a Ceph cluster is configured, for the most part, it can run maintenance free. In most cases, lack of knowledge on how Ceph works leads to major issues, causing cluster-side interference. In this section, we will highlight some of the most common issues and how to combat them in a Ceph cluster.

## Best practices for a healthy Ceph cluster

The following are a few best practices to keep a Ceph cluster running healthy:

- If possible, keep all settings to default for a healthy cluster.
- Use Ceph pool only to implement a different OSD type policy and not for multitenancy, such as one pool for SSDs and another for HDDs.

- *Do not* make frequent Ceph configuration changes. It adds extra workload on the cluster OSDs, reducing the life of HDDs. After each change, let the cluster rebalance data before making new changes.
- Always keep in mind the core count of Ceph nodes when adjusting Ceph threads. Do not let the number of threads become more than the core count.
- In a small Ceph cluster, SSDs will increase write performance. In a large cluster, a higher OSD count will increase performance.
- *Do not* use desktop class hard drives as OSDs in a small cluster.
- Reduce backfill and recovery threads to a minimum to continue recovery without hurting client request performance.

# Stuck inconsistent PGs in Ceph

Over time, Ceph PGs may become inconsistent. The following steps will help us to find the inconsistent PG and repair it:

1. Get PG name:

   ```
   # ceph health detail
   ```

2. Run this command to repair the PG:

   ```
   # ceph pg repair
   ```

# Stuck inactive incomplete PGs in Ceph

If any PG is stuck due to OSD or node failure and becomes unhealthy, resulting in the cluster becoming inaccessible due to a blocked request for greater than 32 secs, try the following:

1. Set noout to prevent data rebalancing:

   ```
   #ceph osd set noout
   ```

2. Query the PG to see which are the probing OSDs:

   ```
   # ceph pg xx.x query
   ```

3. Go to each probing OSD and delete the header folder here:

   ```
   var/lib/ceph/osd/ceph-X/current/xx.x_head/
   ```

4. Restart all OSDs.

5. Run a PG query to see the PG does not exist. It should show something like a NOENT message.

6. Force create a PG:

   ```
   # ceph pg force_pg_create x.xx
   ```

7. Restart PG OSDs.

**Warning !!**
Follow this only if all attempts to restore the placement group or PG have failed. This will cause data loss.

# Error while moving a Ceph journal to another drive

When a Ceph journal is on SSD, it provides the fastest performance in a small Ceph cluster with less than 50 OSDs. If a cluster was created initially with OSDs co-located on the same spinner HDD, then it needs to be moved to SSD for journaling. There are a few steps that must be followed to ensure a Ceph journal can be written onto a new drive. When using SSD as a journaling drive, always ensure not to overload it with too much journals for multiple OSDs. As a rule of thumb, one SSD should be used for every five OSDs. We can allocate multiple partitions on an SSD to store journals for multiple OSDs. If proper steps are not followed to create a journaling drive, the respective OSDs will not be able to start. The following steps will move an OSD journal to another drive:

1. Format the SSD and create a number of partitions based on the number of OSD journals needing to be stored.

2. Stop the OSD using this command:

   ```
   # service ceph stop osd.<id>
   ```

3. Flush the journal for the OSD:

```
# ceph-osd -i <id> --flush-journal
```

4. Create Symlink:

```
# rm /var/lib/ceph/osd/osd.<id>/journal
# ln -s /dev/sdX /var/lib/ceph/osd/osd.<id>/journal
```

5. Create a new journal:

```
# ceph-osd -i <id> --mkjournal
```

6. Start the OSD:

```
# service ceph stop osd.<id>
```

As of Proxmox 5.5, we can start/stop OSDs from the GUI, but we cannot move the journal drive. However, when creating new OSDs through the GUI, we can manually select which drive we want to use as the journaling drive, as shown in the following screenshot:

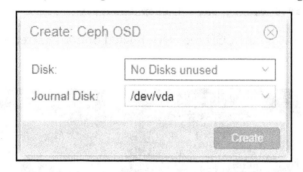

# Ceph node running out of resources during recovery

On day-to-day operations, a Ceph node uses very little resources such as CPU and memory. But during a cluster recovery, Ceph redistributes a large amount of data between OSDs, which uses up a large portion of the node resources. If a node is constantly running out of resources during recovery, check whether there are any VMs running on that node. Those VMs will need to be powered off or migrated to another node until the rebalancing finishes. If this is not the case, then check the available resources of the node. It may be that the node simply does not have enough resources to keep up with the Ceph recovery. Another common reason for running out of resources is that Ceph may be configured with higher performance values, such as a number of threads allocated for recovery or maximum backfills allowed. A great feature of Ceph is lots of the configuration can be applied during runtime, which gets applied immediately. The following are some of the configuration options that need to be checked if nodes are running out of resources during recovery:

To check the recovery values of an OSD, run this command format:

```
# ceph daemon osd.0 config show | grep recovery
```

This command will show all the OSD recovery-related options currently set for OSDs, as shown in the following screenshot:

```
root@pmx-01:~# ceph daemon osd.0 config show | grep recovery
    "osd_min_recovery_priority": "0",
    "osd_recovery_retry_interval": "30",
    "osd_allow_recovery_below_min_size": "true",
    "osd_recovery_thread_timeout": "30",
    "osd_recovery_thread_suicide_timeout": "300",
    "osd_recovery_sleep": "0.01",
    "osd_recovery_delay_start": "0",
    "osd_recovery_max_active": "3",
    "osd_recovery_max_single_start": "1",
    "osd_recovery_max_chunk": "8388608",
    "osd_recovery_max_omap_entries_per_chunk": "64000",
    "osd_recovery_forget_lost_objects": "false",
    "osd_scrub_during_recovery": "false",
    "osd_force_recovery_pg_log_entries_factor": "1.3",
    "osd_debug_skip_full_check_in_recovery": "false",
    "osd_recovery_op_priority": "3",
    "osd_recovery_priority": "5",
    "osd_recovery_cost": "20971520",
    "osd_recovery_op_warn_multiple": "16",
```

From the previous screenshot, we can see that currently the value for `osd_recovery_max_active` is set to 3. This means the OSD recovery will use three threads during recovery. If the Ceph node is struggling, we need to drop the value to one thread using the following command:

```
# ceph tell osd.* injectargs '--osd-recovery-max-active 1'
```

The previous command will change the recovery thread to 1 for all OSDs because we have added a wildcard as the OSD ID instead of specifying one particular OSD. The `injectargs` syntax changes values in real time without needing to restart any OSD or node.

If we want to check the value currently set for max backfills, we can enter a similar command as follows:

```
# ceph daemon osd.0 config show | grep backfills
```

For our example cluster, the command shows the backfills set to 6, as shown in the following screenshot:

```
root@pmx-01:~# ceph daemon osd.0 config show | grep backfills
    "osd_max_backfills": "6",
```

As we can see from the previous screenshot, the backfills are set to a value of 6. This may be too high for a smaller node. This value should be set to 1 if the node is running out of resources during recovery. We are going to change the value using the following command we already have seen for the recovery thread:

```
# ceph tell osd.* injectargs '--osd-max-backfills 1'
```

It is important to note here that besides a node running out of resources, there can also be a network bottleneck due to higher recovery values, such as an extreme slowdown in network connectivity to the point where users will not be able to access their VMs. In such a scenario, these recovery values will also prove very helpful. Lower recovery values ensure that user requests do not get interrupted, yet recovery takes place at a slower pace. If user connectivity is not a priority, for example overnight, we can inject new higher values to speed up recovery, then change them to a lower value before the working day starts.

# Summary

In this chapter, we got to see some of the most common scenarios when things can go wrong and some steps to recover from them. By no means are these the only issues that can bring a cluster down. This list should be expanded through proper documentation as new issues surface and solutions are found.

No amount of reading or study can equal hands-on experience with Proxmox. You may already be a professional in the virtualization field, or you may be just starting out on a networking career and looking for a way to stand out from the crowd, but hopefully, this book will push you in the right direction. Besides the official site and forum, you can also reach out to the author directly to ask questions or to have a discussion, through the author maintained forum at `http://www.masteringproxmox.com/`.

# Index

www.ingramcontent.com/pod-product-compliance
Lightning Source LLC
Chambersburg PA
CBHW060642060326
40690CB00020B/4483